German National Socialism
and the quest for
nuclear power
1939–1949

German National Socialism and the quest for nuclear power 1939–1949

MARK WALKER

Union College, New York

CAMBRIDGE
UNIVERSITY PRESS

Published by the Press Syndicate of the University of Cambridge
The Pitt Building, Trumpington Street, Cambridge CB2 1RP
40 West 20th Street, New York, NY 10011–4211, USA
10 Stamford Road, Oakleigh, Victoria 3166, Australia

First published 1989
First paperback edition 1993

Printed in Great Britain at the University Press, Cambridge

British Library cataloguing in publication data
Walker, Mark
German national socialism and the quest for
nuclear power, 1939–1949
1. Germany. Nuclear power. Research, 1939–1949
I. Title
621.48′072043

Library of Congress cataloguing in publication data
Walker, Mark, 1959–
German National Socialism and the quest for nuclear power,
1939–1949/Mark Walker.
    p.   cm.
Bibliography.
Includes index.
ISBN 0-521-36413-2
1. Nuclear energy–Germany–History. 2. Nuclear engineering–
Germany–History. 3. National Socialism. I. Title.
TK1078.W35 1989
355.8′25119′0943-dc19 88-36458CIP

ISBN 0 521 36413 2 hardback
ISBN 0 521 43804 7 paperback

Contents

Preface

I had always thought of this book as an individual effort, that is, until I came to write this preface. However, the fact that I am indebted to the individuals listed below in no way implies or assumes that they necessarily are in agreement with what I have written. First of all, I was lucky enough to be able to meet and speak with many of the actors in my drama, which can be one of the great benefits of doing contemporary history. The list of my interview partners includes: Erich Bagge, Gerhard Borrmann, Adolf Butenandt, Werner Czulius, Gerhard Dickel, Heinz Ewald, F. Charles Frank, Ewald Fünfer, Wilhelm Hanle, Paul Harteck, Georg Hartwig, Otto Haxel, Julius Hiby, Karl-Heinz Höcker, Willibald Jentschke, Heinz Maier-Leibnitz, Werner Maurer, Wolfgang Paul, Rudolf Peierls, Michael Perrin, Nikolaus Riehl, Stefan Rozental, Kurt Sauerwein, Kurt Starke, Hans Suess, Wilhelm Walcher, Carl-Friedrich von Weizsäcker, Karl Wirtz, and Karl Zimmer. Since this book is a slightly revised version of my 1987 doctoral dissertation for the Department of History at Princeton University, I want to single out those who helped me through six long years of graduate school: Faye Angelozzi, who did more for the history of science graduate students than anyone else, all of my fellow graduate students at Princeton, without whom the Program in History of Science would not exist, and my first, and best, teacher in history, Charles C. Gillispie. I must not forget to thank those institutions that have generously given me financial support, for which I am very grateful: the Friends of the Center for History of Physics, American Institute of Physics; the Bonn American Businessman's Club; the German Academic Exchange Service; Princeton University; and Union College. Several institutions treated me kindly as a guest, and I want to express my gratitude for their hospitality: Martin Klein, who took me on as a participant in a seminar held at Yale University; John L. Heilbron and the entire history of science community in Berkeley, who made the eight months I spent in the Bay Area pleasant indeed; Michael Eckert, Menso Folkerts, Maria Osietzki, Willi Pricha, Ivo Schneider, Helmut Schubert, and Jürgen Teichmann, at the German Museum, and Helmut Rechenberg and the Max Planck Institute for Physics, all of whom went out of their way both to help me and to make me feel at home in Munich; Kristie Macrakis, Hartmut Petzold, and Monika Renneberg all generously entertained me while traveling in Germany. The Archives of the University of Arizona, Erich Bagge in Kiel, the Berlin Document Center in West Berlin, the Federal German Archives in Koblenz, the German Museum, the First Physical Institute of the University of Göttingen, the Hamburg State Archives, the Institute for Contemporary History in Munich, the Karlsruhe Nuclear Research Center, the Archives of the Max Planck Society in West Berlin, the National Archives in Washington, DC, the Niels Bohr Library of the American Institute of Physics in New York City, Wolfgang Paul in Bonn, and the Archives of Renssealaer Polytechnic Institute all generously granted me access to historical materials. Per Als, Finn Aaserud, Gro Naes, and Bartel van der Waerden did me a big favor by translating documents into English. Perhaps most importantly, I must express my indebtedness to those individuals who accepted the greatest of burdens, read preliminary drafts of all or part of this work, and gave me their criticism: Ken Arnold, John Carson, David Cassidy, Ron Doel, Michael Eckert, Paul Forman, Charles C. Gillispie, Mikael Hård, Harold James, George Mosse, Rudolf Peierls, Helmut Rechenberg, Monika Renneberg, R. Steven Turner, Spencer Weart, Karl Wirtz, Karl Zimmer, and the anonymous reader from Cambridge University Press. The congenial environment provided by my colleagues and the Department of History at Union College allowed me to transform my dissertation into a book relatively quickly. Finally, I want to thank three historians who have influenced me more than they know: Paul Forman, Charles C. Gillispie, and Spencer Weart.

This work is dedicated to Linda and my family: Ed, Eric, Jeanne, Mary Jo, Nancy, Peggy, and Wayne.

An earlier version of a part of chapter 2 appeared in the *Journal of Contemporary History*, 24 (1989), 63–89. The author is indebted to Hunter/Fischer Visual Enterprises, Norwalk, CT, for the images used in the jacket design, to Sheila McEnery for her copyediting, and to my editor William Davies and Cambridge University Press for their interest, support, and goodwill.

Since the original publication of my book, I have written two related articles: "Legends surrounding the German Atomic Bomb," published in Teresa Meade and Mark Walker (eds.), *Science, Medicine, and Cultural Imperialism* (London, Macmillan, 1991), pp. 178–204, and "Physics and Propaganda: Werner Heisenberg's Foreign Lectures under National Socialism," *Historical Studies in the Physical and Biological Sciences*, 22 (1992), 339–89. See also David Cassidy's definitive biography: *Uncertainty: The Life and Science of Werner Heisenberg* (New York, W. H. Freeman, 1991).

Abbreviations

NW	*Die Naturwissenschaften*
NYT	*New York Times*
PB	*Physikalische Blätter*
PR	*Physical Review*
PSQ	*Political Science Quarterly*
RMP	*Reviews of Modern Physics*
RPI	The Archives of Rensselaer Polytechnic Institute, Troy, New York
RSI	*The Review of Scientific Instruments*
SCIS	*Science Studies*
SGNY	Private Papers of Samuel Goudsmit, Niels Bohr Library
SI	*Science Illustrated*
SM	*Süddeutsche Monatshefte*
SUAR	*Sudhoffs Archiv*
VB	*Völkischer Beobachter*
WGM	Private Papers of Walther Gerlach, Munich
WHM	Private Papers of Werner Heisenberg, Max Planck Institute for Physics, Munich
WPB	Private papers of Wolfgang Paul, Bonn, FRG
ZGN	*Zeitschrift für die gesamte Naturwissenschaft*
ZP	*Zeitschrift für Physik*
ZPCB	*Zeitschrift für physikalische Chemie B*

Introduction

It would be misleading to suggest that the Nazi government has completely repudiated science and intellect. The official attitudes towards science are clearly ambivalent and unstable. (For this reason, any statements concerning science in Nazi Germany are made under correction.) On the one hand, the challenging skepticism of science interferes with the imposition of a new set of values which demand an unquestioning acquiescence. But the new dictatorships must recognize, as did Hobbes who also argued that the State must be all or nothing, that science is power. For military, economic, and political reasons, theoretical science – to say nothing of its more respectable sibling, technology – cannot be safely discarded. Experience has shown that the most esoteric researches have found important applications.

Robert Merton (1938)[1]

This book investigates science and knowledge as power. But what is power? Power can subsume economic, industrial, military, political, and social forces and refer to the transfer of energy as well. Moreover, it is important to examine how power is wielded and controlled, and by whom. A study of science as power falls into the category of science policy in the broadest sense, and the relationships between scientists and various parts of the modern state will be investigated in this context. This book examines what was an extreme case, the German attempt to exploit the economic and military potential of nuclear fission during the last six years of National Socialist rule, from the perspective of the scientists involved in this research. Although this example is extraordinary, I believe that the phenomena thus exhibited are always present in science policy, and are unusual here only because of their visibility. The cracks in a branch are easier to see when the wood is bent.[2]

The prelude to my story begins at the height of the German Empire. By the start of the twentieth century, Germany had become a world power, particularly in the areas of economics, industry, science, and warfare; she had acquired colonies and was engaged in a naval arms race with Great Britain. The German economy was flooding other countries with exports, the German chemical industry dominated the world, and the German

1

electrical industry was one of the major competitors in the international market. German was the dominant scientific language, German journals set the standard for international scientific research, and Germany rivaled all competitors with respect to the quality, quantity, and institutional support of science.[3]

Moreover, the interests of German industry, science, and the state came together and intertwined during the decades before World War I. Perhaps the best example of this interdependence came with the founding of the Kaiser Wilhelm Society for the Advancement of Science (*Kaiser Wilhelm Gesellschaft zur Förderung der Wissenschaften*) in 1911. This society was funded by private industry as well as the German state – in order that it would not be completely dependent on either – and was intended to foster scientific research outside of the university system by freeing scientists from teaching responsibilities, to benefit German industry by supporting scientific research on topics relevant to industrial application, and to enhance German national prestige. The interests of the German military were also inextricably linked to Germany's science and industry, for science was recognized as an indispensable part of national power on the eve of World War I.[4]

Along with most Germans, many scientists mistakenly believed that Germany had been forced to fight a defensive war in 1914. Thus it was no surprise that German researchers also took part overwhelmingly and wholeheartedly in the enthusiastic wave of German nationalism and militarism, either by enlisting for military service, or by supporting the war effort on the home front. Perhaps the most famous example of this "war of the intellectuals" (*Krieg der Geister*) was the "manifesto to the civilized world". This obtuse and inflammatory document, a reply to accurate accusations of German atrocities in occupied Belgium, was signed by ninety-three leading German intellectuals, including the theologian Adolf von Harnack, President of the Kaiser Wilhelm Society, and the distinguished natural scientists Emil Fischer, Fritz Haber, Felix Klein, Philipp Lenard, Walther Nernst, Wilhlem Ostwald, Max Planck, Wilhelm Röntgen, and Wilhelm Wien.[5]

In their rush to rally to the German flag, some of these scientists – including the distinguished Berlin physicist Max Planck – later said that they had signed the manifesto without having read it. Subsequently Planck did distance himself from the "manifesto to the civilized world", although he never explicitly renounced it, but most of his colleagues did not even go that far. Along with 3,000 other German professors, the Munich physicist Arnold Sommerfeld signed the "declaration of German university instructors," in which the signatories supported the cause of German arms. Sommerfeld, but not Planck, also signed Wilhelm Wien's memorandum against the English, an exhortation for German physicists not to cite Englishmen more often than Germans in their publications. This sincere identification of the interests of German science with Germany's fortunes in the war and refusal to believe any evidence of German wrongdoing – in other words, a naive trust in the German state – had enduring international repercussions.[6]

This faith in the justness of the cause of German victory led some of the leading representatives of German science not only to acquiesce in, but also to advocate German cultural, economic, and political imperialism. Although German cultural imperialism did not begin in 1914, World War I certainly accelerated this process. As the wartime activities of Arnold Sommerfeld demonstrate, the European territory overrun by the German armies provided new opportunities for German cultural expansion. In early 1918, Sommerfeld traveled to France in order to lecture before the soldiers of the German Sixth Army and made an unscheduled stop in Belgium at the former University of Ghent. This institution of higher learning had been turned into a Flemish university by the German occupation authorities in 1916. This German attempt to exploit Flemish nationalism was part of tentative long-range plans to annex part of Belgium.[7]

In late February of 1918, Sommerfeld described his trip to Belgium in the literary supplement of the *Münchner-Augsburger Abendzeitung*. For Sommerfeld, or as he noted, for any German professor, to be able to speak at the "newly blooming" University of Ghent was most satisfying and represented an auspicious event for the future of German-Flemish cultural relations. After all the "ill will" and "slander" which, according to the Munich professor, both German science and the German people had had to endure during the war years, Sommerfeld had been elated to find a place on "old Germanic soil" where before only French had been heard and which had now been retaken for German science. The founding of the University of Ghent was the most effective and promising part of German policy in Belgium, a policy which Sommerfeld believed had grasped the problem by its roots in "Germanic culture." Previously Sommerfeld had not thought that a forced incorporation of Belgium into Germany would be desirable. But after viewing firsthand what was taking place in Flanders and especially at the "nurseries of Flemish culture," this scientist thought that a voluntary incorporation of Flanders, the part of Belgium most valuable to Germany, was possible. After all, he told his Bavarian readers, it would be a shame if Germans had to disappoint the hopes of the Flemish, the "best" of the Belgium nation. Sommerfeld left Ghent with a new opinion on the future of German–Flemish relations. No matter how enthusiastically the Flemish may have welcomed the Germans, Sommerfeld's actions in Ghent, and his retrospective description of his 1918 lecture tour in areas occupied by Germany, both fell into line with the sentiments expressed in the "manifesto to the civilized world."[8]

Besides supporting the war indirectly, German scientists also applied themselves to warfare. By using the Fritz Haber–Carl Bosch process for the production of ammonia, the Germans compensated for shortages of crucial raw materials and thereby saved their country from a certain early defeat. Both Bosch and Haber eventually received Nobel Prizes for their work, but the latter's contributions to the German war effort also earned him a different sort of notoriety. At the start of World War I, the British, the French, and the Germans all were considering the use of chemical warfare, and evidence of the French intention to use tear gas shells on the front fell into German hands during the spring of 1915. Haber transformed the nature of chemical warfare by substituting chlorine for tear gas and by replacing individual gas shells with a chemical cloud that was released from large canisters. On 22 April 1915, a cloud of chlorine gas was released at Ypres on the western front, thereby wreaking havoc in the defending French lines. Several young scientific colleagues were recruited by Haber to serve in the gas warfare corps, including Gustav Hertz, James Franck, and Otto Hahn. Haber also turned his Kaiser Wilhelm Institute for Physical Chemistry over to the military for chemical warfare, thereby expanding the institute manpower from 5 to 1,500 men. Science was clearly a significant part of military power, and German science and scientists were important parts of the war effort.[9]

The formal surrender of German forces was a crushing blow to almost all Germans, including scientists, and the subsequent political revolution and establishment of the "Weimar Republic" provoked great resentment and embitterment within significant and influential portions of the German scientific community. For example, on 27 March 1919 Sommerfeld told his colleague Wien that, because of the "Jewish-political chaos," he was becoming "more and more of an anti-Semite." Anti-Semitic resentment did not lead to anti-Semitism at Sommerfeld's theoretical physics institute in Munich. Sommerfeld had many Jewish students and assistants whom he treated very well. Instead, Sommerfeld's comment to Wien illustrates the latent predisposition towards anti-Semitism that could exist among the scholars of the Wilhelmian and Weimar periods, as well as a tacit identification of the hated political revolutionary forces with the Jews. The reaction of the eighteen-year-old Werner Heisenberg to the events of 1919 was even more extreme. Heisenberg joined a reactionary private militia (*Freikorps*) and fought against the short-lived revolutionary Bavarian republic. The long-term responses among some German scientists to the abdication of their Emperor, to the surrender of Germany's military might, and to the coming of democracy were more complex than the immediate reactions of Sommerfeld or Heisenberg and require an examination of ideology in science.[10]

Scientists generally observe an ideology that can be named "apolitical." Furthermore, this ideology entails a dichotomy between rhetoric and practice. The rhetorical side of this ideology can be summed up succinctly: science and politics are antithetical. The former is objective, the latter is subjective. According to this ideology, the only legitimate routes to status and influence within the scientific community, including the responsibility of representing this community before the rest of society, result from objectively judged, distinguished scientific contributions – the so-called "merit system." With respect to the general interaction between members of the scientific community and the greater society, the principle of separable roles is employed. The roles of "scientist" and "citizen" in the same individual are kept distinct. For example, when a scientist supports a political party, he speaks as a citizen, not a scientist. When a government or industrial representative asks a scientist for expert advice on a scientific or technological matter, he replies as a scientist, without the responsibilities of a citizen. These two roles are not only separable, according to the rhetoric of the apolitical ideology, they should be kept separate.[11]

Take the example of a scientist whose country is at war. As a citizen, he may well feel obligated, or indeed be compelled, to serve his country by contributing to the war effort. When approached by his government as a scientist for expert advice on the feasibility or potential of a weapon, he provides this advice exclusively on professional grounds. The question is not, should this weapon be made available or used? Instead, the scientist asks whether this weapon can be made available or used? Is such a black-and-white division of labor, as well as of responsibility, realistic or acceptable for a society? This example shows that such a black-and-white separation is not always possible. A gray area exists as well, for as the history of the German quest for nuclear power will show, expert advice on the feasibility of a weapon can hardly be divorced from all civic responsibility with respect to its subsequent implementation.

When the rhetorical part of the apolitical ideology is set aside and the adherents of this ideology are observed in practice, the opposite of the above argument appears to be the case. The roles of citizen and scientist are inseparable. The "citizen-scientists" enjoy access to knowledge that concerns the economic, military, and social potential of science and that is denied to most of their fellow citizens. Moreover, citizen-scientists often enjoy enhanced status within this society, precisely because of their expertise. Because "scientist-citizens" are aware of the potential political significance of science and are looked to as experts by their fellow citizens, they bear the responsibility of discharging the duties of a citizen in the process of prosecuting their profession. This argument applies not only to Germany, but to other countries as well.

Scientists and their professional communities are certainly more immune to politics than other professions, but nevertheless are susceptible to the political currents of their social and economic environment, and scientists often successfully attempt to influence their environment in turn, using any and all means at their disposal and certainly taking advantage of their scientific expertise. Yet scientists consistently claim that they and their science are apolitical. How is this apparent contradiction reconciled? Scientific communities may include all or part of one or more scientific disciplines, and may have boundaries that are determined by ideological, national, racial, and other factors. But these groups of scientists also have conventions for acceptable professional behavior that usually are reached through consensus. The key to the apolitical ideology is that this acceptable behavior is *defined* as apolitical. In other words, "apolitical" is used as a synonym for "professional," "political" as a synonym for "unprofessional," and the political/apolitical rhetoric of scientists should be read in this way. Since different scientific communities can have different conventions, in turn dependent on their economic, political, and social environment, there are no universal guidelines for apolitical behavior. It is subjective by definition. Keeping the apolitical ideology of science in mind, let us examine the behavior of some German scientists during the Weimar Republic and beyond.[12]

Many German natural scientists were typical examples of the "German mandarins." The members of this social, cultural, and intellectual elite derived their status from their education, viewed the new materialistic age of democratic mass politics with pessimism, and looked back to the authoritarian, militaristic Wilhelmian era with nostalgia and forward to German democracy with sullen suspicion, if not outright hostility. But the republican government was not the only perceived enemy of German science. In the wake of the Treaty of Versailles and of the enduring resentment that the "manifesto to the civilized world" had provoked among Germany's former opponents, German science was confronted with an international boycott in 1919. Germans were to be barred from international congresses, and even the use of German as the language of international scientific communication was to be avoided.[13]

The pride of German scientists understandably was wounded by this professional ostracism, and they reacted as might have been expected. Any embarrassment caused by revelations of German atrocities in Belgium, for example, was more than outweighed by the resentment felt after World War I by German scientists towards the Treaty of Versailles and the new democratic German government. As a result of this deep and lingering embitterment, German scientists often reacted defensively and came to view science as a replacement for political power (*Machtersatz*). Scholarship and science were now considered to be the sole remaining attributes of a great power that Germany still possessed. Since German scientists generally refused to recognize the Weimar Republic as a legitimate German state – an exception such as Albert Einstein is conspicuous by its uniqueness – they now regarded themselves as the agents, or even bearers, of the true foreign policy of their nation, as well as of true German culture.[14]

These scientists sometimes felt obliged to sacrifice the interests of their profession as well as their own personal interests for the sake of patriotic political posturing. For example, when as a somewhat forced gesture of reconciliation, the International Research Council offered to lift its boycott of German science in 1926, at a time when the Weimar government was actively pursuing a policy of reintegrating Germany into western Europe, the German scientific organizations and societies refused to join this international council. Instead of reestablishing such official international contacts, for such cooperation is a necessary part of modern science, German scientists enthusiastically engaged in unofficial scientific commerce. Individual scientists went out of their way to spread propaganda for German science as well as for their own research, as Sommerfeld's world tour and guest professorship in the United States illustrate.[15]

But even though they might find democracy distasteful, many German scientists were willing to work with the republic if their science would benefit. The great German inflation of the twenties devastated institutional endowments as well as the salaries and savings of individual researchers. German scientists were forced to turn to their government and industry for aid. Although academic researchers had worked with industrial colleagues during the Wilhelmian period, many scientists had also avoided being tainted by public association with German industry. However, the economic and political excesses of the twenties forced scientists into the arms of industrialists, causing a tacit social and political alliance between German industry and academia. Both groups supported the same conservative parties, and both felt threatened by the new democratic order. The German state responded to the scientists' pleas for assistance by establishing the Emergency Society for German Science (*Notgemeinschaft der deutschen Wissenschaft*), an organization which was funded mainly by the state and which funneled money into selected areas of German science. This society was partially responsible for the flourishing of modern physics research during the Weimar Republic.[16]

The ideology of science as a replacement for political power and the attitude of some German scientists towards their government during the Weimar Republic illustrate a parasitic side of German science during the Weimar era. Science exploited the republic for financial support, but generally denied political and social support to the democratic state in return. The political behavior of scientists from the height of the Wilhelmian Empire to the death of the Weimar Republic vividly illustrates the apolitical ideology. An important portion of the scientific community remained consistent in its political views throughout this period by appreciating authoritarianism, militarism, and nationalism while rejecting democracy and internationalism. But while to support the government of the German Emperor and to serve in World War I had been considered by convention apolitical, indeed patriotic, opposition to the Weimar regime was labeled, and indeed justified, as apolitical as well. The few scientists who wholeheartedly supported the democratic government or the international pacifist movement were often attacked by their colleagues as being political. But in 1933 these apolitical German scientists were put to the test, for the republic that they and their conservative and industrial allies had helped to destroy was replaced by a new and extremely political order, a regime that was interested above all in power and its control.

In two consecutive elections during the last six months of 1932, the National Socialist German Workers Party gained more parliamentary seats than any other party, although the latter election did represent a relative decline. On 30 January 1933, Adolf Hitler, the leader of the National Socialist movement, was appointed Chancellor of the German Reich by Reich President Paul von Hindenburg through the political machinations of certain conservative politicians and army officers. This conservative circle believed that it could control and exploit Hitler and his undisciplined supporters, but this conviction was revealed as a delusion. The National Socialist movement quickly and ruthlessly gained firm control over the German state. It was the conservative members of the "National Government of Adolf Hitler"who became the puppets.[17]

If many German scientists were willing to work with the republic they hated, then it should be no surprise that they were prepared to cooperate with the National Socialist regime, which in some respects was ideologically more compatible. Although National Socialism did contain an anti-intellectual element, it was also reminiscent of Germany under the Emperor. (In this regard, the reader is cautioned to contemplate, not the National Socialist state as revealed after 1945, but rather National Socialism as perceived by most Germans during the first few years of the Third Reich.) From the standpoint of these scientists, the relationship between German science and the German state could be seen as more of a continuation from the Second Reich to the Third Reich, including the Weimar Republic as an aberrant, unfortunate, but mercifully brief interlude, than as a sharp divide in 1933.[18]

Nevertheless, there was an obvious dark side to the "National Socialist Revolution," as some contemporaries named it, for the policy of the new masters of Germany was far more extreme than that of either the troubled Weimar Republic or the authoritarian Wilhelmian Empire. Perhaps most relevant for the German academic scientific community was the Law for the Restoration of the Career Civil Service (*Gesetz zur Wiederherstellung des Berufsbeamtentums*) of 7 April 1933, a law designed to purge the civil service – including the universities – of all potential opposition to the new regime. Civil servants who had been appointed during the Weimar Republic, who were of non-Aryan descent, or whose previous political activities did not guarantee that they would serve the new state at all times and without reservation, had to go. In theory, non-Aryans who were in office before the start of World War I, who had fought at the front during this war, or who had had a father or son killed in the war, could remain, although in practice all non-Aryans were quickly harried from office.[19]

The Nuremberg race laws of 15 September 1935 eliminated all exemptions for non-Aryans. A disproportionately high percentage of academic physicists in Germany were Jewish. By 1935 one out of four physicists had been driven from their posts. The Kaiser Wilhelm Society purged its Jews in the spring of 1933, shortly after the Ministry of Interior had informed the Society that the civil service law applied to its employees, although institute directors were exempted. It was left up to each director to fire any non-Aryans under his charge. Fritz Haber, himself a Jew, resigned rather than acquiesce in this purge, but he was notably alone in doing so. The other directors – including other Jews – carried out the instructions of Kaiser Wilhelm Society General Secretary Friedrich Glum and let their people go. The Jewish directors were able to hang on for only a few years more before they too were sacked.[20]

The immediate reactions of individual scientists to these political measures were often quite naive. The chemist Otto Hahn was visiting Canada in April of 1933. When asked by a Toronto newspaper reporter about reports of the purges in Germany, Hahn replied that he considered them to be exaggerated. As the chemist told the reporter, he had reason to believe that all the arrested Jews were also communists. Moreover, Hahn was convinced that Hitler was not responsible for the atrocities that had been attributed to him. In June of 1933, Werner Heisenberg tried to convince his Jewish teacher and colleague Max Born, who had left his professorship, to return to Göttingen. Heisenberg had visited Planck in Berlin and asked what could be done for physics? Planck had spoken with the head of the German government and received the assurance that the government would do nothing beyond the civil service law which could hamper science. Heisenberg understood very well that Born might not want to return to such "ungrateful surroundings," but he nevertheless reminded his teacher of the gratitude that Born's former students still felt for him and exhorted him to return to Germany and to his appreciative colleagues.[21]

The aim of the National Socialist civil service policy was to pacify the German bureaucracy, and this goal was achieved. By purging all non-Aryan and leftist elements and provoking others to resign in protest, the National Socialist government was left with a generally homogeneous, conservative, nationalistic, Aryan, and apolitical scientific and engineering community, that is, was left with researchers who were willing to work with, and within, the National Socialist German state. For example, administrators at the American Rockefeller Foundation were disturbed by the racial purge of German science and attempted to pull out of a commitment they had made to help finance the construction of a Kaiser Wilhelm Institute for Physics. The Kaiser Wilhelm Society responded to the Americans' misgivings by playing them off against the National Socialist government. Kaiser Wilhelm Society President Max Planck and other Kaiser Wilhelm Society members and officials put pressure on the consciences of the Americans not to abandon them. The aged Planck stressed that the realization of the physics institute was his heartfelt wish (*Herzenswunsch*). The society leadership also persuaded the National Socialist government to agree to meet the operating costs of the future institute by exploiting the influential connections that this organization enjoyed with German industry and banking circles and by demonstrating support for the National Socialist regime through passive acquiescence in the purge of the civil service and other policies of the new order. The Rockefeller Foundation tried to avoid payment by making impossible demands of Planck but, with the strong backing of the National Socialist government, he met them. Construction of the institute was finished by 1937. In the eyes of Planck and the rest of the Kaiser Wilhelm Society, the political and ideological concessions that they had made were outweighed by the new state-of-the-art institute.[22]

To many Germans, there was a bright side to the National Socialist Revolution as well as a dark one, an optimism that was summed up in the concept of national renewal. During the first years of the Third Reich, a sympathetic listener could easily filter out the unfortunate excesses – especially if he remained untouched by them – and focus on the rhetoric of a return to traditional German values and to a strong Germany. Indeed, a scientist could well appeal to the apolitical ideology of his community and decide not to become involved in the political purges carried out by the National Socialist state. For example, Heisenberg wrote to Born saying that he knew that there were people among the new political leaders who deserved support. Over the course of time, Heisenberg believed, the ugly would separate itself from the beautiful. Therefore he tried to persuade Born not to see only the ingratitude in Göttingen. Heisenberg hoped that life in Germany would once again become peaceful in the near future.[23]

The National Socialist government did more than just talk about a renewal of national strength. Beginning in the middle of the thirties, the return of universal military service and renunciation of the Treaty of Versailles were accompanied in 1936 by the Four Year Plan, a massive rearmament program under the leadership of Hermann Göring. Many

German scientists were able and willing to take advantage of the renewed emphasis on military might. For example, by 1937 the Hamburg physical chemist Paul Harteck was advising Army Ordnance on chemical explosives and carrying out experiments on benzene-cracking under the auspices of the Four Year Plan. As throughout the Wilhelmian era, during the first years of the Third Reich, German scientists took seriously the commitment of German science to the military strength of Germany. In 1935 Max Planck noted in his capacity as President of the Kaiser Wilhelm Society that, with respect to the universal military service obligation in Germany, it went without saying that any members of the Kaiser Wilhelm Institutes capable of service in the armed forces would volunteer.[24]

By 1936, National Socialism was showing its best face to the world. German power had been reborn. For example, a tourist brochure for the 1936 Berlin Olympics could claim that the nation was no longer "rent asunder" by civil war. Its factories were no longer idle, nor its people anxious and impoverished. Peace and goodwill, faith and confidence had created a contented Germany which now extended its hospitality to all visitors from near and far. The above depiction was blatant propaganda, but more critical observers were impressed by the changes in Germany as well. Max Born returned to Germany for a visit in 1936, and the impressions of his trip, recorded in a letter to Ernest Rutherford, reveal great respect for the successes of the new government. There were so many things in Germany which Born could not help but admire. Unemployment had been eliminated by a kind of "forced labor". But Born had talked to the men who lived in "labor camps " – not concentration camps – and found them well-dressed, clean, well-fed and happy, certainly, the physicist thought, better off than they had been while unemployed. Cleanliness and efficiency impressed Born everywhere he went. The functioning of roads, factories, and trains was excellent. However, Born was disturbed by the insecurity of his non-Aryan relatives, by the obscene anti-Semitic propaganda of *Der Stürmer*, a National Socialist publication, and by the unbelievable things that his colleague Max von Laue had told him about life in the university.[25]

When examining the Third Reich, the historian must be careful with his terminology. The British historian Ian Kershaw has provided a valuable distinction between what he defines as "resistance," "opposition," and "nonconformity" to National Socialism. If "resistance" is considered at one end of the spectrum, referring to an utter rejection of all that National Socialism stood for as well as a planned attempt to work for its complete downfall, then obviously "resistance" forms only a small portion of the scale of attitudes present during the Third Reich. "Opposition," active refusal to cooperate with specific measures or directives of the regime, either by individuals, or by groups, is met with more frequently. Finally, "nonconformity," all signs or forms of discontent which have a political expression, was extraordinarily widespread. But Kershaw notes that what is most striking is the partial nature of most of this opposition or nonconformity. Opinion and behavior were concerned with specific elements of Nazi rule, but were not extended in their implications. Therefore a person's behavior could be both conformist and nonconformist at the same time – nonconformist towards the specific, conformist towards the general nature of National Socialist rule.[26]

With the aid of hindsight, one might be tempted to view the collaboration between German science and National Socialism as a Faustian pact, but such a characterization obscures important realities of German science and society during this period. German science circa 1933 contained powerful anti-Semitic, anti-democratic, imperialistic, and nationalistic currents, which can be traced back to the Wilhelmian Empire, if not further. Moreover, the National Socialists were not aided by supernatural forces. Hitler did not use mirrors to gain control of Germany. Without the support of influential economic, industrial, and conservative circles that desired the end of the republic and to which a considerable portion of the scientific community belonged, and considerable mass appeal, especially from the alienated and devastated middle classes, the National Socialist seizure and consolidation of power is inconceivable.

National Socialism was not something painted on top of the Weimar Republic. This ideology eventually pervaded every aspect of life in Germany during the Third Reich. Therefore, when the question of responsibility for the legacy of German National Socialism is raised, a differentiated analysis is required. Some histories of the National Socialist period have dealt with historical figures whose names are now synonymous with evil, whose "guilt" is clear. Still other histories have shed light on the few, but honorable Germans, who resisted national Socialism actively. But this history of the German quest for nuclear power does not, and cannot, recognize such a black-and-white portrayal of Germans under Hitler. The actors in this historical drama all fell in the gray area in between, where one both opposed, and collaborated with, different aspects of National Socialism. Along with many other victims, German science and scientists were often seduced by the atavistic National Socialist vision of a rebirth of German power.

1 ✣ Lightning war

According to unanimous reports from all over the Reich, the *special news reports of the last few days* have elevated the mood of the population considerably...Even though the people had been prepared for the announcement of a successful operation, the extent and wealth [*Fülle*] of the achievement nevertheless surpassed all expectations...The great successes of German warfare in the East have led a portion of the population to *hope* that *the eastern campaign will end this year*. It is often assumed that after Leningrad falls as expected in the next few days, any further resistance by the main Soviet forces which, as the news reports imply, continue, will be broken...[thus] undoubtedly sealing the fate of the collapsing Soviet regime. Once again, here and there deadlines such as 'four to six weeks' have been set for the end of the war against Russia.

From a secret report by the SS security service (22 Sept. 1941)[1]

Nuclear fission

By the fall of 1938, Germany had lost her contented face and National Socialism had shed its tranquil mask. Aided by the policy of appeasement employed by Britain and France, Hitler's government had considerably strengthened its foreign and domestic position by the annexation of Austria and the Sudetenland region of Czechoslovakia. As Germany continued to press for further territorial expansion in the face of British and French opposition, the specter of European war reappeared. Just as Germany became more of a military threat to her neighbors, the domestic policy of the German government turned more blatantly racist and totalitarian. The "Crystal Night" (*Reichskristallnacht*) of 10 November 1938 brought virulent anti-Semitism back out into the open. Throughout Germany, Jewish shops, homes, and synagogues were looted, defaced, and burned. The reaction of most scientists to the events of 1938, especially if they were not personally involved, was to shut out the growing domestic and foreign pressure by concentrating even more on their teaching duties and research.[2]

Hahn wrote to his friend and colleague Lise Meitner shortly before

Christmas and asked her opinion of a perplexing experiment that he and Fritz Strassmann had just concluded at Hahn's Kaiser Wilhelm Institute for Chemistry in Berlin-Dahlem. By bombarding uranium with neutrons, Hahn and Strassmann had expected to manufacture radium, a neighbor of uranium with respect to mass. But instead of knocking a few particles loose from the uranium nucleus, they appeared to have split it. Hahn and Strassmann found barium in their sample solution, an element almost half the mass of uranium. Meitner, an Austrian Jew, had worked with Hahn for several decades before the events of 1938 forced her flight to Scandinavia. Her immediate response to Hahn's news was cautious, but encouraging. Although the idea of a nuclear explosion was difficult to believe, she was unwilling to say that such a disintegration was impossible.[3]

Hahn's and Strassman's experiment was described in a cautious article drafted by Hahn for the journal *Die Naturwissenschaften*. Up until that time, scientists had assumed that the neutron bombardment of uranium led either to a transuranic element, if the neutron stuck in the nucleus, or to an element with slightly less mass than uranium, if the neutron chipped off part of the nucleus or caused the emission of a nuclear particle. Since this phenomenon fitted into neither category, Hahn, Strassmann, and many other scientists were forced to recognize that nuclei could be split.[4]

Taking advantage of the head start that Hahn's letter had provided her, Meitner and her nephew Otto Frisch quickly used Niels Bohr's "liquid drop" model of the nucleus to explain the new process. The behavior of a heavy nucleus was analogous to the movement of a liquid drop. If this drop was disturbed, then it might divide into two smaller pieces. Bohr also assumed that nuclear matter had a "surface tension" similar to that found in water. But at the nuclear level, surface tension was diminished by increasing nuclear charge. Helium, with charge two, had an extremely strong surface tension, while the surface tension of uranium, with charge ninety-two, was relatively weak. Meitner and Frisch estimated that the surface tension of nuclei, decreasing with increasing nuclear charge, approached zero for atomic numbers on the order of a hundred. Given its low surface tension, the relatively unstable uranium nucleus seemed susceptible to "fission" if bombarded by a neutron.[5]

Researchers in Denmark, France, and Germany – Frédéric Joliot in Paris, Frisch and Meitner at Copenhagen, and Siegfried Flügge and Gottfried von Droste at Hahn's institute – independently predicted that nuclear fission released large amounts of energy. Since the sums of the masses of practically all possible pairs of fission products were considerably smaller than the mass of the original uranium nucleus, the loss in mass had to represent a release of energy, which would cause the fission fragments to move apart at high velocity. Thus these particles should be detectable, either by following their trails in a gas-filled ionization chamber, or by placing a small sheet of metal near the uranium and thereby collecting the fission products. Bohr unveiled the liquid drop theory of nuclear fission on 26 January 1939 at the fifth Washington Conference on Theoretical Physics, touching off a frenzy of activity. By the time the flood of publications began slackening off in March, more than eighteen different research teams from France, Germany, and the United States had independently verified nuclear fission.[6]

As soon as Hahn and Strassmann began thinking in terms of fission products, they realized that the fission process should release neutrons along with the two or three fission fragments. This exciting suggestion was published in a second article on nuclear fission in late January of 1939. By May, more than eleven scientific papers, again from France, Germany, and the United States, had reported the production of "secondary" neutrons. In other words, neutrons were liberated from a uranium nucleus through the collision of a primary neutron with this nucleus. If a uranium nucleus was split into two particles, then the uranium nuclear mass and charge must be divided between the two lighter nuclei. However, the respective fission products would then contain considerably more neutrons than the heaviest stable isotopes with the same nuclear charges. This neutron excess could disappear through one of two processes. Either a neutron was transformed into a proton by the emission of a beta particle, thereby reducing the neutron excess by two, or neutrons were liberated directly during fission.[7]

Fission definitely produced secondary neutrons, moreover these neutrons were ejected at high velocity. Scientists realized immediately that if high-velocity neutrons were produced when a uranium nucleus splits, then an exponentially-increasing, energy-producing, nuclear-fission chain reaction was possible. Once again, several groups of researchers in France, the United States, and Germany independently estimated the average number of neutrons released per fission as between 2·3 and 3·5. Chain reactions appeared promising.[8]

The discovery of nuclear fission and the potential of energy production through nuclear-fission chain reactions caused great excitement in the international physics community. But, at first glance, Hahn's and Strassman's results also appeared contradictory. In 1937, Meitner, Hahn, and Strassmann had shown that uranium sometimes experienced "resonance absorption." Neutrons traveling at certain relatively high velocities were absorbed by the uranium nucleus, but instead of exciting fission, these neutrons remained in the nucleus and led to a heavier isotope of uranium. However, neutrons traveling at thermal velocities (where movement is caused solely by the heat of the system) split uranium nuclei very effectively. Thus the apparent contradiction. If the impact of a slow neutron caused fission, why would a faster neutron strike the nucleus and be captured?[9]

Bohr suggested that these two conflicting phenomena could be resolved by the existence of different uranium isotopes. In particular, he argued that thermal neutrons caused fission in the rare uranium isotope with mass 235, while the far more common uranium isotope with mass 238 was responsible for resonance absorption. Less than two weeks after Bohr had submitted this brief note to the American journal *The Physical Review* in early February 1939, a research team at Columbia University in New York City provided indirect evidence in support of Bohr's proposal. Moreover, Bohr's opinion carried considerable weight in the physics community. By the following summer a contributor to *The Physical Review* noted that uranium 235 was commonly believed to be responsible for the thermal neutron fission of uranium. This belief was reinforced by a thorough article on the mechanism of nuclear fission by Bohr and the American physicist John Wheeler. Their convincing theoretical explanation of nuclear fission and the resulting phenomena attributed the resonance capture process strictly to uranium 238 and thermal neutron fission to uranium 235.[10]

By June of 1939, less than six months after the original publication by Hahn and Strassmann, fission research had progressed far enough to warrant a review article by the theoretical physicist Siegfried Flügge in *Die Naturwissenschaften*, "Can the Energy Content of Atomic Nuclei Be Harnessed?" (Flügge also wrote a popular version for the German newspaper *Deutsche Allgemeine Zeitung*.) For the first time anywhere, Flügge discussed the possibility of constructing an energy-producing "uranium machine" out of uranium and a "moderator". This latter substance would slow down the neutrons released by fission and thereby inhibit the chain reaction. Flügge painted an almost fantastic picture of the great potential of nuclear power. If all the available uranium atoms in 1 cubic meter of uranium oxide could be fissioned, he wrote, then the energy thereby liberated could lift 1 cubic kilometer of water 27 kilometers into the air. If all the available uranium atoms in 4 metric tons of uranium oxide could be fissioned in a uranium machine, then this machine would equal the output of all German coal-fueled power plants for eleven years.[11]

Less than a year after Hahn's and Strassmann's article on nuclear fission, the Princeton University physicist Louis Turner reviewed the nearly one hundred scientific papers that had already appeared on nuclear fission. His survey in *Review of Modern Physics* stressed five important points:

1 nuclear fission releases enormous amounts of energy;
2 nuclear fission emits high-velocity neutrons;
3 thermal neutron fission probably occurred in the rare uranium 235, while uranium 238 experienced resonance absorption;
4 since more than two neutrons appears to be released per fission, there was the possibility of a "catastrophic" chain-reaction which would release terrific amounts of energy in a short time;

5 such chain reactions could be controlled in a "uranium machine" consisting of uranium and moderator.[12]

The next steps towards applied nuclear fission were clear: large-scale uranium isotope separation and the construction of energy-producing uranium machines. Turner's article, published three months after the German invasion of Poland had touched off World War II, clearly illustrated the great potential of nuclear power. The published discussion of nuclear fission had been limited to topics of fundamental scientific interest and electricity production, but the application of nuclear fission to warfare had not gone unnoticed. Behind the barriers of secrecy, researchers in France, Germany, Great Britain, Japan, Russia, and the United States began investigating the military potential of Hahn's and Strassmann's discovery. This book is a history of this effort in Germany, where the story began.[13]

The German nuclear power project

In the spring of 1939, several German scientists brought the economic and military potential of nuclear fission to the attention of at least two different authorities. The Göttingen University physicists Georg Joos and Wilhelm Hanle contacted the Ministry of Culture (*Kultusministerium*), which forwarded the letter to the Reich Research Council in the Ministry of Education. Abraham Esau, a technical physicist in charge of the physics department in the Council, was impressed by the prospects of applied nuclear power and held an organizational meeting for a "uranium club" (*Uranverein*) on 29 April 1939. The industrial physicist Nikolaus Riehl, a former student of Hahn and Meitner and the head of a scientific research department in the Auer Company, brought nuclear power to the attention of the army. Long after the war, Riehl recalled that he had been inspired by Flügge's article in *Die Naturwissenschaften* and immediately became interested in the applications of uranium nuclear fission. The Auer Company, which had experience with radioactivity, luminescence, and rare earths such as cerium, expected Riehl to develop new, marketable products, and he was always alert to the application of science to the marketplace. Riehl contacted Army Ordnance and offered the services of Auer for uranium production. However, at first the army seemed uninterested.[14]

The army was also contacted by their chemical explosives consultant Harteck and his assistant Wilhelm Groth. This letter, written on 24 April 1939, explicitly mentioned the military application of nuclear-fission chain reactions in uranium. In their opinion, the recent developments in nuclear physics might allow the production of an explosive many orders of magnitude more powerful than those then available. Moreover, Harteck and Groth pointed out the political significance of nuclear fission, arguing that the country which first used nuclear explosives would have an "unsurpassable advantage." The question of intent naturally arises here. Why did these scientists bring nuclear fission to the attention of civilian and military authorities in National Socialist Germany? These scientists were not "convinced National Socialists," a complimentary title used by the National Socialist movement when judging the commitment of its members. In fact, Riehl had to conceal his non-Aryan ancestry throughout the Third Reich. These scientists were probably motivated in varying degrees by nationalism, patriotism, and ambition, professional as well as personal.[15]

Harteck had to wait until August for a reply, when Army Ordnance thanked him for his report, noted that it was aware of the scientific work on nuclear fission, and invited him to Berlin for a confidential conference. In a move typical of the National Socialist period, Army Ordnance moved quickly after the start of war to squeeze out the Reich Research Council by setting up their own nuclear power project and ordering the council to halt all such experiments. Esau appealed to his superior, Rudolf Mentzel, but the latter replied that Army Ordnance had been working on nuclear fission for years, and parallel work should be avoided. Esau's objection, that the discovery of nuclear fission was less than a year old, fell on deaf ears.[16]

The seizure of nuclear fission research by the army demonstrated the pecking order of science policy in National Socialist Germany. The armed forces and German industry formed two relatively independent power centers. Both groups had held strong political positions as the National Socialists came to power, and both continued to be indispensable for National Socialist foreign and domestic policy. In exchange for partial collaboration with, and integration into the National Socialist movement – for example, companies often purged any Jewish executives and many industrialists became members of the National Socialist German Workers Party – both the military and industry had considerable autonomy as the war began. However, this relative freedom of movement did not mean that either of these groups necessarily opposed rearmament, the war, or most aspects of National Socialist policy. These groups had some limited autonomy because of their cooperation with, or support of, National Socialism. The Ministry of Education, on the other hand, was one of the weakest agencies in the National Socialist state. There was little doubt who would get the upper hand in any bureaucratic battles between Army Ordnance and the Reich Research Council, especially while the lightning war was scoring impressive victories and German armies occupied most of Europe.[17]

As several German scientists recalled long after the war, the army had a specific utilitarian interest in nuclear fission. Could nuclear power influence the foreseeable course of the war? If not, then the enemy could not surprise Germany with nuclear weapons. If the application of nuclear power to warfare could be a decisive weapon, then the necessity of German research into the economic and military uses of nuclear fission was self-evident. The organization and administration of the research project was entrusted to Kurt Diebner, the expert in both atomic physics and the physics of explosives at Army Ordnance. Whereas in 1914 the German armed forces had reacted condescendingly towards scientific claims of military utility, synthetic ammonia production, the efficient organization and distribution of raw materials and manpower, and poison gas had given the military new respect for science. By 1939, Army Ordnance included weaponry research departments for various scientific disciplines, including physics, which were staffed by good, competent scientists.[18]

One of the first steps Diebner took was to contact the young physicist Erich Bagge. As Bagge recalled long after the war, Army Ordnance had offered him a job in 1938 because of his work on the disintegration of deuterium (a heavy isotope of hydrogen), but Bagge declined in order to become an assistant at Werner Heisenberg's Institute for Theoretical Physics at the University of Leipzig. When Army Ordnance decided to fund nuclear fission research, the army scientists remembered Bagge as an expert on nuclear disintegration. Diebner's decision to consult Bagge influenced the subsequent development of the German nuclear power project, for this young physicist brought his mentor Heisenberg into a research group that had been dominated by experimental physicists and chemists.[19]

In October of 1939, less than two months after the start of war, Army Ordnance informed Kaiser Wilhelm General Secretary Ernst Telschow that the army was requisitioning the Kaiser Wilhelm Institute for Physics for war work. The National Socialist German government would now decide both what type of research would be performed at the institute, and who would work there. Without informing society President Carl Bosch, Telschow took it upon himself to pass on an ultimatum from the government to the Dutch physicist Peter Debye, the director of the physics institute. Either Debye must give up his Dutch citizenship, become a German citizen, and take part in the war work, or he would lose the directorship. Debye, who did not want to change his citizenship, reached a compromise with the Ministry of Education. Debye would accept a standing offer of a guest professorship at Cornell University in the United States, receive a leave of absence from the Kaiser Wilhelm Society, and continue to draw his pay. The National Socialist German government would do whatever it wanted with the physics institute. Diebner became the administrative head of the Kaiser Wilhelm Institute for Physics. Hahn and Heisenberg were brought in to oversee the scientific research into the economic and military applications of nuclear fission, but were subordinate to Diebner.[20]

The loss of the physics institute was only one example of the policy of accommodation pursued by the Kaiser Wilhelm Society during the Third Reich. Political pressure contributed to Planck's decision to resign his presidency in 1936. In order to retain as much autonomy as possible, the society took a conscious step closer to an alliance with German industry, while several society institute directors and administrators joined the Party. Planck was succeeded by the IG Farben industrialist Carl Bosch, and when the latter died, he was succeeded in turn by Albert Vögler, President of one of the largest steel concerns in Germany. This move towards industry was not a step away from National Socialism, rather it represented a further step into the National Socialist system. Both Bosch and Vögler had close ties to the National Socialist German state, and it was these connections that allowed them to be effective presidents. Although Bosch had quarreled with the National Socialists on some issues, he was above all concerned that IG Farben continue to profit from, and play a major role in, the German armament industry. Vögler was an influential supporter of Hitler and his party even before the National Socialists came to power in 1933. Neither Bosch nor Vögler could have been appointed without the approval of Reich Minister of Education Bernhard Rust. Rust chose Bosch over the physicist Johannes Stark, an "old fighter" (*alter Kämpfer*, a long-standing member and supporter of the National Socialist movement) and vocal advocate of National Socialism. Vögler's appointment was supported by Rust as well as Göring, the second man in the National Socialist German state. Moreover, Vögler served as an unofficial scientific advisor for Reichmarshal (*Reichsmarschall*) Göring. By pursuing the same course of partial integration and collaboration that German industry and the armed forces had taken, the Kaiser Wilhelm Society gained a limited degree of independence in National Socialist Germany.[21]

Although the Kaiser Wilhelm Institute for Physics did become the center of the Army Ordnance nuclear power project – indeed most of the uranium machine trials were held there – much of the research was carried out under the direction of a few leading scientists at university institutes scattered throughout Germany. For example, uranium isotope separation was assigned to Harteck, most of the measurement of nuclear constants (various nuclear properties) took place at the Kaiser Wilhelm Institute for Medical Research under the direction of the physicist Walther Bothe, and Heisenberg was asked to work out the theory of chain reactions. Although there was some overlap, by and large this separation held. Along with being compatible with the National Socialist "leader principle" – whereby an individual was assigned a task and given far-reaching powers and absolute control over his subordinates in order to carry out the assignment – this delegation of authority and division of labor was typical of the German scientific community of the time and perpetuated Wilhelmian structures of scientific organization. A German university professor enjoyed a privileged position in German society. If he was the director of an institute, he handled it as a satrap governed his own province, exercising absolute control within the boundaries prescribed by the higher authority, in this case the army.[22]

Heisenberg, a university professor and scientific advisor at the Kaiser Wilhelm Institute for Physics, held an influential position in the nuclear power project. The purge of Jewish scientists during the first years of the Third Reich had hit theoretical physics especially hard. Heisenberg, recipient of the 1932 Nobel Prize for his work on quantum mechanics, was the leading theoretical physicist left in Germany, and he took up the theory of chain reactions with enthusiasm. By February of 1940, Heisenberg had set out a theory of energy production through nuclear fission. Drawing on the same literature that Turner had reviewed, Heisenberg assumed that Bohr's and Wheeler's argument with respect to uranium 235 was correct, studied mixtures of uranium and moderator that would enhance chain reactions by facilitating secondary neutron production, and sought means for incorporating such mixtures into uranium machines. As long as the uranium was combined with an efficient neutron-moderating substance, Heisenberg believed, natural uranium could be employed for energy production in a uranium machine. Water appeared unsuitable, but Heisenberg thought that heavy water and very pure carbon met these specifications. The "enrichment" of uranium 235 – increasing the ratio of isotope 235 to isotope 238 in a given sample of uranium – would facilitate the chain reaction and the manufacture of an energy-producing uranium machine. Enrichment had another application, as Heisenberg recognized, for if almost pure uranium 235 could be produced, then this uranium isotope represented a nuclear explosive of hitherto unknown power. Heisenberg sent his results on to Army Ordnance and selected colleagues, where his reports were greeted with enthusiasm. According to Heisenberg's predictions, Harteck noted that they could not have hoped for more favorable prospects. Two weeks later, Harteck told his friend and colleague Karl-Friedrich Bonhoeffer that it was time to stop being content with "ridiculously small" experiments. Instead, Harteck wanted to set up large-scale investigations as quickly as possible.[23]

Since Heisenberg's theory was based on Bohr's claim that uranium 235 was responsible for thermal neutron fission, the experimental verification published by American scientists in the spring of 1940, that different uranium isotopes exhibit disparate behavior when bombarded by neutrons of a given velocity, gave welcome support to the German nuclear power project. Alfred Nier and his collaborators used a mass spectrograph to separate molecular beams of uranium in an electromagnetic field, producing minute quantities of separated isotopes. By bombarding these isotopes with neutrons, Bohr's theory was borne out. Thermal neutrons clearly excited fission in uranium 235, while resonance capture occurred in the heavier uranium 238. Although the Vienna physicist Willibald Jentschke did not have access to a mass spectrograph, he was one of several Vienna scientists who also substantiated Bohr's claims a month later by observing analogous phenomena in the element thorium.[24]

Up until this time, separation of the isotopes of heavy elements on an industrial scale had appeared so daunting that it had not even been attempted. Because of the inherent difficulties connected with the pure production of uranium 235, the manufacture of nuclear explosives appeared impracticable, if not impossible. But this pessimistic outlook was altered significantly by the recognition that uranium machines could be used to manufacture transuranic nuclear explosives. Bohr's and Wheeler's theory took on new meaning when combined with the possibility of transuranic elements. In other words, uranium machines produced transuranic elements as a by-product of nuclear fission, and these transuranics appeared to be as easy to fission as uranium 235. In 1934, Enrico Fermi believed that he and his collaborators had manufactured a "new" element. The Italian group had bombarded each of the known elements with neutrons, transmuting the former substances into the element with the next higher charge. In order to regain stability, a nucleus that had absorbed a neutron emitted a negatively-charged "beta" particle with practically no mass, while a neutron within the nucleus transmuted into a proton. This process increased the atomic number by one – transmuting the element – while the mass remained practically unchanged. When the members of Fermi's group bombarded uranium, the last natural element, and detected radioactivity, they assumed that this radiation was caused by transuranic elements. Subsequently Fermi backed off from this claim, and most of the radioactive periods that he had observed were attributed retroactively to fission products after the discovery of nuclear fission. However, there was still the matter of the uranium resonance absorption observed in 1937. If uranium 238 captured a neutron, then uranium 239 would be formed. According to measurements, this man-made isotope had a half-life (the period required for half the mass of a given element to decay radioactively) of 23 minutes and emitted beta particles. Thus uranium 239 should transmute into a new element of mass 239 and charge 93.[25]

By 1940 researchers in Germany and the United States were searching for element 93. Edwin McMillan and Philip Abelson used the University of California cyclotron at Berkeley to bombard a thin sheet of a uranium compound with neutrons. As their article in *The Physical Review* reported, the fission products burst out of the layer, while the uranium nuclei which had captured neutrons remained. Along with the known 23 minute half-life, they detected another radioactive half-life of 2.3 days. They assumed that this activity had been caused by element 93, and the American researchers strengthened this claim by demonstrating that the substance with the 2.3 day half-life grew from the uranium 239.[26]

Working at the Kaiser Wilhelm Institute for Chemistry, the young radiochemist Kurt Starke independently discovered element 93 by means of a different method. Since Starke had only weak neutron sources at his disposal, he first enriched the uranium 239 in the irradiated uranium sample. This enrichment was possible because, under certain circumstances, artificially-radioactive isotopes can be separated from the natural isotopes of the same element as if the man-made and natural isotopes were chemically dissimilar. Starke then demonstrated that a substance with a 2.3 day half-life grew from the artificially radioactive uranium. After Starke had succeeded in producing element 93[239], Hahn and Strassmann also turned their attention to the properties of the new element.[27]

Since element 93 emitted beta particles as well, scientists immediately began searching for its daughter product element 94[239]. McMillan and Abelson believed that element 94 should emit "alpha" particles (a particle consisting of two protons and two neutrons). Since they could not find any such emission, the two researchers speculated in their May 1940 article that 94 was a long-lived element with a half-life on the order of a million years. German physicists and chemists also sought element 94, but the lack of a strong neutron source held them back. The Vienna scientist Josef Schintlmeister observed a substance which radiated alpha particles, and he thought that it might be 94, but as Starke remembered long after the war, his colleagues were skeptical. Schintlmeister was unable to demonstrate convincingly that he had found the new element.[28]

The idea of discovering or manufacturing a new element certainly was attractive to German scientists, but there were other reasons why elements 93 and 94 were of interest to Army Ordnance. Several German theoretical physicists independently came to the conclusion that, according to the Bohr–Wheeler theory, transuranic elements were even easier to fission than uranium 235 and therefore were potential nuclear explosives. Siegfried Flügge, Fritz Houtermans, and Carl-Friedrich von Weizsäcker all realized that a uranium machine could be used to manufacture fissionable materials. The application of the Bohr–Wheeler theory to transuranic elements was obvious. If these German physicists had not come to this conclusion themselves, they could have read it in the first 1940 issue of the American journal *The Physical Review*. [29]

In the summer of 1940, Weizsäcker set out the problem in a vivid report to Army Ordnance. Drawing on Nier's experimental results as well as the Bohr–Wheeler theory, Weizsäcker noted that uranium 238 could be fissioned by thermal neutrons and thereby be used as a nuclear explosive. This fission would be the result of not one, but two neutrons deposited successively. The first neutron produced uranium 239, which decayed to element 93. According to the Bohr–Wheeler theory, this transuranic element was easier to fission than uranium 235. (At the time he wrote this report, Weizsäcker was unsure whether element 93 or element 94 would be long-lived, though shortly thereafter the Germans adopted McMillan's and Abelson's view and assumed that element 94 was the stable transuranic.) Weizsäcker also cautioned that the fissionability of these transuranics could only be tested after amounts large enough to be weighed had been produced in uranium machines. In the summary of his report, he noted two important applications of interest to Army Ordnance for these new elements: smaller uranium machines, and nuclear explosives.[30]

By taking advantage of key American and French publications, as well as utilizing their own secret research, the members of the German nuclear power project were able to lay out clearly the military and economic applications of nuclear fission. An energy-producing chain reaction could be achieved through uranium isotope separation, the construction of a uranium machine, or both. Uranium enrichment and uranium machines were complementary, not mutually exclusive. Furthermore, such a chain reaction had two possible applications. As an Army Ordnance spokesman put it, a slow chain reaction in uranium represented a heat-producing uranium machine. A fast chain reaction in uranium represented a very effective nuclear explosive.[31]

In other words, a slow, controlled chain reaction in a uranium machine would produce a continuous stream of heat, and could thereby generate electricity. A fast, uncontrolled reaction in uranium 235 or in a transuranic element would become a nuclear explosive. Furthermore, controlled and uncontrolled chain reactions were simply two complementary aspects of nuclear power. Although an electricity-producing uranium machine could be constructed with enriched uranium and water, any uranium isotope separation method capable of enriching uranium significantly eventually could produce the nuclear explosive uranium 235 through a step process. Any uranium machine, whether composed of enriched uranium and water, or natural uranium and a more effective moderator, could also be used to produce highly-fissionable transuranic elements and thereby nuclear explosives. In practice, research on uranium machines or isotope separation was also research on nuclear weapons. Once this ground work had been laid, these scientists pressed ahead on the three basic problems for the realization of nuclear power: an effective neutron moderator, isotope separation, and uranium machines.

Moderators, isotope separation, and uranium machines

As Siegfried Flügge pointed out in his article in *Die Naturwissenschaften*, a uranium machine needed an effective moderator, a substance that slowed down neutrons passing through it, but did not absorb them. Ideally, the neutrons entered the moderator, experienced a series of collisions with moderator molecules, lost some energy with each impact, and excited the moderator at a much lower velocity. Since this energy loss occurs as a result of nuclear collisions, the smallest nuclei should be the most efficient, and the first successful moderators were paraffin and water, both substances rich in hydrogen. As Werner Heisenberg stressed in his reports to Army Ordnance, only water, heavy water (oxygen combined with deuterium, D_2O), and carbon were feasible moderators for a uranium machine. For a machine to run with ordinary water as moderator, enriched uranium would probably be needed. Although hydrogen was an excellent moderator with respect to energy loss, it also tended to absorb neutrons.[32]

When Paul Harteck learned that carbon was a promising moderator, he immediately suggested to Army Ordnance that solid carbon dioxide be tested for neutron moderation and absorption, since this form of carbon is relatively free from impurities. Without waiting for a reply, Harteck took advantage of his excellent connections with German industry and persuaded IG Farben to provide a block of dry ice (frozen carbon dioxide) free of charge. As soon as the dry ice was secured, Harteck proposed an experimental test of carbon as a moderator, requesting 100 to 300 kilograms of uranium from Army Ordnance as well as a railway car to rush the dry ice to Hamburg.[33]

Army Ordnance agreed to provide the rail transport and at least 100 kilograms of uranium. But there was little uranium available in the spring of 1940, and the scientists at the Kaiser Wilhelm Institute for Physics were planning experiments with uranium as well. Heisenberg wrote to Harteck in late April and told him that, although only 150 kilograms of uranium were on hand in the spring of 1940, by the end of June more than six times as much uranium should be available. Heisenberg had ordered several hundred kilograms of uranium himself, and politely asked Harteck if he could postpone his dry ice experiment. On the other hand, Heisenberg graciously offered to let the Hamburg physical chemist have first crack at the uranium, if Harteck thought it necessary. In any case, Kurt Diebner would make the final decision.[34]

Harteck replied the very next day. The timing of the experiment was crucial. He had to have the uranium by the beginning of June. After that date, IG Farben needed all its dry ice for food storage. Harteck wrote Diebner and stressed that 200 kilograms was the minimum amount necessary for a meaningful experiment. Diebner, trying to keep both sides happy, compromised. Harteck received one third of the 150 kilograms belonging to the Kaiser Wilhelm Institute for Physics and 150 kilograms of freshly-purified uranium from the Auer Company. Nikolaus Riehl delivered the metal to Harteck personally. Given the amount of uranium available, Diebner's distribution of uranium was reasonable and generous. Unfortunately, 200 kilograms nevertheless proved too little to yield significant experimental results.[35]

The next German scientist to examine carbon as a moderator was Walther Bothe in Heidelberg. As part of the measurements of nuclear constants performed at his institute, Bothe studied the neutron absorption of carbon. His first experiments were inconclusive, due to the inhomogeneous quality of his sample of graphite, a very pure form of carbon. The second round of measurements used electro-graphite from the Siemens Company, the purest form of carbon commercially available, and yielded unfavorable results. According to Bothe's measurements and the requirements set out by Heisenberg's theory, a uranium machine would not work with electro-graphite.[36]

Aside from Harteck's brief passing interest, the only advocates of carbon as a moderator were Wilhelm Hanle and Georg Joos. However, the army takeover of nuclear fission research had pushed them, along with Abraham Esau, out of the picture, and both Hanle and Joos were engaged in other war research. Hanle learned of Bothe's discouraging results, carried out his own measurements on carbon, and came to different conclusions. Bothe's results were misleading, though understandable. As Hanle demonstrated, even the Siemens electro-graphite contained boron and cadmium, two strong absorbers of thermal neutrons. When the influence of these impurities was taken into account, carbon appeared to be a much more promising moderator. Hanle also pointed to the cause of Bothe's and Peter Jensen's pessimistic results. In order to measure the impurity content, the Heidelberg physicists had reduced part of the graphite to ashes. But whereas Bothe and Jensen had assumed that neutron-absorbing impurities would not be lost during this combustion, Hanle showed that such a loss was very likely. Finally, Hanle also described methods for producing moderator carbon of sufficient purity.[37]

Even though Hanle remained outside of the nuclear power project, he nevertheless sent his results to Army Ordnance, where they were put to good use. Taking Hanle's research as well as Bothe's results into account, Army Ordnance recognized that carbon could be an effective moderator.

On the other hand, Heisenberg had shown that a machine composed of carbon and uranium would require much more uranium and much more moderator than a heavy water device. In the end, Army Ordnance came to the reasonable conclusion that given the requirements of the German war effort, carbon was not a feasible moderator. Boron- and cadmium-free carbon of sufficient purity could be produced, but only at prohibitive costs.[38]

It was heavy water, not carbon, that excited great interest among German scientists. In 1932, American researchers had discovered that the electrolysis of water also separated hydrogen from deuterium and thereby represented a method for separating "light" water (H_2O) from "heavy" water (D_2O). This discovery was quickly exploited in Europe. On the suggestion of the German physical chemist Karl-Friedrich Bonhoeffer, the Norwegian Hydro Company, a manufacturer of electrolytic hydrogen, began producing and selling heavy water as a sideline. But Bonhoeffer was not the only German scientist who became involved with heavy water. The physical chemist and physicist Karl Wirtz, an assistant to Bonhoeffer at the University of Leipzig before he moved on to the Kaiser Wilhelm Institute for Physics, had done much of his best research on heavy water. Harteck had studied heavy water together with Ernest Rutherford in England. Along with his Hamburg collaborator Hans Suess, Harteck had been searching for ways to mass-produce heavy water before the Norwegian Hydro made this research appear superfluous. Finally, the Munich physical chemist Klaus Clusius had a great deal of experience with heavy water as well.[39]

Heisenberg's discussion of neutron moderators quickly revived Harteck's interest in heavy water. As soon as he received a copy of Heisenberg's report, Harteck asked his Leipzig colleague what was being done about the mass production of heavy water. Heisenberg replied that Army Ordnance had met with Bonhoeffer and Wirtz in Berlin, but electrolysis was the only production method under consideration. Harteck immediately wrote to Army Ordnance, made clear that electrolytic heavy water production was not economically feasible in Germany, and suggested a catalytic conversion process. Although Army Ordnance officials assured Harteck that they were taking care of the matter, the Hamburg scientist nevertheless asked his friend Bonhoeffer if he would be willing to experiment with catalytic exchange processes. Bonhoeffer inquired in turn at IG Farben, and the chemical giant expressed interest in Harteck's suggestion. Further support for large-scale heavy water production came a few months later, when in August 1940 the Leipzig physicist Robert Döpel demonstrated experimentally that heavy water was an excellent moderator, which implied that a machine built from natural uranium and heavy water should work.[40]

The German invasion and occupation of Norway in April of 1940 and the subsequent seizure of the Norwegian Hydro by IG Farben drastically altered Germany's potential for heavy water production. Under German control, the heavy water production was quickly enlarged from a rate of 20 liters per year to 1 metric ton for the same period. This takeover followed the general German policy of setting up defense plants in occupied countries whenever possible. During 1941, the Norwegians were forced to install a catalytic conversion process, designed by Harteck and Suess, which was to boost production to 4 or 5 tons per year. According to the best German estimates for the amount of heavy water required by a uranium machine, Norwegian Hydro therefore could provide the heavy water for one uranium machine per year. Production and installation costs were paid by the Norwegians. The Norwegian Hydro officials were also ordered to use Norwegian contractors and materials whenever possible. As a gesture of goodwill, IG Farben sent Army Ordnance the first shipment of 1,500 kilograms heavy water at cost, and the chemical cartel was offering Army Ordnance a special low rate for Norwegian heavy water by the summer of 1942. Heavy water was produced in Norway instead of Germany because this policy promised to provide for the entire nuclear fission development program as well as the first large-scale uranium machine as quickly and as inexpensively as possible.[41]

Although by the end of 1941 everyone involved with nuclear fission research was committed to heavy water as a moderator, there was disagreement with respect to how heavy water should be produced. Clusius, Harteck, and other scientists pushed for the development of new production processes in Germany that would be more cost-efficient in the long run. In a report written in December of 1941, Harteck surveyed four production methods: electrolysis; a catalytic exchange process between hydrogen and water that utilized the disparate equilibrium constants that existed at two different temperatures; a low-pressure rectification (repeated distillation) column; and the rectification of liquid hydrogen at normal pressure. According to Harteck, electrolysis in Germany entailed prohibitive costs, but cost-efficient large-scale production could be achieved through one of the remaining methods. Each of these processes appeared equally profitable. Specific local conditions – the availability of energy sources, of cooling water, and so forth – would determine which particular process was most suitable.[42]

However, when Harteck came to consider the necessary investment costs, Army Ordnance no longer found him reassuring. Although any one of the new processes could undersell the Norwegian Hydro in time, Harteck admitted that an initial investment of around half a million Reichmarks would be required per metric ton of heavy water. For example, if 2 metric tons were to be produced, then an investment of a million

Reichmarks was needed. Army Ordnance preferred to buy Norwegian heavy water from IG Farben, rather than to invest large sums of money for heavy water production in Germany. If new heavy water production processes were to be developed, they had to be economical and entail relatively low start-up costs. For Army Ordnance, any disturbance of the war effort had to be avoided.[43]

Heavy water was needed for a machine to run on natural uranium as nuclear fuel, but Heisenberg had shown that ordinary water would suffice as a moderator, if enriched uranium could be made available. This conclusion gave added significance to isotope separation. Along with the previously recognized value of uranium 235 as a nuclear explosive, a successful large-scale uranium enrichment process effectively would eliminate the moderator problem. Moreover, Germany appeared to have a promising new method of isotope separation. In July of 1938, the summer before Hahn's and Strassmann's article on nuclear fission, Clusius and his younger colleague Gerhard Dickel had unveiled their "separation tube."[44]

The two Munich physical chemists heated one wall of a vertical tube containing various gas mixtures (see figure 1). Because of a thermo-diffusion effect, the heavier molecules concentrated themselves on the colder wall, while the lighter molecules moved towards the warmer wall. In addition, a thermo-siphon effect caused the gas mixture to rise along the warmer wall to the top of the tube, where it was diverted to the colder wall. The gas then sank along the cold wall to the bottom, moved over to the warmer wall, and rose again along this wall in turn. These two effects combined to form a counter-current cycle that gradually separated the gas mixture into a heavier component at the bottom of the tube and a lighter one at the top.[45]

The Clusius-Dickel separation device consisted of little more than a glass tube and an electric heating coil, but Clusius' and Dickel's brief article in *Die Naturwissenschaften* during the summer of 1938 touched off con-siderable interest in both the German and international scientific communities. By January of 1939, Wirtz and Horst Korsching had modified the Clusius-Dickel tube in order to separate liquids at the Kaiser Wilhelm Institute for Physics. Clusius and Dickel quickly rose to the challenge and manufactured some heavy water by means of their separation tube. Korsching and Wirtz were full of praise for the new isotope separation method. After using the tube to separate the zinc isotopes they commented that the application of the Clusius-Dickel process to liquids could allow the separation of all isotopes of all elements sometime in the future. A year after their initial article on the separation tube, Clusius and Dickel proudly announced that the separation of the isotopes of chlorine, futilely attempted for more than twenty years, had become fact.[46]

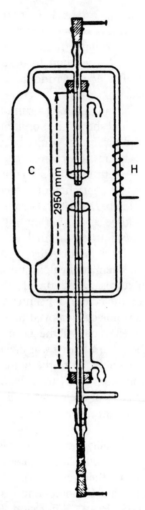

Figure 1 The Clusius–Dickel separation tube.

Note: One wall of a tube containing a gas is heated, in this case by a metal wire coiled around one side. The temperature difference between the warm wall, designated by H (hot), and the colder wall, designated by C (cold), produces both a thermo-diffusion effect – which causes the heavier molecules to concentrate near the colder wall, and a thermo-syphon effect – which causes the gas mixture to rise along the warm wall, to be diverted to, and to sink along the colder wall. These two effects combine to produce a counter-current cycle inside the tube which separates the heavier from the lighter gas isotopes.

Source: Adapted from Klaus Clusius and Gerhard Dickel, "Das Trennrohr," *Zeitschrift für physikalische Chemie B*, 44 (1939), 459.

At first glance, the Clusius-Dickel separation tube appeared far superior to all existing methods of isotope separation. Up until this point, only Gustav Hertz's gaseous diffusion separation process had been able significantly to enrich or separate the isotopes of elements other than hydrogen. Wilhelm Groth compared the efficacy of the two competing methods. Using xenon gas, he found that the Clusius-Dickel tube could be far more efficient and effective than gaseous diffusion. The two Munich physical chemists agreed with Groth's judgment of the superiority of their device, and estimated that the energy, cooling water consumption, purchase cost, and space requirements for a Hertz isotope separation device were from ten to a thousand times greater than for their separation tube. However, they graciously allowed that the Hertz method would probably still be of some use in the future for the processing of very small amounts of gas. Together with Harteck, Groth continued experimenting with the separation tube. Their success in separating the isotopes of mercury suggested that the isotopes of all metal vapors could be isolated by means of the separation tube.[47]

Because of Groth's own striking success with the Clusius-Dickel device, once the Army Ordnance nuclear power project began in earnest, Harteck and his collaborators turned immediately to the separation tube. The Clusius-Dickel device appeared to be one of the shortest paths to the realization of nuclear power, as Rudolf Fleischmann, a physicist at Bothe's institute, concluded independently in 1940. However, the problem of uranium isotope separation obviously was very difficult. Nier had measured the isotopic ratio of uranium 235 to uranium 238 as 1 to 139.[48]

Harteck quickly acquired a sample of uranium hexafluoride, the only stable gaseous uranium compound, proposed to Diebner that the Clusius-Dickel separation tube be used for the uranium isotopes, and began building an 8-meter separation tube for uranium. The army approved Harteck's proposal, Army Ordnance sent 500 grams of uranium to the Hamburg physical chemistry institute for the production of uranium hexafluoride, and Harteck began searching for a suitable tube material. Since uranium hexafluoride is a very corrosive gas, the walls of the separation tube had to be resistant to deterioration. Experiments carried out at IG Farben on Harteck's behalf suggested that nickel was the best metal for a uranium hexafluoride separation tube, but nickel was vital for the war effort and therefore hard to acquire. Harteck ordered his 65 kilogram nickel tube through Army Ordnance, but had to ask the army to intervene for a second time in order to gain approval from the Reich Metals Council. Although these negotiations took time, Harteck did not dawdle. His entire institute was busy with research contracts from the army.[49]

The construction of the nickel tube finally began in October of 1940 and made rapid progress. By the next February, Harteck and his physicist collaborator Johannes Jensen reported to Army Ordnance that prospects were very favorable for uranium isotope separation by means of a nickel separation tube. A project meeting in the spring of 1941 set out two pressing problems: heavy water production and uranium isotope separation. Harteck, who was working on both topics, argued at this time that, for the immediate future, a secure supply of heavy water was more urgent than uranium 235 production or uranium enrichment. Research results had shown that a heavy water machine should run without uranium enrichment, and it appeared much cheaper and easier to manufacture the amount of heavy water needed for a uranium machine than to enrich the isotope 235 in a corresponding amount of uranium by the degree needed to allow a machine to run with ordinary water. Indeed, unless a better isotope separation process was found, Harteck believed that uranium 235 production would only be considered for the manufacture of nuclear explosives, or as he cryptically put it, for "special applications," for which profitability was a "secondary consideration."[50]

But the Clusius-Dickel separation tube quickly lost its appeal. The continuous movement of gas within the tube compounded the problem of corrosion. In the IG Farben experiments, where the gas had simply been confined within a metal container, the uranium hexafluoride had corroded the nickel walls, but this green layer of nickel fluoride had also served as a barrier to further attack. In the Clusius-Dickel separation tube, however, as soon as the hot wall corroded, the corrosion layer traveled to the cold wall, thereby leaving one wall unprotected. Although the problem of corrosion was bad enough, the Hamburg scientists received even more serious news. The corrosion should not have hindered isotope separation, but no enrichment was found in any of the trials with uranium hexafluoride. Since the separation factor of the Clusius-Dickel tube was temperature as well as substance-dependent, Harteck's circle concluded that the separation factor for uranium hexafluoride was practically zero for any useful temperature. In theory, the gas might have a larger separation factor at a higher temperature, but then uranium hexafluoride would be too unstable to use in a Clusius-Dickel tube. By the summer of 1941, Harteck and company were looking for another method of isotope separation.[51]

Other members of the German nuclear power project had been investigating various additional methods of isotope separation. Wilhelm Walcher was developing a high-powered mass spectrograph at Kiel, both for isotope separation and as a means for checking uranium samples for evidence of enrichment. Clusius and Fleischmann independently proposed, and the former developed, an isotope separation method that might be able to exploit the different solubility of isotopes in two non-mixable liquids.

Alfred Klemm tested a separation method at Hahn's institute that used the diffusion of metal ions. Horst Korsching continued to study thermal diffusion in liquids as a way to separate isotopes. Erich Bagge proposed and developed an "isotope sluice," whereby a molecular beam would be sent through rotating blades such that the heavier molecules are periodically cut out of the system and the lighter portion is enriched. But even though a few of these processes showed some promise, their potential was limited. Almost all of the separation methods proposed by researchers outside of Harteck's circle were problematic. Some processes probably would not work with uranium, and the methods that appeared successful were capable of producing only very small quantities of uranium isotopes.[52]

Yet another isotope separation method caught the attention and fancy of the Hamburg group. The Kiel physical chemist Hans Martin had been working on centrifuges since 1933. Just as Harteck's circle had given up on the Clusius-Dickel tube, a talk given by Martin seized their interest. Once again, they lost little time. In August Groth contacted the Kiel Anschütz gyroscope firm, Harteck sent a report on isotope separation by means of ultracentrifuges to Army Ordnance in late September, and in October of 1941 Diebner agreed to let out a contract for the construction of a centrifuge. Groth, who was responsible for most of the day-to-day isotope separation research at Harteck's institute, based his centrifuge design on some recent publications by the American scientist Jesse Beams. Once again, the procurement of necessary materials was hampered by the war. Originally Groth had wanted a centrifuge rotor of high density steel, but the Krupp Company insisted that such an order would take at least eight months to fill. The Hamburg researchers decided to make do with a rotor of a light metal alloy that would be available before the new year. The Anschütz Company was pleased to have the centrifuge contract, but their representative also told Groth that if it ever came to mass production, many more mechanics and engineers would have to be made available to the firm.[53]

The centrifuge had several advantages when it came to isotope separation. Harteck's circle hoped that the centrifuge could avoid some of the corrosion problems apparently inherent in the diffusion of uranium hexafluoride. Since a centrifuge was capable of producing pure uranium 235 in principle, no additional isotope separation process would be needed. Finally, the centrifugal method of isotope separation appeared to be cost-effective, a concern constantly on the minds of Harteck and Army Ordnance representatives.[54]

As the winter of 1941/42 approached, a centrifuge was under construction, but the prospects for large-scale isotope separation, and especially for uranium 235 production, appeared poor. An army spokesman noted laconically that only the Clusius-Dickel process had been tried, and that method had failed. The negative experience with uranium hexafluoride corrosion in the Clusius-Dickel tube had made both Army Ordnance and the Hamburg researchers pessimistic about diffusion processes in general, including Hertz's method. Even Harteck, who was always pushing with both good humor and great vigor for faster and larger development of all aspects of nuclear power, had to admit in December of 1941 that no uranium isotope separation, or even enrichment, had been achieved in Germany, and he went so far as to agree with Army Ordnance that the necessary preconditions for the construction of large-scale isotope separation plants were still lacking.[55]

Army Ordnance was more direct. Although an enrichment of uranium 235 by a factor of two appeared feasible, and such an enrichment of uranium 235 might allow the construction of machines with enriched uranium and ordinary water, the complete separation of the two uranium isotopes from each other – in other words, the manufacture of the nuclear explosive uranium 235 – was not yet within reach. Unless cost-effective isotope separation processes could be found for uranium, Germany's best hope for nuclear explosives and nuclear energy lay with machines composed of heavy water and natural uranium.[56]

Just as Heisenberg's two-part report to Army Ordnance inspired research on heavy water production and gave added weight to uranium isotope separation, his contribution to chain-reaction theory provided the foundation for all subsequent German work on uranium machines. The basic problem was to find, and to construct, a mixture of uranium and moderator that could sustain a controlled, energy-producing, nuclear fission chain reaction and thereby produce heat – which could generate electricity in turn – and breed transuranic nuclear fuel. Drawing on the published results of American, *émigré*, and French scientists, Heisenberg noted that there were two obvious options for uranium machines: either a homogeneous solution, as Hans von Halban, Frédéric Joilot, and Lew Kowarski had used in Paris, or an arrangement of uranium concentrated in large pieces and surrounded with moderator, as Herbert Anderson, Enrico Fermi, and Leo Szilard had constructed in New York.[57]

As soon as the Army Ordnance nuclear power project had been founded, Harteck suggested that a uranium machine with separated layers of uranium and moderator would experience less neutron loss through resonance absorption than a device with a homogeneous mixture of uranium and moderator. Since any neutron loss would hinder a chain reaction, a layer machine might therefore be more effective. After surveying the theory of uranium machines, Heisenberg agreed with his Hamburg colleague. With respect to neutron production, an arrangement that separated the uranium from the moderator would be more effective than a homogeneous solution and, in Heisenberg's opinion, the best design

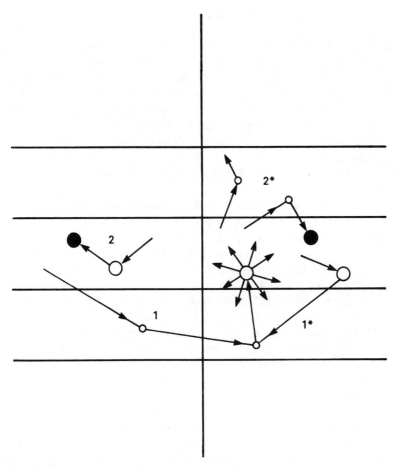

Figure 2 Chain reactions in layer uranium machines.

Note: The smaller circles designate moderator nuclei, the larger circles uranium nuclei, and the arrows represent neutrons in motion which have been released by uranium fission. (1) a neutron enters the moderator layer, experiences a series of inelastic collisions with moderator nuclei, losing energy with each encounter, reenters the uranium layer at slower thermal velocities, and meets a uranium 235 nucleus, exciting fission. (1*) a neutron is deflected by a uranium 238 nucleus into the moderator layer, where it proceeds as (1). (2) a neutron travels within the uranium layer, losing energy by means of collisions with uranium 238 nuclei, until it reaches the resonance velocity and is absorbed by a uranium 238 nucleus. (2*) a nucleus enters the moderator layer only immediately to be reflected back into the uranium layer, where it proceeds as (2).

was probably a series of alternating uranium plates and moderator layers. In the second installment of his report to Army Ordnance, Heisenberg presented the alternating-layer design as the only option for uranium machines.[58]

Layer machines employed either horizontal or spherical layers of uranium and moderator, arranged around a central neutron source (see figure 2). The widths of the uranium layers were chosen so that a neutron released by fission and moving perpendicularly to the layers was likely to enter the moderator before encountering another uranium nucleus. Once inside the moderator, the neutron should remain in the layer long enough to lose most of its initial velocity. In the ideal case (1), the neutron entered the moderator, experienced a series of inelastic collisions, lost a great deal of velocity with each encounter, and finally reentered a uranium layer at thermal velocities. Since there was little danger of resonance absorption for neutrons traveling at this speed, the particle would hopefully bounce around in the uranium until it met with, and fissioned, a uranium 235 nucleus.

But neutrons could be emitted in all directions by fission. If a neutron traveled within the uranium in a direction parallel to the layers, for example, then the neutron would probably collide with a much larger uranium 238 nucleus, lose a small amount of energy, and be deflected away in another direction at slightly reduced speed. The diverted neutron could now move perpendicularly to the layers, enter the moderator, and facilitate further fission (1*), but it could also remain on course within the uranium. After a few collisions with uranium 238 nuclei, the neutron would fall within the resonance absorption energy band for uranium 238 and probably be captured by the heaviest uranium isotope (2). A neutron could also impact with a moderator nucleus and immediately be reflected back into the uranium before losing sufficient energy to avoid resonance absorption (2*). Neutrons which made their way to the exterior of the uranium machine were lost to the chain reaction, and some neutrons might be absorbed by a moderator nucleus. Layer uranium-machine designs had advantages and disadvantages. Since neutrons were emitted in all directions, a certain percentage of fission neutrons were lost through resonance absorption, and the chain reaction was thereby hindered. Although resonance absorption was necessary for the production of transuranic nuclear fuel, a self-sustaining chain reaction was a prerequisite for any significant production of transuranic elements. On the other hand, layer machines were relatively easy to conceive, calculate, and construct.[59]

After he had drafted his two-part report on energy production by means of nuclear fission in the winter of 1939/40, Heisenberg no longer took an immediate interest in uranium machines. He recognized the great potential of applied nuclear fission, but while he avidly followed the development of nuclear power as an administrator, he also left most of the actual theoretical and experimental research to others. Work on the theory of uranium machines continued at the Kaiser Wilhelm Institute for Physics under the direction of Carl-Friedrich von Weizsäcker, but after he had demonstrated the importance of transuranic elements as nuclear fuel, he lost immediate interest as well. Both Heisenberg and his friend and younger colleague Weizsäcker were concerned with fundamental physical problems, not technical or practical matters. Most of the theoretical research on uranium machines was carried out by two of Weizsäcker's graduate students, Karl-Heinz Höcker and Paul Müller.[60]

Höcker and Müller extended and developed the theory of layer machines. Both spherical and horizontal layer systems were considered, the influence of different moderators and of varying temperatures were calculated, and the optimal density of the machine was determined. Bothe also contributed to machine theory by investigating the proper size of the device, the effect of an inwardly-reflecting neutron mantle, and the possibility of using fast neutrons in the chain reaction. This last point was studied by Heisenberg as well. Within the theoretical framework of the layer design, considerable progress was made by the fall of 1941. Metal uranium appeared to be a more effective nuclear fuel than uranium oxide, the use of a reflecting neutron mantle might reduce the necessary size of the machine, and heavy water was the most promising moderator. The preliminary theory of uranium machines was now finished. The next step was to carry out experiments.[61]

Heisenberg's original calculations had shown that very exact values had to be obtained for the various nuclear constants. These preliminary experiments were carried out by around two dozen researchers scattered throughout Germany, although the bulk of the work was done under Bothe's direction in Heidelberg. The measurements, conducted throughout 1941 and 1942, included the ratio of neutrons liberated to neutrons absorbed in uranium, the energy of fission neutrons, the energy distribution for fission fragments, "cross sections" (probability of a given event) for fission by thermal neutrons and for resonance absorption, and neutron increase in different mixtures of uranium and moderator. The results of these measurements were generally encouraging. In some cases, German scientists deliberately repeated experiments which had already been carried out in foreign countries in order to check these results.[62]

Once the preliminary theory and experiments were finished, the next item on the agenda of Army Ordnance was a series of "model experiments." As an Army physicist explained, a uranium machine combined uranium and moderator in order to produce more neutrons than were lost. In effect, a uranium machine was a neutron multiplier. But not every neutron-multiplying design of uranium and moderator was a "uranium machine." A certain minimum amount of materials was needed to facilitate a self-sustaining chain reaction and thereby to allow the significant production of energy and transuranic elements. Smaller designs of uranium and moderator were models of the subsequent self-sustaining machines. The neutron increase or decrease would be measured for various designs in order to correct the theory of uranium machines, establish more exact values for nuclear constants, and provide indispensable experience for the construction, installation, and operation of the next model. Army Ordnance planned trials with increasingly larger amounts of materials and in continually varied form. Once a model could produce more neutrons than were fed into it, the scientists would know that they had found a workable design for a uranium machine. If they increased the scale of this neutron-producing model, eventually they would have a uranium machine capable of sustaining a chain reaction. Model experiments therefore provided an immediate test for the usefulness of a particular uranium and moderator design.[63]

But the model experimental program progressed slowly at first, for very little uranium was available at the beginning of 1940. Once again, the success of the German armies helped the nuclear power project. Tons of uranium compounds were seized from the Belgian Mining Union Company and shipped back to Germany in the wake of the German invasion and occupation of Belgium. However, uranium did not flood into the nuclear power project. The Auer Company had more pressing tasks than uranium production and did not want to commit itself completely to armaments and thereby lose the peace-time market. As far as uranium production went, the orders from Army Ordnance were simply filled as they came in. As always, the army avoided large investments not immediately applicable to the war effort. A uranium-casting plant finally went into operation in early 1941.[64]

The first model experiments (B-I and B-II) were directed by Karl Wirtz during 1940 and 1941 in Berlin-Dahlem and consisted of alternating horizontal layers of uranium oxide and paraffin (see figure 3). Horizontal layers were chosen because they were easy to manufacture and the layer thickness was easy to vary. Höcker had calculated that a layer system of uranium oxide and paraffin or ordinary water as moderator might produce neutrons, and the Berlin-Dahlem physicists under Wirtz decided to test this prediction. Even if the model did not multiply neutrons, the experiment would yield valuable information. In any case, since there was so little uranium and heavy water available, this trial was the only sort of experiment that could be performed at this time. Since the radioactivity from this amount of uranium could contaminate the entire physics institute, an outside laboratory – named the "virus house" to discourage curiosity – was finished in October of 1940. Here the layer design was immersed in a 2 meter, water-filled pit, which was equipped with high-speed pumps quickly to remove the water in case of emergency. Measurements were taken on these model uranium machines, but with negative results. The neutron count was reduced, not increased, by the

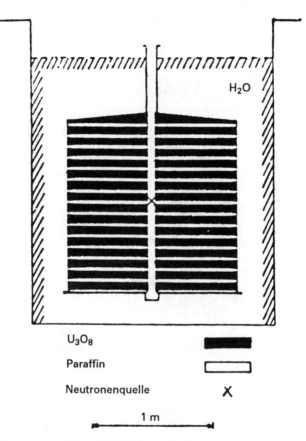

H_2O

U_3O_8

Paraffin

Neutronenquelle   X

1 m

Figure 3 Experiments B-I and B-II (schematic diagram).

Note: Cylinders consisting of alternating horizontal layers of uranium oxide and paraffin, all surrounded by a mantle of water. In the center of the experiment was a neutron source, X (*Neutronquelle*).

Source: Adapted from Walther Bothe and Siegfried Flügge (eds.), *Kernphysik und kosmische Strahlen, Naturforschung und Medizin in Deutschland 1939–1946*, vol. 14 (Weinheim, Chemie, 1948), part 2, p. 152.

model uranium machines. But the measurements nevertheless gave the scientists reason for optimism. Although this combination of uranium oxide and paraffin did not work, it appeared that if heavy water was used as a moderator, then the horizontal layer uranium machine design might achieve a self-sustaining chain reaction.[65]

Complementing the horizontal layer trials in Berlin-Dahlem, Robert Döpel set up a spherical layer system in Leipzig (see figure 4). Layers of uranium oxide and water were separated by aluminum support material sealed with rubber. The design symmetry allowed a high degree of

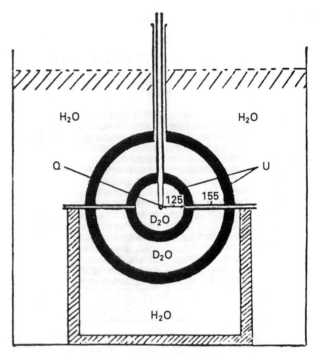

Figure 4 Experiments L-I and L-II (schematic diagram).

Note: Spheres consisting of alternating spherical layers of uranium oxide and water, all surrounded by a mantle of water. In the center of the experiment was a neutron source, Q.

Source: Adapted from Walther Bothe and Siegfried Flügge (eds.), *Kernphysik und kosmische Strahlen, Naturforschung und Medizin in Deutschland 1939–1946*, vol. 14 (Weinheim, Chemie, 1948), part 2, p. 150.

measurement accuracy for small amounts of material. Since the bulk of the uranium was being used in Berlin-Dahlem, Döpel did not have much material to work with. The experiment with water as moderator, L-I, absorbed more neutrons than it produced. On the other hand, it appeared that the spherical machine might "run" with heavy water as moderator, and six months later L-II was underway. Only 150 kilograms of heavy water were on hand, in contrast to the 5 metric tons that the Germans thought a self-sustaining uranium machine would require. More neutrons were absorbed than produced by L-II, but only slightly so. Moreover, the absorption caused by the aluminum support material appeared to be all that was standing in the way of neutron multiplication.[66]

The model experiments were promising, but inconclusive. The tempo of the trials had been dictated by the limited amounts of uranium and moderator. Uranium oxide machines were built with paraffin and water as moderators because so little metal uranium or heavy water was on hand,

and because isotope separation had been unsuccessful. The amount of available materials was influenced in turn by the main concern of Army Ordnance, sticking to cost-efficient, low-investment procedures that would not disturb the war effort. The army was still interested in the military and economic applications of nuclear power, but the success of the lightning war focused their attention on short-term goals.[67]

Nuclear power and lightning war

Was the German quest for nuclear power pursued only in laboratories, on blackboards and desks, and in the minds of scientists? Most of the researchers involved with nuclear fission probably saw their work in this light, but an observer unfettered by the professional blinders that scientists often wear would have seen nuclear power in the consequential context of National Socialist Germany at war, a context symbolized by "lightning war" and "Greater Germany." The nuclear power project was immediately involved in the economic, scientific, and technological plunder of prostrate Europe. Indeed the very start and early progress of this research depended on this exploitation. The first small amounts of uranium oxide were mined in what had once been Czechoslovakia, before tons of uranium compounds were extorted from Belgium by the German occupation authorities. IG Farben made Norwegian Hydro one of its many industrial vassals scattered throughout Greater Germany and thereby controlled the largest heavy water plant in the world. Frédéric Joliot was forced to include several German researchers on his staff at the Paris cyclotron, scientists who were eager to gain experience with one of the few particle accelerators in continental Europe.

These developments were unexceptional for the time. Much, if not most of the lightning war and subsequent German occupation was financed by the plunder of Europe. But not only were these developments unexceptional, they were not new. Belgians in particular must have felt a mild sense of *déjà vu* in 1940 when they saw the second German occupation of their country within a generation. The actions and attitudes of German scientists during the lightning war closely paralleled those of a quarter century before. In contrast to 1914, Germans and German scientists did not generally welcome war in 1939, but the German scientific community nevertheless rallied to the swastika flag once the conflict had begun and successfully rationalized and justified the steady expansion of Greater Germany. The reaction of individual scientists to the cause and effect of the German occupation of Europe strikingly illustrated a continuation and slight adaptation of the "apolitical" ideology. German scientists were often disturbed when faced with the plight of individual foreign colleagues. For example, when Karl Wirtz inspected the Norwegian

Hydro, he saw firsthand the sobering conditions under which old friends and colleagues in Norway had to live. But although individual cases might seem unsettling, in general the scientific, technological, and economic exploitation of Europe was rationalized as an evil necessary for a German victory and Germany's continued prosperity and power.[68]

But scientists did not have the leisure merely to comment on the war. The comprehensive mobilization and conscription in the fall of 1939 greatly disrupted German science – even more than a generation earlier – for although most young scientists had been called up, many had been drafted simply as soldiers, not as scientists, and scientific manpower quickly became scarce. This shortage had an immediate impact on the nuclear power project. Even though Army Ordnance wanted a scientific investigation of nuclear fission, neither this agency nor this task had special priority. Army Ordnance had to compete with other branches of the army for manpower. Moreover, an exemption from direct military service, called *uk* status ("indispensable" – *unabkömmlich*) could be obtained only through the armed forces. The German Army considered the prospects of nuclear power important, and certainly worth a careful investigation, but for the military, this concern was insignificant when compared to the needs of the war effort.

Since Paul Harteck had excellent contacts in the armed forces and German industry – representatives of the latter were often influential middlemen when dealing with the military – he was able to secure service exemptions for all his collaborators. Given his many supporters in German industry, Otto Hahn was in a similar position. Long after the war, Heinz Ewald, a former member of the Kaiser Wilhelm Institute for Chemistry, recalled that Hahn had been able to arrange service exemptions for all the members of his institute. But *uk* status was temporary. It had to be renewed regularly and could be revoked by the military authorities at any time. Karl-Heinz Höcker and Paul Müller were drafted while working on the theory of uranium machines at the Kaiser Wilhelm Institute for Physics. As Höcker recalled long after the war, even though they had been classified *uk*, Kurt Diebner could do nothing to halt the call-up. Carl-Friedrich von Weizsäcker was able to delay the process long enough to allow them to finish their doctoral degrees, whereupon they were sent to the Russian front. This sequence of events vividly illustrated the relative lack of priority enjoyed by the German nuclear power project.[69]

Another group of young researchers found themselves in a similar uncertain position. They, as many other scientists, received *uk* status only while working on specific, limited-term contracts. Depending on the state of the war and the importance of their assignment, they had little security. For example, as Kurt Starke recalled long after the war, he was drafted shortly after he transferred from the Kaiser Wilhelm Institute for Chemistry to Klaus Clusius' Institute for Physical Chemistry at the University of Munich. Only the stubborn efforts of Clusius, who spent an entire day arguing with the military authorities, granted Starke a reprieve. Starke subsequently accepted an offer to work in the group of German scientists at the Paris cyclotron, as much for the additional security this position offered, as for the scientific opportunities it entailed.[70]

In general, researchers with political influence or influential patrons stood a good chance of receiving service exemptions. Without such political influence, it was much more difficult to be classified *uk*. Since it was often easier at this time to remain at a post than to take up a new job, older scientists had a distinct advantage over recent graduates and students. Indeed, the nuclear power project scientists were far better off than most researchers. The contrasting fates of Höcker and Müller demonstrate how uncertain and insecure a position these young scientists found themselves in. Because of poor health, Höcker was able to return to Berlin-Dahlem in 1941 and subsequently received a more secure research and teaching position. Müller died fighting in Russia. However, an attempt by a scientist to avoid front line service through *uk* status did not necessarily imply a lack of support for the war effort or that the scientific war work was uninteresting. *Uk* status provided physicists and chemists with the opportunity to fulfill the military service obligation to the state as a scientist, rather than as a soldier.[71]

For the members of the nuclear power project, this military service obligation was fulfilled in part by nuclear fission research. As the attitude shown by Heisenberg and Weizsäcker towards the theory of uranium machines illustrated, nuclear power quickly became "applied" scientific research, and therefore lost some appeal for certain scientists. But not all members of the nuclear power project had an aversion to applied science. Harteck and Karl Wirtz, two of the most important scientists in the research group, were very interested in the technological application and practical realization of science. The Hamburg physical chemist was one of the strongest driving forces behind the entire nuclear power project. He continually pressed the military, industrialists, and his own colleagues to accelerate the research and development of nuclear power. His younger colleague Wirtz held the main responsibility for the model uranium machine experiments in Berlin-Dahlem.

The senior scientists in the nuclear power project had scientific interests other than nuclear fission, and they did not abandon these other areas of research. For example, although Harteck's institute was completely geared up for the war effort, not all of this research was for the nuclear power project. Harteck was also a consultant for the German chemical industry. Heisenberg devoted most of his time during the first years of the war to cosmic radiation – at that time the only way to investigate high-energy physics experimentally – and after, the physics of fundamental particles. Bothe had devoted most of his time and effort during the pre-war period to the construction of the first German cyclotron. Just as he had finally secured the necessary material and financial backing for this particle accelerator, the start of war put the whole project on hold. As Bothe's negotiations with various governmental authorities dragged on, the members of his institute devoted themselves to nuclear constant measurements for Army Ordnance. Shortly after German troops occupied Paris, Bothe's assistant, Wolfgang Gentner, was sent to head the German group at Joliot's cyclotron. The experience thereby gained was to be put to use later when Gentner returned to Heidelberg.[72]

Hahn and Strassmann continued their comprehensive examination of the nuclear fragments caused by fission. Hahn and his institute made valuable contributions to the military goals of the nuclear power project, as Hahn himself stressed in his reports to Army Ordnance. For example, when Hahn mentioned Starke's successful manufacture of element 93, he also made a point of mentioning the potential of transuranic elements as nuclear explosives by referring to Weizsäcker's report to the army. Although the scientists working for the army on nuclear power were no less enthralled by the great potential of nuclear fission than Army Ordnance, several of these researchers spent a large portion of their time on other tasks, including teaching. This behavior was not passive resistance. These scientists carried out the military research that had been assigned to them – including tasks other than nuclear power – conscientiously and enthusiastically as their part in the German war effort. But a quick German victory was expected, and the question facing Army Ordnance was whether nuclear power could decide the outcome of the war. Nuclear fission research had been well supported and indeed was quite successful. Nevertheless, the nuclear power project had low priority when compared to the immediate war effort. Although good progress had been made, the research status was dependent on the small amounts of material available and researchers involved, in turn a result of the low priority.[73]

Army Ordnance was firmly in control of nuclear fission research. But although the army wanted to be kept up to date on the status of the scientific work, and the scientists were doing their part for the war, neither Army Ordnance officials, nor the scientists, were under great pressure. The German nuclear power research appeared to be far, far removed from the war. No "wonder weapons" were needed. Although the scientists involved with nuclear fission research were well aware of its military potential, they may have believed that they were taking advantage of the war, the military, and the National Socialist government in order to further the cause of their science and their own careers. During 1940 and

1941 it was easy to lose sight of the connection between nuclear fission research and warfare. These new "nuclear weapons" could hardly be of use in this conflict. After all, the war appeared almost won. By October of 1941, almost all of Europe was under German control. Britain was isolated, the United States was neutral, and German armies were rolling on towards Stalingrad and Moscow. Although some Germans had begun to doubt that the war would come to a quick conclusion, most German observers were still looking forward to the inevitable German victory.

2 ✦ The war slows down

The reports of the continual Soviet attacks and the hard defensive fighting on the eastern front have filled the people [Volksgenossen] with increasing uneasiness... The recent news reports do not provide a clear picture of these events. In many cases, the description of a backwards repositioning of the front for strategic reasons originally had an enlightening effect. But since no subsequent statement has been made concerning developments on the eastern front, it is frequently feared that the withdrawal of our troops... might have taken place because of pressure from superior Russian forces... In particular, the people want an explanation why the Russians are still in the position to carry out such attacks, given the previous frequently repeated propaganda about the 'last reserves of the Soviets...'

From a secret report by the SS security service (5 Jan. 1942)[1]

The end of the lightning war

In late November of 1941, the German eastern offensive ground to a halt. The subsequent Russian counterattack brought the lightning war to a definitive end. For the first time, but not the last, Germany was on the defensive. The Third Reich now faced more and tougher opponents. Immediately after the Japanese attack on the American naval base in Pearl Harbor, Germany brought the United States into the European hostilities by a declaration of war. The setbacks in Russia also cost the traditional German military elite much of its remaining independence. Adolf Hitler took over as operational commander of the army a week before Christmas.[2]

Germany's foreign policy reversals had a direct impact on the domestic policy of the National Socialist German government. German public opinion, which had strongly supported the National Socialists and the war as long as Germany was winning and the victorious end appeared near, now became more critical. In response, the internal security apparatus of the government, the secret police (*Gestapo – Geheime Staatspolizei*) and the SS security service (*SD – Sicherheitsdienst der SS*), intensified domestic repression and began implementation of a more extreme racial policy. In general, the control of the National Socialist German government over its citizens became perceptibly tighter.[3]

The military reversals in Russia unexpectedly threatened the heart of the German nuclear power project. Suddenly, both Paul Harteck and Carl-Friedrich von Weizsäcker were called up in January of 1942 for service on the Russian front. In both cases, it was Werner Heisenberg who, by means of patient effort and his close ties to the traditional German military elites, managed to light a fire under Erich Schumann and Army Ordnance and thereby bring about the preservation of Harteck's and Weizsäcker's *uk* status. Heisenberg was aided by Karl-Friedrich Bonhoeffer, whose brother-in-law was an influential figure in the German army. Bonhoeffer, Harteck, Heisenberg, and Weizsäcker all felt as if they and the nuclear power project had dodged a bullet. These scientists were now certainly aware that the war had taken a turn for the worse. As Bonhoeffer wrote to Harteck, they were living in serious times.[4]

The war now shifted gears. Although the German authorities and most Germans still expected to win, any hope of a quick victory was gone, and it now appeared that the war might drag on for a few years. There was a clear and recognized need for a well-ordered war economy, something which the Third Reich had never had. The lightning war had been financed from the plunder of Europe, but Germany now needed to reorganize armaments production, material and supply distribution, and capital investment. It was in this context that the army reconsidered the relevance of nuclear fission research to the war effort. Erich Schumann, a military acoustic physicist and a powerful figure in Army Ordnance, set a reappraisal of the nuclear power project into motion. Schumann was a skillful and powerful science policy maker. For example, as the physicist Georg Hartwig recalled long after the war, Schumann was both a university professor and an army general. When generals visited Schumann, he greeted them in the guise of a German university professor. When scientists visited Schumann, he put on his officer's uniform.[5]

In early December of 1941, Schumann informed the leading scientists in the nuclear fission research group that the continued support of the nuclear power project could be justified only if military applications of nuclear fission could be expected in the foreseeable future. The changing fortunes of war exacerbated both the military demand for manpower and the limited availability of raw materials. Schumann summoned these scientists to a meeting in Berlin and made clear that, as the representative of Army Ordnance, he would make the final recommendation to higher officials with respect to the future status of the nuclear power project. But Schumann and Army Ordnance did not rely exclusively on the reports of Walther Bothe, Klaus Clusius, Otto Hahn, Paul Harteck, and Werner

Heisenberg. Army scientists also prepared a long, thorough, and comprehensive report on nuclear power. The standpoint of these Army Ordnance scientists was expressed clearly in their recommendations. The large-scale industrial exploitation of nuclear power must be attempted, for the great significance that nuclear power could have for the German economy in general, and for the armed forces in particular, more than justified any and all advance research into the applications of applied nuclear fission. Moreover, they believed that this problem was being investigated intensively in America and other enemy countries. These Army Ordnance scientists, who were in the best position to judge the entire nuclear power project in the context of the war effort, desired that this research be supported with all possible means. In particular, they wished to take the considerable and consequential step from laboratory to industrial-scale research and development.[6]

However, a careful reader of this quite enthusiastic report will notice some inconsistencies between the results achieved by the nuclear power project and the proposal to boost the scale of nuclear fission research up to the industrial level of production. For example, the possible application of either uranium 235 or element 94 as a weapon was portrayed dramatically. These nuclear explosives might be a million times more powerful than the same weight of dynamite. Furthermore, a critical mass of only 10 to 100 kilograms would be needed per bomb. But on the other hand, the same authors wrote elsewhere in the same report that a complete separation of uranium 235 from uranium 238 was technologically not yet within reach. In other words, pure uranium 235 was not to be expected soon. As far as element 94 was concerned, the Germans knew neither the amount of element 94 produced by a uranium machine nor the properties of this transuranic precisely enough for an accurate prediction. These army physicists had to concede that only after the first uranium machine had gone into operation or uranium isotope separation was successful on an industrial scale could the feasibility of nuclear explosives production be decided. For the moment, they admitted, there was still a great deal of preliminary work to be done.[7]

Uranium machines did appear promising with heavy water as a moderator, but a close reading of this report would also reveal that, while between 5 and 10 metric tons of both heavy water and uranium were needed per machine, the Norwegian heavy water plant could produce at best 4 to 5 metric tons per year. Electrolysis, the method used in Norway to manufacture heavy water, was too expensive to be used in Germany, and the newer, more efficient methods for producing heavy water had not yet been tested on an industrial scale. According to this report, in theory uranium machines could be used to power tanks, submarines, and planes, but only if enriched uranium or element 94 were available as fuel. In effect, just as was the case for nuclear explosives, these other military applications would have to wait either for large-scale uranium isotope separation or for operating uranium machines. Machines built from natural uranium and heavy water could be used only in ships or as large, immobile power plants.[8]

The Army Ordnance report contained one basic message. The realization of nuclear power in the forms of electricity production or of nuclear explosives was certainly possible, but not close at hand. The step towards the industrial application of nuclear fission would be a very costly one. Indeed, these scientists did not shy away from this conclusion, for their recommendation was ambitious and unambiguous. As soon as the preliminary research was finished, the mobilization of significant amounts of materials and manpower for the nuclear power project was necessary. As soon as all the prerequisites had been achieved, and these scientists did not provide any time scale for accomplishing these goals, the industrial-scale manufacture of heavy water and uranium had to be started as quickly as possible.[9]

Schumann and other leading figures in Army Ordnance were not persuaded by the enthusiasm and zeal of their own experts on nuclear power. Even before the review of nuclear fission research was finished in February of 1942, the army had been leaning towards relinquishing control of nuclear power. A meeting took place in early February between Schumann, Albert Vögler, the President of the Kaiser Wilhelm Society, and General Leeb, the head of Army Ordnance. Schumann's superior informed Vögler that, since the preparatory nuclear power research had come to a "certain formal conclusion," Army Ordnance officials believed that the sponsorship of the project should be transferred to another organization. Leeb proposed that the Kaiser Wilhelm Society take over the research, a suggestion that Vögler happily accepted. Although the nuclear power project had been quite successful, this very success simultaneously had made clear that the practical application of nuclear fission in Germany could not be achieved overnight. For this reason, Army Ordnance concluded that nuclear fission was irrelevant to the war effort and offered the project to the German organization traditionally entrusted with basic scientific research. In the opinion of Army Ordnance, the question raised at the outbreak of hostilities had been answered. Nuclear power could not influence the outcome of the war, from either side.[10]

Given the historical context of the military decision to transfer nuclear fission research, and especially taking into account the almost universal assumption in Germany that the war would last at most only a year or two more, this judgment appears reasonable and justifiable. With respect to electricity production by means of nuclear-fission chain reactions, a neutron-multiplying machine had not yet been built, and the technological step from such a machine to industrial-scale electricity production was clearly very large. Although natural uranium machines with heavy water were promising, their mass production clearly would entail great investment costs which could hinder the immediate war effort. Although enriched uranium machines with water for a moderator might have lower material costs, the construction of these devices presupposed a uranium isotope separation process applicable on the industrial scale that neither existed nor appeared feasible. The production of uranium 235 or of element 94 would be possible only after the realization of a successful process for the industrial-scale separation of the isotopes of uranium or after a self-sustaining uranium machine was in operation and after the related problem of the chemical separation of element 94 from the rest of the nuclear fuel had been solved. The manufacture of nuclear explosives did not appear likely for the foreseeable future.

The German military command was concerned with the practical problems of winning the war. New weapons were welcome, but only if they could be used in the struggle at hand. Schumann and the rest of Army Ordnance most certainly were interested in the application of science and technology to novel weaponry. The army was already supporting the rocket project. After they realized that nuclear fission was irrelevant to the war effort, these same administrators went on to push rocket research even harder. Scientists often feel underpaid, under-supported, and under-appreciated. Moreover, these researchers had their service exemptions to consider. But when the administration of the nuclear power project is viewed in the historical context, Army Ordnance appears as a very competent and – within the constraints of the war economy – generous sponsor. As long as the research was in an exploratory stage, appropriate support was given. When the state of war and the progress of the research made a reappraisal necessary, the army came to the reasonable conclusion that it was neither advisable, nor responsible, to shift the nuclear power project up to the industrial scale, and the project subsequently was transferred to a traditional site for civilian basic research.

Even though the nuclear fission research generally was considered to be irrelevant to the outcome of the war, the army nevertheless agreed to continue its financial support of nuclear power. All parties were of the opinion that this work should be taken further because of its great future military and economic potential. Therefore the research remained "important for the war" (*kriegswichtig*), a designation which meant that the research was important enough to be supported during wartime, not necessarily that it would influence the outcome. After all, the amount of money, manpower, and materials required by the nuclear power project at the laboratory scale was insignificant when compared to the daily costs of running the war. The decision reached by Army Ordnance officials during the first few months of 1942, that applied nuclear fission was irrelevant to the prosecution of the war, was final. Subsequently no one – not the military, German industry, the National Socialist government, or even the academic and military scientists themselves – believed that nuclear weapons could be built and employed during World War II. In particular, this conclusion was never reexamined seriously. But in many respects, this judgment by Army Ordnance was more of a "non-decision" than a decision. The research, methods, and goals remained essentially unchanged. As before, all possible military and economic applications of nuclear fission were investigated and pursued, although these applications did appear to be far away.

Unknown to the Germans, both the Americans and the British had begun their own nuclear fission research programs. Coincidentally, during the winter of 1941–2 American officials made a thorough review of the military feasibility of nuclear power, weighed technical information and scientific research results similar to those achieved in Germany, and came to very different conclusions: nuclear weapons were feasible and could decide the outcome of the war. Moreover, the Allies assumed that the Germans were of the same opinion. Thus the quest for nuclear power became a peculiar sort of race. For one of the two competitors the contest was a potentially fatal sprint, for the other a marathon irrelevant to the war. But the metaphor is apt, for both sides wanted to be the first to discover, control, and wield nuclear power. But let us leave a more detailed comparison of the Allied and German efforts to a later chapter, and return to the German story.

Nuclear power conferences

The abdication by the army of any responsibility for nuclear power made the future of this research program unclear. Whereas some scientists were concerned that the project might not receive the further support it needed, several different organs of the National Socialist German state cast covetous eyes on the economic and political potential of nuclear fission research. Shortly before Army Ordnance offered the nuclear power project to the Kaiser Wilhelm Society, Erich Schumann scheduled a research conference for the end of February 1942 at the Kaiser Wilhelm Institute for Physics. So many talks were submitted to Army Ordnance that a three-day meeting was finally set for late February, including twenty-five lectures. After the research conference had been scheduled, a popular lecture series, sponsored jointly by the army and the Reich Research Council for a restricted audience, was set up to run concurrently and to provide a showcase for nuclear power. The Ministry of Education obviously was still interested in nuclear fission research.[11]

But let us examine the professional conference first of all, for this gathering provides an opportunity to examine the scope and composition of the project at its height. There were never more than seventy scientists connected directly or indirectly with nuclear power, and only around forty of these researchers devoted at least half of their time to nuclear fission research. After the army relinquished its hold on nuclear power, the number of scientists working on applied nuclear fission diminished drastically. Many of the independent researchers, scientists not connected with one of the main institutes, stopped work on nuclear fission, and often these scientists subsequently took up tasks more relevant to the war effort.[12]

These numbers remained stable from this point on. Indeed the limited personnel of the nuclear power project illustrates what was perhaps the greatest impact of National Socialism on scientific research: the lost generation. Most of the youngest members of the nuclear power project had begun their university studies before the National Socialists took office and made admission to higher education dependent on political acceptability. The politicization of the universities curtailed student enrollments. Because of ideological attacks on physics, the natural sciences were hit especially hard. Most importantly, at the start of war the majority of students were drafted and sent to the front. All of these developments combined to reduce drastically the number of trained physicists. By 1940, physics graduate students had practically disappeared, and according to a report by the SS security service, the shortage of physicists was so acute that German industry was hiring physics students who had failed their exams as soon as they left the university. The effect of National Socialism on the German physics community can be seen most clearly here, in the loss of a generation, rather than in the careers of scientists already in place. By the end of the war, physicists and physics students born between the years 1915 and 1925 were practically nonexistent. Although the National Socialist movement was able to exploit the physicists it had inherited, at least in the short run, it was unable to produce its own.[13]

In practice, the nuclear power project was now broken down into three main problems: the production of uranium and heavy water, uranium isotope separation, and uranium machines. Even more than before, the project was split up into several institutes, each dominated by its director and pursuing its own line of research:

1 Walter Bothe (Heidelberg): six physicists; measurements of nuclear constants
2 Klaus Clusius (Munich): around four physical chemists and physicists; isotope separation and heavy water production
3 Kurt Diebner (Army Ordnance lab in Berlin-Gottow): around five physicists; measurements of nuclear constants
4 Otto Hahn (Berlin-Dahlem): around six chemists and physicists;

transuranic elements, fission products, isotope separation, measurements of nuclear constants

5 Paul Harteck (Hamburg): five physical chemists, physicists, and chemists; heavy water production and isotope separation

6 Werner Heisenberg (Berlin-Dahlem as advisor; Leipzig): around seven physicists and physical chemists; uranium machines, isotope separation, and measurements of nuclear constants

7 Hans Kopfermann (Kiel, later Göttingen): two physicists; isotope separation

8 Nikolaus Riehl (Berlin, Auer Company): around three researchers, although the larger reserves of the firm could be drawn upon; uranium production

9 Georg Stetter (Vienna): around six physicists and physical chemists; measurements of nuclear constants and transuranic elements

The scientific results of the January 1942 meeting were mixed. Harteck and Wilhelm Groth sidestepped their lack of success with the Clusius-Dickel separation tube by delivering no talk on isotope separation. The published proceedings of the conference contained a report written by Groth at the end of 1941 which described the failure of the separation tube and also described the planned centrifuge experiments. Other separation methods were discussed at the conference, but no concrete success could be reported. Clusius, Horst Korsching, and Wilhelm Walcher had continued their experiments, while Erich Bagge had begun tests with uranium hexafluoride in his isotope sluice.[14]

Whereas uranium isotope separation had been uniformly disappointing, heavy water production had made modest progress throughout 1941. The members of Harteck's circle lectured on the two heavy water production methods they were pushing for use in Germany, catalytic exchange and a low pressure column, while Clusius and Kurt Starke discussed their laboratory experiments with the distillation of liquid hydrogen. Most importantly, as Karl Wirtz reported, heavy water production in Norway had made some improvement. Although ammonia was still the main product of Norwegian Hydro, heavy water was now being manufactured as a sideline at a rate of $1\frac{1}{2}$ metric tons a year. Harteck and Hans Suess had designed a supplementary catalytic exchange process for the Norwegian Hydro plant that eventually could boost the Norwegian production to around 5 metric tons per year, but this installation was still under construction in the winter of 1942.[15]

As the supply of moderator increased, the prospects for uranium machines improved. The model experiments were now using uranium metal instead of uranium oxide, but as with heavy water, pure uranium was still scarce in Germany. A new series of model uranium machines was underway at the Kaiser Wilhelm Institute for Physics. There alternating

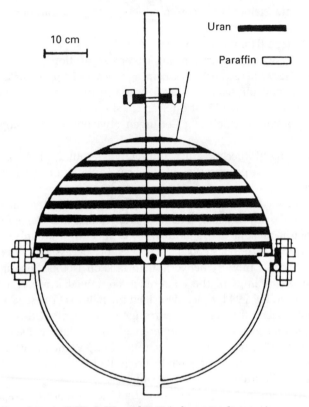

Figure 5 Experiments B-III, B-IV, and B-V (schematic diagram).

Note: Spheres consisting of alternating horizontal layers of metal uranium powder and paraffin, all surrounded by a mantle of water.
Source: Adapted from Walther Bothe and Siegfried Flügge (eds.), *Kernphysik und kosmische Strahlen, Naturforschung und Medizin in Deutschland 1939–1946*, vol. 14 (Weinheim, Chemie, 1948), part 2, p. 154.

horizontal layers of paraffin and metal uranium powder were arranged in a spherical container. Although this design was smaller than the first horizontal layer models, it nevertheless produced more neutrons. (See Figure 5.) But as the participants at the conference learned, Robert Döpel had obtained the most exciting results in Leipzig. Even though there was only enough metal uranium to fill one layer, the Leipzig heavy water machine with uranium powder came very close to neutron production. The first uranium machine seemed in sight. Although model uranium machines received the most attention at the conference, transuranic elements were also topics of considerable interest. Siegfried Flügge lectured on the process of resonance absorption that led to elements 93 and 94, Otto Hahn and Fritz Strassmann discussed the isolation and chemical properties of element 93, and Josef Schintlmeister stressed that element 94 should be relatively easy to fission, perhaps even easier than uranium 235. This three-day conference demonstrated that, with the notable exception of uranium isotope separation, all aspects of the research into the applications of nuclear fission had made good progress.[16]

As already mentioned, a popular lecture series was also held on 26 February 1942 in the "House of German Research" in Berlin-Dahlem before a restricted audience of representatives of the National Socialist German Workers Party, the German state, and German industry. Minister of Education Bernhard Rust, Albert Vögler, and the assembled Reich Research Council were in attendance. The text of the invitation to this event underlined both the possible military and economic significance of nuclear power and the fact that this power was a future concern, not a present matter. A series of important questions in the area of nuclear physics were to be discussed, topics which up until that time had been researched in secret because of their importance for the national defense. Given the "extraordinary significance" that this research one day might have for German armaments and the entire German economy, Rust thought that he could count on considerable interest in the lecture series.[17]

The program of the popular lecture series was designed to be as impressive and persuasive as possible:

1 Professor Doctor Schumann: "Nuclear physics as a weapon"
2 Professor Doctor Hahn: "The fission of the uranium nucleus"
3 Professor Doctor Heisenberg: "The theoretical basis for energy production from uranium fission"
4 Professor Doctor Bothe: "Results of the energy-producing designs examined up until this time"
5 Professor Doctor Geiger: "The necessity of general basic research"
6 Professor Doctor Clusius: "Enrichment of the uranium isotopes"
7 Professor Doctor Harteck: "The production of heavy water"
8 Professor Doctor Esau: "The extension of the research group 'nuclear physics' through cooperation with other Reich departments and industry."

Along with popular talks on the latest research results given by the responsible project scientists, the army representative Schumann discussed the military applications of nuclear fission, the Reich Research Council representative Esau stressed the significance of nuclear power for the state and industry, and Hans Geiger, politically as well as professionally a very conservative experimental physicist, made the connection between research and application.[18]

These lectures gave the members of the nuclear power project the opportunity to "sell" their research and thereby secure financial, material and institutional support. The vivid and suggestive contributions by Hahn,

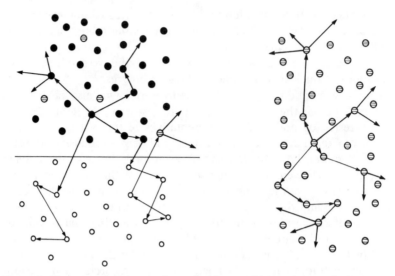

Figure 6 Chain reaction in uranium machines and in nuclear explosives.

Note: The smaller circles designate moderator nuclei, the solid black circles uranium 238 nuclei, and the hatched circles uranium 235, while the arrows represent neutrons in motion that have been released by fission. The left-hand side of the diagram illustrates a controlled chain reaction, in other words a uranium machine, while the right-hand side portrays an uncontrolled chain reaction, in other words a nuclear explosive.

Source: Adapted from Werner Heisenberg, "Die Energiegewinnung aus der Atomkernspaltung," *G-217* (6 May 1943), 30.

Harteck, and Heisenberg were exemplary in this regard. Possibly because of Hahn's audience and the occasion, he avoided any mention of his Jewish former collaborator Lise Meitner in his historical account of the discovery of nuclear fission and described enthusiastically the potential of nuclear-fission chain reactions. As was his nature, Harteck was even more colorful in his justification of heavy water research. From what the Germans knew at that time, heavy water was needed in order to ignite a nuclear-fission chain reaction. Once lighted, no one knew how long or how powerfully this flame would burn, but in any case, Harteck told his audience that the Germans were in a position to produce heavy water in such quantities that this flame could burn for a long time.[19]

Heisenberg used a diagram of the various possible nuclear reactions in uranium and moderator to provide his listeners with a layman's description of how uranium machines and nuclear explosives should work (see figure 6). The left-hand portion of the diagram represents a schematic uranium machine and the various nuclear processes that a fission neutron could experience in uranium. (The solid black circles represent uranium 238, the ruled circles uranium 235, and the small circles moderator). A fission neutron could strike immediately and fission a uranium 238 nucleus – for this isotope could be split, but the incoming neutron had to be traveling at very high velocities – but such fission was very unlikely. After a few collisions, a fission neutron could be absorbed by a uranium 238 nucleus. The neutron could meet and fission a uranium 235 nucleus, but unfortunately that was much less probable. Therefore the desired chain reaction could not proceed in ordinary uranium, so that new techniques were needed in order to "force" the chain reaction.[20]

Heisenberg then made an analogy both in the spirit of the times and tailored to the level of comprehension of his audience. The behavior of neutrons in uranium could be thought of as a human population, where the fission process represented an analogy to a child-bearing marriage and the neutron capture process corresponded to death. In ordinary uranium, the death count overwhelms the birth rate, so that a population must die out after a short period of time. Obviously this state of affairs can only be improved if either: (1) the number of births per marriage can be increased; (2) the number of marriages can be increased, or (3) the probability of death can be reduced.[21]

Heisenberg told his audience that, because the number of neutrons released per fission was governed by a natural law, option number one was impossible. On the other hand, option number two, an increase in the number of fissions/marriages, could be achieved by enriching the uranium 235 in the uranium sample. If pure uranium 235 could be produced, Heisenberg noted, then the processes represented in the right-hand side of the diagram could take place, each one an example of fast-neutron fission. Unless a fission neutron escapes through the outer surface of the uranium, every neutron would cause a further fission after one or two collisions. In this case, the probability of death was vanishingly small compared to the likelihood of neutron increase. If a large enough amount of uranium 235 could be accumulated, then the number of neutrons in the uranium would increase tremendously in a very short period of time. Therefore the isotope uranium 235 undoubtedly represented an explosive of "utterly unimaginable effect." However, Heisenberg hastened to inform his audience of prospective patrons that the explosive uranium 235 was very difficult to obtain. Moving on to the third option, reducing the probability of neutron death, Heisenberg noted that a uranium machine composed of uranium and moderator could facilitate fission in uranium 235 without great danger of neutron absorption by the heavier isotope uranium 238. But once again, Heisenberg noted that large amounts of the moderator heavy water were not easy to obtain.[22]

As Heisenberg's listeners learned, such energy-producing uranium machines had great military and economic potential. They could be used as heat engines to produce energy, could power vehicles and ships, and since a uranium machine does not consume oxygen, it was especially suitable for use in submarines. But these uranium machines had an even more important application. As soon as such a machine was in operation, Heisenberg noted, nuclear explosives took on new meaning. The transformation of uranium in the machine created a new substance, element 94, which most probably was an explosive with the same potential power. Indeed, Heisenberg told his audience that element 94 would be much easier to manufacture than uranium 235, since this new element could be separated chemically from uranium. Heisenberg's summary could have impressed any one of his listeners, no matter how high their station. Uranium enrichment made nuclear energy possible. Uranium 235 was an unimaginably powerful explosive. A uranium machine could both function as a heat engine and produce another unimaginably powerful explosive. On the other hand, as Heisenberg repeatedly had stressed, there was still work to be done before any of these applications could be expected. The nuclear power project required strong financial and institutional support. Tailored to both his audience and the times, Heisenberg's talk illustrated clearly and vividly the warlike aspects of nuclear power.[23]

As Hahn noted in his diary, the lectures before the Reich Research Council made a good impression. Indeed the lecture series was subsequently publicized in a newspaper account under the title, "Physics and National Defense." Although the words atomic, nuclear, energy, or power were not used, a reader would have learned that the meeting dealt with problems of modern physics decisive for national defense and the entire German economy. By the following May, matters had progressed to the point that the physicist Wolfgang Finkelnburg could tell Heisenberg that his lecture before the Reich Research Council and the subsequent press accounts had had a good effect. Finkelnburg had received several inquiries from Party positions concerning the "military importance" of theoretical physics and especially of Heisenberg's work.[24]

In fact, the military potential of nuclear power penetrated into the highest circles of the National Socialist German state. On 21 March, less than a month after Heisenberg's lecture, Reich Minister of Propaganda Josef Goebbels noted in his diary that he had received a report on the latest developments in German science. Goebbels learned that research in the "realm of atomic destruction" had now progressed to the point that it might possibly be used in the ongoing war. "Tremendous destruction," his reports claimed, could be wrought with a minimum of effort, so that the prospects for both a longer, and a subsequent war were "terrifying." Modern technology placed means of destruction in the hands of human beings that The Reich Minister of Propaganda found "simply incredible." It was essential that Germany be ahead of everybody, he recognized, for whoever could introduce such a "revolutionary novelty" into the war had the greater chance of winning it. No one involved with the research or administration of the nuclear power project claimed or believed that nuclear fission could influence the outcome of the war that Germany was fighting. But by dangling seductively the prospect of unimaginably powerful weapons sometime in the future, scientists from the German nuclear power project could, and did, enjoy exceptional political and financial support from several diverse sections of the National Socialist German state.[25]

In fact, the lectures in the House of German Research were so successful that they had an apparently unforeseen consequence. The Minister of Education decided to take the nuclear power project away from the Kaiser Wilhelm Society and give it to his own Reich Research Council, a move that Vögler was powerless to stop. The economic and military future of nuclear fission obviously appealed to Rust. The fate of nuclear power once again reflected the pecking order in the National Socialist German state. Although Army Ordnance could easily force the Reich Research Council out of nuclear fission research, this council similarly was able to supplant the Kaiser Wilhelm Society in turn. This takeover had important consequences for the project scientists, for the new overlords of nuclear fission research intended to control nuclear power as completely as the army had done.[26]

Since Army Ordnance had relinquished its hold on nuclear power, the Kaiser Wilhelm Institute for Physics was to be returned to the Kaiser Wilhelm Society. But since Peter Debye was living in a now hostile country, it appeared unlikely that the former institute director would return to Berlin-Dahlem anytime soon. Both Army Ordnance and the Kaiser Wilhelm Society wanted to appoint a new director. Shortly before Christmas of 1941, Schumann impulsively brought up the matter at a meeting with the institute directors by announcing that he believed that Bothe was the right man for the job. After twenty seconds of silence, Schumann declared that everyone was obviously in agreement and instructed Hahn as the eldest scientist to compose a letter to that effect and to send it on to Schumann. None of the scientists raised any objections during this meeting.[27]

A month later, Ernst Telschow, the General Secretary of the Kaiser Wilhelm Society, was visited by Harteck, Hahn and Max von Laue, all of whom argued that Heisenberg, not Bothe, was the proper choice to head the Kaiser Wilhelm Institute for Physics. Harteck admitted that Bothe was the best experimental physicist in Germany, but argued that Bothe as an experimental physicist did not compare to the status of Heisenberg as a theoretical physicist. A few days later, Hahn and Laue told Telschow that because of Bothe's difficult personality, he was not a suitable director for the Kaiser Wilhelm Institute. For his part, Bothe laconically stated that the other directors had had their chance to vote against him and by their silence had already promised him the directorship. The Heidelberg physicist had had his eye on becoming Debye's replacement as early as 1940. However, Heisenberg had entrenched himself in the Berlin-Dahlem institute by virtue of his research position there, even though he remained subordinate to Kurt Diebner. Telschow responded by telling Harteck that the appointment of a new director should lie in the hands of President Vögler alone.[28]

But the president of the Kaiser Wilhelm Society agreed with Leeb and Schumann that Bothe was the best candidate, for the Kaiser Wilhelm Institute for Physics was to continue comprehensive experimental research in nuclear physics, a task for which Bothe was better suited than Heisenberg. But all of these plans were made before the February nuclear power conferences and the takeover of the research program by the Reich Research Council. In early March, Vögler was forced to tell Leeb that the situation had changed. In a surprising development, Bothe's appointment as Debye's successor was blocked in the Reich Research Council, which now had to give its blessing. Vögler confronted Mentzel, the real power in the Reich Research Council, with a question. Who would direct the institute in the future? Mentzel replied that the Reich Research Council was in complete control. As head of the physics department in this council, Abraham Esau, who had not forgotten the humiliation he had suffered in the fall of 1939, took over as head of the nuclear power project.[29]

National Socialism and German physics

Two months after Walther Bothe's call to direct the Kaiser Wilhelm Institute for Physics was stopped, Werner Heisenberg was appointed in his place with the approval of Rudolf Mentzel. In order to explain this sudden turnabout, a digression is necessary, an examination of the interaction between the German physics community and National Socialism. Whenever the influence of ideology and especially of political ideology on science is discussed, two recent and extreme examples often come to mind: Russian biology under Stalin and the *deutsche Physik* (literally "German physics") movement during the National Socialist period in Germany. Traditionally, this latter movement has been taken as the whole and sole subject of the perversion of physics to the support of the National Socialist regime. In this section, a different approach will be taken with respect to the notorious case of German physics and physicists during the Third Reich. The strident and often incoherent calls for a more Aryan and less Jewish science were not the only examples of the penetration of National Socialist ideology into the practice of physics. On the contrary, the interaction between the physics community in Germany and the National Socialist movement cannot be equated with, or limited to, *deutsche Physik*. Rather the relationships between *deutsche Physik*, National Socialism, and the German physics community provide a fascinating example of the impact that an ideology can have on science as well as of how science and scientists can influence this ideology in turn.[30]

During the early years of the Third Reich, Werner Heisenberg and other supporters of "modern physics" – roughly speaking, quantum physics and the theory of relativity – were attacked politically by the adherents of *deutsche Physik*. Much has been made of the fact that the *deutsche Physik* movement was able to discredit Heisenberg sufficiently to block an attempt to call him to Munich as the successor to his teacher, Arnold Sommerfeld, yet far from proving the strength of the movement, this coup was a good example of winning a battle, but losing the war. The highly-publicized attacks on Heisenberg's honor and the subsequent retaliation by the established German physics community set in motion a careful and thorough reappraisal by the German government of the value of modern theoretical physics in the context of the Second World War. In time, the National Socialist state came to support modern physics as a necessary part of the German war effort, and the German physics community in turn entered into a full partnership with the state for reasons both patriotic and selfish. If seduction played a role in the relationship between German physics and National Socialism, it was reciprocal.[31]

The high tide of "deutsche Physik"

The *deutsche Physik* movement was first and foremost political, not scientific, and should be recognized as such. To a great extent, this movement arose from the frustration and embitterment that two German Nobel Prize winners, Philipp Lenard and Johannes Stark, felt during the Weimar Republic. What Lenard and Stark had been unable to achieve through normal professional channels during the short-lived German democracy, they set out to seize in the political arena during the Third Reich. Both Lenard and Stark were conservative experimental physicists who rejected key aspects of the new quantum and relativity physics. But during the Weimar Republic, as Lenard's objections to Albert Einstein's theory of relativity went unheeded and Stark found himself unable to regain a professorship, their anger was channeled, as with many Germans, into anti-Semitic and anti-democratic sentiments which were congenial to Adolf Hitler's National Socialist German Workers Party.[32]

In 1924, while Hitler was imprisoned briefly for his role in a failed coup in Munich during November 1923, both Lenard and Stark came out in public support of the National Socialist leader. The backing of two internationally known scientists was appreciated by Hitler at this precarious stage in the development of his political movement, and when the National Socialists took over the government in 1933, they did not forget who their friends were within the German scientific community. Without the seizure of power by Hitler and his followers, the *deutsche Physik* movement never would have played a significant role in the politics of the German physics community. But the elderly Lenard had already retired by 1933, and Stark, an ambitious science policy maker who wanted to control as much of German science as possible, soon ran afoul of stronger and politically more savvy opponents within the National Socialist bureaucracy and quickly squandered much of the political support that he had enjoyed at the start of the Third Reich. By the end of 1936, Stark had been stripped of most of his power within the science policy apparatus of the German state. But Lenard and Stark had gathered around them a small group of young scientists who took up the calls of their elders for an Aryan science, and along with Lenard and Stark these adherents of *deutsche Physik* set out to influence the development of German physics under Hitler however they could.[33]

In 1936 Heisenberg was attacked both in an article in the *Völkischer Beobachter*, the semi-official paper of the Party, and in a speech by Stark. Heisenberg published an article in the *Völkischer Beobachter* in response, but his political problems were just beginning. A year later, Heisenberg and other German physicists were attacked indirectly by Stark as "white Jews" and "Jewish in character" in *Das Schwarze Korps*, the newspaper of the SS. A "white Jew" referred to someone who was of Aryan race, yet who also had been tainted by the influence of Judaism, in this case by Einstein's physics. This attack on Heisenberg was timed to block his transfer to Munich as the successor to his mentor Sommerfeld, an appointment which the University of Munich and the Bavarian Ministry of Culture had approved.[34]

Being attacked as "Jewish in character" in the SS newspaper was a serious matter, so Heisenberg took steps to protect himself. Since Stark's article had received at least the tacit support of the SS, Heisenberg took advantage of family connections and appealed directly to the Reich SS leader (*Reichsführer SS*) Heinrich Himmler. By February of 1938, Heisenberg began to be pessimistic both about his call to Munich and his political problems. Indeed he now doubted that he could remain in his University of Leipzig professorship. Heisenberg was not alone in his troubles. A colleague in Königsberg had recently been denounced as politically unreliable as well. As Heisenberg told his old teacher Sommerfeld, it was really too bad, that at a time when physics was so exciting and so much fun, Heisenberg had to devote so much time to these "political things."[35]

The attacks on Heisenberg's reputation also made it more and more difficult for him to do day-to-day physics. For example, after the article came out in *Das Schwarze Korps*, a student who had planned to study with Heisenberg and who had even received a scholarship for this purpose now declined to come to Leipzig. He feared that his course of study might become "political." It was no wonder that students were turning away from theoretical physics. The official organ of the Reich Student Organization, a subsidiary of the Party, harassed this discipline continually. Heisenberg wrote to Sommerfeld that he sometimes lost all hope that the decent people would win out in Germany, but then excused himself for his "perhaps unjustified" pessimism. In April of 1938, Heisenberg was informed by a low-ranking SS officer that the SS could do nothing for him. It seemed to Heisenberg that Himmler and the Minister of Education had decided that Heisenberg should never receive an answer to his requests for both the Munich professorship and the public recognition of his service and loyalty to the fatherland. Heisenberg was now forced to consider emigration, for he saw no alternative to submitting his resignation at Leipzig and leaving Germany. He did not want to emigrate, but he also had no desire to live in Germany as a second-class citizen.[36]

However, influential friends now came to the aid of Heisenberg and the German physics community, including the respected Göttingen aeronautical engineer Ludwig Prandtl. As he sat next to Himmler at the 1 March 1938 meeting of the German Academy for Aeronautical Research, Prandtl energetically argued the case for modern theoretical physics and against *deutsche Physik*. In a letter sent four months later, Prandtl reminded Himmler of his concern. A small clique of experimental physicists, who could not keep up with the recent advances in theoretical physics, had attacked these new developments mainly because significant portions of modern theoretical physics had been created by Jews. Choosing language congenial to the head of the SS, Prandtl admitted that among these non-Aryan researchers there were some of low rank who "trumpet their Talmud-wares" with the "industry of their race." However, Prandtl went on to say that there had also been non-Aryan researchers of the highest rank who strove with great effort to advance science and who had truly succeeded. The Göttingen aeronautics expert also indulged in the apparently obligatory Einstein-baiting. With Einstein, he argued, a distinction must be made between the person and the physicist. The physicist was first-class, but according to Prandtl Einstein's early fame apparently had gone to his head, so that as a person the Jewish scientist had become "insufferable."[37]

Having demonstrated that he was not backing Jews, but rather supporting modern physics, Prandtl went on to plead Heisenberg's case. The central authorities of the National Socialist state and the highest Party offices had to make it clear that they did not agree with Stark, for otherwise the effectiveness of Heisenberg as a teacher would be compromised. In particular, Prandtl suggested that Heisenberg be allowed to publish his views in the journal *Die Zeitschrift für die gesamte Naturwissenschaft*, which was not only the main organ of the Reich Student Organization but was also the major forum of the *deutsche Physik* movement. The Göttingen engineer closed by remarking that he considered the matter important, not because of Heisenberg as a person, but because of his concern for German physics.[38]

Less than two weeks later, Heisenberg and Prandtl simultaneously received good news from the SS in the form of personal letters from Himmler. The intervention by Germany's leading aeronautics engineer had been an obvious success. The Reich SS leader agreed with Prandtl that Heisenberg was a decent man of integrity and that the Leipzig professor should be supported. Himmler personally forestalled any further attack on Heisenberg's name, telling Heisenberg explicitly that he did not approve of the attack made on him in *Das Schwarze Korps*. Furthermore, Himmler invited Heisenberg to come to Berlin in the autumn in order to discuss the matter man-to-man. Heisenberg was also instructed, however, that in the future he was to separate clearly the recognition he gave the results of scientific research from the personal and political standpoint of the researcher. Himmler expected Heisenberg to concern himself with physics, not politics. Reinhard Heydrich, the head of the SS security service, received simultaneous orders from Himmler to support Heisenberg, for Himmler believed that Germany could not afford "to lose by emigration or silence" [*zu verlieren oder tot zu machen*] Heisenberg, who was relatively young and still capable of training a generation of scientists. Heisenberg had obviously been in serious danger.[39]

Heisenberg answered Himmler immediately and agreed to distinguish in the future between a researcher's politics and his science. Physics was to remain apolitical. Furthermore, he would be pleased to discuss this matter personally with Himmler in order to clear up the misunderstandings that had arisen between politics and science. Finally, Heisenberg wanted the SS to make clear in public that the attacks on him had been unwarranted. Heisenberg asked for more than freedom from further attack. He demanded a public rehabilitation as well. Here the matter rested for a few months. In November 1938, however, a messenger from Himmler visited Heisenberg in order to obtain more detailed information about the "physics war," which seemed to Heisenberg to be a good sign. A few days later, Prandtl was told by a Party official that the "struggle" against the theory of relativity had been stopped by somebody high up.[40]

Heisenberg traveled to Berlin several times during the first months of 1939 in order to meet with Himmler, but he was always told that the

Reich SS leader was busy at that moment, and that the interview would have to take place sometime in the near future. Apparently Heisenberg never did meet with Himmler. But Heisenberg did receive sympathy from the SS men he encountered in Berlin. One of his SS interrogators had been examined by Heisenberg in physics during the last year of the Weimar Republic and agreed completely with his former teacher on the subject of modern theoretical physics. Another SS officer, Johannes Juilfs, was a respected experimental physicist, had worked in theoretical physics as an assistant to Max von Laue, and energetically backed Heisenberg in his struggle with *deutsche Physik*. Although Heisenberg could not meet with Himmler, the latter's staff did tell the physicist what the problem was. Rudolf Hess, Hitler's deputy and the political director of the Party, opposed Heisenberg's appointment in Munich. As Heisenberg himself recognized, the question of Sommerfeld's successor had become a political football.[41]

An SS official told Heisenberg that Himmler had pressed for Heisenberg's call to Munich, but Walther Schultze, the head of the Reich University Teachers League (*Reichsdozentenbund*), a subsidiary of the Party, had taken the position that the Party had already decided against Heisenberg on the question of the Munich professorship. If Heisenberg was now called to Munich, the Party would lose face. Himmler did not agree with Schultze, but had little desire to alienate the Party over a professorship. Indeed throughout the Third Reich, a tension existed between the Party – whose headquarters was in Munich – and the National Socialist government in Berlin, especially when spheres of influence and authority overlapped. Himmler was willing to support a prestigious professorship – and thereby a public rehabilitation – for Heisenberg anywhere other than Munich, an offer that the Reich SS leader probably considered the last word on the subject. In June of 1939 Heisenberg was informed by the head of the SS that he would receive a call to a prestigious professorship in Vienna as part of his public rehabilitation and that he would be allowed to express his viewpoint in the *deutsche Physik* journal. Prandtl's recommendations had been followed to the letter. But the German invasion of Poland and the resulting confusion – for example, all the universities were closed temporarily – apparently aborted Heisenberg's call to Vienna. What is important here is not so much the failure to give Heisenberg the Munich professorship in particular, but rather the nature of academic appointments during the Third Reich in general, and the effect that the Byzantine bureaucratic politics of the National Socialist period could have on academic science. In practice, scientists had to work with men such as Himmler and Schultze in order to further their discipline and their own careers. There were not, nor by the very nature of the Third Reich could there be, scientists and scientific administrators who held themselves aloof from the politics of the National Socialist state.[42]

But if Heisenberg was not to be Sommerfeld's successor as professor of theoretical physics in Munich, who would be? By the spring of 1939, rumors were circulating that Wilhelm Dames, a physicist and bureaucrat in the Ministry of Education, was supporting Wilhelm Müller, an aeronautical engineer congenial to the *deutsche Physik* movement, but not a physicist, let alone a theoretician. There were certainly other candidates more capable than Müller but just as acceptable to Lenard's and Stark's clique. Heisenberg believed that the Munich professorship had also fallen prey to a political battle between the Ministry of Education and *deutsche Physik*. According to a rumor, so long as the Ministry was under pressure to appoint an advocate of *deutsche Physik*, Dames was pushing Müller's candidacy in order to mobilize the forces opposing *deutsche Physik* within the state. Even if this opposition was unsuccessful, Dames would have exposed the Lenard-Stark faction to public ridicule by placing someone from their camp in the Munich professorship who would be considered incompetent by almost all concerned. Heisenberg feared that so far as Dames was concerned, the political question of Lenard's influence within the leadership of the Reich University Teachers League was much more important than who received the Munich professorship. If Dames did indeed pursue this strategy, it was a complete success. Müller succeeded Sommerfeld on 1 December 1939 and immediately became the lightning rod for attacks on *deutsche Physik*.[43]

War and the decline of 'deutsche Physik'

As the war became more ambitious and drawn out, both the official policy and the unofficial attitude of the National Socialist state towards modern physics changed. The government, Party, and armed forces became more concerned with scientific education and armaments production than with the influence of Jews in physics, a development that could only harm the cause of *deutsche Physik* and favor scientists such as Heisenberg. In particular, under pressure from German industry and military leaders, the National Socialists now exhibited a willingness to compromise their hard ideological line in return for concessions from the established physics community. The followers of *deutsche Physik*, whose physics had always been barren and who had relied on rhetoric for their influence within the new German order, found themselves cast aside in the rush to mobilize all of German science for the war.

For example, although the number of teaching positions in theoretical physics had contracted during the first six years of the Third Reich, several new professorships and lectureships in this subject were established during the war years. Moreover, these new positions were staffed by young physicists respected by the established physics community, not by adherents of *deutsche Physik*. The founding of the new Reich University of Strassburg (Strasbourg) provided the most striking example of the renewed prestige enjoyed by modern physics. Set in land "reclaimed" by Germany, for the region of Alsace-Lorraine had been seized by Germany after the Franco-Prussian war only to be returned to France as part of the settlement following World War I, this university was to be a showpiece of National Socialism. Only scholars and teachers who could be expected to champion National Socialism energetically were to be called to Strassburg. Perhaps the most extreme example of a scientist who fits this mold was the Strassburg anatomist, Dr. August Hirt, who experimented with the effects of "chemical weapons" on humans under the auspices of the Reich Research Council. The SS provided inmates from the Bavarian concentration camp at Dachau as experimental subjects for this scientific research.[44]

Of course the exact sciences were further removed from the practical applications of National Socialist ideology than the biological sciences. But physics – like all subjects taught at Strassburg – was nevertheless expected to support and propagate National Socialism. However, just as Müller's call to Munich illustrated the high-point of *deutsche Physik*, the 1941 Strassburg appointments in physics represented a major defeat for the Lenard-Stark clique. Each of the three professorships established at Strassburg was filled by talented scientists opposed to *deutsche Physik*. For example, Rudolf Fleischmann, a former student of the respected Göttingen experimental physicist Robert Pohl and former assistant to Bothe, and Wolfgang Finkelnburg, who already held a less prestigious professorship, both became associate professors (*Extraordinariat*) in experimental physics.[45]

Viewed in the context of the *deutsche Physik* debate, the new associate professorship in theoretical physics represented more than a job opening. It was a matter of prestige. The university wanted to appoint Carl-Friedrich von Weizsäcker, but his candidacy was rejected by Party officials. Although nothing explicitly detrimental was known about him, he appeared completely uninterested in the political events of the time, and given his apparent disposition, he could not be expected actively to take part in the National Socialist movement in the future. This characterization of Weizsäcker was mistaken. Although he held himself aloof from politics in the strict National Socialist sense, he was both very interested and very involved with politics in general, for example German foreign policy. This Party judgment showed exactly how well Weizsäcker could play the politics of the Third Reich.[46]

But the University of Strassburg wanted Weizsäcker and did not give up so easily. The Reich Ministry of Education, a University of Strassburg dean, and Weizsäcker's father – a state secretary in the German Foreign Office

(*Auswärtiges Amt*) – all collaborated to bring the physicist Weizsäcker to Strassburg. Thus Ernst von Weizsäcker requested a reexamination of his son's case from the Chancellery of the Party, pointing out that his son belonged to the National Socialist German Teachers League (*National-sozialistischer Lehrbund*) and had volunteered for labor and military service. The University Teachers League also supported Weizsäcker's appointment. Although this Party agency agreed that the teachers at Strassburg must be willing to champion National Socialism, they backed Weizsäcker because so far as theoretical physics was concerned, personally and scientifically he was undoubtedly one of the best of his generation.[47]

The University Teachers League pointed out that Weizsäcker had performed voluntary military service and had been classified indispensable by Army Ordnance, and suggested that an energetic University Teachers League representative in Strassburg might be able to persuade Weizsäcker to play a more active role in the National Socialist movement. Alfred Rosenberg's Office for Foreign Policy of the Party (*Aussenpolitisches Amt der Nationalsozialistischen Deutschen Arbeiterpartei*) agreed that Weizsäcker should be called to Strassburg, but did not go along with the naive belief that Weizsäcker could be brought to political activity on behalf of the Party. Citing the physicist's political inactivity with respect to National Socialism, Rosenberg's representative expressed no misgivings about bringing Weizsäcker to Strassburg, so long as there was no applicant of equal scientific stature, but who also was politically reliable. Scientific credentials were by now more important than mere political acceptability. Both the state and Party realized that apolitical scientists were not only acceptable; in the absence of a sufficient number of researchers who were both capable and absolutely loyal to National Socialism, apolitical science was a necessity.[48]

Weizsäcker was hired by the University of Strassburg, but his appointment was put in perspective by a subsequent attempt to bring him back to Berlin. The university in the Reich capital had an opening for an associate professorship in physics and was considering Weizsäcker along with two other scientists. The University Teachers League provided reports on all three candidates. Once again, Weizsäcker was their first choice because of his scientific abilities and performance. He was touted as both an internationally known physicist and the best of the younger generation. Furthermore, he was a good teacher and had been greatly appreciated by the Berlin students when he had taught there previously. But, as before, his lack of political consciousness in the National Socialist sense was a drawback. A second physicist was neither politically nor scientifically acceptable. On the other hand, the remaining physicist was a good, competent, and respected scientist, a very good teacher and, most importantly, he was a "good National Socialist." Weizsäcker did not get the job.[49]

Nevertheless, as Weizsäcker's call to Strassburg underlined, by 1941 the advocates of *deutsche Physik* were in retreat. Indeed Heisenberg felt that Weizsäcker's appointment brought "fresh wind" to German physics. A year earlier Finkelnburg, an influential member of the University Teachers League, had taken the offensive against the followers of Lenard and Stark by arranging a debate on modern physics in Munich under the auspices of the League. By the end of this conference, the members of the *deutsche Physik* movement had been coerced into a five-point compromise agreement:

1 theoretical physics, with all its mathematical tools, was a necessary part of physics;
2 the facts drawn from experience and put together by the theory of relativity belonged to the resources of physics; however, the certainty of applying the special theory of relativity to cosmic relations was not so great that a further investigation was unnecessary;
3 the four-dimensional representation of natural processes was a useful mathematical tool; but it did not signify the introduction of new concepts of space and time;
4 every connection of the theory of relativity with a general relativism was rejected;
5 the quantum- and wave-mechanics were the only tools known at that time for a quantitative comprehension of atomic processes; a penetration beyond the formalism and its directions for interpretation to a deeper understanding of the atom was desired.[50]

The outcome of the Munich debate was a clear victory for the established physics community. The champions of *deutsche Physik* had had to discuss physics, not politics, and a Party agency, the University Teachers League, had officially recognized the theory of relativity and quantum physics as valid parts of German science. The back of *deutsche Physik* had been broken. Although Munich remained one of their few strongholds, the followers of Lenard and Stark increasingly became isolated. In December of 1941, Heisenberg could write to his old teacher that he believed that in the coming year there would be an improvement with respect to *deutsche Physik*, in fact Heisenberg was "thoroughly optimistic" in this regard. The last gasp of *deutsche Physik* came at a "physics retreat" – political indoctrination retreats were common during the Third Reich – held under the auspices of the University Teachers League in Seefeld, Tyrol during November of 1942.[51]

The few followers of Lenard and Stark who attended this retreat were outnumbered and cowed, and with good reason. Along with several long-time vocal opponents of *deutsche Physik* such as Finkelnburg, Heisenberg, and Weizsäcker, the industrial scientist Carl Ramsauer represented the interests of industry and the military by lecturing on the dangerous decline of German physics. Moreover, the attendance of Johannes Juilfs also made it clear which side of the *deutsche Physik* controversy the SS favored. The compromise program of the 1940 Munich debate was adopted by the physics retreat. The theory of relativity and quantum mechanics were recognized as important parts of German physics. The significance of this victory by the physics establishment cannot be overestimated. The state had been forced to back down on the ideological purity of physics education in order to receive the full support of the German physics community.[52]

But political support was not free during the Third Reich. In exchange for a free hand for the physics establishment in the teaching curriculum and faculty staffing of university physics, some concessions to politics and ideology had to be made. The publication of Sommerfeld's lectures in physics during the Third Reich provides just one example among many of the sort of compromises that German physicists were forced to make on a daily basis. In the fall of 1942 Heisenberg's acquaintance, who had been indispensable to the established physics community during the *deutsche Physik* controversy, had a request for Heisenberg's former teacher. Sommerfeld had mentioned Einstein "quite often" in the section of his lectures devoted to the theory of relativity. Could Sommerfeld not take the "spirit of the times" more into account? Heisenberg passed on this suggestion to Sommerfeld and added that he personally believed that one had to be content with stating that the theory of relativity was correct. A strong emphasis on Einstein could only complicate the relations between physicists and the political authorities.[53]

Sommerfeld wrote to his editor and mentioned the request by Heisenberg's acquaintance. After pointing out that the request to expunge Einstein's name must have originated with the publisher, Sommerfeld left it up to the editor to make whatever changes appeared necessary. For Sommerfeld, removing Einstein's name went against the "honor" of an author. He had mentioned Einstein five times in the text of his lectures. Although the first three citations that dealt with the special theory of relativity could go, of the remaining two references to the general theory of relativity, the first absolutely had to stay. The second could go, though the Munich physicist preferred to see it remain. In the end, Sommerfeld left it up to the editor.[54]

The definitive and authoritative exposition of the guidelines for modern physics under National Socialism was provided by Heisenberg's article in the *Zeitschrift für die gesamte Naturwissenschaft*. The article was written in 1940, but Heisenberg waited until after his public political rehabilitation in 1942 to submit it to the SS. The editor of the *deutsche Physik* journal stalled publication for a while, but Heisenberg's article, "The Value of 'Modern Theoretical Physics'" (Die Bewertung der "modernen theoretischen Physik") finally appeared in 1943.[55]

The attacks by Stark and others on his scientific name and national loyalty had angered Heisenberg, but the loss of the Munich professorship and of the right to succeed his mentor Sommerfeld embittered him. As the harsh and blunt tone of his article made clear, Heisenberg had been waiting a long time for revenge. Instead of the distinctions used by the adherents of *deutsche Physik* during the previous few years, such as pragmatic versus dogmatic, realistic versus unrealistic, and clear versus formalistic, Heisenberg proposed a simpler distinction for judging physics: right or wrong. His sarcasm was evident as he tossed aside the claims that modern theoretical physics had not yet been strictly proven through experiment. Even though the sun had risen every morning and the laws of mechanics had always stood the test, it could not be "strictly" proven that the sun would rise tomorrow. Nevertheless, Heisenberg noted that most people were convinced that the sun would rise tomorrow and in practice were content with this degree of certainty.[56]

As Heisenberg demonstrated, both the special theory of relativity and quantum mechanics had been successful. Taking the offensive, Heisenberg taunted his opponents – who, as Heisenberg stressed, had been unable to keep up with the developments in experimental and theoretical physics of the past twenty years – to prove modern physics wrong. Only contradictory experimental evidence could overturn scientific theories, not philosophical discourse or polemics. As Heisenberg argued in the language of the times, experiment had to be "at the Front!" The last sentence of Heisenberg's article expressed his distaste for the tactics of *deutsche Physik*. The use of anything besides scientific arguments and tools in a scientific discussion was unworthy of the dignity of German science.[57]

However, the support of the SS, without which this article would never have been published, did not come cheaply. Heisenberg and the rest of the German physics establishment had to disown Einstein's contribution to modern physics, often in a humiliating fashion. German physics had to be separated from Jews at all costs, as Heisenberg proceeded to do. First of all, by citing an article written during the Weimar Republic by the *deutsche Physik* advocate Hugo Dingler, in which Dingler had spoken favorably of Einstein, Heisenberg attacked the *deutsche Physik* clique for support of Jewish physics. Then Heisenberg went on to show that he had taken his own advice to Sommerfeld to heart. A physical theory made statements about reality, and that was all. Reality existed independent of theories, no matter how they arose. Even if Columbus had never lived, Heisenberg argued, America would have been discovered. The theory of electrical phenomena would have been found without James Clerk Maxwell, and electric waves without Heinrich Hertz, since the discoverer cannot change reality. Similarly, the special theory of relativity would have come about without Einstein. Then Heisenberg noted that other scientists had examined similar questions, including Hendrik Antoon Lorentz, and Henri Poincaré, and had come very close to discovering special relativity. With respect to the correctness of a theory, Heisenberg argued, its history should be ignored.[58]

Heisenberg's colleagues were heartened by his article and the official recognition of modern theoretical physics that it implied. The Munich physical chemist Klaus Clusius, who had to deal with the influence of *deutsche Physik* in the university on a daily basis, vividly expressed his disgust for the followers of Lenard and Stark. After comparing Heisenberg's piece in the *Zeitschrift für die gesamte Naturwissenschaft* article to Daniel entering the lion's den, Clusius told his physicist colleague that he subscribed to the *deutsche Physik* journal in order to keep up with the "drivel" and "spurts of venom" from their opponents. This "nauseating and repulsive" task was necessary, for one must know the enemy. Clusius hoped that perhaps this "generation of vipers" finally would give them some peace. The once-powerful *deutsche Physik* movement was now little more than an isolated clique that occasionally caused some aggravation.[59]

The treatment of Einstein's legacy to modern physics by the established German physics community was put into perspective by an exchange of letters between Max von Laue on one hand and Rudolf Mentzel and Carl-Friedrich von Weizsäcker on the other. Mentzel received an official report that Laue had mentioned the theory of relativity while speaking in Sweden without also emphasizing that the established German physics community had explicitly distanced itself from the Jew Einstein. Mentzel was no friend of *deutsche Physik*, but he was obliged as an official in the Ministry of Education to censure Laue and stress that in the future Laue should separate the theory of relativity from Einstein, in other words, that Laue should abide by the guidelines set down at the Munich and Seefeld meetings. Since he knew that Weizsäcker was interested in the official recognition of the theory of relativity, Laue sent his younger colleague a copy of Mentzel's letter. Weizsäcker answered promptly by summing up the compromise reached at the Seefeld retreat: the theory of relativity would have been discovered without Einstein, but it was not. Laue replied that he had submitted a paper using the theory of relativity to a scientific journal, and that would be his answer to Mentzel. After all, Laue continued, he had only mentioned the theory of relativity once or twice while in Stockholm.[60]

Laue could afford to ignore Mentzel, but another encounter with a higher official was more serious. Shortly after the war was over for Germany, Paul Rosbaud, a consultant to the journal *Die Naturwissen-*

schaften and someone who held Laue in the highest regard, related the following incident. Minister of Education Bernhard Rust confronted Laue at a dinner party and expounded his views on *deutsche Physik* and Jewish physics. When Rosbaud subsequently asked Laue how he had replied, the physicist said that he had kept his mouth shut. The intention here is not to question Laue's courage, but rather to give an accurate picture of life and physics under National Socialism and of the significance of *deutsche Physik*.[61]

Power over ideology

The clash between ideology and power within the German state can be seen clearly in the continuing counterattack against *deutsche Physik*. On 4 September 1939, just before Heisenberg was drafted by the German Army as part of the research program into the military and economic applications of nuclear fission, he wrote to Sommerfeld from his summer house in Bavaria that he was expecting his call-up, which "strangely enough" had not yet come through. Heisenberg had no idea what would happen to him, and his family would stay in his summer house in the mountains until the war was over. Heisenberg believed that Sommerfeld's successor would remain undecided until the "mastery of Europe" had been decided. As he told his former teacher, Heisenberg hoped that the path to this end would not cost too many lives, but this wish went unfulfilled. Three years and many lost lives into the Second World War, Heisenberg was called to the directorship of the Kaiser Wilhelm Institute for Physics in Berlin-Dahlem. His appointment in the spring of 1942 was seen by the SS as well as by Heisenberg himself as the fulfillment of Himmler's promise.[62]

Since Heisenberg could now draw upon the considerable political backing of the SS, it was no surprise that his appointment in Berlin-Dahlem was rubber-stamped by Rudolf Mentzel and the Reich Research Council. Although as a Ministry of Education official, Mentzel previously had been able to block the appointment of the physicist Walther Bothe as director of the Kaiser Wilhelm Institute for Physics in order to place the institute more firmly under the control of the council, Mentzel, himself a member of the SS, now had to take Himmler's declaration of support for Heisenberg seriously. Heisenberg did not take the directorship away from Bothe, the first choice of General Leeb and Albert Vögler, rather only Heisenberg's appointment could be forced through in the face of Mentzel's opposition. Just as Heisenberg lost the Munich professorship because of political intrigue against him, six years later he gained two more prestigious positions – a professorship at the University of Berlin went along with the directorship at the physics institute – because of newly-found political support for theoretical physics and for the established physics community within National Socialist Germany. Heisenberg certainly deserved the two Berlin appointments on scientific grounds, but his professional competence was not why he received them.[63]

The controversy caused by Müller's appointment in Munich had not been settled by Himmler's promise of a professorship for Heisenberg. The fact that a once important German center of theoretical physics would now be staffed by someone incapable of teaching physics stuck in Prandtl's craw and prompted him to join with industrial allies to make yet another, more vigorous assault on National Socialist policy towards physics. This time Prandtl, the most respected aeronautical expert in Germany, entered the politics of military power by taking his case to Reichmarshal Hermann Göring, second in command to Adolf Hitler and head of the German Air Force. Prandtl complained to Göring that because of the attacks on theoretical physics, physics education had deteriorated to the point where Germany was in danger of falling perilously behind the Americans in this militarily and economically important area. Focusing on Müller in particular, Prandtl called his appointment "sabotage."[64]

But one of Göring's secretaries informed Prandtl that the Reichmarshal was unfortunately too busy to deal with his request – the engineer subsequently realized that Göring had probably been involved with the preparations for the German invasion of Russia – and suggested that he confront Minister of Education Rust directly about this matter. Prandtl responded a week later by pointing out that since Rust had personally approved Müller's appointment, any attempt to approach the minister would be pointless. Moreover, Prandtl had in the meantime learned that Rust had not acted voluntarily in filling this professorship, rather he had been coerced by overwhelming pressure from the Party. Indeed, Rust had opposed Müller's appointment – though he had obviously acquiesced and may have been outmaneuvered by his subordinate Dames – considering the appointment harmful for German science, but he had also felt powerless in the face of pressure from the Reich University Teachers League.[65]

Göring did not respond to Prandtl, but Vögler suggested another path to power – through the German military by way of German industry. Prandtl accordingly enlisted two influential and willing industrial physicists for his cause: Georg Joos, chief physicist at the Zeiss optical works, and Carl Ramsauer, a leading physicist at German General Electric (*Allgemeine Elektricitäts-Gesellschaft*) and newly chosen head of the German Physical Society. Ramsauer had the advantage of being a former student of Philipp Lenard – though he had parted company with his old teacher – and could not be accused of being under the spell of Jewish physics. Ramsauer had recently chosen the respected academic experimental physicist Wolfgang Finkelnburg as his deputy. Finkelnburg appealed to

Ramsauer because of the former's active advocacy of theoretical physics. Moreover, the industrial scientist considered it necessary to have a moderate member of the Party in the governing committee in order better to finish off the "extreme" colleagues. For his part, Joos remarked that just as Kepler had to sustain a "witch trial" for ten years on his mother's behalf, so they might also have to endure a long trial on behalf of "mother physics" against wickedness and superstition.[66]

Germany's misfortune in war also played into the hands of Prandtl, Ramsauer, and company. Shortly after the Russian defense had frozen the lightning war in its tracks during the winter of 1941, the realization that the entire German war economy had to be reorganized and made more efficient trickled down through every part of the German state. Ramsauer now succeeded in convincing General Friedrich Fromm, commander of the German reserve army and chief of armaments production, that German physics, and with it Germany's ability to wage war, was in grave danger. Fromm promised Ramsauer that the army would support his proposals for reform. Two weeks later, Prandtl contacted Field Marshal Erhard Milch, Göring's deputy in the Ministry of the Air Force. By early December of 1941, Prandtl had received a favorable response, for Milch had read Prandtl's letter with great interest. The air force considered the state of physics education to be most important and recognized the connection between academic physics and the industrial production of modern weapons. Milch agreed with Fromm that the German armed forces and, if possible, other Reich agencies should support Prandtl's cause.[67]

After assembling such powerful political backing, Ramsauer took a step designed to force an official reappraisal of the value of theoretical physics. He submitted a twenty-eight page memorandum with six appendices on the sorry state of German physics to Minister of Education Rust. Neither Ramsauer, Joos, nor Finkelnburg expected Rust to react in any way, but the Ministry of Education was not their main target. The scientists were confident that the Party and the German military would get the message. As head of the German Physical Society, Ramsauer informed Rust that he considered it his duty to bring his concerns about the future of German physics to Rust's attention. German physics had lost its earlier supremacy with regard to American physics and was in danger of falling even further behind. Although the Americans did apply much more material, money, and manpower than the Germans to physics, in Ramsauer's opinion there was another reason for the German decline, one just as important as material support. The Americans had been able to train a numerous, strong, and carefree generation of young researchers who took pleasure in their work, who with respect to individual performance were equal to any of Germany's products from the best of times, and who outdid the German physicists in their ability to work together.[68]

The German universities received only a fraction of the money needed for research and education in physics, Ramsauer argued. Moreover, one of the most important branches of this discipline, theoretical physics, had been pushed into the background. Taking care to fulfill the ritual requirement of personal attacks on Einstein, Ramsauer protested that the "justified struggle" against the Jew Einstein and against the "ravings of his speculative physics" had been wrongly carried over to the whole of modern theoretical physics. In particular, Ramsauer stressed that professorships were not being staffed on the basis of professional performance and that the academic career for a physicist had lost much of its earlier distinction and attraction. The struggle within German physics had to be aborted, Ramsauer argued passionately, if this science was to heal itself. The letter to Rust closed with the suggestion that the two physics factions meet on neutral ground in order to discuss their differences and that the financial support of German physics be increased considerably. The industrial physicist also went out of his way to tell Rust that he had already won the support of both Fromm and the Ministry of the Air Force, that the armed forces were willing to increase the amount of money flowing into physics, and that a copy of this memorandum had been sent on to the Reich University Teachers League.[69]

The appendices to Ramsauer's memorandum elaborated several points crucial to his argument. The claim that American physics had outstripped its German counterpart was demonstrated convincingly by a statistical comparison of the numbers of American and German physics publications, Nobel prizes, papers in nuclear physics – the field with the "greatest future prospects" – and cyclotrons. On all counts, Germany had either lost most of an earlier considerable lead or was already trailing the Americans. The decisive strategic importance of modern theoretical physics was under-scored by a blatant reference to the military significance of physics and especially of its most warlike application, nuclear power. Ramsauer insisted that there was more at stake than a difference of scientific opinion, namely, perhaps the most important question for the future of the German economy and armed forces: the liberation of new energy sources. The known potential of classical physics and chemistry in this regard had been exhausted. Only nuclear physics held out the hope of new sources of energy and explosives.[70]

In other words, *deutsche Physik* could not provide terrible new weapons. Only modern theoretical physics could do that. It was ideology versus power, and given the strained state of the war, the latter had a definite advantage. The message of this memorandum was clear. German physics should be well supported and left alone, not because the physics community opposed National Socialism, for it did not, but rather in order that German physicists could better help Germany win the war and regain Germany's position as a world power.[71]

The Ministry of Education did not react directly to Ramsauer's criticism, but his memorandum circulated in wider circles with great success. Prandtl was confident that the military would exert the pressure on the *deutsche Physik* movement that Rust had been unable or unwilling to provide. Both Heisenberg and Sommerfeld were very impressed by the influence Ramsauer's memorandum had in military circles. Moreover, the highest agencies of the government now seemed to have great interest in theoretical physics. Because of the realities of a drawn-out war and the insistence of German industrialists, the Party, the military, and the German state now clearly understood the connections between physics instruction, research, and the science and technology of war. But Rust did in fact react decisively to Ramsauer's emphasis on the military potential of nuclear physics, for it was a little more than a month after Ramsauer had submitted his memorandum that the Minister of Education took nuclear power away from the Kaiser Wilhelm Society.[72]

The initiative by Prandtl and Ramsauer produced a ripple effect that spread throughout the Third Reich. As he recalled long after the war, Albert Speer, the newly appointed Minister of Armaments and Munitions, was contacted by both Fromm and Vögler on behalf of German physics in the spring of 1942. Just like Ramsauer before them, Fromm and Vögler cited the nuclear power project as an example of the potential military and economic utility of science and especially of modern physics. Speer had ridden the reorganization of the war economy close to the pinnacle of power in Germany. Having to a large extent benefited from the plans and innovations of his late predecessor Fritz Todt, Speer now emerged as one of the most important patrons for German science and engineering in 1942. The Minister of Armaments and Munitions had sweeping powers within the German war economy as well as a very high opinion of science and technology.[73]

Vögler criticized the support given by the Ministry of Education to German science in general and to physics in particular, but this complaint was misleading. The Reich Research Council had been even more generous than Army Ordnance had been. Moreover, the army continued to fund nuclear power. Vögler wanted the Kaiser Wilhelm Society to have more autonomy at the expense of the Ministry of Education. Speer approved the request from Vögler – whose influence with the Reichminister had more to do with the industrialist's presidency of Germany's largest steel concern than his comparable role in the Kaiser Wilhelm Society – and arranged the transfer of the entire Reich Research Council from Rust to Göring. This move represented an apparent victory for Vögler, a gain for Göring, and a loss of prestige for Rust.[74]

After the Reich Research Council had been placed under the authority of Germany's highest-ranking air force officer, Speer and several high-ranking members of the German Armed Forces met with representatives of German physics in the offices of the Kaiser Wilhelm Society. Among other lecturers, Heisenberg spoke on some of the applications of nuclear fission. Although the text of this talk has not survived, Heisenberg's speech was probably similar to the lecture that he had delivered six months earlier on 26 February 1942 before the Reich Research Council. Long after the end of the war, Speer recalled that he asked the physicist whether nuclear weapons could be used in the war. There was nothing extraordinary about this question – Heisenberg probably encountered it whenever he spoke on nuclear power before a lay audience – and by Speer's account, Heisenberg repeated faithfully the assessment made by the German army some six months before. Nuclear weapons were a matter for the future, not for the conflict that Germany found herself engaged in. Moreover, this meeting with Speer and important members of the Armed Forces came at the second crest of the German military campaign. Rommel was advancing in North Africa, the submarine warfare was slowly starving Great Britain, and German armies were closing in on Stalingrad and Moscow. Once again, at this time no wonder weapons appeared to be needed.[75]

Speer was impressed by the future military and economic prospects for nuclear power and took a personal interest in the research. The institute directors of the Kaiser Wilhelm Society were instructed to provide the Ministry of Armaments and Munitions with one or two-page reports written for a general audience – probably for the minister himself – and Speer offered to assist the research being carried out in Heisenberg's institute in any way he could. Speer's potential support was immense. His office controlled the distribution of materials and manpower, wartime construction, and the crucial priority ratings. The war had passed beyond the stage where money alone was sufficient. Without the proper priority rating, no materials could be acquired, no workers could be assigned, and no research could be conducted. But Speer's interest in nuclear power – something which he considered irrelevant to the war effort – was genuine and intense. Just like many people before him and many more yet to come, Speer was seduced by the terrible and wonderful promise of nuclear power.[76]

Along with the substantial influence of the SS, the new-found industrial, military, and governmental allies of the established physics community also played a role in Heisenberg's appointment at the Kaiser Wilhelm Institute for Physics. For it was one thing to be nominated by the Kaiser Wilhelm Society for the directorship of the physics institute with Mentzel's blessing, and quite another matter to get and keep this appointment. During the Third Reich any potentially politically sensitive move had to be ratified by the state – here represented by the Ministry of Education – and the Party. Heisenberg and Vögler apparently considered the matter of Heisenberg's appointment to be closed by the summer of 1942, but this call to the Berlin-Dahlem institute touched off a reexamination by the state and Party of the value of theoretical physics. *Deutsche Physik* was out, modern physics was in.[77]

The advocates of modern physics had used the inherent military potential of their discipline to ensure its ideological acceptability. The Education Ministry stressed the importance of Heisenberg's appointment for the national defense by claiming that Heisenberg was practically the leader of the German atomic physics community, and emphasizing that both Speer and the German Armed Forces had the "greatest interest" in this research. Alfred Rosenberg's office put science before politics, echoed Ramsauer's memorandum by arguing that German atomic physics must not be allowed to fall behind the science of foreign countries, and laconically stated that the Party could not intervene in the "difference of opinion" between Lenard's and Heisenberg's schools of theoretical physics.[78]

By this time the National Socialist government had come to view the *deutsche Physik* controversy as intramural. It was a professional debate between two groups of German physicists loyal to the state and supportive of the war effort. In particular, opposition to *deutsche Physik* was not considered opposition to National Socialism. When the National Socialist University Teachers League was asked for a report on Heisenberg, they responded by demonstrating his "exemplary" character. Heisenberg had fought in a counter-revolutionary private militia against the short-lived Munich Soviet Republic in 1919 and had volunteered for military service during 1938, at a time when war with Czechoslovakia appeared imminent. But Heisenberg was hardly a convinced National Socialist. His political conduct could hardly be described as positive, instead he was no doubt the "apolitical-scholar" type. However, in this connection the University Teachers League referred to the fact that the Reich SS leader had personally called the political attacks on Heisenberg to a halt. Heisenberg could be attacked as a white Jew in 1937, but could also be defended as a nationalist and anti-communist five years later. More importantly, the established physics community now had powerful support from the SS, the Ministry of Armaments and Munitions, and the armed forces. By exploiting the heightened concern with the war effort and using nuclear power as its exemplar for the military value of science, physics had taken the fancy of several sections of the state. Conservative and nationalistic scientists had been influenced by Prussian and German militarism ever since the unification of Germany, if not earlier, but now the military and state were being seduced by science as well.[79]

Lenard's and Stark's clique did influence the relationship between German physics and the German state, but the appointment of Müller in Munich was a Pyrrhic victory. The success of *deutsche Physik* during the years 1933 to 1938 stood in stark contrast to its fall from grace during the war. When faced with the realities of warfare – especially after the war turned sour for Germany – powerful forces in the state listened to Prandtl's and Ramsauer's emphasis on the military power of applied science, even in the form of science education, and to their calls for the support of an apolitical physics in the service of the war. The fine line between Einstein-baiting and obstruction of physics education necessary for the war effort was manipulated successfully by the German physics establishment to their benefit.

The relationship between German physics and National Socialism became one of *compromise* and *collaboration*. Indeed every branch of the state – including the Party, the Secret Police, the SS, the Armed Forces, and the various ministries – had competent, loyal scientists in their employ, and their loyalty was first and foremost to their organization, for example the SS, rather than to "science" or "physics." For these researchers, along with the "straight" scientists, for whom "physics" was their organization, this loyalty was not only an end in itself but rather also represented the means to advance both themselves and some of the goals of National Socialism. Instead of viewing the interaction between National Socialism and science in terms of black and white, in terms of "nazis" and "enemies/victims of the nazis," the gray areas must be investigated, where scientists both opposed and supported certain aspects of National Socialist policy, and where all the members of the German nuclear power project belong.

The struggle against *deutsche Physik* illustrates the dilemma of scientific research and instruction in a totalitarian (or fascist) state. No goals can be pursued without collaboration with the state/Party and the advancement of its goals, and for this reason the validity and significance of a distinction between researchers loyal to the regime and apolitical scientists is limited. The apolitical established physics community successfully waged an uphill battle against the politicized science embodied by *deutsche Physik*. Ironically, however, in order to defeat the followers of Lenard and Stark, scientists like Finkelnburg, Heisenberg, Prandtl, Ramsauer, and Weizsäcker moved within, and thereby gave support and legitimacy to, the National Socialist system, an extremely political act. Once involved in this system, it was difficult for someone to withdraw. Further compromises would have to be made, for the system demanded them, including actions far more serious than the sacrifice of Einstein's name. The ever-worsening war placed German scientists in a position where their freedom of movement shrank even further and both they and their science were expected to help forestall defeat and secure victory for National Socialist Germany. Keeping the struggle against *deutsche Physik* and its repercussions in mind, let us return to the German quest for nuclear power.

Progress and infighting

Neither the takeover by the Reich Research Council of nuclear fission research, nor Werner Heisenberg's subsequent appointment as Director of the Kaiser Wilhelm Institute for Physics, had an immediate impact on the nuclear power project. Heavy water production at the Norwegian Hydro progressed very slowly during the spring of 1942. Although the Norwegian engineers and scientists were under considerable pressure from the German authorities to increase heavy water output as quickly as possible, their colleagues in Berlin and Hamburg were quite reluctant to give the Norwegians more than the minimum access to the German research. In general, the Norwegians were left on their own to expand heavy water production. For example, the Norwegian Hydro staff did not receive the reports composed by Paul Harteck and Hans Suess on the very catalytic exchange process the Norwegians were forced to install. The information that the Germans did pass on often seemed to want far more testing in the laboratory. The Hydro heavy water output was cut off due to insufficient water power in the spring of 1942 and because of the construction necessary for the eventual expansion during the following September. Since the Norwegian Hydro had not been producing the amounts of heavy water that the Germans wanted, Army Ordnance suggested the seizure and conversion of an additional Norwegian electrolysis plant at Saaheim. In response, Harteck agreed that such a move was desirable, since it could provide an additional metric ton of heavy water per year.[80]

The German physical chemists had not abandoned their plans to produce heavy water in Germany. The Clusius-Linde liquid hydrogen rectification process was put forward again in 1942 as a way to produce heavy water economically in Germany. If enough enriched water was available, in other words, water with an abnormally high percentage of deuterium, then the rectification method could produce large amounts of heavy water while avoiding prohibitive investment costs. Enriched water was often a waste product of electrolysis plants, but there was only enough such concentrate in Germany to produce around half a metric ton of heavy water per year. However, if enriched water could be found outside of Germany as well, then the Clusius-Linde process might be worthwhile, and both Abraham Esau and Harteck had their eyes on several industrial plants in Italy. A delegation of German scientists was sent south in late 1942 to inspect the Italian installations.[81]

This interest in Norway and Italy represented a continuation of previous science policy. Large investments in Germany for matters not immediately relevant to the war effort were to be avoided at all costs. Whenever possible, someone else, such as Italians or Norwegians, should pay. However, because of the well-known inherent connection between neutron moderator and nuclear power, German industrial circles also had a definite interest in heavy water. An IG Farben physical chemist named Herold attended the February conference at the Kaiser Wilhelm Institute for Physics, was inspired, and afterward discussed heavy water production on an industrial scale with Karl-Friedrich Bonhoeffer, Harteck, and Suess. Indeed the chemical giant was interested enough to erect a pilot plant in Germany, free of charge, using Harteck's catalytic conversion process. The industrial physical chemist Heinrich Bütefisch, one of the youngest members of the IG Farben managing board and a major in the SS, wrote Harteck personally and agreed to build a plant capable of enriching water up to 1 percent deuterium and requiring a maximum investment of 150,000 marks. But Bütefisch did have his price. IG Farben expected all access to all aspects of nuclear power, including a share in patent rights. Both Army Ordnance and the Reich Research Council agreed, and construction began. Once again, the German government was not making a large investment for something exclusively of future interest, rather IG Farben was gambling with a small part of the incredible profits the company had been making from the economic exploitation of Europe since the start of the war.[82]

The promise of natural uranium machines with heavy water, coupled with the failure of the Clusius-Dickel separation tube, led to a de-emphasis on uranium isotope separation. Harteck was disturbed by this shift in policy, and with the blessing of Kurt Diebner, the Hamburg physical chemist argued forcefully in the summer of 1942 for more support of centrifuge research, thereby contradicting the priorities that he had set out a year previously. As Harteck sketched out the problem for Army Ordnance, there were two paths to nuclear power: machine type number one, containing around 5 metric tons of heavy water and equal amounts of natural uranium, and machine type number two, needing smaller amounts of enriched uranium and less heavy water or even ordinary water. The German nuclear power project had taken the first path, but Harteck warned that the Americans might have chosen the second, and only experience could determine which method was best. The second path had some potential advantages, Harteck stressed, for it could lead to smaller devices suitable for army vehicles, and furthermore this method came closer to the production of explosives. Harteck closed his report by referring to the recent success achieved by Groth's centrifuge experiments and emphasized that uranium isotope separation should be supported.[83]

With the help of Dr. Konrad Beyerle of the Kiel Anschütz company, Groth had made up for lost time. Although there were some setbacks – Groth noted in his diary that the centrifuges had a tendency to explode – by the end of June he had successfully shifted the ratio of xenon isotopes in a given sample by means of a centrifuge. A month later, Groth used a

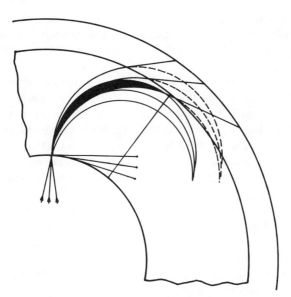

Figure 7 Heinz Ewald's electromagnetic isotope separator.

Note: A stream of isotopes is injected into a magnetic field. The strength of this field allows only the heavier masses in the stream to reach the other side of the container and be collected, thereby separating the isotopes.

Source: Adapted from Walther Bothe and Siegfried Flügge (eds.), *Kernphysik und kosmische Strahlen, Naturforschung und Medizin in Deutschland 1939–1946*, vol. 14 (Weinheim, Chemie, 1948), part 2, p. 99.

centrifuge to enrich a small amount of uranium 235 very slightly, which represented the first success Harteck's circle had had with uranium isotope separation. Groth traveled to Sweden during November and December of 1942 in order to consult with Swedish centrifuge experts in Stockholm and Uppsala. The Swedish colleagues were very helpful, and Groth returned to Germany with the conviction that the German scientists were on the right track.[84]

At about the same time that Harteck was arguing for the support of centrifuge research, Heinz Ewald, a young physicist at Hahn's institute, proposed yet another method of isotope separation: an electromagnetic isotope separator. Mass spectrographs had already been used to separate isotopes magnetically, but the output of these devices was very limited. Ewald's method offered the promise of much higher yields. An ion stream of homogeneous energy would enter a homogeneous magnetic field at a certain angle. The strength of this field allows only the heavier masses in the stream to reach the other side of the chamber and be collected there (see figure 7). Ewald pointed out that this separation process might be suitable for uranium 235 production and enrichment, but he did not pursue the matter further. Manfred von Ardenne, a scientific entrepreneur, learned of Ewald's idea and began building a prototype electromagnetic isotope separation device under the auspices of the German Postal Ministry.[85]

Along with advances in heavy water production and uranium isotope separation, the prospects of uranium machines grew even brighter during the course of 1942. The series of metal uranium powder–paraffin layer models at the Kaiser Wilhelm Institute for Physics was brought to a close in late October. The improvement in neutron production caused by the substitution of uranium metal for uranium oxide was greater than expected. As predicted by theory, the neutron production depended on the thickness of the uranium layers. It appeared that an enrichment of uranium 235 to around 11 percent of the entire uranium sample would allow a uranium machine with a layer design to run with paraffin or ordinary water as moderator. But these experiments had a human cost. Blood tests of Wirtz's research team revealed that Erich Fischer had suffered serious radiation damage and that Fritz Bopp had experienced damage to a lesser degree.[86]

The most striking success was achieved in Leipzig. Robert Döpel finally built a model machine with a layer design that produced more neutrons than it absorbed, a system that incorporated two spherical layers of metal uranium powder as well as several shells of heavy water (see figure 4). Trial "L-IV" provided experimental evidence in the summer of 1942 that energy- and explosives-producing uranium machines could be constructed. It appeared that an enlargement of this design to around 5 metric tons of heavy water and 10 metric tons of metal uranium would lead to a machine capable of sustaining a nuclear fission chain reaction for a considerable amount of time.[87]

Döpel's enthusiasm was marred by a major accident. The previous fall his mechanic had severely burned his hand while filling a sphere with uranium. This metal oxidized very quickly when in powdered form, emitting flammable hydrogen gas and causing the accident. However, shortly after experiment L-IV was finished, the Leipzig researchers had a more dangerous experience. The model machine had been immersed under water for twenty days when a stream of hydrogen gas suddenly was observed. Since the stream soon stopped, Döpel went on with his measurements. At the end of the experiment, they opened up the layer system to check whether too much moisture had entered the uranium. About three seconds after the mechanic Paschen had removed one of the rubber-lined aluminum covers, he and Döpel heard a sound similar to air rushing into a vacuum and watched as flames shot out of the machine. Inside the machine the uranium continued to burn, and by evening the temperature had risen to the point where an explosion was imminent.

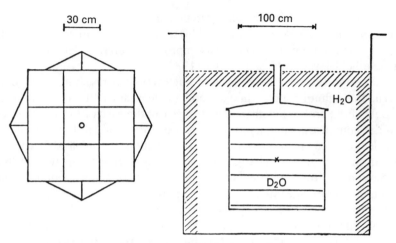

Figure 8 Experiments B-VI and B-VII (schematic diagram).

Note: Cylinders consisting of alternating horizontal layers of cast uranium metal plates and heavy water, all surrounded by a mantle of water. In the center of the experiment was a neutron source, X.
Source: Adapted from Walther Bothe and Siegfried Flügge (eds.), *Kernphysik und kosmische Strahlen, Naturforschung und Medizin in Deutschland 1939–1946*, vol. 14 (Weinheim, Chemie, 1948), part 2, p. 156.

Heisenberg arrived just in time to flee the building as the outer sphere buckled, showering burning uranium. Explosive bursts of flame continued for several hours. The Fire Department was called, but the fire nevertheless continued for another day and a half. As Döpel noted in his report, this experiment clearly had demonstrated the advantages of cast metal uranium over powder.[88]

In the light of the stimulating research carried out in Berlin-Dahlem and Leipzig, Heisenberg sat down to plan the next large-scale experiment, which would include 1.5 metric tons of heavy water and 3 metric tons of uranium in the form of large cast-metal plates (see figure 8). Furthermore, in order to reflect more neutrons back into the machine and to increase the likelihood of a self-sufficient chain reaction, Heisenberg suggested using a mantle of carbon instead of water. Since this design might go "critical," the problem of machine stability had to be taken seriously for the first time. Because the metal uranium plates would be heated to high temperatures and this time be in direct contact with heavy water, the metal had to resist corrosion. Like French scientists in 1939, Heisenberg suggested that rods of cadmium could be used to keep the chain reaction under control. But the large uranium plates that Heisenberg wanted caused problems for the Auer Company. Although sheets of uranium could be readily cast at a factory in Frankfurt, hardened metal tools were needed to cut the sheets into plates. In the summer of 1942 Auer could neither produce such tools alone nor find another firm willing to help manufacture them. In October, an Auer employee, Karl Zimmer, told Heisenberg that, unless the priority rating for uranium production was improved, uranium plate production would be delayed until March of 1943.[89]

Although the scientific aspects of nuclear fission research were going well, the administrative changes and unclear distribution of authority troubled the project members. The transfer of the Reich Research Council to the administrative domain of Hermann Göring had little effect on the nuclear power project. If anything, the position of Rudolf Mentzel was strengthened by this change. Vögler brought nuclear power to the attention of the Reichmarshal, but Göring remained uninterested. Abraham Esau and Mentzel reasserted their control of nuclear fission research, despite Heisenberg's appointment in Berlin-Dahlem. Relations within the research project rapidly deteriorated to the point that Diebner told Ernst Telschow that a meeting had to be arranged between himself, Walther Bothe, Esau, Harteck, Heisenberg, Albert Vögler, and Erich Schumann.[90]

Esau and Bothe both wanted the next large-scale model experiment to take place at a neutral site, in other words, not at Heisenberg's institute. Bothe probably still remembered the events of the previous winter, and, in any case, he considered himself more capable than Heisenberg of directing experimental work. Because of the tension between Esau and Heisenberg, a month after Heisenberg's official appointment at the Kaiser Wilhelm Institute for Physics he and Telschow were considering asking Army Ordnance to take back nuclear fission research. The Kaiser Wilhelm Society had changed from being a dependent research subsidy for the army to being even more dependent under the auspices of the Reich Research Council. The fact that Heisenberg and Telschow considered going back to Army Ordnance – if the army would have them – illustrates how little autonomy and freedom of movement the Kaiser Wilhelm Society and its scientists had. Heisenberg was also uncomfortable at the prospect of moving into Debye's house, since he did not want to give the impression that he had forced out his colleague, but Telschow told him that no other housing was available.[91]

In May of 1942, when applied nuclear fission apparently had great future potential, but little immediate relevance, Heisenberg was approached by a physicist in the employ of the giant armaments manufacturer Krupp. This firm knew of Siegfried Flügge's article on the harnessing of nuclear fission. Moreover, Krupp had been informed by Vögler that a research group under Heisenberg was investigating the applications of nuclear power. The scientific research department at Krupp was looking for new areas of research, and the technical applications of nuclear processes appeared quite promising to Krupp, especially nuclear energy production on an industrial scale. Would he be interested in cooperating with Krupp, Heisenberg was asked, if the company could contribute to the advancement of nuclear power research?[92]

This unsolicited proposal offered exactly what was needed to boost nuclear fission research up to the industrial scale. Krupp could provide large amounts of manpower and engineering experience, precisely what the nuclear power project lacked. Heisenberg laconically replied that yes, his group was investigating nuclear fission, but immediately added that this research was naturally secret, so that he was not allowed to discuss it. Although this claim was correct in principle, Heisenberg could certainly have received such permission through Vögler. However, Krupp did not press the matter. Heisenberg also noted that he believed it unlikely that Krupp could promote such research during wartime, but did hold out the hope that matters might be different after the war. By this time Heisenberg considered it irresponsible to invest large sums of money, materials, and men in nuclear power.[93]

Although Esau did not favor Heisenberg, the Minister of Armaments and Munitions was on bad terms with Esau and had been impressed by the new director of the Kaiser Wilhelm Institute for Physics. Albert Speer's strong support of the Kaiser Wilhelm Society gave this organization some leverage in its territorial dispute with the Reich Research Council. In general, the distribution of authority in the nuclear power project was very unclear and the project scientists were caught in the middle. Speer's favor allowed the Kaiser Wilhelm Society to begin building an underground "bunker" laboratory for the uranium machine trials. Vögler received the highest priority for this construction, a privilege denied to Esau. Speer's patronage also extended to include Bothe's cyclotron, even though no one had ever claimed that it had military applications. Bothe immediately set to work on his long-delayed project and henceforth devoted most of his time and effort to the Heidelberg cyclotron, not nuclear power. Unfortunately, the Siemens company told Bothe that not even the new priority rating could accelerate the delivery of the cyclotron magnet.[94]

Esau was concerned first and foremost with the German war effort. Late in November of 1942 he informed Mentzel that although the nuclear power project had made steady progress during the preceding few months, increasingly the project researchers had been forced to take up tasks more relevant to the war. A week later, Esau was planning to pack in the whole project by January or February of 1943 at the latest. It was obvious to him that the solution of this problem could not decide the outcome of the war. Nuclear weapons appeared far off. But Esau soon had reason to change his mind.[95]

3 ✧ The war comes home

According to the available reports from all parts of the Reich, at the moment the people feel that their emotional [*seelischen*] powers of resistance have been put under great strain. *The people* [*Volksgenossen*] *lack any real basis for the optimism demanded of them*...The reports show clearly that the great majority of the population *is not convinced that a victory is within our reach*, rather sees the state of the war approximately as follows:...the enormous deployment of material and the apparently inexhaustible human reserves of the Soviets could lead *this winter* to a new catastrophe *in the East*. Germany – now also the southern and southeastern regions of the Reich – *has been left defenseless* to air terror. Many still place hopes on *revenge*, others do not dare to believe in it. The evacuation of millions of people has in turn encroached upon the 'private sphere within four walls' of other millions, [an area that] up until now had remained untouched by the war...

From a secret report by the SS security service (16 Aug. 1943)[1]

Wonder weapons

Although nuclear weapons at best appeared to be irrelevant to the war effort and at worst represented a potentially dangerous drain on the war economy, the future military and economic promise of nuclear power not only justified continued support, it also made this research into a valuable science policy asset. The state agency that controlled nuclear power could anticipate considerable returns in the future on any investments made during wartime. Reichmarshal Hermann Göring had begun to lose some of his political influence by this stage of the war, but he nevertheless controlled a huge empire and extensive funds. On 8 December 1942, Abraham Esau was named Göring's plenipotentiary for nuclear physics, a position that embodied far-reaching powers, included control over a generous budget, and in theory entailed complete control over the nuclear power project. This type of bureaucratic solution, placing an individual with almost absolute powers in charge of a problem or important area, was favored in the National Socialist period with its "leader principle," but was hardly what Vögler had had in mind when he set this administrative reshuffle in motion six months earlier by complaining to the Minister of Armaments and Munitions.[2]

Rudolf Mentzel had proposed Esau's appointment as plenipotentiary. Despite Heisenberg's call to Berlin-Dahlem and Speer's patronage of the Kaiser Wilhelm Society, the Reich Research Council was determined to control nuclear fission research. Army Ordnance went along with this rearrangement of the nuclear power project. Kurt Diebner and the rest of the army scientists who had been involved with nuclear fission research were transferred to the Imperial Physical-Technical Institute, where Esau was president. In practice, Diebner continued to handle the bulk of the administrative paperwork for the nuclear power project. Both Erich Schumann and Esau personally wrote to all the institute directors involved with nuclear fission. The former noted that nuclear fission research now lay solely in Esau's hands, while the latter announced that the nuclear power project had been transferred definitively to his authority. Esau also noted that there would be some changes during his administration. Although the nuclear power project had made good progress under the direction of Army Ordnance, in view of the now strained nature of the war economy and the current status of the research, Esau felt that it was necessary to set narrower goals than had been previously held.[3]

Esau's gain in power and influence came at the expense of the Kaiser Wilhelm Society. Since this organization could not ignore these changes, a meeting was held in February of 1943 at Albert Vögler's office in the United Steel Works (*Vereinigte Stahlwerke*). During this discussion Esau, Mentzel, Vögler, and Ernst Telschow reached a compromise with respect to the subject of money and materials. The Kaiser Wilhelm Society would fund the research carried out at its institutes, while the Reich Research Council financed the rest of the nuclear power project. The Kaiser Wilhelm Society would continue to enjoy the support of the Reich Minister of Armaments and Munitions, and while Esau did not have such support, the Reich Research Council would nevertheless control all equipment and research materials. The nuclear power project appeared ready to split in half, and relations between the two factions deteriorated rapidly. Less than a month later, Vögler and Telschow both complained to Mentzel and insisted that another meeting was needed – this time with a representative of Albert Speer present. Mentzel replied that he would be glad to attend such a meeting, but only if Esau invited him. On the last day of March 1943 Army Ordnance severed its last ties to nuclear power. The finance section of the army had objected to the continuing cost. However, Army Ordnance generously donated all equipment and materials used for their nuclear fission research to the Reich Research Council. Moreover, the nuclear power project did not suffer financially because of the withdrawal of the army, for Göring's ministries more than made up for the loss.

Mentzel instructed Esau to submit a new budget, although he took care to remind his subordinate that the Kaiser Wilhelm Institutes would not be funded.[4]

But the effects of all these administrative changes on nuclear fission research were insignificant when compared to the influence of the ever-worsening war. Just as the German military campaigns had crested in the summer of 1942, the war turned sour for Germany during the following winter and spring. By October of 1942, Rommel's forces were retreating in North Africa, and they had surrendered by May. American and British troops landed in Morocco during November of 1942 and eight months later were in Sicily. In May of 1943, Admiral Karl Dönitz declared the submarine war had been lost, and by July of the same year Germany was being racked by massive Allied bombing raids. However, the most damaging setbacks for the morale of the German people came in the east. Russian troops encircled a great number of German troops in Stalingrad during November of 1942. Forbidden by Hitler to attempt to break free of their trap, the remnants of these German armies finally surrendered in February of 1943 after months of suffering. Germany's sinking military fortunes were paralleled by a drastically deteriorating public opinion back home. As soon as it became clear during the course of 1942 that the eastern offensive would not come to a quick conclusion, the war began to lose its appeal for the general population. The revelations about Stalingrad were all the more devastating because of the misleading propaganda that had preceded them. By this stage in the conflict, the general optimism among Germans with respect to the war had been replaced permanently by an increasingly fatalistic certainty that the war was lost. In recognition of this loss of faith, the state turned the crank even harder, including the strident call for "total war" by Josef Goebbels, the Minister of Propaganda.[5]

Pessimism in Germany was accompanied by growing optimism among their enemies. In late January of 1943 the Allies called for an unconditional German surrender. This Allied demand was no idle boast. By 1943 the armaments war had turned against Germany and in favor of her qualitatively and quantitatively superior enemies. All branches of the German Armed Forces had to reckon with powerful opponents in 1943. The Russian Red Army enjoyed a double to triple quantitative advantage over Germany in tanks and other war materials. Allied radar brought the German unrestricted submarine warfare to a disastrous close. By the end of 1943 Germany's opponents were producing five aircraft for every one manufactured in the Reich. It was in this environment that the myth of German wonder weapons was born. The quantitative advantage of German enemies would be matched and overcome through qualitative superiority.[6]

The German inferiority in air warfare had a destructive consequence.

American and British planes began to bomb the western part of the Reich. According to a report by the SS security service, during the summer of 1943 these attacks unleashed great bitterness and hate against England and America among Germans. The National Socialist leadership learned that the public desired revenge with "any and all means" against the Allies. But as was often the case under the Third Reich, this enthusiasm had to a large extent been created by the regime. The confidence held by the greater part of the population in the effectiveness of wonder weapons was due to repeated, vivid assurances by leading figures in government that Germany would have its revenge. Among the many new weapons rumored to be in production was something that sounded like nuclear power. Stories of a "new bomb" were circulating within the population. Twelve of these bombs, which used the principle of "atomic destruction," would suffice to destroy a city of a million inhabitants. Moreover, these rumors had had their intended effect, for the false reports of terrible new weapons had renewed German hopes for a final victory.[7]

Several members of the nuclear power project became involved in this irrational quest for wonder weapons. Werner Heisenberg and other prominent German scientists were called upon to judge proposals for inventions. While Heisenberg was plagued by inventors all his life, at this stage of the war such irritating contacts with self-styled scientists became dangerous. As the war worsened the National Socialist leadership took great interest in the inventive potential of Germans and especially of the front-line soldier. In September of 1942, for example, Heisenberg was asked by Mentzel to examine three scientific papers from an inventor in Vienna. Heisenberg replied that the first paper, on ether and atomic structure, was nonsensical and worthless. The other two treatises dealt with acoustics and ethics, two areas outside of Heisenberg's professional expertise, but Heisenberg also doubted that they contained any new or useful ideas. Ten months later, Heisenberg received a paper entitled "The psycho-rational constitution of nature, its recognition, and its mastery." Heisenberg replied that he was appalled by the author's vague "number-mysticism" and especially by his irresponsible claim that his invention could be decisive to the war effort and therefore deserved financial support.[8]

However, in at least one case Heisenberg was not so easily rid of an inventor. In July of 1943 the Ministry of Armaments and Munitions asked Heisenberg for his opinion on the invention of a motor that ran without fuel. The Ministry admitted that as a rule such suggestions were considered to be perpetual motion machines, but nevertheless wanted Heisenberg to make a careful examination of the proposal, sent in by an engineer named Günther. Heisenberg replied two days later that the author's claim to be able to create energy from nothing was false and added that the proposal was so incoherent that Heisenberg found it very difficult to read. A few months later, Heisenberg heard from the Ministry once again. Günther had been left unsatisfied by Heisenberg's criticism and had complained directly to Adolf Hitler. The Ministry spokesman asked Heisenberg if he could perhaps reconsider the matter. Heisenberg was even asked to meet with Günther.[9]

Heisenberg replied with a cold, formal letter and stated tersely that since Günther obviously was one of the typically stubborn inventors of perpetual motion machines, an interview appeared pointless. In January of 1944 Heisenberg was contacted about Günther's invention by a much higher official from Speer's renamed Ministry for Armaments and War Production (*Ministerium für Rüstung und Kriegsproduktion*). This Captain Bahr requested a copy of Heisenberg's reply to Günther's proposal, but the physicist replied that he had not answered the inventor, that he considered him to be a charlatan, and referred Bahr to Heisenberg's two previous letters to the Ministry for any further information. In the end Bahr summoned up the courage to reject Günther's perpetual motion machine, but even then he acted with considerable tact and restraint. Among other things, this episode reflects the increasing degree of hysteria and desperation attached to winning the war. Even perpetual motion machines were being considered to help fuel the German war effort.[10]

As the quest for wonder weapons began in earnest during late 1942 and 1943, one of the few novel scientific developments not considered seriously by German science policy makers was a nuclear explosive of unimaginable power. With the aid of hindsight, this apparent lack of interest in the military applications of nuclear fission appears to be paradoxical. But when the behavior during this period of the scientists involved with nuclear power and, more importantly, of the project administrators is examined, this relative lack of emphasis becomes understandable. To the men who oversaw nuclear power as well as diverse other research projects, it was clear that nuclear explosives – however powerful they might be – could not be manufactured in significant quantity in time to win the war. After all, the strained German war economy and reserves of raw materials scarcely seemed capable of lasting more than a few years. If Germany could not win quickly, Germany would not win. However, as the war turned for the worse, the search for wonder weapons became more and more frantic. In this environment hardly any German science policy maker would have wanted to promise something he could not deliver.

Such an attitude is found among the leaders of the German nuclear power project. In stark contrast to the optimistic, militaristic reports on nuclear fission research that were submitted by Esau and others throughout the first three years of the war, when Göring's plenipotentiary for nuclear physics described the status of nuclear fission research in late

1942, he mentioned only the exploitation of nuclear power in the form of "heat engines." As Mentzel passed Esau's report on to Göring's office, the former also avoided any reference to nuclear explosives and referred only to the use of the "unbelievable" amount of energy in a nucleus for a heat engine powered by "atomic energy." In fact, Mentzel qualified his statement even farther. This research group had been very successful, but these achievements simultaneously demonstrated that what Mentzel now characterized as the "practical problem," the creation of a heat engine for submarine propulsion, would not be solved in the near future. However, even though the uncrowned head of the Reich Research Council now referred to nuclear power as basic research, he nevertheless argued that this work was so important that it deserved support during wartime.[11]

A year and a half later, Mentzel became even more defensive about the nuclear power project. While forwarding Esau's latest progress report on to Fritz Görnnert, one of Göring's subordinates, Mentzel added a disclaimer. As Görnnert could see for himself, the research had received considerable support during the last few months. If the work could not lead to useful heat engines or explosives in the near future, Mentzel went on, the research results did ensure that the enemy could not surprise Germany with such weapons. After years of vivid propaganda on behalf of the terrible military potential of nuclear power, it is doubtful that anyone believed that the German industrial, military, or political elites would suddenly forget about nuclear explosives, and they did not. Esau and Mentzel were simply pursuing good science policy. They pushed new weapons that appeared feasible – for both of these men continued to devote themselves vigorously to the war effort – and played down research that was of intrinsic interest, but only of future importance.[12]

There was also a noticeable change in the way the project scientists portrayed their own work. A second popular lecture series on nuclear power was held before the Air Force Academy in May of 1943. In a sense, by demonstrating the usefulness of modern physics, these lectures were part of the continuing battle against *deutsche Physik*. A month earlier, Carl Ramsauer had repeated his arguments about the dangerous decline of German physics before this same sympathetic audience. Ramsauer had kindled the interest of academy members in nuclear physics, so Heisenberg was asked to arrange a lecture series on this topic. But nuclear fission research was still subject to military secrecy, and Esau was still in charge. Heisenberg tried to go around the plenipotentiary for nuclear physics by asking Erich Schumann directly for permission to hold the lectures, but the latter reminded Heisenberg that if Esau wanted to hold the lectures, then he would ask Schumann himself.[13]

When Heisenberg gave in and suggested that Esau head the lecture series, all difficulties vanished. The plenipotentiary opened the lecture series with a status report on the nuclear power project and followed it with a talk on the production of luminous paints without the use of radium, a pressing topic for the manufacture of aircraft dials. Otto Hahn spoke on the artificial transmutation of elements – and this time, before a less political audience, mentioned Lise Meitner by name – Klaus Clusius discussed isotope separation, and Walther Bothe lectured on the research tools of nuclear physics. All of these speakers stressed the utility of physics as well as the need for increased governmental support.[14]

Heisenberg's contribution was almost the same as his 1942 lecture before the Reich Research Council. But a comparison of the two talks does bring out some striking differences. Heisenberg's characterization of the military applications of uranium fission took both the decision by Army Ordnance that nuclear power was irrelevant to the war effort and the deteriorating state of the war into account. The director of the Kaiser Wilhelm Institute for Physics did state that a chain reaction in uranium 235 would produce large amounts of energy "explosively" (*explosionsartig*), but that was as close as he came to mentioning nuclear explosives. The word "explosive" (*Sprengstoff*) was not used. The only application of uranium burners (*Uranbrenner*) that he described was for ship propulsion. Moreover, the very terminology employed, "burner" instead of "machine," seemed calculated to play down the military potential of nuclear fission.[15]

The summary of Heisenberg's lecture clearly represented a radical departure from the tone and content of his speech before the Reich Research Council. In his summation, Heisenberg noted that the first step towards a very important technical development had been taken. Given the available experimental evidence, it was clear that nuclear power could be liberated for large-scale applications. On the other hand, Heisenberg added that the practical execution of this process was greatly hindered by the strained economy and the great "external difficulties" presented by the war. Once again, the contrast with earlier descriptions of nuclear power is stark. From this point on, everyone involved with nuclear fission research, whether as a scientist or as an administrator, avoided the word "explosive" and only advocated weapons that seemed within reach. As the war deteriorated and the pressure for wonder weapons grew, the position of scientists and science policy officials associated with rumored weapons of "unimaginable effect" became less and less desirable.[16]

Uranium machines in Berlin-Gottow

Abraham Esau's enhanced status provided the nuclear power project with financial and political support, but it also facilitated a reform in uranium machine design. Werner Heisenberg's appointment as director of the

Kaiser Wilhelm Institute for Physics had an important consequence. Army Ordnance physicist Kurt Diebner had to leave the institute. Although the exact details are unknown, it is clear that considerable personal animosity developed between Diebner on one hand and Heisenberg's inner circle – Heisenberg, Carl-Friedrich von Weizsäcker, and Karl Wirtz – on the other. But as is quite often the case with personal feuds among scientists, the personal conflict between Diebner and Heisenberg almost always assumed a professional guise. Diebner would be attacked as a mediocre physicist, or Heisenberg's circle would be accused of performing second-rate experiments. In fact, the researchers on both sides were capable scientists doing their best to make the nuclear power project a success, even though each of the two factions was quite ambitious and believed sincerely that it was better suited to conduct uranium machine experiments. Although Kaiser Wilhelm Society president Vögler had been very happy with Diebner's work in Berlin-Dahlem, the army scientist quickly found himself ostracized by the new administration at the Kaiser Wilhelm Institute for Physics.[17]

But Diebner had something to fall back on and could continue his personal quest for nuclear power. At the very beginning of the war, he had gathered together a group of young physicists who had recently completed their doctoral degrees, put them under contract to Army Ordnance, and set them to work on nuclear physics at the army laboratory in Berlin-Gottow. Whatever these scientists might have lacked in experience was outweighed by their enthusiasm. At about the same time that Diebner left Berlin-Dahlem, the scientists under his direction began their own uranium machine model experiment.[18]

By the summer of 1942, most researchers had switched over from uranium oxide to the more efficient metal uranium powder and a large amount of the former uranium compound had been accumulated by Army Ordnance. The Gottow group decided to attempt their own model experiment with the cast-off uranium oxide and took as their starting point the basic design of alternating horizontal layers of uranium oxide and paraffin. Because these researchers wanted to avoid all neutron absorption due to support material, they tried, and failed, to press the uranium oxide into a compact, solid form. Since the uranium oxide was so hard to handle, a slight change was made in the design in order to facilitate the construction of the model. Instead of uranium oxide, layers of uranium oxide cubes embedded in paraffin were used (see figure 9). The length of the sides of the cubes was chosen so that a neutron released by uranium fission probably would escape from the uranium and enter a paraffin layer before it encountered another uranium nucleus.[19]

The construction of this experiment required tedious, painstaking labor. A disk of paraffin was laid down, then another was cast on top of it with wooden cubes inserted as forms. Once the paraffin had set, the forms were

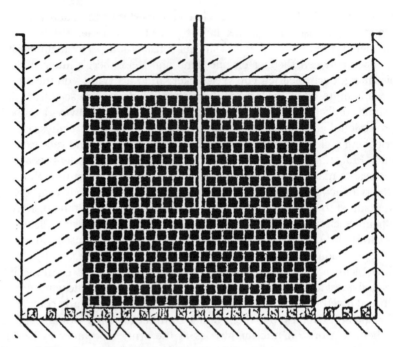

Figure 9 Experiment G-I (schematic diagram).

Note: A cylinder consisting of alternating horizontal layers of paraffin and layers of uranium oxide cubes arranged in a lattice, all surrounded by a mantle of water.

Source: Adapted from F. Berkei, Werner Czulius, Kurt Diebner, Georg Hartwig, W. Herrmann, Gerhard Borrmann, Karl-Heinz Höcker, Heinz Pose, and Ernst Rexer, "Bericht über einen Würfelversuch mit Uranoxyd und Paraffin" G-125 (before 26 Nov. 1942), 19.

removed and the uranium oxide was added, spoonful by spoonful. Uranium oxide was recognized as an extremely dangerous chemical poison, so this entire procedure had to be carried out with dust suits, rubber boots, rubber gloves, and facial masks. Experiment G-I contained more than 4 metric tons of paraffin and 25 metric tons of uranium oxide distributed among 6,800 cubes. But it was worth the effort. This model experiment yielded a higher rate of neutron production than any of the earlier uranium oxide trials.[20]

The Gottow group lacked a theoretical physicist. Once the promising experimental results of G-I became known in 1942, Heisenberg asked Karl-Heinz Höcker to make a theoretical evaluation of this trial. Thus Höcker, who after his return from the Russian front had accompanied Weizsäcker to the University of Strassburg as the latter's assistant, took up the problem of uranium machine design once again. Replacing cubes with spheres in his calculations, Höcker found that a lattice design would produce more neutrons than a layer machine of comparable size. But he went further and did what no German had done up until that time. He conducted a general examination of the internal geometry of uranium machines that did not restrict itself to alternating-layer designs.[21]

The main goal was to maximize neutron production by minimizing neutron absorption, and Höcker analyzed these processes in terms of a trade-off between two factors: a "boundary capture effect," and resonance absorption within the original mass of uranium. Assuming the ideal case, where neutrons are not absorbed by the moderator substance and do not escape to the outside of the design, one of three events would take place (see figure 10). The fission neutron is successfully moderated to thermal velocities without experiencing neutron capture and subsequently excites fission in a uranium 235 nucleus (1). The fission neutrons are absorbed within the initial mass of uranium before these particles enter the moderator layer (2). A boundary capture effect: immediately upon entering the moderator layer, the fission neutron would collide with a moderator nucleus and be deflected back into the initial uranium mass, where it is absorbed (2*).

Resonance absorption within the initial mass of uranium could be minimized by using uranium spheres with a radius on the order of the neutron mean free path in uranium (the average distance that a neutron travels in a given substance between collisions). But for a given amount of uranium, a design that used uranium spheres would have a relatively large amount of uranium surface area and thereby would also entail a relatively high boundary capture effect. If this same amount of uranium was broken up into layers with a thickness on the order of the mean free path, then this design would have a relatively small amount of surface area and thereby would also have a relatively low boundary capture effect. But these layers would also facilitate a much higher rate of neutron capture within the initial uranium mass than would be found in the sphere design.[22]

Taking this trade-off into account, for a given fixed amount of uranium Höcker found that a lattice of cubes or spheres embedded in moderator would always provide a much higher rate of neutron production than an arrangement of alternating layers of uranium and moderator. The former design exploited nuclear reactions occurring in all directions more effectively than the latter. A lattice design would therefore require less uranium 235 enrichment in order to run with water as a moderator than would a layer machine. However, difficulty of construction, especially a problem for a lattice of cubes or spheres, had to be taken into account as well. In practice, a sphere lattice would be much harder to set up and manipulate than an alternating-layer design. Höcker therefore suggested that cylinders of uranium represented an effective compromise. Both

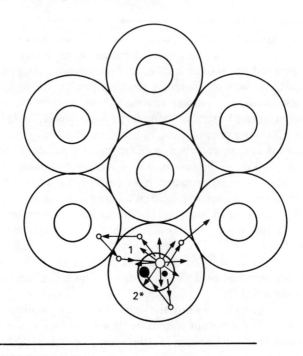

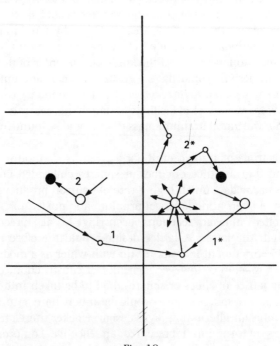

Fig. 10.

Höcker and the Gottow group believed that the question of the best uranium machine design had been thrown wide open.[23]

The Gottow physicists needed access to metal uranium and heavy water if they were to continue their research, but the bulk of the heavy water available at that time was under Heisenberg's control. However, the escalating tensions between Esau and Heisenberg worked to the benefit of Diebner's research team. A week after the Gottow group was transferred from Army Ordnance to Esau's Imperial Physical-Technical Institute, the plenipotentiary for nuclear physics informed Heisenberg by phone that the 600 liters of heavy water stored in the cellar of the Kaiser Wilhelm Institute for Physics would be moved to the Imperial Chemical-Technical Institute (*Chemisch-Technische Reichsanstalt*) on Esau's order. Heisenberg had no option other than acquiescence. The official reason for this transfer was that, until the bunker laboratory was completed, the heavy water was vulnerable to attack from the air. In fact, the Gottow group had already made plans to conduct a low-temperature model experiment with heavy water in the Imperial Chemical-Technical Laboratory.[24]

The Gottow researchers had decided to carry out another uranium machine trial without support material. A lattice of metal uranium cubes was frozen in heavy water, with a surrounding layer of light ice acting as a reflecting mantle. The Gottow scientists had come to the conclusion independently of Höcker that a lattice of cubes would be more effective than a layer design for neutron production. A symmetric spherical arrangement – almost a perfect lattice – was chosen in order to facilitate accurate measurement (see figure 11). The experiment contained 189 kilograms of heavy ice and a similar amount of uranium distributed among 108 cubes. According to Höcker's theory, cubes with a side of 6·5 centimeters would be optimal, but since the cubes had to be formed from 19 by 11 by 1 centimeter sheets, 5 centimeter cubes were chosen in order to get the most out of each plate. This experiment, conducted at -10 C, was very difficult to adjust. Just as the first Gottow experiment had been very difficult to construct, G-II was far away from a practically useful device. However, G-II did produce neutrons at one and a half times the rate

---

Figure 10 Chain reactions in spherical and layer uranium machines.

Note: The smaller circles designate moderator nuclei, the larger circles uranium nuclei, and the arrows represent neutrons in motion which have been released by uranium fission. (1) a neutron enters the moderator layer, experiences a series of inelastic collisions with moderator nuclei, losing energy with each encounter, reenters the uranium layer at slower thermal velocities, and meets a uranium 235 nucleus, exciting fission. (1*) a neutron is deflected by a uranium 238 nucleus into the moderator layer, where it proceeds as (1). (2) a neutron travels within the uranium layer, losing energy by means of collisions with uranium 238 nuclei, until it reaches the resonance velocity and is absorbed by a uranium 238 nucleus. (2*) a nucleus enters the moderator layer only immediately to be reflected back into the uranium layer, where it proceeds as (2).

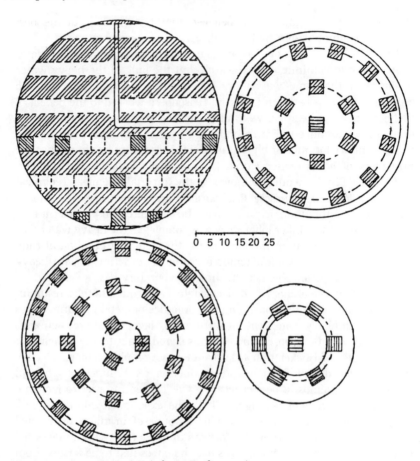

Figure 11 Experiment G-II (schematic diagram).

Note: A sphere consisting of alternating horizontal layers of frozen heavy water and metal uranium cubes arranged in a lattice, all surrounded by a mantle of ice.
Source: Adapted from Kurt Diebner, Georg Hartwig, W. Herrmann, H. Westmeyer, Werner Czulius, F. Berkei, and Karl-Heinz Höcker, "Bericht über einen Versuch mit Würfeln aus Uran-Metall und schwerem Eis," *G-212* (July 1943), 13.

of L-IV, making the latest Gottow experiment the best heavy water trial performed up until this time.[25]

Esau's seizure of the heavy water that Karl Wirtz had been guarding provoked Heisenberg to call again for a nuclear power project meeting, with Albert Vögler present, to decide which experiments would be performed, who would conduct them, and how the scarce materials would be distributed. Such a conference was indeed held a little more than a month later, but this meeting was held at the Imperial Physical-Technical Institute with Esau presiding and Vögler absent. The participants included

Walther Bothe, Esau, Paul Harteck, Heisenberg, Höcker, and Weizsäcker as well as Werner Czulius and Diebner from the Gottow group. At this meeting Heisenberg found himself being attacked on two fronts. Höcker argued that Heisenberg's evaluation of experiment L-IV had been too optimistic, a view backed by Bothe. Although previously he had agreed with his younger colleague Höcker on this point, Heisenberg now remarked that he believed that the experiment had been evaluated correctly. Esau stated that any further model experiments should take the most recent experimental results into account, a clear reference to the Gottow experiments, but Heisenberg replied that he had not changed his plans for experiments at the Kaiser Wilhelm Institute for Physics. Diebner brought up the promising new lattice design, and on cue Esau remarked that the next experiment should be carried out with the best design for neutron production, which obviously used cubes, not layers.[26]

Heisenberg disagreed, for several reasons. First of all, he argued that the small scale of the experiments performed up until that point precluded definitive results. Moreover, the Auer Company was geared up for uranium plate production and Heisenberg pointed out that a change in the order might disturb the firm. Heisenberg believed that the plates should be cast and that the layer experiment should be carried out. Afterward, the plates could be cut up and reassembled in the form of cubes. In any case, there was only enough heavy water available for one large-scale model uranium machine experiment at a time. Bothe agreed with Heisenberg that the large plate experiment was important, although the Heidelberg physicist also noted that he considered the lattice design to be basically superior. But the decision was Esau's to make. A few weeks later, the plenipotentiary for nuclear physics announced that although in general it was agreed that a lattice was superior to layers for neutron production, he had agreed to Heisenberg's compromise proposal. The Auer Company was able to produce both cubes and plates at the same time – indeed the firm went out of its way to keep both sides happy – so Esau scheduled two experiments: a plate arrangement would be set up at the Kaiser Wilhelm Institute for Physics to test the thermal stability of a uranium machine, and a further lattice design would be built in Gottow to achieve as high a rate of neutron production as possible. There was still not enough heavy water to go around, but this problem soon disappeared.[27]

In the fall of 1942, Bothe had started an experiment with small uranium plates of varying thickness in order to determine the optimal ratio of uranium to heavy water in a uranium machine. Actually, Bothe's younger colleague Erwin Fünfer performed most of these tests, since Bothe was busy with his cyclotron. But Fünfer's experiment was delayed because of problems in uranium plate production. In order to manufacture pieces of uniform thickness, the uranium plates had to be cast and then planed to the desired state. Because normal implements were quickly worn down by the uranium, this manufacturing process required hardened metal tools, which were hard to come by for the Auer Company. However, by the fall of 1943 enough small plates had been produced for Bothe and Fünfer to determine the optimal plate thickness for a layer machine and to conclude that the uranium machine needed roughly equal amounts of uranium and heavy water.[28]

The plates for the large-scale experiment at the Kaiser Wilhelm Institute for Physics presented much greater difficulties for the Auer Company. Given the size and number of these plates, special hardened metal tools were an absolute necessity. But no such implements were available. By July of 1943 the Auer Company had a large supply of cast plates on hand, but no tools to process them. An Auer representative asked two other firms if they could provide such tools, but one company said no, while the other one did not even bother to reply. The main difficulty was the steadily deteriorating state of the war. As the war economy became more and more strained, it also became very difficult to convince a firm to take the time and effort necessary to process a special order. Not even the highest priority rating could guarantee service, for by now most firms had a backlog of projects that enjoyed such status. Auer Company scientist Nikolaus Riehl asked Heisenberg if he could do something. Heisenberg appealed in turn to Vögler, noting that production at the Auer Company had been held up for two months, and the plate experiment had been delayed for three. By September of 1943 a firm that was willing to provide the tools had been found. Three months later, Nikolaus Riehl and Karl Zimmer could promise delivery of the uranium plates by the middle of January.[29]

While the Kaiser Wilhelm Society was waiting for the large uranium plates that Heisenberg had ordered, the Gottow group cheerfully began their third model experiment. Since the uranium cubes cast by the Auer Company needed relatively little processing, this lattice experiment was not delayed. While this trial was underway, two other physicists on Esau's staff tested Höcker's theory of uranium machine design. Using pressed uranium oxide and paraffin, Heinz Pose and Ernst Rexer compared the effectiveness with respect to neutron production of designs using plates, rods, and cubes. Their results fitted Höcker's predictions perfectly. Cubes were better than rods, which in turn were more effective than plates. Since cubes were hard to handle, in practice a design using rods appeared to be the best.[30]

Although heavy ice had had some advantages as a neutron moderator, it was impractical, so the third Gottow experiment was held at room temperature. Once again, neutron-absorbing material was avoided wherever possible. The metal container used in the previous two

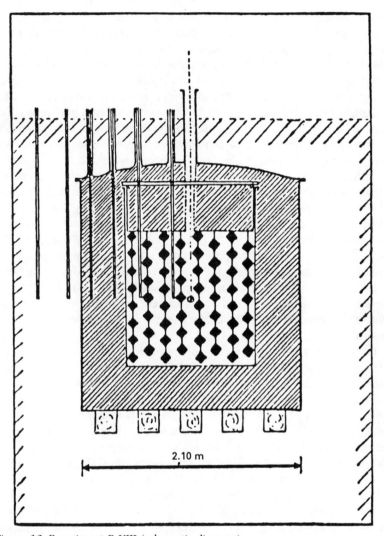

Figure 12 Experiment B-VIII (schematic diagram).

Note: A cylinder (in the case of G-III a sphere) filled with heavy water, into which a lattice of metal uranium cubes is suspended, all surrounded by a mantle of carbon (in the case of G-III a mantle of water).

Source: Adapted from Walther Bothe and Siegfried Flügge (eds.), *Kernphysik und kosmische Strahlen, Naturforschung und Medizin in Deutschland 1939–1946*, vol. 14 (Weinheim, Chemie, 1948), part 2, p. 159.

experiments was replaced by a hollow paraffin sphere. The metal uranium cubes, coated in order to resist corrosion, were suspended by wires of an aluminum-magnesium alloy in a perfect lattice and immersed in the heavy water; 180 cast cubes were supplemented by 60 more made up from plates. Each cube was hung at the same distance from its twelve nearest neighbors. (See figure 12, which illustrates a subsequent cylindrical experiment). Most importantly, given the relatively small scale of the design, G-III yielded an exceptionally high rate of neutron production. This model experiment was far superior to anything that had been built in Berlin-Dahlem, Heidelberg, or Leipzig when it came to facilitating nuclear fission chain reactions.[31]

Even Karl Wirtz, who was to conduct the long-delayed plate experiment at the Berlin-Dahlem physics institute, began to have second thoughts about alternating layer uranium machines. As Heisenberg lay sick in bed during November of 1943, Wirtz wrote to him and described a conversation he had had with Höcker while visiting Strassburg. The young theoretical physicist believed that a lattice machine would always produce more neutrons than a layer design. Choosing his words carefully, Wirtz told Heisenberg that although Höcker might not be right, he nevertheless feared that the plate experiment might turn out poorly. By this time, Heisenberg was practically alone in his opposition to the lattice design.[32]

Heisenberg recognized the value of both Höcker's theoretical work and the experiments by the Gottow group, but remained unwilling to abandon his layer design. Part of this intransigence should be attributed to personal differences with Diebner and Esau. It is also possible that pride played a role. The spectacle of a group of young, relatively inexperienced physicists bettering both Heisenberg's own theoretical work and the experimental results of the research teams under his authority could have inclined Heisenberg to cling more stubbornly to his own plans. However, the main reason for Heisenberg's behavior was that he spent very little of his own research time on nuclear fission. His scientific interests during this period were the physics of elementary particles and cosmic radiation – both fundamental problems – and not nuclear power. His interest in the project as a science policy maker was keen, but someone else would have to do the calculations and conduct the experiments. As a physicist, Heisenberg had lost touch with the day-to-day work. Moreover, by this stage of the war nuclear power had no immediate military or economic relevance. There was no pressing need for Heisenberg personally to take part in the research. Heisenberg was certainly capable of mastering the new theory and design. He did not bother to try. However, as we shall see, a great deal of Heisenberg's time and effort was taken up by other activities during 1943.[33]

Greater Germany and cultural imperialism

At first glance, the subject of this section, Werner Heisenberg's lecture tours in Greater Germany and Switzerland during the years 1942, 1943, and 1944, appears to represent an even greater digression than *deutsche Physik*. In fact, this vignette is very relevant to the history of German nuclear power and will facilitate a better understanding of the environment of science under National Socialism as well as during World War II. In particular, this examination of Heisenberg's role as a guest lecturer will provide a better understanding of the commitment made by German scientists to a German victory in World War II, of the way in which National Socialism and German physics interacted, and of the subsequent postwar ostracism of German scientists by their foreign colleagues. Heisenberg was not the only scientist who gave talks outside of Germany during the Third Reich. Klaus Clusius, Paul Harteck, Max von Laue, Max Planck, and Carl-Friedrich von Weizsäcker, for example, lectured abroad as well, but no other physicist enjoyed as much prestige as a guest speaker or spoke abroad as often. So far as surviving documentation allows, Heisenberg's role as a goodwill ambassador for Germany and German science will be examined.[34]

As the struggle against *deutsche Physik* demonstrated, Heisenberg's appointment in Berlin-Dahlem entailed far more than the directorship of a physics institute. Heisenberg had been rehabilitated publicly by the National Socialist German state. It was therefore no coincidence that the newly appointed director of the Kaiser Wilhelm Institute for Physics quickly became a sought-after guest speaker inside and outside of Germany. Heisenberg, already internationally known as a recipient of the Nobel Prize for physics, was now considered politically acceptable throughout Greater Germany as well. But it was difficult for a German academic to leave Germany for any reason during the war. Without the support of the Ministry of Education, a foreign lecture was impossible.[35]

If the Ministry of Education considered a scholar to be a good representative of Germany, German science, and German culture, then a foreign visit might be approved. If this trip was sanctioned, then the German Foreign Office, the foreign branch of the National Socialist German Workers Party, the German Academic Exchange Service, and, where relevant, the German Cultural Institute (*Deutsches Wissenschaftliches Institut*) located in the host country would be informed. These institutes were centers of pro-German cultural and political propaganda in countries occupied by, or obedient to Germany. These institutions cooperated closely with the various German occupation forces and were often the forums in which the visiting German scholar would present his lecture. The aim of German Cultural Institutes was to contribute to the "Germanization" or

"Aryanization" of these countries by exposing the natives to the cultural and scientific achievements of Germany as well as to leading German scholars and scientists. Once such a bearer of German culture arrived in the host land, he had orders to contact the representative of the German Academic Exchange Service or the German Cultural Institute immediately. Such visits were closely controlled by the occupation forces.[36]

By the spring of 1943, German Cultural Institutes existed in Belgium, Bulgaria, Denmark, Greece, Hungary, Portugal, Romania, Serbia, and Spain, foreign branches of the German Academic Exchange Service were found in Italy, Croatia, Holland, Norway, Sweden, and Slovakia, and a "German Institute" operated in France. Both the Party office in the host country and the institute or branch of the Exchange Service provided the visiting scholar with detailed instructions on how he should represent Germany and German culture. Any papers that were to be taken across the German border had to be submitted beforehand for inspection by the Ministry of Education, including the text of the lecture. Furthermore, the Ministry might choose to require the traveling scientist to submit a report on the trip, including the general impressions of the scientist's visit, news of any contacts with foreign colleagues, and intelligence with respect to the attitude towards Germany and German policy found in the host land.[37]

In the spring of 1942, Heisenberg received an invitation to speak before the Swiss League of Students. The Swiss physicist, Paul Scherrer, who had recommended his German colleague as a lecturer to the Swiss students, also asked Heisenberg to give a talk before the physicists at the Technical University (*Eidgenössische Technische Hochschule*) as well. Once it became known that Heisenberg might come to Switzerland, he was inundated with offers for speaking engagements. In the end, he agreed to lecture before the Science Faculty of the University of Geneva, the Swiss Physical Society, and the student organizations of Bern and Basle as well. Although Heisenberg had not solicited these invitations, they naturally pleased him, especially since they would provide an opportunity to visit old colleagues in Switzerland. Heisenberg requested permission from the University of Leipzig and the Ministry of Education for the trip, and this lecture tour was sanctioned by the Ministry in late October, although the Party did remind him of his obligation to call upon its foreign branch while in Switzerland.[38]

Fortunately for the historian, the report on this Swiss visit that Heisenberg submitted to the Ministry of Education has survived and is a fascinating historical source. However, an important question of interpretation arises when these reports are used by a historian. Did these reports accurately represent Heisenberg's intentions and impressions, or were they instead mere fabrications designed to tell the Ministry officials in Berlin what they wanted to hear, or – perhaps most likely – were they a little of both? No one, not the historian, not Heisenberg's family and friends, nor even Heisenberg himself as he sat down a few years before his death to write his memoirs, can or could hope to know all that was in Heisenberg's mind as he traveled outside of Germany during the last years of the war. Therefore, let us temporarily suspend judgment on Heisenberg's intent, and rather focus on what he did and the repercussions and contexts of his actions, as reconstructed from contemporary documents. We shall return to the question of intent in the end and thereby try to reach some conclusion about Heisenberg's role as a representative of the National Socialist Germany.[39]

On 17 November 1942, Heisenberg arrived in Zurich and was met by the head of the Swiss Students League. Later that afternoon Heisenberg paid a visit to a colleague at the University of Zurich. The next day Heisenberg spoke at a university colloquium on the observable variables in the theory of elementary particles. Afterward he visited his old colleague Scherrer at the Technical University. Heisenberg's next lecture came before the Swiss Physical Society on 19 November, including dinner afterward as the guest of the president of this society. On 20 November, Heisenberg traveled to Basle, paid a courtesy call on the physicists there, and in the evening spoke before the local student organization on the current goals of physical research. The next day Heisenberg returned to Zurich and was fêted once again by the Swiss Physical Society. Two days later, Heisenberg held an evening lecture before the Zurich student organization on changes in the foundation of the exact sciences. On 24 November Heisenberg traveled to Bern, visited both the German ambassador to Switzerland and the representative of the Party, was the guest of a colleague at the university during the early evening, and finally lectured before the Bern student organization on the current goals of physical research. The next day, Heisenberg ended his busy trip to Switzerland and returned to Germany. As required by the Ministry of Education, Heisenberg also reported on the mood of his visit. He was treated in a very friendly fashion in Switzerland, and not just by old colleagues, but by all Swiss with whom he came into contact. He had encountered frequent political condemnation of the German "re-ordering" of Europe while in Switzerland, but this ill will did not carry over to personal relationships. His lectures had attracted great interest.[40]

Less than a week after his return to the Reich, Heisenberg traveled to Hungary for another speaking engagement. Accompanied by his colleagues Max Planck and Carl-Friedrich von Weizsäcker, Heisenberg took part in a lecture series sponsored jointly by the Kaiser Wilhelm Society and the German Cultural Institute in Hungary. On 30 November 1942 Heisenberg arrived in Budapest and joined Planck and Weizsäcker as the guests of the Budapest institute. Planck and Weizsäcker spoke on the first two days of December, respectively. Heisenberg had lunch with the director of the German Cultural Institute on 2 December, then had tea with the German ambassador to Hungary, and that evening lectured on the current goals of physical research. An informal party at the institute brought the activities of the day to a congenial close. The three German physicists met the Professor of Physics at the University of Budapest for lunch on the following day as well as joining his counterpart at the local technical university for dinner. Finally, Heisenberg returned to Germany on 4 December. When Heisenberg reported his impressions of the political climate in Budapest, he noted that many Hungarians had attended his lectures. Heisenberg believed that the German Cultural Institute had succeeded in keeping alive the Hungarian interest in German "cultural goods" (*Kulturgut*) in a most auspicious fashion.[41]

In February of 1943 the Slovakian University in Pressburg (Bratslava) sent an invitation by way of the Reich Ministry of Education for Heisenberg to lecture in the Slovakian Protectorate. The Ministry did more than approve the trip. A ministry official told Heisenberg that they wanted him to accept the invitation, and Heisenberg agreed to go. On 28 March Heisenberg was met at the train in Pressburg by the President of the local technical university, the Dean of the Slovakian University, and a representative of the German Academic Exchange Service. That afternoon Heisenberg was the guest of the President, while in the evening the physicist joined the President and the Dean at the opera. Heisenberg had an even busier schedule for the next day, including an audience with the German ambassador during the morning, lunch with the Dean and the President, an evening lecture on the state of atomic physics, and finally a late dinner with some Pressburg scientists. On 30 March the mayor of Pressburg gave Heisenberg a morning tour of the old town hall, the physicist met the Dean, the President, the local head of the German Academic Exchange Service, and the German ambassador for lunch, in the evening he visited the Pressburg University physics institute as well as lecturing on cosmic radiation before a small group of scientists and students, and finally ended the day by dining with Pressburg scientists and a visiting Italian mathematician. On the last day of his visit, Heisenberg called on a few acquaintances in the German colony in Pressburg during the morning, met some physics students at the university in the afternoon, and left for Germany in the evening. The Pressburg scientists had been very friendly to Heisenberg. He reported that the relations between Germans and their Slovakian colleagues were very good.[42]

One of Heisenberg's most interesting trips abroad, and one for which a relatively large amount of documentation has survived, was his visit to occupied Holland in 1943. Sometime in late 1942 or early 1943, the Dutch physicist Dirk Coster contacted Heisenberg and Max von Laue on behalf of the parents of Samuel Goudsmit. This Jewish colleague and friend of Heisenberg had emigrated from Holland to the United States of America. The German occupying authorities had ordered that Goudsmit's parents, along with all other Dutch Jews, would be removed from Holland and sent to a concentration camp.[43]

Heisenberg responded by drafting and sending a letter to Coster that was designed to help Goudsmit's parents as much as possible. First of all, Heisenberg noted that Goudsmit was an internationally known physicist, implying that the fate of his parents would attract attention outside of Germany and Holland and might be politically embarassing. Next Heisenberg indulged himself in a white lie by exaggerating grossly Goudsmit's affection for Germany and Germans. Finally, Heisenberg closed with a perilous personal statement. He would be very sorry, if for reasons unknown to him, "difficulties" were to arise for Goudsmit's parents in Holland. It is difficult to imagine that Heisenberg could have done anything more for Goudsmit's family than this public declaration of sympathy and support. In any case, drafting and signing such a letter in the spring of 1943 was a dangerous step for someone in Heisenberg's position to take. Whether such an intervention could have made a difference is a moot question. The letters from Heisenberg and Laue arrived after Goudsmit's parents, like many other Jews, had been forced from their homes by the German occupation forces and sent to the concentration camp at Auschwitz.[44]

A few months after Heisenberg had written to Coster, the Berlin physicist received a very different sort of request from Holland. Heisenberg was contacted by the SS, an organization with which he had been in frequent contact during the struggle against *deutsche Physik*. In 1942 the first "SS-House" (*SS-Mannschaftshaus*) outside of the Reich had been established in Leiden. Himmler had given this institution the tasks of providing Dutch students with a Germanic education and of establishing contact with intellectual circles in Holland. The Dutch should become acquainted with German "ideological goods" (*Ideengut*).[45]

The director of the SS-House believed that he and his colleagues had made a good start towards their cultural and political goals, but he also recognized that the German military setbacks of the previous winter as well as political developments inside Holland had created difficulties which now had to be overcome. For this reason the SS had decided to invite leading German scholars to Leiden in order to demonstrate German intellectual prowess to Dutch academics. Heisenberg was asked whether he could visit Leiden in a few weeks time. The Berlin-Dahlem physicist declined the invitation. His calendar for the next few months was too full. On the other hand, he suggested that they ask again in the fall, but the SS apparently did not contact him a second time. Nevertheless, the invitation to speak at the SS-House demonstrated how much Heisenberg's professional and political reputation had changed since the 1937 attack in *Das Schwarze Korps*. Rather than being labeled "Jewish in character," he was now considered to be one of Germany's leading cultural figures by the most powerful and most extreme ideological force in Greater Germany.[46]

In June of 1943, the collaborationist Dutch Ministry of Education sent Heisenberg yet another invitation to visit Holland. The Reich Commissioner for the Occupied Dutch Territories, the highest German official in Holland, made it clear that Heisenberg should come. The Reich Ministry of Education thought that the proposed trip was a good idea, especially since the invitation had come from the Dutch Ministry. Heisenberg told the Ministry in Berlin that he was willing to visit Holland in principle, but only under certain conditions. He had asked the Dutch officials to tell him which of his Dutch colleagues wanted to see him and what the exact details of his itinerary would be. Heisenberg wanted to know what his Dutch colleagues – including friends and former students – thought of the idea before he committed himself.[47]

An official in the Dutch Ministry called in his countryman Hendrik Antony Kramers, a physicist and close friend of Heisenberg, and showed him Heisenberg's letter. Kramers then wrote to his friend in Berlin and personally described the context of Heisenberg's invitation. In many respects the working conditions for Dutch academics were unsatisfactory. A Dutch Ministry of Education official had proposed that this situation might be improved by reestablishing personal scientific contacts between Dutch and "international" – in other words, German – colleagues. The Dutch and German authorities wanted Heisenberg to spend a week in Holland. He would visit all the physics institutes, meet with his Dutch colleagues, and give talks drawn from his own research before small groups of Dutch physicists. Kramers also carefully added that he had discussed this matter with Hendrik Casimir and other Dutch scientists. All were sympathetic towards a visit by Heisenberg. Kramers hoped that he had explained the matter so clearly that Heisenberg understood that he was truly welcome, which, as Kramers recognized, was very important to him.[48]

For obvious reasons, Kramers had played down what he described in his letter as unsatisfactory working conditions. The economic, political, and social oppression of the Dutch at the hands of the German occupation forces was exceptionally harsh. Even though Dutch university instructors were certainly better off than many of their countrymen, these academics had not been spared. For example, the physics laboratory at the University of Leiden, where Kramers was Professor of Theoretical Physics, had been seized and closed. The scientific equipment was to be shipped to Germany as war booty and the Dutch scientists were barred from the laboratory.[49]

As soon as he received the letter from Kramers, Heisenberg wrote to the

Reich Ministry of Education, agreed to visit Holland, and implied that the personal invitation that he had received from his Dutch colleague had been a crucial factor in his decision. Heisenberg simultaneously wrote to Kramers and expressed his pleasure at visiting Holland under the circumstances that his friend had described. Kramers replied in kind. The Berlin officials passed on Heisenberg's acceptance to the German occupation authorities in Holland, but these latter officials were disturbed by the previous chain of events. They were pleased that Heisenberg was coming, but also displeased that Kramers had become involved. As they informed Heisenberg, the majority of Dutch academics either rejected, or mistrusted, German views and ideas, but nevertheless were prepared to prevent the severing of professional ties. Kramers belonged to this majority. The German occupation officials informed the Berlin physicist that although he was free to see Kramers informally, the latter would not be an official participant in the program of Heisenberg's visit. Furthermore, Heisenberg was ordered to visit the German occupation authorities at the very beginning of his visit in order to be briefed on the "political" state of the Dutch universities.[50]

On 18 October 1943 Heisenberg traveled to Holland and met with collaborationist officials from the Dutch Ministry of Education as well as with some representatives of the German occupation authorities. The following day Heisenberg traveled to Utrecht, paid a courtesy call on the physics institute there, and dined with the theoretical physicist Leon Rosenfeld in the evening. In the morning Heisenberg journeyed to Leiden, visited the famous Kammerlingh-Onnes Laboratory, and met his friend Kramers. On 21 October Heisenberg gave the first talk of his trip, a lecture on the theory of elementary particles in a small colloquium at the Leiden physics institute. Heisenberg spent the next few days in Delft and visited his colleague Kronig as well as the nearby technical university. On 24 October Heisenberg as well as physicists from the Phillips Company and the University of Leiden attended an informal colloquium presented by Kramers at Rosenbeld's house. The following day Heisenberg traveled to Amsterdam, visited his colleague at the university there, and participated in some experiments on cosmic radiation, a topic dear to Heisenberg's heart. Finally, on 26 October, Heisenberg discussed the experiences of his visit with Dr. Seyss-Inquart, the German Commissioner of Holland.[51]

When examining Heisenberg's reports to the Reich Ministry of Education for his trips to Switzerland, Hungary, and Slovakia, the reader might have been tempted to assume that these accounts bore little resemblance to Heisenberg's own impressions. They might have been merely what Heisenberg believed he should write and what the Ministry officials in Berlin wanted to hear. But the frank report that Heisenberg submitted at the end of his trip to Holland and his subsequent involvement with the

German occupation authorities and his colleagues in Holland both make such an interpretation doubtful. There are reasons for accepting Heisenberg's reports at face value. But let us continue to suspend judgment with respect to intent, and follow Heisenberg's odyssey further. When Heisenberg came to the end of his report on the trip to Holland, he provided his usual observations on the general political climate of his visit. Everywhere he had gone in the Netherlands, he had met with a most cordial reception. Heisenberg admitted that he had avoided politics wherever possible, but added that whenever this subject had nevertheless been brought up, his Dutch colleagues had harshly rejected the German standpoint. However, Heisenberg struck an apolitical note at the end of his report by assuring the officials in Berlin that cooperation with the Dutch on a purely scientific basis definitely was possible.[52]

In the case of Heisenberg's 1943 visit to Holland, the historian is especially fortunate. An excellent source exists for Dutch reaction to, and perception of Heisenberg as a spokesman for Germany and German science. Shortly after the end of the war, the Dutch physicist Hendrik Casimir was questioned by the astronomer Gerard Kuiper, a former countryman of Casimir and now a member of the American Armed Forces. Kuiper's subsequent report vividly captured the impression of callous nationalism that Heisenberg had made on his Dutch colleagues. According to Casimir, when Heisenberg visited Holland in 1943 he told his Dutch colleague that history legitimated Germany to rule Europe, and later the world. Casimir reported that Heisenberg had been aware of the German concentration camps and the looting of other countries, but nevertheless wanted his country to control Europe. Heisenberg justified his position to Casimir by arguing that only a nation which ruled "ruthlessly" could maintain itself. Democracy was too weak to rule Europe. Therefore, in Heisenberg's opinion, there were only two possibilities: Germany and Russia. Heisenberg, showing great insensitivity to the plight of his colleagues in occupied Europe, then drew the logical conclusion from his argument: a Europe under German leadership might well be the "lesser evil."[53]

However, Kuiper's report must be read with just as much caution as Heisenberg's letters to the Reich Ministry of Education. The scientists who were suffering under the yoke of the German occupation could hardly have been objective observers when a nationalistic German colleague rational-ized the German occupation and exploitation of Europe as necessary for the German victory-in-arms that he wanted so badly. In particular, one must point out that while, like most Germans, Heisenberg probably was aware in 1943 that German concentration camps existed, that Jews, leftists, and others were imprisoned there, and that these camps were hardly pleasant places, Heisenberg nevertheless could not have known that these camps would develop into human slaughterhouses during the last years of the war. Heisenberg's Dutch colleagues did not appreciate the message that he gave them, that Germany had to win the war, but it is also clear that Heisenberg could not, or would not, understand how or why he had alienated them. Heisenberg believed that his visit to Holland had gone well, despite all the politics. In fact, Heisenberg's visit to Holland poisoned his relations with many of his Dutch colleagues.[54]

But there is another important aspect to Heisenberg's tour through the Netherlands. He had been asked by his colleagues to visit their country in order to improve their working conditions, and that is exactly what he did. Because of Heisenberg's intervention, for example, his colleague Leon Rosenfeld received permission to visit his mother in Belgium. Kramers and the Leiden physicists benefited as well. After Heisenberg's visit, the German occupation authorities suddenly announced that the Dutch scientists might be allowed to retain some scientific instruments vital to their research. Kramers and his colleagues immediately submitted a modest list of apparatus they wished to keep. There was in fact direct evidence of Heisenberg's influence. Shortly after this announcement, a German official visited Kramers, mentioned that he had spoken with Heisenberg in Berlin, and claimed to have been surprised to find out that the Leiden laboratory was still closed. This official now ostentatiously lifted the ban on research and promised that the Dutch physicists would be told as soon as possible what equipment would not be removed. Obviously the German occupation forces were willing to make minor concessions in order to encourage cultural collaboration between Dutch and German scientists. Heisenberg's Dutch colleagues were sincerely grateful to him, and thanked him.[55]

Just at the end of his visit to Holland, the German occupation authorities – who wished to encourage a fruitful collaboration between Dutch and German scholars – had asked Heisenberg how his visit might be extended. For a long time, Heisenberg felt unable to answer this question, but he finally gave an apolitical response. Given the state of the war, further visits did not appear to him to be a good idea. Heisenberg counselled the occupation authorities to wait patiently for a while. But he also noted that he considered his trip to have been a success, since it had reopened channels of scientific communication between himself and Dutch physicists. Indeed, his recent correspondence with Kramers had been very valuable. Heisenberg told his countrymen in Holland that he was convinced that scientific relations between the Germans and the Dutch would resume very quickly once the war had come to a happy end.[56]

A little more than a month after returning to Germany from Holland, Heisenberg traveled east to speak at the German Institute for Eastern Work (*Institut für Deutsche Ostarbeit*) in the General Government, a region that had formerly been part of Poland. In April 1940 this institute was founded in place of the former University of Cracow. With very few exceptions, the Polish faculty of this university had been arrested by the German occupation forces and sent to the concentration camp in Sachsenhausen. Hans Frank, the governor of this German satrapy, was also the founder and promoter of the German Institute for Eastern Work. This institution was to provide scientific support for the German colonization of eastern Europe at the expense of other peoples (*Lebensraumpolitik*). For example, the institute section for astronomy and mathematics employed the forced labor of Russian prisoners of war and concentration camp inmates for mathematical research. Coblitz, the director of this institute, argued in 1941 that the Eastern Jewish question required scientific investigation as preparation for the final postwar solution of the European Jewish question. Heisenberg may have been unaware of the exact details of the scientific research carried out at the German Institute for Eastern Work, but such work nevertheless was prosecuted in Cracow.[57]

Heisenberg's invitation to speak in Cracow had originated from the governor himself. Frank had been a schoolmate of the Nobel Prize winner and may well have wished to show off one of the scientific institutes under his control to his scientist friend. But when Coblitz asked the Ministry of Education in 1941 for permission to hold a lecture by Heisenberg at the German Institute for Eastern Work, the request was rejected, even though Heisenberg had been willing to take part. In the spring of 1943, after Heisenberg's public rehabilitation, Coblitz submitted a second petition, which was approved. The Ministry made so prompt a decision, and informed Heisenberg so quickly, that he wrote to Coblitz and reaffirmed his willingness to speak in the General Government even before the director of the German Institute for Eastern Work had sent him an official invitation.[58]

At around the same time, Heisenberg received recognition from the east of his enhanced professional prestige in another form. He was awarded the Copernicus Prize for excellence in physics by Hans Frank's Cracow institute. Both Heisenberg and Gustav Borger, a Party official from the University Teachers League, saw this honor as yet another blow against the forces of Lenard and Stark. In fact Heisenberg's lecture tours in Greater Germany also contributed to the continuing campaign against *deutsche Physik*. Borger sent Heisenberg his hearty congratulations, since this award represented yet another gratifying official recognition of Heisenberg's work and thereby of theoretical physics. Heisenberg replied that this prize especially pleased him, because it could be interpreted as an official "rehabilitation" [*Rehabilitierung*] of theoretical physics. As Germany's position in the war grew worse, Heisenberg's prestige as a scientist in Germany rose higher and higher.[59]

For various reasons, Heisenberg's visit to Cracow was delayed until the end of the year. Frank was either busy or on vacation throughout the summer. Heisenberg had to wait until the dates of his trip to Holland were set in October. A month later, Heisenberg became ill. The guest lecture was finally scheduled for the second week of December, and Coblitz took care to remind the "in-house physicist" at the German Institute for Eastern Work to attend. Especially since Frank, who was a "close friend" of Heisenberg, had personally invited him and would be at the lecture. Heisenberg gave this talk, and thereby lent his personal prestige to German policy in occupied Poland, though his report to the Ministry of Education on the trip apparently has not survived.[60]

The last foreign lecture that will be discussed here took place at the Copenhagen German Cultural Institute during the spring of 1944. In January of that year Heisenberg learned that the Niels Bohr Institute for Theoretical Physics had been closed by the German occupation authorities, and the Danish physicist Jørgen Bøggild had been arrested. Once the physicists at Bohr's institute realized that their German colleagues had not been responsible for the German takeover, they decided to tell Heisenberg about the occupation and asked Hans Suess – who was passing through Copenhagen on his way south from Norway – to pass on the message. Heisenberg learned of the occupation from Suess on 5 January 1944 and arranged to be part of the German commission that would investigate whether the research at the Niels Bohr Institute had been contributing to the Allied war effort.[61]

During the previous year Bohr and the other Jewish or partly Jewish members of the institute had been forced to flee occupied Denmark in order to evade deportation to a concentration camp. Weizsäcker learned that the German officials in Copenhagen were considering appointing him the new director of Bohr's old institute, and he hastened both to tell his friend Heisenberg that he would be very unhappy in such a position and to ask him to use his influence to kill this plan. In the company of Kurt Diebner and others, Heisenberg traveled to Denmark on 24 January and met with the plenipotentiary of the German Reich in Copenhagen. The German authorities were debating whether to staff the Bohr institute with German physicists, to force the Danish scientists at this institute to contribute to the German war effort, or to strip the Institute of Theoretical Physics in Copenhagen of any equipment that was in demand in Germany.[62]

Heisenberg wanted to arrange as beneficial a settlement as possible for the Danes, and for this reason conducted a tour of the institute, and especially of the high-voltage equipment and the cyclotron, that the Danes believed was designed to show how complex the construction of such equipment was, and thereby how difficult these devices would be to ship and to reassemble. On the very next day the German authorities informed the Danish Foreign Office that the Bohr institute would be reopened without conditions and released Bøggild. Heisenberg subsequently told

Johannes Jensen, a colleague who, like Heisenberg, had many friends and acquaintances at the Bohr institute, that the Danes had been very happy about this solution.[63]

A month after his visit to Denmark, Heisenberg received an invitation to return to Copenhagen. The plenipotentiary of the German Reich wanted him to speak at the German Cultural Institute, which was located very near to the Bohr institute. Heisenberg spoke there in April, and although his subsequent report to the Ministry of Education apparently has not survived, correspondence between Heisenberg and Höfler, the director of the German Cultural Institute in Copenhagen, is available. The German Cultural Institute had been very hospitable to Heisenberg. The Berlin physicist had tried to reconcile some of the differences between the physicists still at the Bohr institute and Höfler's institute while visiting Copenhagen. In his report to the Ministry of Education, Heisenberg had supported energetically Höfler's plans for the future development and responsibilities of the German Cultural Institute.[64]

Heisenberg's association with German Cultural Institutes in occupied countries during the Third Reich raises one obvious question. Was his support a reflection of an acquiescence in National Socialism, or something else? In order to answer this question, we must jump ahead in time to the postwar era, when Heisenberg was free to speak his mind. In 1949 Höfler applied for a teaching position at the University of Munich and prompted a university official to ask Heisenberg whether Höfler had strictly limited himself to scholarship while in Copenhagen, or had engaged in "cultural propaganda?" Heisenberg's evasive answer provides insight into his naive perception and continued support of the German Cultural Institutes. First of all, Heisenberg claimed that he had never met Höfler personally, and that the latter had been out of town when Heisenberg had visited the German Cultural Institute. Although this account may have been accurate, it contrasts starkly with both Heisenberg's letter to Höfler in the spring of 1944 and a letter that Höfler sent to Heisenberg in 1947, in which the former reminded the physicist of how much he had enjoyed Heisenberg's visit.[65]

Next Heisenberg asserted that the Copenhagen German Cultural Institute had not had an entirely bad reputation and that it had not been a source of explicit National Socialist propaganda. Heisenberg defended the director of this Copenhagen institute. If the Danes had stopped frequenting the German Cultural Institute, that was not Höfler's fault. Heisenberg claimed that he had never heard criticism of Höfler by the Danes, although he did admit that the Danish scientists would hardly have expressed such complaints to him. Long after the war, Stefan Rosental, a collaborator of Bohr, contradicted some of Heisenberg's claims. According to Rosental, the Danes never patronized the German Cultural Institute and did criticize

Höfler in Heisenberg's presence. Heisenberg closed his report on Höfler by noting that even if the latter had not been as successful as the director of the Budapest German Cultural Institute, Heisenberg nevertheless believed that Höfler had not left a negative impression behind in Denmark. Heisenberg obviously had few misgivings either about his association with, or the goals of, these institutes.[66]

Now we can return to the question of Heisenberg's intent. Heisenberg never spread vulgar National Socialist propaganda. Every one of his official visits was strictly restricted to a scientific talk before a professional or lay audience. However, it is clear that the German authorities deliberately used Heisenberg as a propaganda tool. He represented the better side of National Socialist Germany, a good German who publicly had opposed the Party and the SS in the *deutsche Physik* controversy, but also someone who could travel to Holland after the Dutch Jews had been shipped to concentration camps, experience firsthand one of the dark sides of the German war effort and German imperialism, the occupation and plunder of Europe, and nevertheless feel compelled to try to convince his foreign colleagues that the German re-ordering of Europe was a necessary evil. It is difficult to imagine any fuller support for the German war effort. Heisenberg's intent could be broken down into three concerns: (1) aiding colleagues, friends and acquaintances wherever and however possible, and; (2) keeping science and scientists apolitical, and; (3) helping Germany win the war and regain its status as a cultural, economic, and political world power. The Third became dominant, and forced Heisenberg to rationalize elements of his behavior that contradicted the other two, for it was precisely the expansion of German power that threatened both his colleagues and apolitical science.

Heisenberg's lecture tours also provide insight into another aspect of science during the Third Reich: National Socialism overlapped with, and partially or completely assimilated, existing German ideologies and traditions. Many of these lectures were held under the authority of German Cultural Institutes or the German Institute for Eastern Work. In fact, as long as he could lecture in German, Heisenberg accepted all offers of speaking engagements at such institutes. In the eyes of many native scientists, these institutes were centers of scientific and cultural collaboration with the policy of National Socialist Germany as well as symbols of the German occupation and exploitation of their homeland.

These visits alienated and deeply disappointed many of Heisenberg's foreign colleagues, but Heisenberg was either unable or unwilling to understand the cause and effect of this alienation. Heisenberg repeatedly aided foreign colleagues in trouble when he could, often at considerable risk to himself, and they were very grateful. However, this gratitude could not make up for the alienation caused by Heisenberg's close association with German aggression. Heisenberg supported wholeheartedly the efforts of these institutes to "sell" German culture and science to the natives and found nothing wrong with visiting and speaking at these forums. He thereby legitimated the National Socialist policy of cultural imperialism and Germanization by means of the considerable weight of his professional prestige. Heisenberg's reports on his lecture tours were hardly objective accounts, but they do demonstrate how useful he was to the German government. Heisenberg neither desired nor intended to participate in cultural propaganda for National Socialism, but it was a role he played all the same.[67]

Heisenberg's lecture tours demonstrated German nationalism equal to any extreme reached by German scientists during the Wilhelmian Empire and Weimar Republic, and his trip to Holland was strikingly reminiscent of the visit that his teacher Arnold Sommerfeld paid to occupied Belgium and France during World War I, although the respective political contexts were very different. From his standpoint, Heisenberg was not buttressing National Socialism, but he certainly supported German imperialism willingly and knowingly. Heisenberg and his German colleagues may have made a distinction in their own minds between their duty to Germany and service for National Socialism, but their colleagues at the wrong end of the stick, Jews, leftists, and scientists from countries occupied by or struggling against Germany, could not and did not appreciate so fine a distinction.

The perception of Heisenberg's foreign colleagues may have been biased, but it existed nevertheless. With so many goals and methods in common, German nationalism could not be separated from National Socialism, whether those individuals involved wanted to, or not. From the perspective of the victims and enemies of Germany, the war, the military occupation, the economic exploitation, and the political repression were not carried out by National Socialists, rather by Germans. Although by 1943 Heisenberg no longer believed a German victory likely, he, like most of his countrymen, continued to aid efforts to stave off a German defeat and to perpetuate German power. How else can his behavior in Greater Germany be understood? But let us return to the German quest for nuclear power.[68]

Death from above and betrayal from within

The war came home to Germany with a vengeance in 1943, as the irrational search for wonder weapons and the difficulties experienced by the Auer Company in their attempts to produce uranium plates both demonstrated. But the two other branches of the nuclear power project, heavy water production and uranium isotope separation, reflected the new state of siege most vividly. Allied attacks on the Norwegian Hydro forced the Germans to abandon heavy water production in Norway, and Allied air raids drove the isotope separation research out of Hamburg and Kiel in search of a safe haven. The scientists in the nuclear power project were well aware of the danger that enemy attack represented for their research. Paul Harteck and Karl Wirtz had called attention to the precarious position of the Norwegian Hydro as early as October of 1941. The Norwegian installation was easy to damage or destroy, especially by means of sabotage. In the minds of these heavy water experts, this threat of sabotage was yet another reason why heavy water production should be supported in Germany.[69]

In January of 1943, the German intelligence service reported an English plot to destroy the Norwegian power plant and electrolysis installation in Vemork. A subsequent investigation by the SS security service – which acted as the Secret Police in areas occupied by Gemany – included a search of every house in the nearby city of Rjukan and came to the conclusion that the leading Norwegian officials at the Hydro as well as the general Norwegian population believed that the English were planning a raid in order to damage the vital nitrogen production at the plant. The SS security service found no unusual uneasiness in the Vemork plant. The Norwegian engineers appeared to be preoccupied with increasing the heavy water output.[70]

But in late February the part of the Norwegian Hydro devoted to heavy water production was blown up by saboteurs. 900 kilograms of solution containing anywhere from 15 percent to pure heavy water had been lost. The Norwegians would need six weeks to repair the installation, and it would be four months before pure heavy water could be delivered. An official of the German Army High Command in Norway, which oversaw the Norwegian Hydro along with other branches of Norwegian industry, reacted to this attack by suggesting that both the heavy water and the heavy water production installation be transferred to Germany. In the meantime, the Germans would continue the construction of heavy water plants at Saaheim and Notodden, but the German authorities in Norway asked Army Ordnance and the Reich Research Council to make a decision as soon as possible. Should the Norwegian heavy water production continue?[71]

On 1 March 1943 Swedish radio broadcast news of the sabotage. According to this source, the attack had hit the German war potential in a sensitive area. The goal had been the heavy water installation, the radio announcer claimed, since heavy water was desperately needed in Germany for the production of high-quality explosives. A German army official now remarked that the sabotage should not have been a surprise. Because of the great interest that the German military had shown in the Norwegian Hydro, it had become almost a Norwegian national sport to help destroy this factory. Under these circumstances, it was difficult for the security service to find the guilty party. In order to speed up the repair work, the SS was asked to release some Norwegians who had been on the job at the time of the attack and subsequently were arrested. The German military authorities in Norway realized that if full heavy water production was resumed at the Norwegian Hydro, then a second British attack might follow. If the Germans made sabotage impossible, then the entire plant might be bombed as soon as the heavy water installation had been rebuilt.[72]

The scientists and administrators of the German nuclear power project recognized the significance of the sabotage in Vemork. Their sole source of neutron moderator was endangered, and apparently the Allies believed that heavy water could be used for the production of explosives. Indeed Harteck asked Kurt Diebner whether any further investment at the Norwegian Hydro made any sense. Abraham Esau made his own position clear at a meeting held in May. Any further expansion of the heavy water production there would be abandoned, since an attack or air raid on the plant threatened nitrogen output in Greater Germany. Therefore, Esau continued, heavy water production in Germany had to be accelerated. The remaining enriched Norwegian heavy water would be sent to the IG Farben pilot plant at Leuna in the Reich. If the IG Farben experiments turned out favorably, then this catalytic exchange separation process would be set up on a larger scale. Esau also decided to have another look at the Clusius-Linde liquid hydrogen distillation process. The Germans originally had planned to test this method, but they had chosen to use the available materials at the ill-fated Norwegian Hydro instead.[73]

Less than a week after this meeting, Esau and Harteck traveled to Italy to inspect the Montecatini electrolysis works in Meran. The Germans hoped to be able to produce water containing 1 percent heavy water in Italy, since this value was the minimum enrichment that the Leuna pilot plant needed in order to produce pure heavy water. Harteck thought that by combining the potential of the Italian plants with the IG Farben pilot plant, production of heavy water at a rate of 0.5 metric tons per year could begin within a relatively short period of time. However, when the Italian water samples subsequently were examined at the Kaiser Wilhelm Institute for Physics, the levels of heavy water were disappointingly low. Moreover, the cause of the low values would be very difficult to ascertain.[74]

On 16 November 1943, the Vemork electrolysis plant was bombed by Allied planes. Although no essential part of the heavy water installation was damaged, the German and Norwegian board members of the Hydro were very disturbed by the raid. The Norwegian head of the plant told Diebner, Hans Suess, and other representatives of the nuclear power project that his company did not want to produce any more heavy water. The claim made by Esau's subordinates, that heavy water was irrelevant to the war effort, was besides the point. The Allies obviously saw heavy water as a threat. If the Norwegians resumed heavy water production, then they had to expect another air raid that would leave them with neither heavy water nor nitrogen. The head of the Hydro did not want to expose his workers to unnecessary danger or to invest millions of crowns in the heavy water installation only to lose it during the next bombing run. Most importantly, Bey, the German IG Farben official and the real power at the Norwegian Hydro, was in complete agreement with his Norwegian vassal. The diluted Norwegian heavy water, no more than one metric ton in all, would be shipped to Germany for further processing, but the Norwegian heavy water production had come to an end.[75]

The German options for heavy water production had now been whittled down to IG Farben. At the end of September, Karl-Friedrich Bonhoeffer, Diebner, and Harteck discussed this problem with the "gentlemen of the IG." The heavy water pilot plant using the Harteck-Suess catalytic exchange process was about to go into full operation. Harteck reported that the pilot plant was very impressive. But the gentlemen of the IG made quite a different impression when it was a matter of money. The price they quoted for a large-scale heavy water plant utilizing this process was, in Harteck's words, "improbably high," and stood in stark contrast to the original estimates of cost. The IG Farben scientists were also pessimistic about the Clusius-Linde process. The great amount of electricity that this method required would be difficult to justify at this stage of the war. Moreover, IG Farben proved itself to be a demanding business partner. As soon as it was clear that the nuclear fission research was now dependent on IG Farben for heavy water, Heinrich Bütefisch personally requested all materials necessary for the patent applications process from the pleni-potentiary for nuclear physics.[76]

Diebner, Esau, and Harteck could sympathize with a reluctance to invite further attack at the Norwegian Hydro. Berlin, Hamburg, and many other major German industrial centers experienced frequent and devastating blows from the Allied air forces in the summer and fall of 1943. Most members of the nuclear power project eventually were forced to evacuate their institutes away from the major cities and into the countryside. Since Hamburg was well within range of the Allied planes based in Britain, Harteck's circle was the first group to become refugees. Although by this time heavy water production had been taken out of their hands, Harteck and his collaborators were nevertheless kept busy by the centrifuge research.

In February of 1943, Paul Harteck and Johannes Jensen proposed a new centrifuge design. A "rocking-process" (*Schaukelverfahren*) would be used to multiply the separation effect in a centrifuge. The drum of the centrifuge (see figure 13), which rotates around a central axis, would be divided up

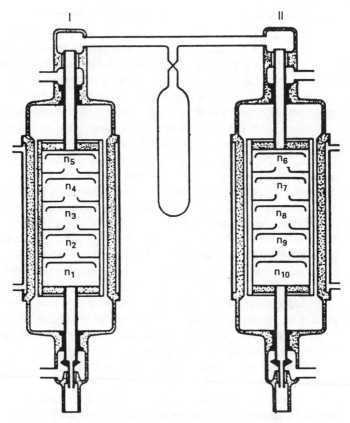

Figure 13 The double centrifuge (schematic diagram).

Note: Two centrifuges, here designated I and II, are connected and divided up into chambers, here
named n_1 through n_{10}. These chambers are connected with each other in turn by channels such
that only gas near the outer edge of the chamber can pass into the chamber above, and only gas near
the middle of the chamber can pass into the chamber below. When the centrifuges are in operation,
the heavier gas in each chamber will concentrate near the outer edge, the lighter gas near the center.
Normally the two centrifuges revolve at the same rate, and in this case there is no transfer of gas
between chambers. Periodically, the velocity of one centrifuge is altered, the resulting difference in rate
of revolution between the two devices causes a sudden drop in pressure, and gas is pushed (or pulled)
into the neighboring chamber such that the heavier and lighter isotopes are separated.
Source: Adapted from Konrad Beyerle, Wilhelm Groth, Paul Harteck, and Johannes Jensen, *Über
Gaszentrifugen: Anreicherung der Xenon-, Krypton- und der Selen-Isotope nach dem Zentrifugenverfahren*
(Weinheim, Chemie, 1950), p. 9.

into chambers such that the portion of one chamber near the axis
communicates with the part of the next chamber near the outer wall. As
the gas is centrifuged, the heavier portion would tend to concentrate itself
on the outer wall of each chamber. Next, the gas is periodically pushed (or
pulled) from one chamber to the next by means of an oscillating gas

stream. This oscillation is achieved by connecting two centrifuges. Most of the time, the centrifuges run at the same number of revolutions per minute. But the rate of revolution of one centrifuge is periodically altered, creating a sudden drop in pressure. This regular change in pressure causes the gas stream to oscillate in turn, thereby pushing (or pulling) the gas near the outer wall of one chamber into the central region of its neighbor. Thus a sort of separation column is produced, which multiplies the separation effect of a single centrifuge. Harteck reported to Diebner in April that the centrifuge experiments were going very well, but Wilhelm Groth noted in his diary that these devices had a tendency to explode.[77]

Esau asked Harteck in July of 1943 if he had made enough progress to be able to provide Walther Bothe with small amounts of enriched uranium for an experiment. The Hamburg physical chemist quickly replied that the work was going very well, but had not yet reached the stage of enriched-uranium production. A small centrifuge was being built at the Anschütz Company in Kiel and a larger double centrifuge was under construction in southwestern Germany. Since the Allied air raids on Hamburg had made scientific work almost impossible, Harteck had begun evacuating his institute to Freiburg. Harteck's circle had been more concerned with the achievement of a stable operating centrifuge than with the production of enriched uranium samples, and the former task unfortunately had taken more time than they had expected. Harteck told Esau that the Kiel centrifuge could be used for separation experiments within a week and the Freiburg double centrifuge was scheduled for completion in a few weeks. But Harteck recognized the urgency of Esau's request and instructed his staff to produce small probes of enriched uranium as quickly as possible.[78]

A month later, Harteck sent a large portion of his Hamburg institute south to Freiburg. Army Ordnance provided the truck, but the scientists had to do their own driving, loading, and unloading. Shortly thereafter all work in Harteck's Hamburg institute was halted by an especially hard air raid. The members of the institute were very lucky to escape unscathed. Groth traveled to Freiburg immediately after the bombing in order to resume research as soon as possible, bringing the apparatus necessary for the centrifuge experiments with him. By the middle of September, Groth could telegraph Harteck with good news. Positive uranium isotope separation had been achieved.[79]

Towards the end of 1943 the southern branch of Harteck's institute moved into a factory in nearby Kandern. By this time the Freiburg experiments with a small single centrifuge had reached a daily production rate of $7\frac{1}{2}$ grams of uranium with the isotope 235 enriched by around 5 percent. By extrapolating from the single to the double centrifuge, Harteck thought that his research group might soon be able to produce more than 20 grams per day of uranium with an even higher degree of enrichment.

For this reason, he abandoned any further work on the single centrifuge model and committed his institute to the double centrifuge, which they hoped to have in operation by January of 1944. Although the working conditions became harsher and harsher for the members of Harteck's circle, they only tried all the harder.[80]

As the war deteriorated for Germany, and even though the potential of nuclear weapons appeared to be irrelevant to the war effort, the nuclear power project continued to receive exceptional support from various patrons in the National Socialist state. Kaiser Wilhelm Society President Albert Vögler's contacts with other industrialists were indispensable for the procurement of materials and equipment, but the delay often became absurd. At the end of 1943 a company representative told Heisenberg that they could fill an order in eighteen months, but only if the matter enjoyed the highest priority. Albert Speer's Ministry for Armaments and War Production continued to support research at the Kaiser Wilhelm Society, but cuts nevertheless had to be made. In April of 1943 this ministry informed the Kaiser Wilhelm Society that priority was being removed from the less important institutes and given to the most important, including the Kaiser Wilhelm Institute for Physics. Heisenberg was instructed to submit a list of his needs to the Ministry of Armaments and War Production. Speer's ministry also ordered that, in order to cut short delays caused by air raids, duplicate pieces of important apparatus be constructed wherever possible.[81]

The German state belatedly took up Ramsauer's arguments about the role of science in the national defense. While 10,000 fewer soldiers at the front would not influence the fighting, 10,000 more scientists working on the home front might win the· war. As in World War I, the German military did not defer to the needs and demands of the scientific community until the war situation became so adverse that the need for the full and willing mobilization of science for warfare was evident. A small number of scientists were allowed to return from the front, some as the result of the "Osenberg Action," named after an SS officer who had been assigned the task of coordinating scientific research by Göring in 1943. This development obviously helped scientific research, and given the casualty rate at the Eastern Front, was especially pleasing to the scientists involved. For example, Bothe received his former collaborator Heinz Maier-Leibnitz, and Julius Hiby, an old friend of Karl Wirtz, went to work for the Kaiser Wilhelm Institute for Physics. But while many saw this project as an attempt to save what was left of the younger scientific generation as well as contributing to the war effort, it was not that simple. Willibald Jentschke recalled, long after the war, that some of the young scientists who had been sent to Vienna as part of the recall were subsequently reassigned to the front. Although the return of young scientists from the front was welcomed by all concerned, the scope of this transfer was very small. For many young scientists, this action came too late.[82]

The Allied air raids on Germany in 1943 caused terror in the general population and hampered both armaments production and materials distribution. Moreover, these attacks brought the war home to the members of the nuclear power project, in many cases for the first time. Their reaction was to close ranks in the face of this new peril. Max von Laue wrote Heisenberg in August with the news of a massive attack on Berlin. For three solid hours, Laue had to endure the "sinister sound" of Allied planes. He complained to Heisenberg that Germany was only a passive contestant in the air war. Harteck both told Diebner that his Hamburg institute and collaborators had escaped disaster narrowly and commiserated with Heisenberg's position in the Reich capital. Upon learning of an especially powerful attack on Berlin, Harteck expressed the hope that all was well with Heisenberg and his institute. As a "Hamburger," he knew what an air raid meant. Foreign colleagues also expressed their concern. Leon Rosenfeld wrote from occupied Holland, hoped that Heisenberg's family had been spared, and added his wish that the splendid scientific institutes in Berlin-Dahlem had not been damaged. Robert Döpel reported that 75 percent of all the scientific institutes in Leipzig had been severely damaged by the air raids and Heisenberg's house had been destroyed. Karl-Friedrich Bonhoeffer told Harteck that he did not believe that Leipzig could be healed within his lifetime.[83]

The air raids made scientific research in Berlin very difficult, if not impossible. The Kaiser Wilhelm Institute for Chemistry was incapable now of making any sort of precision measurement, so Otto Hahn asked his colleague Heisenberg if they could use a small portion of the soon-to-be completed bunker laboratory. These scientists did not respond to adversity with fatalism, but instead made even greater efforts. All scientific research, including military research, was pushed even harder, whenever and wherever possible. Even Bothe, who was preoccupied with his cyclotron, was not neglecting the war effort. He finally received the cyclotron magnet in March of 1943, Wolfgang Gentner was recalled from Paris, and together they began the construction of their long-awaited particle accelerator in Heidelberg. Moreover, Bothe reported to Esau in June of 1943 that the German group at the Paris cyclotron was considering a program of experiments on radiation protection as well as the related use of short-lived radioactive elements in gas warfare.[84]

Nuclear power prospered under Esau's direction, despite the rivalry within the project and the worsening war. Esau showcased his achievement by holding a large conference on nuclear physics, a meeting that was broken up into a session on nuclear power before a restricted audience and a second sitting that was both open to a larger circle and devoted to nuclear physics in the broadest sense. Although the Army Ordnance designation of nuclear power as irrelevant to the war effort did cause the number of researchers involved with this narrow research project to contract, Esau had taken his job title literally, had interested himself in all applications of nuclear physics, and had expanded both the number of researchers involved with nuclear physics as well as the amount of research sponsored and conducted. His conference included forty-one speakers and thirty-four presentations.[85]

The first, more restricted session demonstrated that the nuclear power project had made considerable progress during Esau's tenure. Erwin Fünfer described the experiments he had conducted with uranium plates and heavy water at Bothe's institute. Heinz Pose and Ernst Rexer set out their experimental investigation of internal uranium machine geometry. Karl-Heinz Höcker lectured on the dependency of energy production in a uranium machine on its geometric design. Fritz Bopp and Erich Fischer of Heisenberg's institute lectured on the beneficial effect of an inwardly reflecting mantle of water or carbon on a uranium machine. Karl Lintner reported on the fast-neutron experiments in Vienna. Harteck and Johannes Jensen lectured on the resonance absorption. Eduard Justi and Walter Fritz from the Imperial Physical-Technical Institute discussed the theory behind energy production in a uranium machine. Erich Bagge reported on his isotope sluice, and Harteck's circle discussed the progress made with the centrifuges. Although the needs of the German war economy had restricted nuclear fission research to a relatively small scale, the nuclear power project had thrived under Esau. Neither Werner Heisenberg, Carl-Friedrich von Weizsäcker, nor Karl Wirtz spoke at Esau's meeting, but even if they had, they would have had little to report. Weizsäcker had long ago stopped all work on nuclear power, Wirtz's research had been held up by the problems with uranium plate production, and Heisenberg had been busy with other matters.[86]

The larger session was devoted to a wide range of topics that were connected directly or indirectly with nuclear physics: experimental and theoretical nuclear physics, particle accelerators, properties of heavy water and uranium, and radiobiology and radio-medicine. Many researchers took part who were no longer involved with nuclear power, if indeed they had ever been part of the project. The newest topic covered in this session was the application of the latest developments in nuclear physics to biology. Protection against radiation, artificial radioactive isotopes as biological indicators, and preliminary experiments on radiation therapy were all discussed, including contributions from Walther Bothe and Karl Zimmer. Esau's conference was even larger than the meeting held in February of 1942.[87]

Esau was an efficient administrator, but as Kurt Starke recalled long after the war, there was a dark side to his character as well. An unfortunate confrontation between Esau and Starke during this conference exhibited some of the pressures that these scientists and administrators were under by this stage of the war. Starke had asked Diebner, his immediate superior, if he could accompany his physicist colleagues from the Paris group and report on his work with Joliot's cyclotron. Diebner replied that it was up to Starke, but refused to assume any responsibility. Starke did attend the meeting, only to be thrown out of the session by Esau. The head of the nuclear power project threatened Starke with a transfer to the Russian front – hardly a pleasing prospect in the fall of 1943 – if he ever came uninvited to a restricted meeting again.[88]

The deteriorating state of the war had made the German home front truly dangerous by the end of 1943, as Starke's anecdote corroborates. But there was another reason why every German now had to take great care with everything he or she did or said. Growing public discontent with the state of the war had been met with repression of increasing intensity by the German secret police. As opposed to the first years of the Third Reich when, within certain limits, German citizens enjoyed considerable personal freedom of movement and expression, every careless remark – no matter who made it – now became a potentially fatal matter. One of the most disturbing aspects of life in Germany at this time was the fear of betrayal. Along with distrusting the officials of the police, secret police, government, or military, Germans had to suspect any fellow countryman of being a potential informer.

In the late summer of 1943, a confidential report on Paul Harteck was submitted to the secret police, accusing the Hamburg scientist of "morally-undermining" remarks. Therefore, the report concluded, Harteck had openly revealed himself as an enemy of the state and had to be both removed from his position as a university instructor and immediately prosecuted by the police. The secret police contacted the local Party official in charge of the university faculty, but he replied that he knew nothing about any such behavior by Harteck. The report had to be an exaggeration. Harteck was from Vienna, was a Catholic, was perhaps a little politically unstable because of his world view and of his temperament, but in any case this Party official found Harteck tolerable as an instructor. The secret police nevertheless paid a visit to Harteck in his apartment.[89]

The informer was the Hamburg experimental physicist Peter Paul Koch. Although he had been well respected by his peers while in his prime, by 1943 it had been a long time since Koch had made an original contribution to physics. Koch was a dedicated National Socialist, but did not support the *deutsche Physik* movement. This betrayal of Harteck by Koch may in part have been the result of personal and professional differences. Harteck had thrown his considerable professional prestige behind an attempt by several Hamburg physicists to force Koch into early retirement and to call a young nuclear physicist to Hamburg in his place.[90]

Long after the war and shortly before his death, Harteck described the chain of events that led to his investigation by the secret police, although Harteck did not mention Koch by name. Unknown to Harteck, one of the mechanics in his institute was an informer for the secret police. But Harteck's outgoing, joking demeanor brought him good fortune. The informer/mechanic became so fond of his boss that he revealed himself and assured Harteck that he would not betray him. This story also demonstrates the importance of treating one's staff well. When Koch betrayed Harteck, the latter was forewarned by his mechanic of the visit by the secret police. Thus when the dreaded Gestapo agents arrived and interrogated Harteck, the latter could say that if there had been a complaint, then it must have come from Koch, who detested Harteck. In other words, Harteck claimed that Koch's accusations were due to personal enmity, not because of any misbehavior on his part, and the secret police acknowledged at once that Koch had been the informer. Afterward, much to Koch's discomfort, Harteck openly told his colleagues that Koch had betrayed him. Fortunately for Harteck, apparently the police investigation went no further. But this episode must be placed in the proper perspective. Few Germans who dealt with the secret police enjoyed such good fortune. Furthermore, Harteck was not simply cleared of all suspicion. He probably considered himself to be under surveillance and in constant danger of some reprisal until the end of the war. Like all German scientists, the members of the nuclear power project were now daily faced with death from above and with betrayal from within. Their apolitical reaction was to lower their heads, bury themselves in their work, and try to hang on to the end.[91]

4 ❖ The war is lost

The available reports unambiguously emphasize the *great seriousness* expressed ... by the population. A considerable depression [*Bedrückheit*] exists, especially with respect to the continued air terror, the hard fighting on the eastern front, and the threatened invasion in the West. But confidence frequently is expressed, supported by a recognition of the necessity of our victory and trust in our fighting forces and in our leader. Even if an absolute certainty of victory does not exist, the view prevails [among the population] that we have to 'clench our teeth' and keep our nerves steady. At the same time, fearful expressions of doubt about our further ability to hold out have become loud. Nevertheless, the population generally shows an *unconditional will to hold out*, which as before remains unshaken.

From a secret report by the SS security service (6 Jan. 1944)[1]

Evacuation and self-preservation

Although both the German war fortunes and the home front had deteriorated steadily throughout 1943, the worst was yet to come. The winter of 1943/44 was marked by military defeats and bombing raids, as well as by ever-increasing pessimism. Moreover, the German nuclear power project experienced yet another administrative purge. Hermann Göring and Rudolf Mentzel were coerced by Albert Speer into letting Abraham Esau go. Mentzel then offered Esau's two posts, plenipotentiary for nuclear physics and head of the physics section in the Reich Research Council, to a candidate who met with Speer's approval, the Munich physicist Walther Gerlach. But Esau did not submit so easily. Less than a week after he had been forced to resign, several high-ranking air force officers intervened with Göring on Esau's behalf and represented Esau's dismissal as an inadmissible intrusion by Speer in Göring's domain. Mentzel hastened to abort this intrigue, showing once again his flexibility and administrative talents.[2]

Mentzel had always been ambivalent about supporting Esau. He had abandoned Esau in the face of opposition from Army Ordnance in 1939, had backed him against the Kaiser Wilhelm Society once the Reich

Research Council had regained control of nuclear fission research, and now under pressure from Speer failed Esau yet again. Mentzel admitted to an official in Göring's ministry that Speer was behind the move, but also provided an impressive list of German science policy makers who would greet Esau's departure with "special pleasure". Albert Vögler and Carl Ramsauer, the same combination that had helped bring down *deutsche Physik*, were glad to see Esau go. (However, Esau was no supporter of Lenard and Stark). Given the powerful enemies that he had made, it is surprising that Esau managed to last as long in office as he did. But Mentzel did placate Esau by offering him as compensation the well-paid position of Göring's plenipotentiary for high-frequency technology. The scientist already holding this position was fired summarily. Esau agreed to trade his two physics positions for control of high-frequency research, so long as Speer had no objections, for he did not want to be "shot at" from that direction again. The Minister of War Production agreed to this administrative reshuffle, and Esau took up responsibility for radar, a branch of research for which he was well suited, and continued his devotion to the war effort.[3]

Esau's departure from the nuclear power project met with a mixed reception from the project scientists. As might have been expected, Werner Heisenberg was pleased and spoke of the many new opportunities that had been thrown open by Esau's dismissal. But not all scientists agreed with Heisenberg or had such a negative opinion of Esau as an administrator. Paul Harteck went out of his way to stay on good terms with Esau as well as with Kurt Diebner and Gerlach. For some scientists, Klaus Clusius for example, the major concern was stable leadership. Upon hearing of Gerlach's appointment, the Munich physical chemist expressed the desire that this bureaucratic change should be a long-term solution. Clusius considered the turnover in the administration of nuclear fission research to be wasteful. In fact, Esau had provided strong support and capable oversight for the nuclear power research, even though he could also be a difficult person to deal with.[4]

Esau could boast of many successes during his tenure: the solution of the best uranium machine design, uranium isotope enrichment by means of a centrifuge, the application of nuclear physics to biology and medicine, and a proliferation of particle accelerators of diverse types. Research that was closely connected with the clique that surrounded Heisenberg suffered because of tensions between Heisenberg and Esau as well as rivalry within the nuclear power project, but the work of Heisenberg's inner circle was only one part of the German effort to harness nuclear power. The 1943 budget of the plenipotentiary for nuclear physics provides at least a partial explanation of why the Reich Research Council was so interested in nuclear power. The total 1943 budget was set at 3 million Reichmarks.

Esau could draw upon a discretionary fund of over 150,000 Reichmarks alone. In order to provide the reader with a sense of how generous this budget was, it should be noted that Wolfgang Riezler, head of the German group at the Paris cyclotron, received a yearly salary of only 8,000 Reichmarks from Esau. There was no lack of funds. At the end of the fiscal year over 400,000 Reichmarks remained. The Reich Research Council profited from having such a well-endowed and prestigious research project under its authority. Besides its future economic and military potential, nuclear power was already big business.[5]

Gerlach set up shop in the Berlin-Dahlem Kaiser Wilhelm Institute for Physics with Diebner as his administrative assistant. Diebner's re-appointment in Berlin-Dahlem was something of a triumphant return. Moreover, he had been the administrative anchor of the German nuclear power project throughout the war. Although Gerlach had had no prior connection with nuclear fission research, he had worked extensively with the military throughout the war, for example in a ship de-magnetizing program. Gerlach now took up a post that he characterized after the war as the "emperor of physics."[6]

Harteck congratulated Gerlach on his new appointment, noted that the Hamburg circle was pleased by this administrative solution, and stressed what by this time was the realistic goal of the German nuclear power project. Harteck hoped that the first experimental demonstration of the great potential of nuclear fission, a self-sustaining chain reaction, would take place in Germany, where Hahn and Strassmann had made their discovery. But the Hamburg scientist went on to remind, or inform, Gerlach of the patronizing treatment (at least in Harteck's opinion) that he had endured at the hands of some of his physicist colleagues in the nuclear power project. The small Hamburg circle had dedicated itself completely and with "great pleasure" to the quest for nuclear power and never shied away from questions apparently of "secondary importance," so long as the greater project thereby was served. With justification, Harteck considered himself well qualified to carry out the more important and prestigious aspects of nuclear power research, including uranium machine experiments, even though this opinion was not shared by all of his physicist colleagues.[7]

Gerlach was a competent, though not industrious administrator. By March of 1944, Mentzel was forced to remind his subordinate that monthly progress reports on nuclear physics were due for December through February and that Gerlach's budget could not be approved unless the plenipotentiary submitted a list of the research contracts that he planned to let out. Belatedly, Gerlach proposed a 1944 budget for over 3 million Reichmarks, including twenty-one contracts distributed among individual researchers, institutes, and companies, and Mentzel rubber-stamped Gerlach's proposal. No less than his predecessor Esau and his assistant Diebner, Gerlach was firmly committed to the German war effort and to staving off defeat at the hands of the Allies. But whereas during 1942 and 1943, when the war still held some promise for Germany, this concern far outweighed any other for Esau, Gerlach's appointment coincided with the rise of a new concern, just as important as, and quite compatible with, support of the German war effort: survival and self-preservation. As defeat crept ever closer, scientists and scientific administrators were not above abusing the priority status which went along with their research in order to insure that they would live to see the end of the conflict. For this reason, these scientists hastened to arrange the evacuation of themselves and their institutes away from Berlin, Hamburg, and other large cities and into the relatively peaceful countryside.[8]

Despite heroic efforts and the underground protection afforded by the bunker laboratory, the impotence of the German Air Force and the resulting daily devastation from above made scientific research in Berlin close to impossible by the winter of 1943/44. As early as the summer of 1943, Heisenberg began searching for a more peaceful site for his institute. Kaiser Wilhelm Society President Albert Vögler ordered that the Kaiser Wilhelm Institutes be evacuated, but what was far more important, Minister of War Production Albert Speer continued to grant special favors to one of his pet research projects. In principle, evacuation from Berlin or another troubled urban center was discouraged if not forbidden, lest this transfer contribute to panic or flight among the greater population. Many scientists had no option except to sit tight and hope for the best, but Speer allowed the evacuation of certain Kaiser Wilhelm Institutes as well as the rest of the nuclear power project. With support from Werner Osenberg as well as from Speer, Harteck moved most of his institute to Freiburg and then on to nearby Kandern. Otto Hahn's and Heisenberg's institutes were evacuated to Tailfingen and Hechingen, respectively, two small cities in southwestern Germany near Stuttgart. Clusius' institute and the Gottow group sought and found safer quarters outside of Munich and Berlin respectively, while Walther Bothe's and Hans Kopfermann's institutes remained in relatively peaceful Heidelberg and Göttingen. By September of 1943, a third of the Kaiser Wilhelm Institute for Physics was already in Hechingen. By April of the following year, Heisenberg himself had moved south.[9]

Even after permission to evacuate had been granted, there were great obstacles to overcome. Materials and manpower were in short supply at the evacuation sites. Julius Hiby, now entrusted with moving the Kaiser Wilhelm Institute for Physics south, reported to Heisenberg and Karl Wirtz that there was a bottleneck in construction labor in the Hechingen area. The only labor force available was the Hitler Youth – a mandatory political organization for German boys – or the Polish slave labor it controlled.

Poles were not the only nationality or race forced to work for the German nuclear power project. Bagge's isotope sluice was moved and reconstructed with the help of slave labor from Russian prisoners of war who were controlled by the Bamag company. Around 2,000 female inmates from the concentration camp at Sachsenhausen – including many Jews – were used as slave laborers at the Auer Company Works at Oranienburg, where uranium oxide was produced.[10]

The use of forced labor under appalling conditions was typical of the German economy throughout the conflict, but was intensified during the last years of the war. By 1943 the proportion of foreigners – including prisoners of war – in the Greater German work force had stabilized at around 25 percent. In fact, the longer the fighting went on, the greater the ravenous appetite of the German war economy for forced labor became. By the end of 1944, more than 400,000 concentration camp prisoners were working as slaves for German industry. The attrition rate of these workers, in other words, the number of slaves worked to death, was often as high as 20 percent per month, and the work conditions of the forced foreign labor often were not much better. All of German industry depended on foreign workers, and some of the most prestigious representatives of German business used concentration camp slave labor. Moreover, neither the SS nor the German government forced these workers on the giants of German industry. Instead, these firms solicited the SS for even more of this especially cheap labor. By the end of the war a German had to be quite unobservant to miss the slavery aspect of German industry and the war effort.[11]

Although the evacuation of research institutes made the survival of scientists and apparatus much more likely, it also hampered, delayed, and sometimes ended research. Several scientists spent the last year and a half of the war packing, repacking, and never coming close to being able to work. Since the war now appeared lost, some German scientists gave up any hope of a German victory and for the first time began to look forward more to the postwar period. Gerlach, Harteck, Heisenberg, and others took great care to shelter scientists wherever possible. For this reason, the nuclear power project scientists insisted on being evacuated to the southwest rather than to the east, because they – like most Germans – preferred the prospects of meeting American troops rather than Russian soldiers. However, although the scientists involved with nuclear power naturally were concerned about their own survival, they also continued to work with all the strength they could muster, until the very end.[12]

The isotope sluice that Erich Bagge had proposed in 1940 began to bear fruit three years later. With the assistance of the Bamag company, in August of 1943 he constructed an isotope sluice that was capable of processing uranium hexafluoride. After eight months, Bagge fled the Reich capital with his isotope separation device and began to reconstruct the sluice in Butzbach. The uranium hexafluoride isotope sluice finally went into operation in early June of 1944. But even though Bagge's device broke down after only two hours of operation, it appeared promising enough for Diebner to allow the construction of a larger isotope sluice in Hechingen. In August Bagge was able to report success. By working around the clock, he and his colleagues had managed around 120 hours of unbroken operation with the sluice and thereby had produced about $2\frac{1}{2}$ grams of enriched uranium hexafluoride. Bagge was not the only researcher working on uranium isotope separation in Hechingen. Horst Korsching set up his thermal diffusion apparatus there, and once Hiby had finished directing the evacuation of the institute, he took up isotope separation as well. Due to the shortage of metal uranium, Korsching and Hiby had to restrict themselves to research using uranium oxide.[13]

Although Walther Bothe had not been forced to flee his Heidelberg institute, the sad story of his cyclotron continued. Construction of the particle accelerator was finished by January of 1944. In May of that year, Albert Speer paid a personal visit to Heidelberg and inspected the cyclotron. Four months later, Bothe received a welcome financial award from German industry. However, the Allied invasion of France forced the German research group at the Paris cyclotron to return to the Reich on very short notice. In October of 1944, Wolfgang Riezler reported to Bothe that Frédéric Joliot had been revealed as a leader of the French "communist terrorist group." Near the end of the same month, Mentzel laconically reported to Vögler that all the particle accelerators and high-tension apparatus west of the Rhine were unavailable. Bothe labored on his cyclotron throughout 1944 and 1945, desperately trying to get it running.[14]

The one-sided air war quickly turned Germany into a wasteland. A few weeks before Christmas of 1943, Robert Döpel wrote to his colleague Heisenberg with the bad news from Leipzig. Three-fourths of all scientific institutes had been damaged, including Döpel's own institute. But these attacks did more than disturb scientific research. They took a personal toll as well. Döpel's apartment had burned down and Heisenberg's Leipzig house was destroyed. A month later, Friedrich Hund, Heisenberg's friend and successor in Leipzig, had more of the same to report. Only the cellar and ground floor of the University of Leipzig Institute for Theoretical Physics still remained intact. Hund, who had sent his children into the countryside for safety, described how the air attacks had affected him. From a standpoint of understanding, he had not yet comprehended what had happened and for the moment would not comprehend. Hund wondered whether his attitude was a form of "natural self-protection." By April, Leipzig appeared to be almost completely destroyed. Döpel refused even to attempt an experiment under these conditions. Heisenberg visited the city himself and was shaken by the scale of the destruction. A few months later, he had a similar opportunity while changing trains in his beloved Munich. There Heisenberg saw the surroundings of the train station. Even in Berlin, such destruction was rare. How long would it take to wipe away the trace of this "madness," he asked himself?[15]

The Kaiser Wilhelm Institute for Physics had better luck with the bombs, although Berlin-Dahlem did not escape punishment. Otto Hahn's Kaiser Wilhelm Institute for Chemistry and Peter Thiessen's Kaiser Wilhelm Institute for Physical Chemistry were both hit and ignited by fire-bombs. It took the combined efforts of all the scientists in Berlin-Dahlem to contain the fires and limit the damage. Heisenberg and his institute staff had the advantage of having a bunker laboratory that also served as an air raid shelter, but this asset also led to unpleasantness. Neighbors of the physics institute asked Heisenberg if they too could seek shelter in the laboratory, but because this institute was conducting secret war research, this request had to be denied.[16]

Harteck was disturbed by the Allied air attacks as well. In 1944, for the first time in many years, he did not travel to Vienna for Christmas. Because of the state of the German railway system, the train journey from Hamburg to Vienna now took over seventy hours. In the spring of 1944 all leave for city and state officials was canceled, and as Harteck wrote to his friend and colleague Karl-Friedrich Bonhoeffer, who knew what would happen by August? As the war came closer and closer to home, research and indeed life became more and more difficult. In October of 1944 Harteck requested a delivery bicycle for his institute, since firms could no longer deliver goods within Hamburg. In November the bombing cut off all heat in his institute, so Harteck requisitioned a stove and coal.[17]

No matter how oppressive the dictatorial German police state had grown since the first days of the National Socialist period, the failed attempt to assassinate Adolf Hitler on 20 July 1944 made matters much worse. The German state responded to the rebellion with a bloodbath that shook all aspects and levels of German society. As with many developments during the Third Reich, the German scientific community was touched by the aftermath of 20 July. Long after the war, Heisenberg recalled how several members of a Berlin social group that he had frequented, the Wednesday Club, were implicated in the conspiracy. Heisenberg vividly recounted his own feelings upon learning that several men with whom he had dined the previous Wednesday had been executed and realizing that his own life might now be in danger.[18]

As the war drew closer and closer to an end, more and more Germans were drafted into the Armed Forces. Sixty-year-old men, fourteen-year-old boys, and all males in between were now called upon to defend German soil from the invading armies. The members of the nuclear power project had been able to avoid conscription up until this point, but this danger was ever present. Harteck spared no effort to ensure that he and his collaborators could keep their *uk* status and bombarded Gerlach, Osenberg, and the Reich Research Council with requests and pleas. For example, the industrial scientist Kwasnik, the IG Farben employee in charge of uranium hexafluoride production, was called up suddenly without warning in late 1944. As Kwasnik told Groth, IG Farben gave him no support and had kept the call-up strictly secret until the very last moment. Fortunately for Harteck's centrifuge research and Kwasnik's health, Gerlach managed to secure Kwasnik's position on the home front by placing a large order for uranium hexafluoride that carried the highest priority.[19]

Even nuclear power felt the pinch of approaching defeat. Mentzel passed on a June 1944 decree from the Minister of War Production, commenting that in the future, only new, revolutionary developments that could give Germany an advantage over the enemy would be supported. However, Speer did not intend to dismantle existing scientific research, rather to concentrate it. Research workers would not be drafted, rather the scientists and engineers that were still left in the research sector were to be placed in a position to be able to carry out the most important research with the greatest possible intensity and bring it to the fastest possible conclusion. Walther Gerlach responded by slashing the number of projects that were given the highest priority through the Reich Research Council. Once again, the nuclear power project was protected. Among the few research projects that were supported to the very last were uranium machines, centrifuges, and heavy water production. Nuclear fission research continued to receive exceptional support from powerful patrons. As Albert Speer wrote to Gerlach shortly before Christmas in the winter of 1944, he ascribed "exceptional significance" to nuclear physics research and followed this work with "great expectations." Gerlach could always count on Speer's support to help overcome any difficulties that might hinder the research. Despite the exceptional demands that the now desperate war effort made on the German economy, Speer was still prepared to satisfy the relatively small needs of the nuclear power project.[20]

The new year 1945 brought with it the German "people's storm" (*Volkssturm*), the last stand of practically all males capable of any sort of military service in the local militia. The members of the nuclear power project could not avoid this call-up, but Gerlach managed to obtain a decree from Martin Bormann, the head of the Chancellery of the National Socialist German Workers Party and one of the most powerful men in Germany, that stipulated that these scientists could not be forced to serve outside of their immediate area. The Reich SS leader Heinrich Himmler already had forbidden the call-up of 14,000 other scientists and engineers. He considered that the demolition of Germany's scientific research would be "madness." There were good reasons why powerful men such as Bormann, Himmler, and Speer were willing to protect the nuclear power project to the bitter end. Gerlach coupled his sincere belief that Germany was ahead of all competitors in the race for nuclear power with misleading, hypocritical statements that implied that nuclear weapons might yet bring National Socialist Germany victory. Gerlach walked a fine line between promising too much, and thereby being expected to deliver what he knew he could not, the defeat of the Allied powers, and using the vision of nuclear power to ensure the survival of himself and his researchers. Even as late as December of 1944, the German emperor of physics did not hesitate to dangle the unimaginable potential of nuclear power before Bormann's eyes. Gerlach told Bormann that nuclear power might unexpectedly decide the outcome of the war, and blatantly added that the Americans were making great efforts toward the same goal. However, even though the German research appeared "vanishingly small" when compared to the American effort – actually Gerlach had no idea of how large the Allied efforts were – the plenipotentiary for nuclear physics relayed his sincere conviction to Bormann that Germany still had a "considerable advantage" over America. But time for Germany was almost up.[21]

The heavy water dries up

At the beginning of 1944, the German nuclear power project suddenly awoke to the fact that heavy water production was in serious trouble and that the supply of heavy water in Greater Germany was insufficient for their needs. The Gottow group was the first major casualty of the Allied attacks on Norwegian Hydro. Kurt Diebner and his collaborators had planned to carry out an enlarged version of G–III, an experiment that they believed might be able to achieve a self-sustaining chain reaction, but at the start of 1944 there was not enough moderator for this larger lattice design. Albert Vögler was very disturbed by these developments and expressed disbelief that greater stocks of heavy water were not on hand. But the indefatigable Harteck nevertheless was optimistic. Despite the loss of the heavy water production capacity at the Norwegian Hydro, he still believed that the flow of heavy water into the nuclear power project could be resumed within a short period of time. The transfer of authority from Esau to Gerlach came at an inopportune time for Harteck. Esau had just offered the Hamburg physical chemist all responsibility for heavy water production as Esau's personal representative. This opportunity disappeared with Gerlach's appointment, even though the new plenipotentiary for nuclear physics had great respect for Harteck as well.[22]

Although the IG Farben representatives in Norway were unwilling to risk any further disturbance of the Norwegian nitrogen production, they were quite willing to send all of their enriched water on to Germany via a suitably safe and inconspicuous route. Harteck also discussed the procurement of additional 1 or 2 percent heavy water concentrate from other industrial installations inside and outside of the Reich with the German director of Norwegian Hydro. Both men agreed to discuss such possibilities only orally in the smallest possible circle, in order that the news not leak out and thwart their plans yet again.[23]

While visiting Norway in early 1944, Harteck learned that the Norwegian Hydro had received no payment for the heavy water it had produced and that the native Norwegian officials had resigned themselves to writing off the whole program as a loss. Harteck now chided his superiors in Berlin. The Hamburg scientist felt that he should not have to explain how counterproductive this situation was, both for the prestige of the German authorities in Norway and the Norwegian willingness to deliver heavy water concentrate to Germany in the future. Army Ordnance and the Reich Research Council already had agreed to pay over $2\frac{1}{2}$ million Norwegian Crowns to the firm, but the Allied attacks on the plant had produced over 16 million Crowns worth of damage. Since Norway was considered occupied enemy territory, the German government refused to pay for the destruction. This cost had to be borne by Norwegian industry itself. Taking these considerations into account, Harteck urged that at the very least the $2\frac{1}{2}$ million Crowns be paid.[24]

Unfortunately for the nuclear power project, the heavy water situation in Norway continued to deteriorate. In early March the project scientists learned that a ferry carrying the heavy water concentrate from Norway had been sunk with great loss of life. All the evidence pointed to sabotage. The Norwegian plant director at the Hydro fled Norway at the same time as the ferry was attacked. Traditionally this Allied attack has been celebrated as an act of heroic resistance on the part of the Norwegians and the British. While this interpretation should not be denied, it does not represent the full story. By this time, there was no chance that Germany could have produced nuclear weapons before the foreseeable end of the war. In other words, the heavy water that had been sunk could not have been used effectively by the German nuclear power project to make nuclear explosives. It is very likely that the individuals who carried out the sabotage had been told only that the destruction of the heavy water would be a crippling blow to Germany's ability to wage war. It is easy to understand why they felt that these raids were both necessary and worth the loss of life. Nevertheless, as the members of the German nuclear power project themselves were aware, by the time the first acts of sabotage took place in Norway, the threat of German nuclear weapons was only a German fantasy and an Allied bad dream. However, the Allied sabotage of

Norwegian heavy water production did have an important and disturbing consequence. The German nuclear power project now depended on IG Farben for its supply of neutron moderator.[25]

The obvious Allied fear of German heavy water, however, confused and troubled the officials in charge of the German nuclear power project. The German conviction that explosive nuclear fission chain reactions could not be achieved during the war, combined with intelligence reports that the Americans were manufacturing heavy paraffin as an explosive, led Walther Gerlach and others to take seriously the possibility that the Allies had explosives that utilized nuclear fusion reactions. Large bomb craters in Berlin were examined for traces of radioactivity, and several researchers at the Army Ordnance performed a few inconclusive experiments on the ignition of nuclear fusion reactions by means of conventional explosives.[26]

Not even the sinking of the ferry laden with heavy water could disturb Harteck's boundless optimism. He now told his superiors in Berlin that it was fortunate that German researchers had attacked the problem of heavy water production from so many different angles. Given the loss of the Norwegian Hydro heavy water production and recent successes with model uranium machines, Harteck now recommended that one heavy water production method be chosen and an installation capable of producing 2 tons per year be built inside of the Reich. Harteck's proposal underlined the limited goals of the nuclear power project in 1944. Before the war ended, the Germans hoped to achieve a self-sustaining chain reaction in a uranium machine. Anything further was out of the question.[27]

However, the German nuclear power project was not finished with the Norwegians. In early 1945 Harteck paid another visit to Norway, met with the German IG Farben officials in control of Norwegian Hydro, and asked them to produce water containing 1 percent heavy water in Norway for shipment to Germany. This low level of heavy water concentrate could be obtained easily as a waste product from the Norwegian Hydro electrolytic nitrogen production and it was much cheaper and easier to manufacture pure heavy water from this level of concentrate than from scratch. But Harteck had to agree with his industrial colleagues that any such attempt would quickly lead to further sabotage or bombing and thereby endanger a crucial link in the Greater German armaments industry. If the Norwegian Hydro nitrogen production failed, then Germany would have to supply nitrogen to Scandinavian industry, itself a vital part of the Greater German war economy. Since the nitrogen plants in Germany had been severely damaged, any diversion of the nitrogen necessary for the production of explosives was irresponsible.[28]

But neither Harteck nor the IG Farben officials in Norway were prepared to give up on heavy water. As Harteck reported back to Berlin, he and the Germans in control of the hydro had worked out a compromise. One percent heavy water would be drawn off and stored at Norwegian Hydro by the Norwegians, ostensibly for their own use. After enough time had passed so that the Norwegians would not connect Harteck's visit with an IG Farben proposal for heavy water, von der Bey, the German in charge at Norwegian Hydro, planned to suggest that the Norwegians store this heavy water concentrate for their own economic benefit. Of course, the Germans had every intention of seizing this concentrate at a later date. For this reason, Harteck urgently requested that the Berlin authorities keep these plans confidential and that the Norwegians not be approached directly or indirectly about heavy water without first consulting with Harteck or Bey. Otherwise the Norwegians might with justification fear that their heavy water concentrate would one day be confiscated. Harteck also reminded his superiors that an electrolytic high-concentration apparatus had been removed from the Norwegian Hydro plant and shipped to Berlin without any "private agreement" having been signed. It would enhance the prestige of German business in Norway, Harteck noted, if the Reich or a private firm under contract would pay a lump-sum royalty for the use of the Norwegian device.[29]

Harteck had other business of quite a different sort in Norway. In January of 1944, Paul Rosbaud, a consultant to the scientific journal *Die Naturwissenschaften*, contacted the Hamburg physical chemist on behalf of Odd Hassel, a Norwegian colleague. Rosbaud passed on to Harteck part of a letter from another Norwegian that described Hassel's problem in language that betrayed the seriousness of the matter. Hassel had been unable to carry out any scientific work during the last two months. He was suffering from an "illness" which forced him to be "very quiet" and to be isolated. The Norwegians were all very worried about him. This "sickness" was a euphemistic description of imprisonment by the German occupation authorities in Norway. Rosbaud asked Harteck to do what he could for Hassel when the Hamburg scientist visited Norway again, for he wanted to make sure that Hassel recovered as soon as possible. Harteck replied to Rosbaud immediately. Of course he would look into Hassel's illness. Since Harteck had had frequent dealings with the highest German authorities in Oslo and moreover had often played bridge in Hamburg with the German admiral now stationed in Oslo, he was in a good position to intervene. A few weeks later, the physical chemist traveled to Norway and discussed the problem of Hassel as well as other business with the German authorities there.[30]

Upon his return to Hamburg, Harteck reported to Rosbaud that he had been successful, although it had been difficult. The Norwegians distrusted all Germans and did not speak freely. But Harteck also discussed Hassel with Bey, who suggested that the interned Norwegian be employed at the Norwegian Hydro, and with a young man from the Oslo SS security service, who promised to keep his eye on the Norwegian scientist. As usual, Harteck was optimistic and thought that, as long as someone in Norway pursued the matter, suitable working and living conditions could be found for all Norwegian scientists. Rosbaud was very grateful for Harteck's intervention. If Hassel could not go to Norwegian Hydro, perhaps Rosbaud could bring Hassel to the Berlin area for saftey.[31]

Harteck had still further dealings with the SS in 1944. An SS member named Clasen had studied physical chemistry under Harteck during the first few years of the war, specializing in isotope separation. Clasen had been a soldier in the military branch of the SS (*Waffen SS*) and was one of only 450 SS members who were released from direct military service and classified *uk* for scientific research. Harteck could have had Clasen back in his institute, and wanted him, but Gerlach rejected the idea on political grounds. The plenipotentiary wished to keep a little distance between the nuclear power project and the SS, which by this time was expanding its influence aggressively throughout German industry, science, and technology. Therefore Harteck warmly recommended Clasen to his friend and colleague Karl-Friedrich Bonhoeffer.[32]

Just like Heisenberg's lecture tours in Greater Germany, Harteck's role in the German exploitation of Norwegian Hydro deserves close scrutiny. At first glance, Harteck's behavior appears to be contradictory. Harteck went out of his way to aid foreign colleagues in trouble, acts which entailed considerable risk. He also wanted the Norwegians to be paid for the confiscated heavy water and apparatus. But Harteck was one of the driving forces behind the confiscation and forced production of heavy water in countries allied with, or dominated by, Germany. Indeed Harteck went so far as to, at the very least, acquiesce in the deliberate deception of his Norwegian colleagues for the good of the German nuclear power project. Apparently Harteck was unable, or unwilling, to appreciate the Norwegian position, just as Heisenberg had been unsympathetic towards his Dutch colleagues during his 1943 trip to Holland. These two men had a great deal in common. Both were unusually talented and ambitious scientists in the prime of their careers. Both were nationalistic, patriotic, conservative, and anti-communist. The very narrow and limited sense of sensitivity and responsibility exhibited by Heisenberg in Holland and by Harteck in Norway is striking.

Both Harteck and his assistant Hans Suess attempted to reassure and persuade their Norwegian colleagues that the heavy water was of purely scientific interest. Let us give these two scientists the benefit of the doubt for the moment and assume that any such attempt took place only after the decision by the Army Ordnance in early 1942 that the industrial-scale production of nuclear weapons would not be attempted. Harteck's and Suess's actions are examples of the German scientists' apolitical perception of their position and responsibility. There is no reason to doubt their sincerity, no reason to doubt that they wanted to reassure their colleagues in Norway, but it is quite easy to understand why the Norwegians remained unconvinced. Informal assurances by German colleagues could hardly have offset the effect caused by the machine gun nests, barbed wire, minefields, and armed soldiers at the Norwegian Hydro as well as the periodic dawn investigations by the SS security service. Yet one cannot and should not ignore the fact that these German scientists themselves were convinced that their word should have been enough. The Norwegians needed only to trust them, and everything would work out.

The production of pure heavy water would now have to take place inside of the Reich. Since partially enriched heavy water would be proportionally easier than ordinary water to convert to pure heavy water, German and Italian industrial plants were searched for refuse water that contained unusually large amounts of deuterium. Graduate students proposed new methods for heavy water production. Harteck's student Karl-Hermann Geib, an employee at IG Farben, suggested an exchange that used hydrogen sulfide, while Bonhoeffer's student Herbert Hoyer carried out experiments with an exchange process that would be facilitated by bacteria. Although the pilot plant that used the Harteck-Suess exchange process had been abandoned because of the high price quoted by the IG Farben representatives, this same firm was asked to construct a large-scale heavy water production plant with an electrolytic high-concentration process developed by a member of the IG Farben staff. This plant was scheduled to begin operation by June of 1944, but because of lack of space and to the dismay of Harteck, IG Farben planned to set up the new plant in Upper Silesia, close to the ever-receding eastern front and the ever-advancing Russian armies.[33]

Harteck hastened to try to convince the IG Farben scientist Herold that the recent sabotage had drastically altered the situation and that the Upper Silesia plant was a bad idea. Heavy water is in constant danger of dilution by means of water condensing from the air. By 1944 the German nuclear power project desperately needed the capability to refine solutions as low as 90 percent heavy water back up to near purity. Harteck argued that there was space for such a small-scale plant closer to Hamburg and Berlin, in other words, farther away from the eastern front. He also asked Herold to prepare a cost estimate for a heavy water production plant that used Geib's exchange process and could produce 5 metric tons of heavy water per year. Harteck also apologized for taking up so much of Herold's valuable time. The nuclear power project would not have diverted the attention of IG Farben away from the war effort if Harteck and the other project scientists had not been determined to set up a large-scale heavy water plant during wartime as long as both parties could agree on a process that entailed bearable operating costs and could be realized within an acceptable period of time. In April of 1944, IG Farben agreed to build the plant. Construction would take at least three months, and, in line with their previous pricing policy, Gerlach would be told how much it cost only after the installation was finished.[34]

Now that IG Farben enjoyed a heavy water monopoly, the firm once again brought up the matter of patent rights and registered a patent application for heavy water production by means of exchange processes. These steps provoked an angry reaction in Hamburg. Harteck's circle quickly took steps to cut IG Farben off from the work of the Hamburg institute. Harteck accused the chemical giant of blatant industrial espionage. Part of the IG Farben patent application came from a secret 1942 report from Harteck's institute. The rest of the application drew heavily upon information that Harteck, Suess, and others had furnished to IG Farben over the course of their collaboration. Moreover, Suess implied that the chemical giant had an ulterior motive for such a patent application. The section of the application that dealt with the current state of technology listed practically every heavy water production method that the Hamburg physical chemistry institute or indeed anyone else had suggested. By including all these suggestions in the patent application, IG Farben had in effect made them public property. Suess did not expect this firm to try to patent all these other methods, which represented years of work by scientists in Harteck's institute. Instead, IG Farben apparently wanted to make it impossible for Harteck, Suess, or anyone else to patent any of these processes, especially once the war was over. The Berlin authorities agreed with Harteck that IG Farben had overstepped its authority. Harteck and Suess hurried to file their own patent applications for heavy water production and listed the German Reich as the beneficiary.[35]

IG Farben had now gone too far and had alienated Gerlach as well as Harteck. The German nuclear power project prepared to cut the cord with IG Farben. One separation method would be chosen from among low pressure columns, the Clusius-Linde liquid hydrogen distillation process, the Harteck-Suess catalytic exchange process, and Geib's exchange process. This method should require as little energy as possible, construction and operation costs had to be kept down, the material demand must be small, and the installation had to be kept as safe from sabotage and aerial attack as possible.[36]

Gerlach drew up a new heavy water program that was designed to deal more effectively with the realities of war as well as to put distance between

IG Farben and nuclear power. It no longer made sense for IG Farben to try to set up the planned high-concentration installation, since the enriched water that this plant required as raw material was unavailable. Therefore Gerlach decided to support the Clusius-Linde process and the low pressure column method of heavy water production, and to provide the Kaiser Wilhelm Institute for Physics with a small high-concentration apparatus in order to refine the heavy water that had been diluted during experiments. The scientists at the physics institute had to scramble to gather together the necessary materials for this device. Gerhard Bormann recalled long after the war that he had to use connections with a relative in order to procure the large steel container that this apparatus required. Once again, war booty played an important role in the nuclear power project. An alternating-current generator that was needed for the high-concentration device was shipped in from occupied Russia, and parts of the Norwegian Hydro high-concentration installation found their way to Berlin-Dahlem as well. This small-scale heavy water device was scheduled for completion in July of 1944, but difficulties arose. Lüde, the firm that had received the order for this apparatus, refused to take responsibility for the installation. Since all the members of Heisenberg's institute were otherwise occupied, Kurt Diebner had to struggle to find an electrical engineer to handle the installation. Lüde finally finished the device in late August, and it was installed in Berlin-Dahlem shortly thereafter.[37]

Because of this small electrolysis device, the researchers from the nuclear power project now could keep pure whatever heavy water that they had. The next step towards independence of IG Farben was to interest a different firm in heavy water production. Harteck asked the Linde firm for an estimate of the costs for a plant using the Clusius-Linde process. This production method had one great advantage, for the patent rights were held jointly by Klaus Clusius and Linde. Less than two weeks later, Harteck reported to Gerlach that by coupling the Harteck-Suess catalytic exchange process to the planned hydrogen rectification plant, Linde had made an attractive offer. The total costs, including energy, compared favorably with all other prospective processes. The investment required per ton of heavy water per year was approximately the same as for the other methods, as long as the "overly generous" calculations made by IG Farben were taken into account. Furthermore, Harteck hammered home the main reason for turning to Linde. It was vitally important for the nuclear power project that the planned Linde heavy water plant be completed as quickly as possible, because the unpleasant dependency on IG Farben would thereby be eliminated. Moreover, Linde had made a generous offer – they too were interested in heavy water and nuclear power – and Harteck believed that once the Clusius-Linde process went into operation, IG Farben would be forced to drop their quoted price for heavy water.[38]

However, the Clusius-Linde process required considerable amounts of electricity. While a plant capable of producing a few metric tons of heavy water per year was feasible, such an installation on a larger scale was out of the question. It would be irresponsible to divert so much electricity away from the war effort. In any case, Harteck recommended that Gerlach cancel the order for a large-scale electrolytic high-concentration plant from IG Farben. Between the electrolysis unit at the Kaiser Wilhelm Institute for Physics and the planned Clusius-Linde plant, large-scale electrolysis was superfluous – something that Harteck had been arguing since 1940. On the other hand, Linde needed one and a half years before full operation could be expected. In late July of 1944 Allied air raids severely damaged the Linde plant in Munich. Harteck tried to cheer up Klaus Clusius by noting that the Anschütz plant in Kiel that was building Harteck's centrifuges had been leveled as well. A few weeks later, Harteck informed Clusius that Gerlach had decided to go ahead with the Clusius-Linde process. Harteck's annoyance with IG Farben came out yet again in this letter. Despite their recent experiences with IG Farben, Harteck assumed that Clusius knew Linde well enough to be certain of "unconditional cooperation."[39]

This step away from IG Farben took place at first without the knowledge of the firm. As late as May of 1944, Herold was writing to Gerlach that IG Farben was still willing to produce heavy water, as long as Gerlach could provide the necessary support. But, a few months later, Herold received an unexpected message from the plenipotentiary for nuclear physics. Since the Norwegian heavy water had been cut off and the Italian concentrate was too weak, the nuclear power project did not need the IG Farben electrolytic high-concentration plant. Gerlach then explained his new proposal to Herold. IG Farben would build only the advanced high-concentration stage of the plant. This stage was capable of enriching 10 percent heavy water up to purity with a yearly output of $1\frac{1}{2}$ metric tons. The 10 percent heavy water concentrate would be produced by the low pressure column plant that IG Farben had already agreed to build. Gerlach then informed the chemical giant that its heavy water monopoly was over. The Linde company had been granted a contract to produce $1\frac{1}{2}$ metric tons of heavy water per year by means of the Clusius-Linde process. Herold's reply was humble and accommodating. IG Farben was happy to build the reduced high-concentration installation, would locate it wherever Gerlach wanted it, and was very interested in further cooperation with the nuclear power project.[40]

However, this sudden change of heart came too late to win over Harteck. By now he was also dissatisfied with the progress that IG Farben was making with his low pressure column process for heavy water production. In late November of 1944, the firm told Harteck that an experimental column would be up by the end of the year, but added that even with the highest priority ratings, the full-scale plant could not go into full operation before the summer of 1946. Harteck had anticipated this bad news by asking representatives of the Bamag company, with Gerlach's blessing and without the knowledge of IG Farben, if they were interested in the low pressure column method of heavy water production. Bamag subsequently made the nuclear power project a very generous offer.[41]

Rumors about American interest in heavy water as a weapon persisted. In the fall of 1944, Harteck was asked to judge an intelligence report on a heavy water plant in the United States, but came away unimpressed. The installation featured in the report was merely a pilot plant capable of producing only 4 liters per year and was no more efficient than the Norwegian Hydro. But if Harteck believed that the Americans had nothing to teach the Germans when it came to heavy water, the new year of 1945 also brought with it sober forecasts for heavy water production in the Reich. The amounts of German heavy water would be frozen for years.[42]

The history of heavy water and its role in the German nuclear power project is Paul Harteck's story. With the support of his younger colleagues Wilhelm Groth and Hans Suess, Harteck was always ready with an answer to a new problem, he knew the right people to contact for assistance and support, and he pushed consistently for greater and faster heavy water production.

Harteck's circle, centrifuges, and special experiments

Despite Harteck's great efforts to provide heavy water, most of his time was devoted to uranium isotope separation and enrichment by means of centrifuges. But these two aspects of nuclear power, moderator and isotope separation, are intertwined as complementary aspects of nuclear power. Moreover, this fact explains Harteck's sudden interest in uranium machines during the spring of 1944. Harteck still remembered the patronizing treatment that his 1940 dry ice experiment had received, and given the checkered progress of the model uranium machine experiments, believed that he could do better. In March of 1944 Harteck ordered 400 5-centimeter uranium cubes from the Auer Company for a "special experiment"[43]

Harteck enlisted the help of the accomplished theoretical physicists Karl-Heinz Höcker and Johannes Jensen in order to complement his own experimental expertise. This trial would use ordinary water as moderator – and thereby did not compete for the scarce heavy water – and would be operated at relatively low temperatures. The goal of this experiment was not to achieve a self-sustaining chain reaction. Instead Harteck wanted to examine the financial side of nuclear power. In other words, this special experiment would facilitate a study of the relationship between the amount of material required, the cost of operation, and the energy produced. Given the modest but steady improvement in uranium isotope enrichment by means of centrifuges, this low-temperature experiment was also a preliminary step towards machines built from enriched uranium and ordinary water. This trial was also a typical demonstration of Harteck's skill and drive. He took whatever was available in terms of materials and manpower and pushed it to the limit. But, unfortunately for Harteck and his collaborators, this experiment never went beyond the planning stages.[44]

At the same time that Harteck's interest in uranium machines reawakened, the success of the centrifuge experiments under the direction of Wilhelm Groth rekindled speculation about isotope separation within the nuclear power project. In light of the problems with heavy water production, the demonstration of uranium isotope enrichment, even on a modest scale, revived interest in the potential of enriched uranium machines. Hans Martin's parallel, yet independent, centrifuge research in Kiel was hampered by the inability of Krupp to process and deliver special orders. By the summer of 1944, Martin had been absorbed into Harteck's research group in Freiburg/Kandern. All the parts for the definitive double centrifuge model had arrived a few months earlier, and as Harteck wrote to Diebner, they were waiting with "great expectation" for the results from the new centrifuge model. By the end of March, this centrifuge had survived a test run without damage and had yielded 70 percent of the isotope enrichment predicted by theory. By this time there were ten double centrifuges set up under the direction of Groth and Harteck.[45]

The centrifuge program experienced problems common to the entire nuclear power project. There was a chronic shortage of materials and machinery. Harteck and Gerlach discussed this concern with the military commander of the Freiburg armaments commando, and he advised them to visit a "booty camp" (*Beutelager*). Throughout Germany, confiscated machines and materials poured into these camps from Greater Germany, only to be redistributed on a monthly basis to interested parties throughout the German war economy. Since such a camp was located conveniently in nearby Strassburg, representatives from the Hellige and Anschütz companies visited the Strassburg camp with blessing of Walther Gerlach and found exactly what they needed. But these industrial scientists also learned that the tool-making machines could not be ordered directly. Any such request had to pass through the German military bureaucracy. Harteck asked Kurt Diebner to pressure the responsible authorities in Berlin to speed up the delivery of these machines.[46]

There were also difficulties with the factory site that Harteck had been allocated in Kandern. As late as March of 1944, the local military officials in Freiburg had not yet received official orders concerning Harteck's institute. Moreover, the owners of the factory buildings understandably were trying everything in their power to stop their forced eviction. Harteck's group finally moved into the Kandern site in May. By early June ten to fifteen double centrifuges had been set up in the Vollmer Furniture Factory and the small single centrifuge model was in constant operation in order to test new rotors and other pieces. A few weeks later, the double centrifuges were running around the clock. Harteck hoped that by the start of 1945 all construction would be finished and the centrifuges would be in full operation.[47]

However, in late July of 1944 the Anschütz company in Kiel was bombed, and exactly the portion of the plant that had been working on centrifuges was devastated. Since the Anschütz laboratories were destroyed completely, Konrad Beyerle, the company scientist in charge of centrifuge research, moved south and merged with Harteck's group in Freiburg/Kandern. Harteck shared his buildings, materials, and electricity with his industrial colleague. The Hamburg institute had moved south in order to avoid the air raids, but by September of 1944 the war had found them again. It appeared that the Freiburg area would soon be on the front.[48]

The nuclear power project had always had a military flavor, but as the war became more and more desperate and as more and more Germans were mobilized for defense against the invading armies, all aspects of German society became increasingly militaristic, including nuclear fission research. During the summer of 1944 Harteck brought the matter of discipline to Gerlach's attention. The Hamburg scientist had noticed that the intensity and duration of work varied greatly between different factories and institutes. A subsequent discussion of this problem within Harteck's circle reached the conclusion that a certain minimum daily period of work should be, and would be, required of all members of the institute, whether the individual was an academic or not. Furthermore, each member was to carry a diary of his working hours, keep it up to date, and show it regularly to the institute director. Although Harteck admitted that these strict measures broke with academic custom, given the state of the war and the obligations that went along with a *uk* classification, he believed that these rules were necessary for the entire nuclear power project. Although each of the institute directors was free to follow Harteck's example on his own, the physical chemist pointed out that a general directive by Gerlach to this effect would greatly facilitate matters. Gerlach agreed wholeheartedly with his subordinate. It was especially unpleasant for all concerned when representatives of Werner Osenberg's Researh Planning Board or Albert Speer's Ministry of War Production found a vacuum in the scientific institutes while visiting at non-academic working hours.[49]

Since the approaching western front now made the Freiburg area appear unsafe, Harteck and Groth moved their centrifuges once again to Celle, a city two and a half hours away from Hamburg by train. The Middle German Spinning Company provided a suitable workshop as well as the floor space that the institute needed. Betraying impatience, Harteck asked Gerlach again about the tool-making machines that had been promised him. These devices had been set aside for Harteck in Strassburg, and Harteck saw no reason why they should not be delivered to him. He hoped that the verse from Faust, "He that has right on his side and patience, his time will come," also held true in this case. However, in the middle of October an official from the Ministry of War Production informed Harteck that the machines had to go through regular channels before he could receive them. Apparently he never did.[50]

Even more vividly than the story of heavy water production in Norway, the booty camp episode exhibits a dark side of the German scientific and technological achievement during World War II: the exploitation of Europe. Although Harteck has been featured in this regard, just as the lecture tours made by Werner Heisenberg have been focused upon, this emphasis is partially due to a bias in the available historical sources. In general only institute directors and other administrators composed and signed official letters and reports, and apparently only in the cases of Harteck and Heisenberg have large portions of the institute papers relevant to nuclear power survived the war. Heisenberg was not the only German nationalist in the nuclear power project, and Harteck no exception when it came to taking advantage of war booty in the name of science. For example, Kurt Diebner often accompanied Erich Schumann on trips to occupied countries in order to seize laboratory equipment on behalf of the nuclear power project. But perhaps the most striking comparison is with the attitude of German scientists towards war booty during World War I. Harteck's behavior differed little from that of many of the most distinguished members of his teachers' generation.[51]

By the beginning of 1945, the centrifuges in Celle were finally in operation. Lack of technicians, materials, and the tool-making machines had hindered progress, but Harteck's circle had finally managed to overcome all the obstacles and finish the reconstruction and installation by themselves. By late spring, the double centrifuges were processing uranium at a rate of 50 grams per day with an enrichment of 15 percent more isotope 235 than normal. Just as with the story of heavy water production, the centrifuge isotope separation project in Germany was largely due to the impressive skill, energy, and devotion of Paul Harteck and his assistants Wilhelm Groth and Hans Suess.[52]

Uranium machines and rock cellars

During the course of 1944, the deteriorating war and approaching defeat narrowed the goals and hopes of the German nuclear power project down to one experimental result: the realization of a self-sustaining nuclear fission chain reaction in a uranium machine. But before this last push could be made, the outmoded large-scale uranium plate experiment had to be finished. This experiment finally was ready to go at about the same time as the Kaiser Wilhelm Institute for Physics was getting ready for its annual Christmas party. Several researchers from Walther Bothe's institute joined the group under Karl Wirtz for these trials, although they were unenthusiastic about leaving peaceful Heidelberg for war-torn Berlin.[53]

The Berlin-Dahlem scientists had been waiting for the delivery of the large uranium plates from the Auer Company and the construction of a bunker laboratory. The 2-meter concrete walls, reinforced by steel, gave the laboratory security against air raids and promised to contain the radioactivity that a self-sustaining chain reaction might produce. The bunker design included an experimental pit in the main laboratory, air circulation and heating systems for the entire underground area, storage rooms for both the heavy water and the heavy water concentration unit, a workshop, and several smaller laboratories for the preparation of the metal uranium, the testing of the heavy water for purity, and other tasks.[54]

Experiment B-VI consisted of horizontal layers of uranium plates and heavy water, surrounded by a cylindrical container of a magnesium-aluminium alloy that was designed to resist neutron absorption. By varying the widths of uranium layers and moderator, the researchers were able to corroborate the earlier estimate by Walther Bothe and Erwin Fünfer for the optimal ratio of uranium to heavy water. This model uranium machine did produce more neutrons than had been fed in, but it nevertheless was inferior to the last Gottow experiment. Bothe had long ago suggested that a reflecting mantle of carbon might be more effective than water, a proposal that was now supported by a recent theoretical evaluation by Fritz Bopp and Erich Fischer. Thus the next experiment B-VII used layers set in the optimal ratio of uranium and moderator and surrounded by a layer of carbon. With respect to neutron production, this experiment was better than the performance of any previous layer design, but still was far below that of the best lattice design.[55]

Up to this point, the experimental results of the research team under Karl Wirtz had always fallen behind the work by Robert Döpel, at Bothe's institute, or by the Gottow group. But Wirtz's relatively modest success was not due to a lack of skill or effort. He never had many collaborators, indeed his research team was much smaller than the Gottow group. Although Wirtz was an expert on heavy water, for various reasons he was unable to conduct a uranium machine model experiment with heavy water before 1944, five years into the war, and any trials that used paraffin or water as moderator were doomed to mediocrity. But the real millstone around Wirtz's neck was the uranium machine layer design. As an institute assistant, Wirtz was in no position to overrule Heisenberg on the question of the optimal uranium machine design, even though by the end Wirtz was clearly unhappy about the horizontal plate design. If any progress was to be made, then the layer design had to go.[56]

Once the results of experiments B-VI and B-VII were in, Walther Gerlach came to the same conclusion that Abraham Esau had reached. When it came to neutron production, a lattice of cubes was better than a layer design. By the spring of 1944, the representatives of the Kaiser Wilhelm Institute for Physics agreed. Even before B-VII was finished, Wirtz tacitly accepted and praised Karl-Heinz Höcker's arguments on uranium machine geometry by placing an order with the Auer Company for 700 uranium cylinders with both length and diameter of 7 centimeters. When Gerlach informed Albert Vögler of the experimental results, the latter took the opportunity to remind Heisenberg that both he and the Minister of War Production were prepared to aid the research effort in any way they could.[57]

Allied air raids during August and September of 1944 slowed down uranium production at the Frankfurst casting plant. In January of 1945 conditions had become so intolerable that the plant was evacuated twice and was never able to resume production. Since the supply of heavy water and uranium was now frozen, only one large-scale model uranium machine experiment could be run at a time. Despite their recent success, the Gottow group could not compete with the Kaiser Wilhelm Institute for Physics when it came to prestige. Gerlach gave the bulk of the heavy water and uranium to Wirtz's research team for the next attempt at a self-sustaining uranium machine. The researchers under Diebner's direction, in the meantime, evacuated to Stadtilm, south of Berlin, began preparation for a low temperature experiment using uranium and a carbon-hydrogen compound (C_5H_{10}) as moderator. As might have been expected, the idea behind this trial came from Harteck. By using a carbon-hydrogen compound at relatively low temperatures as a moderator, Harteck hoped to achieve a self-sustaining chain reaction in a uranium machine without the use of heavy water. Unfortunately for Diebner, Harteck, and the rest of the Gottow group, this experiment never progressed beyond the planning stages.[58]

Because of the underground protection that the bunker laboratory had afforded, Wirtz's group had remained in Berlin long after most of Heisenberg's institute had been evacuated to Hechingen. But research in Berlin eventually became impossible, so that Wirtz came south and set up what would prove to be the final German uranium machine experiment in a rock cellar in the nearby picturesque village of Haigerloch. By this time Höcker and Weizsäcker had fled Strassburg and joined the Hechingen branch of Heisenberg's institute, although the researchers from Bothe's institute had returned to Heidelberg.

The form of the Haigerloch experiment, machine B-VIII, was a product of both experience and necessity (figure 12). The German war economy had deteriorated to the point that new parts could not be ordered, and raw materials could not be acquired. The researchers had to make do with what they had at hand. The cylindrical magnesium-aluminum container that had been used for the previous two experiments was now filled with a uranium cube lattice immersed in heavy water. Since the Auer Company had been unable even to begin production of the uranium cylinders that Wirtz had ordered, the scientists were left with around 700 uranium cubes. The container was surrounded by a carbon reflecting mantle, in turn surrounded by water. B-VIII was a dangerous experiment. Safety precautions were conspicuous by their absence. But this lack of security was not due to ignorance or carelessness. The Germans knew the dangers of radioactivity and how to avoid them. The lack of safety precautions was the result of the step-by-step deterioration of the war along with the step-by-step progress with the model uranium machines. By the time that these scientists were close to achieving a self-sustaining chain reaction and these safety measures were needed, they were also impossible. The members of the nuclear power project recognized that time was running out. At all costs and before the end came, they wanted to be the first to tap into the source of nuclear power.[59]

On the first day of March 1945, Heisenberg sent a telegram to Berlin. A ten-fold neutron increase had been achieved. They were on the brink of a self-sustaining chain reaction. Wirtz's group needed just a little more uranium and heavy water in order to enlarge the machine slightly and thereby ignite the chain reaction, but by this time the transportation of materials within the Reich was practically impossible. This rock cellar experiment was carried out under extremely difficult conditions and brought the nuclear fission researchers very close to their goal, a uranium machine that could achieve and indefinitely sustain a chain reaction. But along with the other main branches of the nuclear power project, heavy water production and uranium isotope separation, the model uranium machine experiments were brought to a sudden and definitive end.[60]

5 ✛ The German achievement in the American shadow

What can one make of it, when there is nothing to compare it with!

Fernand Braudel[1]

The Alsos Mission

Nuclear fission research had not been a German monopoly at the start of World War II, and vigorous efforts were made to control and apply nuclear fission in Great Britain and the United States of America throughout the war. The American Armed Forces, understandably concerned about the threat of a German nuclear weapons project, established an extraordinary intelligence gathering unit in the fall of 1943, named the "Alsos Mission." Although the main target of this espionage was nuclear fission research in Germany, the Alsos Mission was empowered to investigate a broad range of other scientific topics as well. General Leslie Groves, the director of the "Manhattan District" in the Army Corps of Engineers (the American nuclear power project), appointed Colonel Boris Pash as the military and administrative commander of the Alsos Mission, while Vannevar Bush, the head of the Office for Scientific Research and Development (an agency empowered to organize and coordinate the American scientific war effort), nominated Samuel Goudsmit as the highest ranking scientific member of the mission. Goudsmit was well suited for this position. Although he was an accomplished nuclear physicist and well versed in European languages, he was not connected with the American nuclear power project in any way. Presumably, Goudsmit could be given limited access to information concerning the American nuclear weapons project and thus be prepared to search for, and to recognize, any German progress in this field without being able to betray the American efforts to harness nuclear fission.[2]

On 25 August 1944, an advance party from the Alsos Mission entered Paris in the company of the advancing Free French forces and began searching for the French physicist Frédéric Joliot. Although mines and sniper fire hindered their efforts, Pash and his men eventually located the French expert on nuclear power. After taking part in Joliot's interrogation,

Goudsmit was convinced that his French colleague had told them all that he knew, but unfortunately he had known little of value. Joliot asked in turn for information concerning any American nuclear weapons effort, a request that was denied. The Alsos Mission entered Brussels on 5 September, found the offices of the Mining Union Company, and learned that most of the Belgium uranium had been shipped to Germany in 1940. The relatively small amount of uranium that had remained in Belgium was confiscated by American and British forces.[3]

While the Alsos Mission was waiting impatiently in the fall of 1944 for the Allied armies to invade Germany, Goudsmit traveled to Holland and paid a visit to his parents' house. It was an unhappy homecoming. Shortly after the war, Goudsmit described how he felt upon his return:

I dreamed that I would find my aged parents at home waiting for me just as I had last seen them. Only I knew it was a dream. In March, 1943, I had received a farewell letter from my mother and father bearing the address of a Nazi concentration camp. It had reached me through Portugal. It was the last letter I had ever received from them or ever would...As I stood there in that wreck that had once been my home I was gripped by that shattering emotion all of us have felt who have lost family and relatives and friends at the hands of the murderous Nazis – a terrible feeling of guilt. Maybe I could have saved them...I wept for the heavy feeling of guilt in me. I have learned since that mine was an emotion shared by many who lost their nearest and dearest to the Nazis. Alas! My parents were only two among the four million victims taken in filthy jampacked cattle trains to the concentration camps from which it was never intended they were to return. The world has always admired the Germans so much for their orderliness. They are so systematic; they have such a sense of correctness. That is why they kept such precise records of their evil deeds, which we later found in their proper files in Germany. And that is why I know the precise date my father and my blind mother were put to death in the gas chamber. It was my father's seventieth birthday.[4]

Pash finally entered Strassburg on 29 November and arrested several German scientists, including Rudolf Fleischmann and Werner Maurer from the nuclear power project. Karl-Heinz Höcker and Carl-Friedrich von Weizsäcker had already fled from Strassburg and the advancing western front. Since Fleischmann's institute was part of the university medical school, he and his colleagues had tried unsuccessfully to pass themselves off as medics. This encounter was the first time that Goudsmit found himself face to face with German scientists presumably at work on the military applications of nuclear power.[5]

The German captives were uncooperative. Fleischmann insisted that his research had been exclusively fundamental and had had nothing to do with military applications. He told Goudsmit that he knew nothing about the activities of other German scientists except for rumors, which he was unwilling to discuss, and he also refused to reveal the location of the Kaiser

Wilhelm Institute for Physics. When Goudsmit asked Fleischmann why the Germans were constructing so many particle accelerators, he replied that there were many more such devices in the United States. When confronted with a University of Strassburg course catalog that listed him as teaching a course on isotope separation, the German physicist merely stated that the class had not been held due to lack of interest and admitted performing isotope separation experiments, but only with nitrogen and carbon. Fleischmann made no mention of his own research on uranium isotope separation. Since the other captives were not much more helpful, Goudsmit concluded that the Strassburg scientists were unreliable informants and recommended that they be transferred to the United States for further questioning.[6]

But while the Germans remained silent, their documents betrayed them. The correspondence and papers that Goudsmit found in the offices of the University of Strassburg physics institutes provided him with a clear picture of the scope and scale of the German nuclear power project. On the last day of January 1945, Goudsmit reported back to Washington that there was evidence that the Germans were investigating the economic and military applications of nuclear power, but added that the German research was on a relatively small scale. He characterized the status of the German effort at that time as still being in the experimental stage. Moreover, although it was clear that the Germans had considered the application of nuclear power in the form of nuclear explosives, Goudsmit had gained the impression that the production of energy by means of nuclear fission was the more immediate German goal.[7]

Although Goudsmit drew the obvious conclusion from this evidence, that there was no danger of German nuclear weapons, certain information led him astray with respect to the reasons behind the relatively modest German nuclear power program, a misunderstanding that one day would come back to haunt Goudsmit. In early November of 1944, the Alsos Mission had interrogated a German chemist who claimed to have secondhand intelligence concerning German nuclear weapons. Supposedly, a Berlin inventor had learned from a member of Otto Hahn's institute that the minimum mass of a uranium bomb was eight tons. The Berlin inventor obviously did not have genuine inside information from the nuclear power project, although he may have confused reports of model uranium machine experiments with a nuclear weapon.[8]

Goudsmit found an anonymous report in Strassburg, presumably written by Fleischmann, that appeared to corroborate this claim. The author of this report speculated that a uranium machine could be used as an oversize "fizzing" bomb. The image employed here is of a uranium machine, capable of spurting out deadly radiation, somehow being hurled out of an airplane. Goudsmit rightly recognized that such a machine would be a most improbable weapon. It is not clear why Fleischmann, if he was the author of this unsigned report, would have so confused a conception of a bomb that employed a nuclear explosive. He had been at Walther Bothe's institute until 1941, and throughout the war had remained in close contact with his other colleagues in the nuclear power project. He should have known better, but if he was the author, apparently he did not, and thus unintentionally provided Goudsmit with convincing, yet misleading, evidence that the Germans did not understand how to build a nuclear fission bomb.[9]

Although Goudsmit was now certain that the fear of German nuclear weapons had been unfounded, the American military, and especially General Groves, remained unconvinced and wanted further confirmation. Groves was also concerned that the United States should control any region that contained part of the German nuclear power project. The Allies anticipated their victory over Germany by agreeing in February 1945 that the Third Reich would be divided into four zones of occupation. Most of the German nuclear fission research was located by chance in the future American, British, or French zones, and since Britain was America's partner in nuclear power and American troops could be sent into the French sector ahead of the advancing French forces, the last two cases did not represent a problem for the United States. But the Auer Company uranium processing plant in Oranienburg was located fifteen miles northeast of Berlin and lay in the future Russian zone. Russian troops were going to reach the plant first. In order to deny the uranium factory to the Soviet Union, Groves arranged for the Auer Company works to be bombed flat. All above-ground portions of the plant were completely destroyed. Nikolaus Riehl, who was at the Oranienburg site shortly after this attack as a Russian captive, recalled long after the war that the Russians had known exactly why the Americans had destroyed this factory. But nuclear power was not an exception in this regard. In the aftermath of World War II, American forces systematically sought to deny all relevant German science and technology to the Russians, and to a lesser degree, to the French and British as well.[10]

At about the same time as the attack on Oranienburg, the Alsos Mission entered Heidelberg and captured Walther Bothe's institute. Goudsmit found his senior German colleague to be friendly, correct, and willing to discuss almost anything except his own secret military research until the war was officially over. Despite the standing order to destroy any secret documents when threatened with capture, Bothe had wanted to save his scientific reports on nuclear power, but fear of betrayal by scientists from a neighboring institute caused him to burn all classified reports when American troops advanced on Heidelberg. Nevertheless, Bothe was more cooperative than his former assistant Fleischmann. The Heidelberg physicist provided Goudsmit with a list of the scientists who had been involved with nuclear fission and revealed that research into uranium isotope separation was being conducted under the direction of Paul Harteck.[11]

Bothe also shared his personal view of the potential of nuclear power with Goudsmit. Although no element with an atomic number higher than ninety-three had been definitely discovered in Germany, the Heidelberg physicist recognized that since element 93 emits beta-particles, eventually it must transmute into element 94. Bothe repeatedly expressed his opinion that the uranium machine was decades away from realization as a source of energy, and that uranium was impractical as an explosive. However, Bothe did believe that such machines could be valuable sources of strong neutron radiation. Under questioning, the Heidelberg physicist also admitted that the cyclotron had been considered as a source of radioactive material for bombs. Wolfgang Gentner independently verified Bothe's testimony and was convinced that the inherent difficulty of uranium isotope separation made nuclear weapons impossible.[12]

The Alsos Mission entered Stadtilm on 12 April 1945 and captured the remnants of the Gottow research group. Goudsmit discovered copies of Walther Gerlach's periodic progress reports to the Reich Research Council among Kurt Diebner's papers, documents that confirmed and reinforced the conclusions that he had drawn from the Strassburg material. Unfortunately, Goudsmit also found evidence that he could fit into his erroneous picture of German nuclear weapons in the form of a letter from Gerlach that referred to the necessity of acquiring tons of uranium. The German physicist was referring to the uranium machine trials, not to nuclear weapons, but Goudsmit took this exchange to be further proof that the German concept of a bomb was far off the mark.[13]

Less than a week later, the Alsos Mission located the German centrifuges in Celle, although Harteck was nowhere to be found. Shortly thereafter, Pash's forces recovered the bulk of the Belgium uranium from a storehouse in Stassfurt, located in the future Russian zone of occupation. This uranium, which had been confiscated by the Germans during the early years of the war, was now seized by British and American troops and shipped back to America. Since the Alsos Mission had taken possession of the only source of nuclear fuel available to Germany – the Americans had reliable intelligence that the mines in Czechoslovakia had not been worked for uranium – the threat of German nuclear weapons was revealed now to have been only a bad dream. This good news reached the highest levels of the American military on 23 April 1945, when General Groves informed his superior General Marshall that the danger of German nuclear power was past. By the end of April, the Alsos Mission was engaged in mopping-up activities. The chief concern of the American military was to prevent any important scientific and technological information from falling into the hands of foreign governments.[14]

Goudsmit, Pash, and the other mission members now prepared to capture the main prize, the Kaiser Wilhelm Institute for Physics at Hechingen and Haigerloch. French troops had advanced more quickly than had been expected and were threatening to beat the Alsos Mission to Werner Heisenberg's institute. In order to forestall this possibility, Pash requested and received an extraordinary group of support troops and hastened to overtake the French. The Alsos Mission entered Hechingen on 23 April and began interrogating scientists. Pash narrowly missed Heisenberg, who had set off the day before on his bicycle in order to be with his family in the highlands of Bavaria.[15]

Carl-Friedrich von Weizsäcker and Karl Wirtz had been left in charge at the Hechingen institute, but at first they were unwilling to discuss anything unless Heisenberg was present, and claimed that all the scientific documents had been burned. Before Heisenberg left, he had given strict instructions to bury the uranium and to conceal the heavy water. However, Wirtz agreed in time to reveal the whereabouts of these materials, while Weizsäcker eventually admitted that the scientific reports had been encased in a metal cylinder and submerged in a cesspool. These documents, the heavy water, and the uranium were all recovered by the Alsos force and sent back to the United States by way of Paris[16]

Since the scientific experts in the Alsos Mission wanted to study the methods of isotope separation developed by Erich Bagge and Horst Korsching, these instruments were disassembled and confiscated. After the Haigerloch uranium machine was photographed and dismantled, the empty pit was destroyed. Goudsmit was now faced with the problem of what to do with the scientists in Hechingen. Technically, he was under orders to capture and intern all German scientists who were involved with nuclear weapons, but Goudsmit had felt that it was unnecessary to imprison Bothe. But whereas Heidelberg lay in the future American zone of occupation, Hechingen and Haigerloch would eventually be turned over to the French, and Goudsmit was unwilling to hand over a large portion of the German nuclear power project to the French. Weizsäcker and Wirtz were arrested, Bagge and Korsching were forced to join them because of their isotope separation research, and Max von Laue, who had been involved only indirectly with nuclear power, was brought along because Goudsmit wanted him to discuss the future of German physics with American authorities. As soon as the Alsos Mission withdrew, French Moroccan troops entered, accompanied by French officers who wanted information concerning nuclear power.[17]

Otto Hahn's institute in nearby Tailfingen was the next target for the Alsos Mission. The military forces supporting the mission clashed with a strong enemy force before entering the town. The mayor of Tailfingen tried to incite the local militia against the Americans, and after the brief struggle that ensued, the mayor was taken prisoner and his assistant had been shot. The scientists in the Alsos force found Hahn to be more accommodating than his colleagues in Heidelberg and Hechingen, not to mention the local politicians. When asked about nuclear power, Hahn immediately produced a set of 150 scientific reports concerning research on nuclear fission, uranium, isotope separation, and transuranic elements. Under questioning, the chemist stated his belief that a nuclear fission bomb was not feasible and added that the Germans had reached this conclusion as early as 1942. However, Hahn did believe that the uranium machine could be developed within a few years into a useful source of energy. He acknowledged that an energy-producing uranium machine would also manufacture element 93, that this man-made substance must decay into element 94, and that this latter transuranic element could be used as a nuclear explosive. Hahn, whose joint publication with Fritz Strassmann had touched off the German quest for nuclear power, was imprisoned and joined Wirtz, Laue, and the others.[18]

Walther Gerlach, Kurt Diebner, and Werner Heisenberg were rounded up separately in Bavaria during the first three days of May. Each physicist made a different impression on his captors. Gerlach appeared to be fully cooperative, Diebner remained silent, and Heisenberg was both actively anti-National Socialist and nationalistic. Paul Harteck was picked up in Hamburg a few days later. In stark contrast to the rest of his colleagues in the nuclear power project, the Hamburg physical chemist recognized that the Allies knew a great deal about nuclear power, probably more than the Germans, and made a good impression on Goudsmit by giving a complete account of what he knew, including the intelligence that he had received concerning the American nuclear power effort.[19]

The Alsos force finally reached the end of the line on 30 July 1945, when mission members inspected what Russian troops had left of the Kaiser Wilhelm Institute for Physics in Berlin-Dahlem. In early August, Goudsmit suddenly was ordered to return from Berlin to the American military headquarters in Frankfurt. He soon learned the reason for his abrupt departure. The Americans and British were about to publicize their nuclear weapons program, and the American military representatives feared that the Russians might capture Goudsmit and thereby obtain restricted information pertaining to the American nuclear weapons project. American policy towards German nuclear power reflected the desire to establish and perpetuate a nuclear weapons monopoly. However, the American obsession with secrecy in the field was not entirely rational. The United States government published an official report on the American nuclear power effort in the summer of 1945 (the "Smyth Report") that was exhaustive and detailed when it was a matter of basic scientific and engineering principles, but was of little help with respect to the industrial-scale realization of nuclear power technology. No member of the Alsos Mission, Goudsmit included, could have been of more help to a foreign power than Henry Smyth's report on "Atomic Energy for Military Purposes."[20]

Goudsmit reported back to Washington that the general attitude of the captured German scientists towards him and the rest of the Alsos Mission was antagonistic. This mood was sometimes more resigned, sometimes more defiant, but the relationship was that between conqueror and subject, not between colleagues. With the exception of Harteck, the Germans, and especially Gerlach and Heisenberg, believed that their work on nuclear power was more advanced than any Allied effort to control nuclear fission. Goudsmit did not correct this mistaken impression, indeed he encouraged it, but he also did not create it. Although throughout the war these Germans had brought up the military potential of American physics as ritual justification for more support, they also were convinced that nuclear power was a German monopoly.[21]

Farm Hall

Eventually the ten German scientists who had been arrested by the Alsos Mission were brought to England and interned in an old country estate named Farm Hall. These Germans were given good provisions. They had books, newspapers, a radio, a piano, and could use a small athletic field that was located behind the house. Their only complaints were that they were prisoners and that they could not communicate with their families back in Germany. At first the reason for their imprisonment was unclear to them, although they assumed that it had something to do with their attempts to harness nuclear power. They soon learned that this assumption was correct, but was not the whole story.[22]

Shortly before eight o'clock on the evening of 6 August 1945, one of the British officers who were guarding the German scientists joined his captives for dinner and told them what he had already mentioned to Otto Hahn. According to the six o'clock news, the Americans had dropped an "atomic bomb" on Hiroshima, Japan. Understandably, a lively discussion followed the British major's remarks. A few Germans expressed the opinion that, if any part of the radio report could be trusted, then an atomic bomb referred to something other than nuclear weapons as the Germans had conceived them. The American atomic bomb had nothing to do with nuclear fission. A skeptical, yet curious, group of scientists impatiently awaited the nine o'clock news.[23]

The second broadcast shattered their disbelief, yet increased their confusion. Now the Germans learned that uranium had been used to make a bomb as powerful as 20,000 tons of high explosives. Moreover, the interned scientists were told of the massive scale of the American and British nuclear power project. A hundred-and-twenty-five-thousand people helped to build the factories, and 65,000 were required to keep them running. When faced with the news that the Americans and British had exerted an effort a thousand times greater than their own, there was little left for the Germans to doubt.[24]

The great impact that this revelation had on the ten imprisoned scientists must be emphasized. The world in which they had been living for five years suddenly was shattered and spoiled. Their proud achievement now appeared insignificant in the face of the American and British effort, but the American attack on Hiroshima cast a long dark shadow over the German nuclear power project. Disturbing questions of responsibility that had been long left unanswered, or even unasked, now became all too clear. The different reactions to the news of the atomic bomb were as varied as the personalities of the scientists themselves. Hahn was calm and pleased that he had not taken part in the construction of such a "murderous weapon." A few of the younger scientists accused Walther Gerlach of being a failure as plenipotentiary for nuclear physics, criticism which wounded the Munich physicist. On the following day, Gerlach wrote an introspective passage in his diary. All the work towards training physicists for education and industry had been for nothing, he thought. Perhaps the "rescue" of German physicists would be appreciated, he hoped, or perhaps not. Obviously one could no longer be certain that intellectual achievement helps humanity. Must everything which helps mankind simultaneously bring its destruction, he asked himself?[25]

Max von Laue had not been involved directly with nuclear fission research, although as the acting director of the Kaiser Wilhelm Institute for Physics, he had been aware both of the nuclear power project and of its military implications. The news of the atomic bomb filled Laue with excitement and exhilaration. He remarked to his considerably younger colleague Erich Bagge that when he himself was young, Laue had wanted to do physics and witness history. He had done physics, and now, as he grew older, he could truly say that he had made history. Werner Heisenberg was frustrated by the superficial nature of the radio broadcasts. These popular reports were so sketchy in detail that Heisenberg was unable to glean a clear understanding of what went on inside of the American atomic bomb, even though he and the others had their own wartime research to fall back upon. Heisenberg believed that the news releases had been kept vague in order to make such an understanding impossible.[26]

The interned scientists not only were shocked by the American demonstration of nuclear power. They also were annoyed by the sensationalist accounts of nuclear power in the British press, especially when they misrepresented the German achievement in this area. According to the American President Harry Truman, for example, the Germans had worked "feverishly" to find a way to use nuclear power, but had failed. The British press could not resist attacking the racial policies of the now prostrate National Socialist state by overemphasizing Lise Meitner's role in the discovery of nuclear fission almost to the point of excluding Hahn and Fritz Strassmann, for example with the title "a Jewess Found the Clue." In addition, the sabotage of the Norwegian Hydro was portrayed falsely as having been the crucial blow by which British intelligence and the Norwegian resistance had brought German nuclear power to its knees.[27]

The Germans at Farm Hall drew up a press release, both as a response to the shocking news of the first attack with nuclear weapons as well as an attempt to tell their own side of the story. The surviving manuscript of this memorandum, set down in Heisenberg's handwriting, is an important historical source, for it represents the German reaction to the revelations of the American atomic bomb before the ten scientists at Farm Hall knew how it had been accomplished. They were aware only that uranium had been used in the device and that production of the bomb had required a huge industrial effort. The purpose of this memorandum was clear. Since the British and American press reports of the German work on the uranium problem were "partially incorrect," the Farm Hall scientists intended to describe briefly the development of their work.[28]

First of all, they stressed that Hahn and Strassmann, not Meitner, had discovered nuclear fission and moreover characterized this discovery as the fruit of "pure" science that had had nothing to do with practical applications. They gave Meitner credit for her contribution to the understanding of nuclear fission, but drew the line at any contribution to its discovery. The great energies released by nuclear fission were predicted and measured by several researchers, the Germans noted, but certainly first of all by Meitner and Frisch. However, they added pointedly that Meitner had left Berlin half a year before the discovery. No mention was made of the reason why Meitner had left Germany, nor was there any other allowance for the obvious political nature of the emphasis that the British press had placed upon the Jewish physicist.[29]

The Farm Hall press release was also concerned with the professional reputation of Paul Harteck. The German efforts to manufacture heavy water in Norway were portrayed as a success up until the point that Allied attacks cut off the supply of Norwegian heavy water. The memorandum also stressed that the Germans had recognized that, provided enriched uranium could be manufactured as nuclear fuel, ordinary water would suffice as a moderator in the uranium machine. Moreover, the Germans had achieved enrichment of uranium 235 on a small scale. But these reasonable statements were followed by a laconic and potentially misleading passage with respect to the question of intent. Isotope separation on a greater scale, the Germans wrote in their memorandum, was not taken up.[30]

Something was missing here. No mention was made of the German recognition of the explosive potential of relatively large amounts of uranium 235. The known connection between the ability to enrich or separate the isotopes of uranium and the capability to produce nuclear weapons was omitted. The authors of this memorandum portrayed the German work on isotope separation as having been concerned exclusively with energy production by means of enriched uranium machines. But it is difficult to believe that Harteck had forgotten his 1939 letter to Army Ordnance, as well as his many other references during the war to the potential of uranium 235 as a nuclear explosive. The fact that uranium isotope separation remained at a small scale throughout the war was not due to any lack of interest on the part of Harteck, Kurt Diebner, Abraham Esau, or Walther Gerlach. No portion of the nuclear power project was pushed harder than isotope separation, and no one wanted to see the application of nuclear fission in Germany on an industrial scale any more than Harteck.[31]

The preliminary research that had led to the model uranium machine experiments was portrayed in a biased fashion by the authors of this memorandum. They noted laconically that the products of uranium fission were investigated at the Kaiser Wilhelm Institute for Chemistry and that this research was published during the war. Relevant information was omitted here. Researchers at Hahn's institute also had conducted research of immediate relevance to the manufacture of nuclear explosives, for example studies of isotope separation, resonance absorption, and transuranic elements. The work carried out at Hahn's institute was no different from important portions of the research that was performed in America as a prerequisite to the manufacture of nuclear weapons.[32]

The Farm Hall memorandum also mentioned theoretical work on chain reactions in mixtures of uranium and heavy water, the experimental demonstration that heavy water has a very low rate of absorption for neutrons, and experiments on the neutrons liberated by fission. The last phrase of this passage implied that the German research had had nothing to do with weapons. As the ten interned scientists had done throughout this memorandum, they portrayed the final goal of their research exclusively as the realization of an energy-producing, neutron-increasing, uranium machine. The potential of such a machine as a source of highly fissionable transuranic elements suitable for deployment as nuclear explosives, a potentiality known to these ten German scientists, was omitted.[33]

Although the Farm Hall scientists took great pains to distance their work from nuclear weapons, they did include a description of their stance towards the possibility of such weapons in the memorandum. Towards the end of 1941, the preliminary research had made it clear that nuclear energy could be exploited for the operation of uranium machines. However, at this time these researchers believed that the prerequisites for the manufacture of a nuclear weapon had not been, and could not be, fulfilled. This statement would have presented an accurate and realistic picture of the German attitude towards the military applications of nuclear power, but these scientists did not limit themselves to this sober account. Immediately following this passage in the memorandum came a sentence which, depending on how it is read, could alter subtly the meaning of the entire passage. Therefore, the Farm Hall scientists argued, the work "concentrated" on the problem of the uranium machine. Was this passage merely a logical statement of fact, or did the authors intend to imply that these scientists willfully decided not to pursue the construction of nuclear weapons? It may well be that some of these German researchers preferred the image of electricity-producing nuclear power plants to the specter of nuclear explosives. But every member of the German nuclear power project nonetheless was aware that any of the paths to electricity production by means of nuclear fission, whether by machines built from enriched uranium and water, uranium and carbon, or uranium and heavy water, also embodied the potential of nuclear explosives.[34]

It is difficult to believe that Carl-Friedrich von Weizsäcker had forgotten his 1940 report on transuranic elements to the Army Ordnance, Werner Heisenberg his vivid 1942 lecture before the Reich Research Council and the Army Ordnance, Kurt Diebner the Army Ordnance report on nuclear power that was written in January of 1942, Paul Harteck his repeated references to nuclear explosives throughout the war, Otto Hahn the remarks that he had made less than six months previously to Samuel Goudsmit, and so forth. The authors of the Farm Hall press release coupled an accurate assessment of the poor prospects for the industrial-scale production of nuclear weapons within the confines of the German war economy to a misleading emphasis on the "peaceful" applications of the uranium machine and an omission of the potential warlike nature of such machines and isotope separation.[35]

The word "bomb" was used for the second and final time in a curious passage in the press release. The authors stated that they knew of no other German research group that had had the manufacture of nuclear weapons as an "immediate goal," implying that they themselves also had not had this objective. The key phrase here is "immediate goal," and this point is subjective. If "immediate" work required actual attempts to build the factories necessary for the production of fissionable material on an industrial scale, for the production of the detonation devices that would be necessary for a nuclear fission bomb, and so forth, then the efforts of the scientists in the German nuclear power project were not "immediate." If "immediate" work referred to theoretical and experimental investigations of highly fissionable materials that were known to have the properties of nuclear explosives as well as attempts to produce these materials in steadily increasing quantities as quickly as possible without disturbing the German war effort, then the work of the German nuclear power project was "immediate." The question, did the Germans try to make nuclear weapons, has no single answer.[36]

The Farm Hall prisoners ended the press release with their own comparison of the German work to the Allied efforts to harness nuclear fission. The resources that were made available to the nuclear power project by the German authorities appeared "vanishingly small" when compared to the vast resources that were mobilized by the Allies. Indeed, the number of people who participated in the German research project never exceeded a few hundred during any phase of the war. This comparison was fair, but it should be added that, given the demands of the war effort, the German authorities who oversaw nuclear fission research were quite generous and did not fail to appreciate the military and economic potential of nuclear power. The tone of this memorandum was both apolitical and amoral. The German scientific community never advocated the industrial-scale manufacture of nuclear weapons during the Second World War. The production of such terrible weapons for use by the National Socialist government might have raised difficult moral questions for these scientists, but they were spared them. The members of the nuclear power project never found themselves in a position where this potential dilemma had to be faced. However, these scientists were not content with this explanation. This memorandum marks the birth of the Myth of the German Atomic Bomb.[37]

The Smyth Report

Shortly after the attack on Hiroshima, the United States government released the official American statement concerning "Atomic Energy for Military Purposes," also known as the "Smyth Report." This oversized press release quickly provided the members of the German nuclear power project with a great deal of information on the successful Allied efforts to control nuclear fission. Werner Heisenberg cited this report in his first published account of the German nuclear power project in late 1946, and a German translation of the Smyth Report was available in Switzerland a year later. The Smyth Report is used here in order to compare the German and American efforts to harness nuclear fission. Moreover, this comparison will be presented as the German scientists themselves might have reassessed their own work in the light of Hiroshima. Henry Smyth's review of the Allied nuclear power effort omitted all classified information and was hardly a definitive account of this work, but since this book is concerned with the German attempt to master nuclear power, and not the American efforts, this comparison will emphasize what the Germans learned of the American work and will not attempt to present a full and balanced account of the Allied nuclear weapons project.[38]

Finally, the reader is cautioned to weigh the various aspects of this comparison carefully. In particular, even though the qualitative and quantitative superiority of the American and British scientific and technological efforts will be stressed, it is argued that this disparity – although clear and undeniable – was not *responsible* for the lack of German nuclear weapons or for the relatively modest scale of the German achievement. After reading this section, a reader may well argue that, even if the Germans had tried to manufacture nuclear weapons on an industrial scale, the superiority of American science would have ensured that the Americans nevertheless would have won the race for nuclear weapons. Of course a reader is entitled to his or her opinion, but such a comment is ahistorical. In fact, for the reasons discussed above, the Germans did not make such an attempt, and the historian cannot then conclude that if the National Socialist government had made a greater effort, that the Germans necessarily would have fallen short, or that they necessarily would have been beaten by the Americans and British – maybe, but maybe not. This history is concerned with other questions.

The Smyth Report began with a review of the experimental and theoretical work on nuclear fission that had been published during the first few years of the war. Smyth noted that this information was generally known in June 1940, both in America and abroad. Looking back on the year 1940, Smyth saw that all the prerequisites for a serious attempt to produce nuclear weapons and control nuclear power were at hand. All of the results cited by Smyth, for example, the average number of neutrons emitted per nuclear fission, had either been achieved or recognized early on by members of the German nuclear power project.[39]

The author of the Smyth Report drew a somber picture when he described the state of nuclear power research in America at the beginning of the war. With the exception of hydrogen, large-scale isotope separation had never been realized. The choice of moderator for the "nuclear pile" (an American name for uranium machine) lay between beryllium, carbon, water, and heavy water. Unfortunately, at this time no more than a few grams of impure uranium and a few pounds of beryllium had been produced in the United States, the total amount of heavy water in America was not much greater, and carbon of the required atomic purity had never been produced in such large quantities. The situation in Germany basically was the same at the start of the war, although thanks to the German occupation of Belgium and Norway, slightly greater amounts of uranium and heavy water were available.[40]

With respect to nuclear piles, the Americans had already made significant progress by the end of 1940. The lattice design, using lumps of uranium embedded in moderator, had been chosen for the Allied uranium machines. Several methods had been proposed to control the chain reaction. The Americans recognized that as long as the ratio of isotope 235 to isotope 238 was increased within the uranium sample, or if "plutonium" (the American name for element ninety-four) was used as nuclear fuel, ordinary water could be used as a neutron moderator in a uranium machine. The Germans were aware of mechanisms for controlling the chain reaction as well as of the virtue of enriched uranium fuel, but in contrast to the Allies, the German scientists clung to the relatively ineffective alternating-layer design until the winter of 1942/43, when the Gottow group and the theoretician Karl-Heinz Höcker implemented the lattice design.[41]

American scientists recognized during the summer of 1940 that plutonium had the same explosive potential as uranium 235, but could be separated chemically from uranium. Shortly thereafter, the nuclear physics research group under Ernest Lawrence at the University of California transformed its powerful cyclotron into a plutonium-producing machine. This instrument was used to accelerate protons to high velocities. The protons were then fed through certain substances where they could collide with, and eject, high-velocity neutrons. The scientists at Lawrence's laboratory then bombarded uranium with these uncharged particles, thereby producing transuranic elements, and subsequently demonstrated that plutonium was susceptible to fission by means of slow neutrons. Enough plutonium was extracted painstakingly for American chemists to begin a radiochemical study of its chemical properties during the winter of 1940/41. Shortly thereafter, chemical processes were developed to remove plutonium from the fuel in a nuclear pile.[42]

Several German physicists recognized the military significance of transuranic elements. The Germans attempted to produce element 94 by means of a particle accelerator, but they never got the cyclotron in Paris running properly, and the Heidelberg cyclotron was still being tested when the end of the war came. Lacking a high-energy neutron source, the Germans were unable to produce element 94 and only managed to manufacture very small amounts of element 93 (named "neptunium" by the Americans) with great difficulty.[43]

Both sides realized that industrial-scale plutonium production required large nuclear piles and great amounts of an effective neutron moderator. The Americans developed a number of methods for the production of heavy water during the course of 1940 and manufactured a few liters for experimental purposes. With respect to carbon, the situation was very different. Several hundred tons of graphite were produced in the United States each year. The difficulty, Smyth noted, lay in the manufacture of carbon with the necessary atomic purity in sufficient quantities, particularly in view of the expanding needs of the American war economy. However, authorities in the United States believed that the development of nuclear power could be carried far enough to determine whether a nuclear fission chain reaction could be achieved in a lattice of uranium and graphite.[44]

At this early stage of the war, heavy water production in Germany was at almost the same stage as in America, and the Germans had the same concern as the Americans. They could not allow the costs of graphite or heavy water production to interfere with the war economy. Since the manufacture of graphite with the required degree of purity appeared to be prohibitively expensive in Germany, the Germans committed themselves to heavy water as a moderator, which at this time appeared to be both inexpensive and easily obtainable from occupied Norway. Just as the Americans were optimistic about a graphite nuclear pile design, the Germans believed that they could achieve a chain reaction in a system of uranium and heavy water without disturbing the German war effort unduly.[45]

A self-sustaining chain reaction was seen on both sides of the Atlantic as a necessary preliminary step. It was needed to convince skeptical scientists, industrial representatives and military officials. Smyth pointed out that there were different ways to achieve this end. An elaborate series of preliminary measurements and calculations could have been carried out, the optimum design for a nuclear reactor (another name for nuclear pile) determined, and finally this design built. An empirical approach was possible as well, whereby uranium would be combined with moderator in various configurations and then examined for neutron production. The researchers who were involved with uranium isotope separation faced a similar choice. Although both the Americans and Germans recognized that the former method represented the ideal approach, compromise solutions were chosen in both countries because of delays in the production of uranium and moderator.[46]

In June of 1940, the Americans decided to test a series of model nuclear piles, although these experiments were delayed for many months by lack of materials. At this stage of the war, one major difference between the American and German nuclear pile experiments was the choice of neutron moderator. While the United States concentrated its efforts on carbon, Germany had committed itself to heavy water. The first American lattice of uranium and carbon was set up at Columbia University in New York City during the summer of 1941, a graphite cube 8 feet on edge and containing around 7 tons of uranium oxide. Eventually the Germans did adopt the lattice design, but not until 1943. The Columbia pile experiments used much greater amounts of uranium than the first comparable uranium machine trial in Germany, but since carbon nuclear reactors require much more uranium than designs that use heavy water, the Americans did not yet have a great advantage in materials. Although the experimental results of the Americans were superficially identical to those registered by Robert Döpel in Leipzig at around the same time, the American experimental design and analysis was already far more refined than the German approach.[47]

In May of 1941, Ernest Lawrence, the head of the Radiation Laboratory in Berkeley, reported an "extremely important possibility" for the military application of nuclear fission to a committee of the National Academy of Sciences, a small group of eminent American scientists that had been asked by the government to judge the military potential of nuclear fission. The distinguished Berkeley physicist emphasized the military significance of plutonium as well as of uranium 235, adding that the transuranic element could be manufactured in nuclear reactors and subsequently separated out from the nuclear fuel by chemical means. As Lawrence emphasized, the properties of plutonium open up three important possibilities: (1) uranium 238 could be exploited for energy production; (2) smaller nuclear piles could be built with plutonium; and (3) large amounts of plutonium could be used to sustain a fast-neutron chain reaction, which he described as a "super bomb." Lawrence's 1941 memorandum bears a striking resemblance to Carl-Friedrich von Weizsäcker's 1940 report to Army Ordnance, indeed they are practically translations of each other. The subsequent report of the National Academy Committee also included a reference to the use of fission products as a particularly "vicious" form of poison gas. For their part, German scientists suggested the use of a cyclotron to produce radioactive gas, although apparently neither side attempted to implement these latter proposals.[48]

The Americans benefited from the work of their British colleagues on nuclear power, and especially from the British success with isotope separation. In the summer of 1941, British scientists relayed their conviction to the Americans that uranium isotope separation by means of gaseous diffusion was feasible (the "Maud Report"). Coincidentally, the members of Paul Harteck's Hamburg circle discounted diffusion methods in general because of the failure of the Clusius-Dickel tube to work with uranium hexafluoride gas and turned their attention to centrifuges.

Although the Germans had not tried gaseous diffusion, they were convinced that centrifuges represented the best approach. Lawrence's laboratory was well equipped for the technology of particle acceleration and thus the Berkeley researchers had ready access to the materials, apparatus, and experience required for electromagnetic isotope separation. In late November of 1941, the largest cyclotron at Berkeley and in the world was dismantled and adapted for isotope separation. By early December, Lawrence was able to report that a microgram of uranium 235 had been deposited. The Germans were aware of this possibility, Manfred von Ardenne, Heinz Ewald, Wolfgang Paul, and Wilhelm Walcher had all worked on this problem as well, but the Germans lacked the powerful magnets as well as the technology and experience that went along with them. At this time, Walther Bothe still was waiting for the cyclotron magnet that he had ordered before the start of the war.[49]

After conducting a thorough review of isotope separation, the Americans concluded that centrifuges and gaseous diffusion plants represented the two most promising means of separating the isotopes of uranium. Each method had been demonstrated experimentally by the end of 1941, in other words, single-stage separation units had enriched the isotope 235 in a sample of uranium to the degree that had been predicted theoretically. Because of the dead end experience with the Clusius-Dickel separation tube, Wilhelm Groth did not achieve comparable enrichment of uranium 235 before 1942. But the huge step from single-stage separators in the laboratory to the industrial-scale production of uranium 235 or enriched uranium was daunting. Smyth reported that in 1941 the Americans had estimated that a gaseous diffusion plant that was capable of producing a kilogram of uranium 235 per day would need 5,000 stages, made up of several acres of diffusion barrier and costing tens of millions of dollars. A comparable centrifuge plant would require 22,000 high-speed, separately-driven, three-foot-long centrifuges at a similar expense. The Germans never progressed far enough to concern themselves with estimates of the scale and costs of an industrial centrifuge plant for isotope separation.[50]

Although the Americans committed themselves early on to the large-scale production of moderator-grade carbon, as Smyth emphasized in his report, they were also unwilling to overlook any possibility of producing nuclear weapons. For this reason, research continued into the manu-facture of heavy water, although on a relatively modest scale. American researchers investigated heavy water production by means of catalytic exchanges, exactly what Harteck and Hans Suess were doing at the same time in Hamburg. Small amounts of metal uranium were manufactured during 1941 in America, but production was still in the development stages. Graphite manufacture did not look much better. Carbon of sufficient purity could not yet be obtained on an industrial scale. By the end of 1941, there was no reason for the Americans or the Germans to believe that the procurement of materials in sufficient quality and quantity for a successful nuclear weapons project was impossible, but there were difficulties in production that still had to be solved.[51]

But there was more to the efforts to control nuclear power than calculations, experiments, and materials. Psychology played an important role as well. In late 1941, Smyth noted, some American scientists traveled to Great Britain in order to get a firsthand view of the British efforts to harness nuclear fission, although this was not the first such contact between the Americans and the British. Upon their return, the Americans passed on the sense of urgency that their British colleagues felt. The British knew that Germany was receiving heavy water from Norway, and since they could not imagine a military application of heavy water other than nuclear power, they feared that if the Germans got the atomic bomb before the Allies, the war might be over in a few weeks.[52]

The British fear had a definite effect on their more skeptical and secure American colleagues. Yet the contrast between the mentality of the German scientists and that of their British and *émigré* colleagues was much more striking. During the fall of 1941, as the German lightning war devoured most of European Russia, most German scientists were looking forward to a quick, victorious end to the war by means of conventional weapons. The British, and to a lesser extent the Americans, were threatened by the specter of German military expansion and domination, and for this reason found the prospects of even more terrible German weapons appalling. The German perspective was decisively different. It appeared that their country would soon emerge from the war victorious and be in a position to consolidate its economic, military, and political control over Greater Germany. As far as these German scientists were concerned, the economic and military uses of nuclear power would be relevant only in the postwar period, not in the conflict then raging in Europe.[53]

On 6 November 1941, at perhaps the height of the German 1941 eastern offensive and more than a month before America was caught unawares by the attack on Pearl Harbor, the National Academy Committee submitted a memorandum to Vannevar Bush on the status and potential of nuclear power research. The Americans owed a considerable debt to British researchers and the "Maud Report," which suggested that uranium isotope separation was feasible. Since this committee deliberately wrote a conservative report, they limited themselves to results that had already been achieved and featured uranium 235 as a nuclear explosive instead of plutonium. The memorandum emphasized the destructive potential of uranium. The critical mass for an explosive chain reaction lay somewhere between 2 and 100 kilograms and each kilogram represented the explosive potential of around 300 tons of TNT.[54]

But the exact destructive potential of a kilogram of uranium 235 or plutonium was not crucial. The two pressing questions were, how long would it take to manufacture such bombs, and could these weapons decide the outcome of the war? The answers to both questions appeared positive to the Americans. If all possible effort would be devoted to the program, nuclear fission bombs might be available in significant quantity within three to four years. Although the calculated expenses of the nuclear weapons project were enormous, they nevertheless appeared to be in line with the other American war expenditures. As Smyth noted, the psychological factor was perhaps even more important than the positive scientific results. Apparently the British and the Germans, both grimly at war, thought that the problem was worth undertaking. Furthermore, the whole American psychology had changed. Although the attack on Pearl Harbor was yet to come, the threat of war was much more keenly felt than before, and expenditures of effort and money that would have seemed enormous in 1940 were considered obviously necessary precautions in December 1941. Thus, Smyth noted, it was not surprising that Bush and his associates felt that it was time to push the uranium project vigorously.[55]

Both the German and American sides carefully reviewed the feasibility and potential of nuclear power during the winter of 1941/42, and it is at this point that a comparison of the German achievement to the American effort is most instructive and relevant. Even though the American research had been qualitatively superior to that conducted in Germany, their German colleagues had performed the same sort of experiments, had made the same type of calculations, and had come to similar conclusions as the Allies – for example, the estimate of explosive critical mass mentioned by the Germans in January of 1942, 10 to 100 kilograms, is comparable to the American estimate reported in December of 1941, 2 to 100 kilograms. Arguably the Americans and British were more confident that the lower limit was correct, while the Germans – who apparently never made more exact calculations of critical mass – inclined more to the upper limit, but the Germans nevertheless were close to their Allied rivals. What was perhaps most important was the enthusiasm and dedication of the Germans, even if they probably did not match the determination of the Allied scientists.[56]

However, there were differences between nuclear power research in Germany and in America, especially with respect to technology and perception. Because of the ready availability of cyclotrons as well as of scientists, engineers, and technicians trained to construct, modify and operate particle accelerators in the United States, the Americans were able to produce small amounts of plutonium and determine that this transuranic element could be separated chemically from uranium. Once a chain reaction had been realized and controlled, the road to plutonium production was clear. Moreover, the isotopes of uranium could be separated by means of electromagnetic fields. It would be staggeringly expensive, but the production of uranium 235 in America was merely a matter of time and money, for the technology and engineers were available. In contrast, the Germans could only claim that the production of uranium 235 and element 94 should be possible. At this time, the prospects of isotope separation appeared bleak in Germany. The failure of the Clusius-Dickel tube had dampened everyone's enthusiasm for isotope separation, even Harteck's. This distinction is important, for it makes quite a difference to be able to tell a skeptic that isotope separation or plutonium production has already been achieved, instead of asserting merely that these goals can be reached in theory.[57]

Why did America have so great an advantage over Germany in the field of particle accelerator techology? Ernest Lawrence perfected his first cyclotron at about the same time as the National Socialist movement seized power in Germany and instituted a sharp reduction in the state funding of academic science. But this explanation alone is insufficient to explain the lack of particle accelerators in Germany. Once German rearmament hit its full stride in 1936, large sums of money again flowed from the state into the coffers of German science. In addition, the United States was far superior to the rest of the world in this area. As part of his tireless efforts to build a cyclotron in Germany, Walther Bothe surveyed the number of cyclotrons in the world as of December 1938:

USA: nine finished, twenty-seven under construction

England: two finished

Japan: two finished

Denmark: one finished

Sweden: one under construction

Switzerland: one under construction

France: one under construction

Russia: one under construction

National Socialism cannot be blamed for the relatively meager number of cyclotrons in every country other than the United States. The American dominance in particle accelerator technology was just one example of a developing American strength in what one day would be called "big science." Science took on an industrial scale and form, while industry became more scientific. But this development lies far beyond the boundaries of this history.[58]

The difference in perception on the two sides of the Atlantic is easier to explain than, and arguably subsumes, the technological disparity. By this time, the Americans had actually manufactured very small amounts of nuclear explosives. The Germans had not. The Americans assumed that it would take several years to subdue Germany and Japan, and planned accordingly. Even after the first reversals on the Russian front during the winter of 1941, most Germans – including scientists – still believed that they could win in a year or two. Whereas the Americans estimated that the costs of nuclear weapons would stay in line with other war expenditures, although the Germans had not attempted such detailed estimates of costs, they nevertheless believed that the expenses of these new nuclear weapons could not be justified in the context of the German war economy.

All these areas of contrast came together to form a stark difference in perception that had serious consequences. Since the Germans did not believe that nuclear weapons could influence the outcome of the war, or that such weapons could be realized in the near future, they made no connection between nuclear weapons and World War II, and had no fear of American atomic bombs. They wanted a negotiated end to the conflict as soon as possible, and they naturally expected that Germany would obtain the favorable terms that a victor deserves, but these hopes were not tied to the terrible potential of nuclear fission. To them, nuclear power was a future, postwar issue.

The Americans, the British, and *émigré* scientists saw matters in quite a different light. The Allies believed in the feasibility of nuclear weapons that could determine victory in the world war, and therefore viewed any evidence of German interest with grave concern. Vannevar Bush and James Conant put this conviction quite clearly in their 17 June 1942 report to the President of the United States. With respect to nuclear power, it seemed likely that, granted adequate funds and priorities, full-scale plant operation could be started soon enough to be of military significance. It also appeared certain that the desired end result, nuclear weapons, could be attained by the enemy, provided he had sufficient time.

In short, since the Americans thought that nuclear weapons were feasible, they assumed that the Germans did as well, and acted accordingly. Since the Germans thought that nuclear weapons were not feasible, they assumed that the Americans did as well, and acted accordingly. When compared at the crucial period of review and decision, the American and German efforts to harness nuclear fission illustrate how comparable scientific and technological results could lead to opposite, yet in their own contexts eminently reasonable and justifiable, science policies. Whereas Vannevar Bush decided in December of 1941 that the possibility of obtaining atomic bombs for use in the war was great enough to justify an "all out" effort to develop them, officials in Army Ordnance came to exactly the contrary conclusion. In order for Germany to have the best chance at winning the war, they believed that the nuclear power project should be left at the laboratory level.[59]

The Smyth Report goes on to describe the successful American nuclear weapons program, but beyond the summer of 1942 (at the latest) any comparison between America and Germany is invalid. The United States government shifted its efforts to control nuclear power up to the industrial scale, but the Germans did not. After President Roosevelt had approved the recommendations submitted by Bush and Conant, General Leslie Groves was ordered to take command of the "Manhattan District" in the Army Corps of Engineers, the code name for the American nuclear power program. Although Groves successfully carried out the task that had been given to him, neither he nor anyone else in the American military was responsible for the great disparity between the work in Germany and America to wield nuclear fission. The greater availability of materials, technology, and manpower in America was important here, but the difference in perception was crucial.[60]

Perhaps the most striking contrast between the German and American efforts can be seen in the industrial production of uranium and moderator. At the end of 1941, only a few pounds of impure uranium were available in America. However, by July of the following year, uranium dioxide of high purity was being delivered at a rate of 30 tons a month. Eight weeks later, the Westinghouse Company had stockpiled 3 tons of metal uranium and expected deliveries of uranium at a rate of 500 pounds a day by the end of the year. Compared to this performance, the efforts of the Auer Company were insignificant. But this stark contrast cannot simply be attributed to the superiority of American industry. The Americans tried to produce huge amounts of high purity uranium, and succeeded. The Germans did not manufacture large amounts of such materials, but they never tried. One cannot conclude that German industry or the German war economy would have been incapable of matching, or even surpassing the American success, for no such attempt was made.[61]

The availability of uranium dictated the pace of model uranium machine experiments in America as well as in Germany. In July of 1942, a group of researchers under the direction of Enrico Fermi built a uranium oxide-graphite lattice in Chicago and unknowingly matched the results that Robert Döpel's less sophisticated experiment L-IV yielded at almost exactly the same time. Both sides had built a neutron-multiplying machine. However, immediately thereafter the gap widened quickly. Six months later, Fermi oversaw the construction of what he still considered a "small" nuclear pile. This nuclear reactor contained close to 380 tons of graphite and 46 tons of uranium and uranium oxide and was incomparably larger than anything that the Germans were able to put together during the war. An even more vivid disparity can be seen in the number of personnel. Twenty-nine scientists worked under Fermi on this one nuclear pile experiment, as many as, if not more than, the total number of German scientists who devoted at least half of their time to nuclear power between 1939 and 1945. On 2 December 1942, the

Americans achieved a self-sustaining nuclear fission chain reaction and thereby attained the goal that the last desperate German efforts in the spring of 1945 failed to reach.[62]

As if beating the Germans to a chain reaction was not enough, the Americans unwittingly added insult to injury. Heavy water had been dismissed early on as a moderator, but the Americans nevertheless erected production plants for heavy water, built a nuclear pile from uranium and heavy water, and achieved a self-sustaining chain reaction in this uranium machine during the summer of 1944. Even the glory of having made the most progress with a nuclear reactor design that used heavy water was denied to the Germans. A cast-off sideline of the Manhattan Project easily outdid the entire German nuclear power project, demonstrating how great the gulf between American and German nuclear power had become by 1944.[63]

In the final section of his report, Smyth described the industrial-scale production of plutonium and uranium 235 as well as "bomb physics," the applied science and technology behind the construction of the atomic bomb and its detonation. Smyth also made some unflattering references to the German efforts to wield nuclear power. After pointing out that the destructive potential of the atomic bomb was beyond the "wildest nightmares" of the imagination and that this weapon was so ideally suited to sudden unannounced attack that a country's major cities might be destroyed overnight by an ostensibly friendly power, Smyth made a clear allusion to the German efforts to control nuclear fission. The American weapon, he noted, had not been created by the "devilish inspiration of some warped genius," but by the "arduous labor" of thousands of "normal men and women" working for the safety of their country. Before the surrender of Germany, Smyth explained, there had always been a chance that German scientists and engineers might develop atomic bombs and alter the course of the war. Therefore, he went on, the Allies had no choice except to work on them as well. Initially many American, British, and *émigré* scientists working in the United States could and did hope that atomic bombs would prove inherently impossible, but this desire gradually faded away. Fortunately for the Americans, during the same period the recognition of the great magnitude of the necessary industrial effort weakened the fear of German success even before the end came.[64]

Finally, when comparing the German nuclear power project with the American and British effort, the historian should also take note of the generally favorable impression that the German achievement made on some of their American colleagues. Enough evidence has survived for a fairly clear picture of how experts from the Manhattan District judged the work of their German rivals. Nuclear power research in Germany can be broken down into three main branches: uranium machines, isotope separation, and the production of heavy water. The Americans paid Paul Harteck the highest possible compliment by offering him a position in the United States during the early fifties. Once Harteck had decided to emigrate to America, Samuel Goudsmit put him in contact with the scientists who were working on heavy water in the United States.[65]

When Jesse Beams, the American expert on isotope separation by means of centrifuges, studied the efforts of Beyerle, Groth, and Harteck to separate the isotopes of uranium, he emphasized a German conclusion that he considered correct. Centrifuges represented the best method for separating uranium isotopes. Beams judged that the German work at the very end of the war was far behind what the Americans had achieved by the end of 1943. But he also noted why the German progress was relatively modest. The Allied air war had kept the factory that had been intended for the manufacture of the German centrifuges from getting beyond the planning stages.[66]

Lothar Nordheim and Alvin Weinberg, both members of the Manhattan District, reviewed the German nuclear reactor program. They claimed that the German experimental work had run pretty much parallel to research carried out in America. As far as the theory of a uranium machine was concerned, the German calculation of optimal lattice dimensions was understood and followed pretty much the same lines as the American work. Generally, Nordheim and Weinberg thought that the German approach was in no way inferior to their own, in fact, in some respects it was superior. The Germans knew how to design a nuclear reactor which would work, and from the practical standpoint, that was all that mattered.[67]

One of the reasons why Nordheim and Weinberg wrote this report was to take part in a debate raging in America over the amount of governmental and especially military control of science. These two American scientists wanted to argue that it was pointless to try and keep scientific secrets, for researchers in other countries would achieve the same results anyway. Nordheim and Weinberg therefore exaggerated the strength of the German achievement in relation to the Manhattan Project. Just as the rock cellar experiment in Haigerloch cannot be compared with the massive plutonium plants in Hanford, the spinning factory full of centrifuges in Celle and the various half-finished heavy water factories that were scattered throughout Germany appear insignificant when compared with the huge uranium isotope separation plants in Oak Ridge and the military nuclear weapons laboratory in Los Alamos.[68]

But Nordheim and Weinberg were right to be impressed by their German colleagues. When the different economic, ideological, and political environments in America and in Germany are taken into account, and the comparative juxtaposition is restricted on the American side to the effort made before Bush decided to shift the research up to the industrial level, the modest success of the German nuclear power project should not be denied or placed completely in the shadow of the American nuclear weapons program. Nordheim's and Weinberg's conclusion should be taken as sincere and insightful. The general impression from the German reports was that the Germans were on the right track and that their thinking and developments paralleled the Allied project to a surprising extent. It was also clear that the total German effort was on a much smaller scale than the American program. But the fact remained, Nordheim and Weinberg emphasized, that an independent group of scientists, of much smaller size than the Manhattan Project, and operating under much more adverse conditions, achieved so much.[69]

The final paragraph of Nordheim's and Weinberg's report carried with it a hint of frost from the approaching Cold War. They had to assume that anyone knowing what was in the German reports could establish a chain reaction, provided sufficient materials were available. The published Smyth report would provide very helpful additional information. The time when other countries could establish a chain reaction therefore was no longer a matter of scientific research, but a matter of procurement. It seemed to Nordheim and Weinberg that the policies of that American authorities must be formulated with a clear realization of these facts. Without pause or interruption, the race to control and wield nuclear power shifted from an American – German to an American – Russian duel. Just as Germany had been one of the main combatants, it now became one of the battlegrounds for the continuing political conflict.[70]

6 ❖ The legacy of German National Socialism

[No] different from their allied counterparts, the German scientists worked for the military as best their circumstances allowed. But the difference, which it will never be possible to forgive, is that they worked for the cause of Himmler and Auschwitz, for the burners of books and the takers of hostages. The community of sciences will be long delayed in welcoming the armorers of the Nazis, even if their work was not successful.

From Philip Morrison's review of *Alsos* (1947)[1]

The occupation of Germany

When the victorious Allies finally accepted the unconditional German surrender, what was left of the former Reich was in sad shape. Although with respect to loss of life and general destruction the Germans were better off than many of their neighbours, especially Poland and Russia, the future for Germany did not appear bright. Large portions of the major cities were in rubble, the shrunken Reich was swollen by refugees from parts of former Greater Germany, and there were grave shortages of food and shelter. The Yalta Conference of the Allies in February of 1945 decided on a four-way division and occupation of Germany: the Russians in the east, the British in the north-west, the French in the south-west, and the Americans in the south, with Berlin being split into four pieces. America and Russia emerged into the postwar world as the two great powers. Conflict between two nations with so different ideologies was probably inevitable, but the escalating tensions between east and west also led gradually, and perhaps not necessarily, to a permanent division between eastern and western Germany.[2]

The American Zone

American military authorities seized the major scientific and technological prizes in Germany, notably the rocket and jet plane research teams, and in general tried to draw scientific talent into their zone of occupation and keep it there. The Americans were not concerned with bringing the German nuclear power researchers to the United States – after all, Hiroshima had exhibited the American superiority in nuclear weapons – but they did not want these Germans to fall into the hands of the Russians, or even the French. Throughout the period of occupation, the American authorities brought German scientists to the United States. Although these Germans eventually may have been pleased to have gone to the United States, at the time they had little choice. The line between "voluntary" and "involuntary" cooperation was very fine. For those who had not held secure positions in Germany, or those who had lost such positions, the choice was often either to hunger in Germany or be paid somewhere else.[3]

There were often professional reasons for going abroad. On his way to America in early 1946, Willibald Jentschke wrote to Walther Bothe that his only wish was to be able to do real scientific work, something impossible in Austria or Germany. Wolfgang Ramm had spent the first part of the war constructing and modifying the high-tension generator at the Kaiser Wilhelm Institute for Physics. Even since Heisenberg and the other researchers had been evacuated to Hechingen, this apparatus had remained in packing crates and Ramm had been unable to work. Since the future of the Hechingen institute was doubtful, and given the huge strides that had been made in experimental physics equipment in the United States, Ramm did not have the courage to attempt competitive scientific research with this outmoded piece of equipment, and could not afford to pass up the opportunity of working in America. Heisenberg was naturally understanding, but was also sad that his former institute gradually was being scattered to the winds.[4]

American offers were not always welcome. The physicist Helmut Volz received a letter from the American War Department – Munich Branch – informing him that he had been suggested for a position in the United States and that henceforth any change of residence had to be reported to the American occupation authorities. It was not clear from the letter whether the American offer was voluntary or compulsory. When Volz finally learned the exact conditions of the American offer, he was even less inclined to go. On the one hand, his family in Germany would receive better care and higher rations than the average German family. On the other hand, he would be allowed to correspond only with relatives, he was to obey all orders, he could not leave a fifty mile radius of his station, at least for the time being, and he had to sign up for at least six months. Worst of all, he could return after this time only with the permission of the employer. This last "very dark point" in the contract was enough to dissuade Volz. In the end, the United States managed to siphon off a considerable part of the best scientific and engineering talent in Germany. Heisenberg had been able to find only one exceptional physics student since returning to Germany, but because of the economic problems and political instability in Germany, this young physicist had taken an assistant position in Canada. Paul Harteck visited Rensselaer Polytechnic Institute in 1950 and decided to stay in America. For years Harteck had wanted to escape the scientific isolation of Germany and catch up on what he had missed.[5]

Whereas the German scientists who moved to America found good living conditions there, those who stayed behind in the American zone were not so lucky. When Walther Bothe took stock in November of 1945, he had little reason for optimism. His plundered institute had practically disappeared, including the loss of a collection of measuring devices that had represented years of Bothe's work. All he had left was his cyclotron – which he was forbidden to use – and two store rooms full of the remnants of various apparatus. In late 1945, Bothe tried to gain permission for some medical research, but the American occupying authorities were still suspicious of his role in the German nuclear power project and left him with little hope of success.[6]

In March of the following year Bothe received good news and bad news. He was reappointed to the University of Heidelberg professorship that he had lost at the start of the Third Reich, but at the same time his last room in the Kaiser Wilhelm Institute was taken away from him. If the loss of his institute was not bad enough, Bothe had even worse experiences to come. Because of a case of mistaken identity, the occupation authorities imprisoned him for two and a half months before realizing their error. By March of 1947, the institute had been released and then confiscated for a second time, while Heinz Maier-Leibnitz, Kurt Starke, and many others of Bothe's younger collaborators left for North America. As Bothe wrote to a colleague, the situation did not appear very hopeful.[7]

However, there were some small consolations for Bothe. Several American physicists reestablished contact after the fall of National Socialism. One scientist sent Bothe the copies of *The Physical Review* that had piled up for him in America once Germany had declared war on the United States, while another asked Bothe whether he could use anything from America. Bothe's answer illustrates just how far away from scientific work his thoughts were: he asked for some long black shoe strings, flints for his lighter, and a pair of suspenders. In March of 1947 Bothe finally received permission to use the cyclotron for medical experiments, and one of his younger colleagues came back. Maier-Leibnitz was one of the very few German scientists to return to Germany once his contract ran out, arriving back in the spring of 1948. Finally, in February of 1949 the cyclotron – designed by Bothe and Gentner before the war and by now dwarfed by the latest particle accelerators in America – was running as well as it had in 1944.[8]

The drain on German science and the importation of German scientists into America – whether under coercion or not – raised objections on both sides. Goudsmit, H. Slack, and Hans Bethe debated this policy in the 1947 issue of the *Bulletin of the Atomic Scientists*, showing that some American scientists had not yet forgiven their German colleagues. As Goudsmit summarized the two opposing points of view in the United States, a number of good enemy scientists was the military equivalent of a few new enemy warships, the economic equivalent of enemy gold caches, and the industrial equivalent of a new source of raw materials. But Goudsmit nevertheless argued that in most cases it was morally wrong for American scientists to collaborate with imported German colleagues.[9]

The rumors of preferential treatment being given to German scientists – possible citizenship, preferred treatment of their families, permanent employment in American universities or industrial laboratories – also disturbed Bethe and Slack, for these unconfirmed reports suggested that the United States planned to make use of the services of the imported scientists beyond the stage of merely bringing the American Armed Forces up to date. Bethe asked what impression this policy would make on the rest of the world. Men who had had preferential treatment under the National Socialists were again to be offered special treatment. Must that not hurt any German democratic feeling still alive, they questioned, or then being born? Did Americans want science at any price?[10]

Although this opinion was certainly widespread in America, not all American scientists were as unforgiving as Bethe and Goudsmit, both of whom had suffered personally because of National Socialism. But what is more striking is a comparison of this veiwpoint with the German reaction to the American policy, for leading German scientists often objected to the same things, but for completely different reasons. In late February of 1947, the recent Nobel prize winner Otto Hahn and Friedrich Rein, President of the University of Göttingen, wrote a newspaper article entitled "Export of Scholars to America" and alienated the American occupation officials in the process.[11]

Hahn and Rein made a distinction between the first American job offers to "specialists" – probably referring to the German engineers and scientists who had been involved with jet plane and rocket research – and the more recent importation of German university professors. The export of the former researchers did not bother the Göttingen scholars as much as the loss of academic scientists, who Hahn and Rein believed were unfairly labeled deserters by the German public, while the leading American scientists treated them as unwanted invaders. What was most upsetting to the Germans – in stark contrast to Bethe's and Slack's major concern about importing National Socialism – was that the German scientists who were being shipped to America saw the road to positions at the American universities and other "sanctuaries of pure science" closed to them. Instead, they were forced to work in military-oriented institutes for applied science. Hahn and Rein disingenuously announced that they would not bring up the American seizure of German patents and complained that German science and scientists were being treated as "reparations." Centuries ago, German princes forced peasant children into service as plantation laborers or soldiers, Hahn and Rein noted, but now scientists were "impressed" into foreign service.[12]

Neither the German nor the American scientists recognized, nor wanted to recognize, how much the relationship between the military on one hand and science and engineering on the other had been changed by one of the biggest lessons of World War II, the proven effectiveness of science as a weapon. The American military and government – just as the British, French, Russian, and National Socialist governments – were or had been interested first and foremost in military, economic, and political power and advantage, not the maintenance and support of "pure" science. Germany had exploited unscrupulously the science and technology of prostrate Europe from 1939 to 1945, and although the Allied occupation of Germany is not to be equated with the National Socialist policy in Greater Germany, at the end of the war each of the four Allies nevertheless desired and expected some sort of scientific reparations.

The Russian Zone

Even before the American attack on Hiroshima, the Russian government took a keen interest in all German science and engineering, and especially rockets, jet planes, and nuclear physics. Russian troops stripped the former Kaiser Wilhelm Institute for Physics in Berlin-Dahlem down to the floors and sent the equipment back to the Soviet Union. Desirable scientists were often lured, coerced, or seized and carried off to Russia. In contrast to the United States, the Russians definitely had a use for scientists with experience in, or with potential ability for, applied nuclear fission research. Such scientists were sought after and gathered together by the Russian occupation authorities. Long after the war, Werner Czulius, a former member of the Gottow group, recalled his "invitation" to go to Russia. He was "invited" by an armed guard to meet with an important Russian general in Berlin. Once in Berlin, Czulius was told that the general was in Moscow, so the meeting would have to take place there. Once in Moscow, Czulius was told that the general was busy, so he could get right to work. Nikolaus Riehl, his colleagues Günther Wirths and Karl Zimmer, and his entire Auer Company laboratory were seized and sent to Russia.[13]

On the other hand, several German scientists volunteered to go east, including Manfred von Ardenne, Robert Döpel, Gustav Hertz, Heinz Pose, and Peter Thiessen, the former head of the Kaiser Wilhelm Institute for Physical Chemistry. In general, all German scientists were treated well in Russia – Nikolaus Riehl entitled the memoirs of his years in Russia as "Ten Years in a Gilded Cage" – and received better rations and care than the general Russian population. But, just as with their colleagues in the other zones, the Germans who found themselves under Russian rule had to deal with the occupation authorities and the harsh living conditions. When faced with hunger and no other chance of scientific work, the Russian offers were hard to turn down. As in the American zone, the distinction between "voluntary" and "involuntary" collaboration was unclear.[14]

Although the Americans and British had gathered together most of the members of the nuclear power project, the Soviets did manage to gather together some scientists useful for their nuclear weapons project. But even though German researchers made important contributions to the Russian effort to harness nuclear fission, the Soviet success was primarily a Russian achievement. These Germans were used for specific, isolated aspects of the project, often in advisory roles. For example, Riehl ran a uranium factory. By the time that the first Soviet atomic bomb was detonated in 1949, the Russians already had learned all they could about nuclear power from their guests. Russians trained by the Germans now took their place.[15]

Just as the western allies tried to keep German scientists and engineers out of the Soviet zone, the Russians were very interested in drawing scientists into their zone – as well as bringing them to Russia – and keeping them there. However, since most Germans preferred working for the Americans, British, or French, there was a general flight from, and shortage of, scientists in the east and overcrowding in the west. The Russians often resorted to cloak-and-dagger operations to lure Germans east.[16]

Heisenberg himself received a mysterious invitation from the east in the summer of 1946. Heinz Pose wrote to Heisenberg from Russia, lauded the working conditions and the available resources there, emphasized the great Russian interest in nuclear power, and noted that the Russians showed German scientists the fullest confidence and no hostile attitude towards Germans existed. Furthermore, the Russians naturally were very interested in Heisenberg and his work. Pose's letter had been delivered by hand. If Heisenberg was interested in working with the Russians, he either could give a message to the courier, or write to Pose directly. Pose ended his message by noting that his own part in this plan was restricted to making contact with his colleague in Göttingen.[17]

Heisenberg wrote to Pose and declined the Russian offer politely. But the message in his letter was meant for the British. Heisenberg wanted to stay in Germany for the time being, as long as it was possible to do science under fairly satisfactory conditions and to nourish and bring up his children. Only if matters became so hopeless that one of these two conditions was not met would Heisenberg consider moving to another country. Heisenberg told Pose that he would like very much to hear about his work and plans in Russia, where of course no one would mind if this information was shared with the English "gentlemen" in Göttingen. Apparently Heisenberg was not contacted again.[18]

The German physicists who remained in the Russian zone were overworked and alienated. For example, Seelinger, professor at the University of Greifswald, complained to Heisenberg by asking why no physicists came to the Russian zone? Heisenberg provided a list of young physicists who were both suitable for a professorship and who had no such position in the west, but added that he considered it very doubtful that any would go to the east. Noting that the sudden abduction of a colleague from the University of Jena had dampened considerably the enthusiasm for the Russian zone, he answered Seelinger with the parable of the fox and the bear: the fox notices that many trails lead into the cave of the bear, but none come out. But Heisenberg nevertheless advised some young physicists to go to the eastern zone or to stay there, for the overcrowding of physicists in the west made a career in physics seem impossible for many young scientists. Also, it was not at all clear at this time that Germany would be divided definitively between east and west, although this division appeared more and more fixed as the period of occupation went on. The Russians abducted German scientists, but the Americans did as well. United States intelligence personnel removed scientists and engineers from Saxony and Thuringia – some against their will – as the American troops withdrew to the boundary between the American and Russian zones of occupation. If specialists were not brought to the United States, they were kept in the American zone and forbidden to relocate, until this policy was changed in 1948.[19]

Two of Heisenberg's former colleagues were still in Leipzig at the end of the war, and both Karl-Friedrich Bonhoeffer and Friedrich Hund gave Heisenberg a harsh description of the basic living conditions and scientific and academic life in the Soviet zone. However much hardship and hunger one could find in the three western zones, things were worse in the eastern portion of Germany. In general, Russian policy was similar to the managerial strategy employed by the Americans: neglect in Germany, but exploitation of German science and technology at home. But whereas the Russians had to rely mainly on military and physical force towards this end, the Americans could often afford the luxury of more subtle economic persuasion.[20]

As the Cold War turned bitter, and the divide between Russia on one side and America, Britain, and France on the other gradually deepened, the scientists in the eastern zone felt more and more cut off from their colleagues in the west. Bonhoeffer had been offered a job in Göttingen, but in the spring of 1946 considered it unlikely that the Soviet occupying powers would allow his transfer to another zone, so long as the western powers in turn continued to forbid the return of the professors who actually belonged in the Russian zone and who were removed by the Americans. But what was more disturbing to these scientists was the attitude of many of their colleagues in the west. The eastern scientists felt abandoned. As Bonhoeffer told Heisenberg, the main impression he received from his last visit to the western zones was a "little sad." Bonhoeffer noticed that many people – even if they were discussing something completely different – "inwardly" had already written off the eastern zone. With the founding of the two rival German states in 1949, German scientists in east and west were cut off from each other, except for the passage through Berlin. Indeed Bonhoeffer, Hund, and many of the Germans who worked on nuclear power in Russia eventually came to the west in this way, until this gate was shut in 1961. The unity of German science fell victim to quarrels among the great powers.[21]

The French Zone

The French government was given the smallest and least industrial zone by the Americans and British. Furthermore, by the time French troops occupied their portion of Germany, the Americans already had removed the best scientific and technological prizes. But the French Zone nevertheless did contain a fair number of scientists and a sizeable amount of scientific equipment, since several research institutes had been evacuated from Berlin to southwestern Germany during the last years of the war. One of the biggest French prizes was the Hechingen branch of the Kaiser Wilhelm Institute for Physics. As soon as the Alsos Mission had withdrawn from Hechingen and Haigerloch, French officials entered and interrogated the remaining scientists. Fritz Bopp had been left in charge of the Hechingen institute and described the initial French attitude towards the institute as having three inseparable levels: exploitation, forced evacuation to France, and a search for, and seizure of, documents and materials. The French Naval Commission was the main advocate of exploitation. They cleared out one nearby research institute, seized an electron microscope from Tübingen, and would have taken the Hechingen ultracentrifuge and other valuable devices to France if the influential biochemist Adolf Butenandt had not intervened.[22]

Shortly thereafter, the French physicist Frédéric Joliot arrived as the representative of the French government and all crude attempts at pillage were stopped. This same pattern was repeated in all four zones. At first science policy was carried out ruthlessly by military personnel, then subsequently scientists took over – often colleagues or former students of the Germans concerned – and instituted a much more sympathetic policy. But the French navy did not give up. In order to put pressure on Bopp, the French imprisoned him for five days. The very flimsy grounds for his arrest came only after the fact. Afterwards, a French naval official named Rochard came to Bopp and tried to force him to agree to the evacuation of the institute to France. Bopp refused, claiming that he had no such authority, whereupon Rochard threatened him with further imprisonment if he did not change his mind.[23]

Fortunately for Bopp, Rochard soon disappeared, and the other French representatives did not employ such crude tactics of persuasion. But while Bopp was in prison, he was removed as head of the institute by the French and replaced by the spectroscopist Schüler. The latter scientist enjoyed the full confidence of the French, although not of the Germans, and his appointment caused considerable tension, both between the nuclear physicists and the spectroscopists in the institute as well as within the Kaiser Wilhelm Society itself.[24]

The British wanted Heisenberg to set up his institute in their zone, specifically in Göttingen. But difficulties arose when Heisenberg attempted to reunite his institute. The French refused to send the Hechingen institute to Göttingen, while the British refused to let the Farm Hall captives return to the French zone. The prospects for combining the two institutes in Göttingen were not good, and Heisenberg was in no position to bargain. By May of 1946 he doubted that he would receive a single screw from the Hechingen institute. Butenandt met with French officials on Heisenberg's behalf and reported back that the French definitely were interested in the physics institute, and were willing to support it, but for this very reason were unwilling to see part or all of it move to another zone. Indeed Butenandt believed that any further attempt to transfer the institute would be misguided if not dangerous. The question of who should be the institute head was not open for discussion. The French trusted Schüler and wanted him to stay. Indeed Schüler also wanted to remain as head of an independent institute in Hechingen and unsuccessfully asked the Kaiser Wilhelm Society and Heisenberg to give him their blessings.[25]

The Hechingen institute survived as long as the French occupation lasted, although the scientists had already begun to trickle away to various universities and industrial laboratories throughout Germany. By the start of the Federal German Republic, Schüler had been given a "Research Institute for Spectroscopy" by the new Max Planck Society, and the physics institutes had been reunited in Göttingen under Heisenberg's leadership. French occupation policy was not qualitatively different from the American or Russian strategies. It was merely on a smaller scale. What the French could not remove to France, they were willing to let run – under close supervision – in the French Zone.[26]

The British Zone

About two months after Hiroshima, Otto Hahn, Werner Heisenberg, and Max von Laue were taken to London to discuss with British authorities the return of the Farm Hall scientists to Germany and the support of German science. The Americans and British were willing to let the researchers return, but only to one of their zones. Travel to the areas occupied by the French or Russians was forbidden. Instead, the British wanted the scientists to form a "crystallization seed" for the rebuilding of German science in the British zone. Great Britain had been planning their occupation policy since 1944, and in contrast to their three allies, they adopted a policy of exploiting German industry, science, and technology in their portion of Germany instead of importing it to Britain. However, for this policy to work, portions of German science and industry had to be rebuilt.[27]

With the start of the new year, 1946, the Farm Hall scientists were shipped back to Germany. Perhaps the most important support Britain gave to German science was the sponsorship of the Kaiser Wilhelm Society and its successor the Max Planck Society. The new society President, Otto Hahn, and the General Secretary, Ernst Telschow, labored mightily to keep the Kaiser Wilhelm Society alive in the postwar period – the Americans, French, and Russians considered the society dead – and therefore argued that the society had remained immune from National Socialist influence, had not been part of the German war machine, and had not taken part in the scientific plunder of Europe.[28]

It is understandable that Hahn and Telschow considered that any connection between the Kaiser Wilhelm Society and National Socialism or the military conquest and industrial plunder of Europe would harm their efforts to rebuild German science, which they believed was a good cause. But these claims nevertheless were false. Setting aside the very disturbing indirect roles that the Kaiser Wilhelm Institutes for Anthropology, Brain Research, and Psychiatry played in the inhuman medical experiments at concentration camps and German health care institutions – for what scientific plunder could be worse than that of the corpse of a murder victim – the German nuclear power project, including the Kaiser Wilhelm Institutes for Chemistry, Physics, and Medical Research, depended on, and benefited from, materials and apparatus plundered from prostrate Europe.[29]

Moreover, Telschow was aware both of this plunder and of his own falsehood. In 1948 the Belgian universities and others inquired officially about the research carried out at the Kaiser Wilhelm Institutes during the war. Telschow asked Heisenberg to draw up a half page summary, directing further that since the Belgian Embassy had been informed that during the war the Kaiser Wilhelm Society had adhered to its tradition of basic research to the "broadest extent" and that "goal-oriented" research had been carried out only to an "extremely small" extent, it was unnecessary to go into the war work in greater detail. Telschow clearly did not want to stress the tons of uranium compounds confiscated from the Belgian Mining Union Company, processed in Germany, and incorporated into the uranium machines at the Berlin-Dahlem Kaiser Wilhelm Institute for Physics. This episode was typical of the apolitical response made by German scientists to the inquiries of the Allied authorities. By misrepresenting their research during the National Socialist period and portraying it as academic "pure" science, the Germans misled their conquerors deliberately, repeatedly, and successfully.[30]

The Americans and British agreed that the Kaiser Wilhelm Institutes for Physics and Chemistry should be relocated in the British zone, and Heisenberg and his Farm Hall colleagues had little choice. Their British colleagues were making great efforts to provide reasonable working conditions for the scientists in the British area of occupation, but Heisenberg was forbidden to move permanently to the American zone. Nuclear fission research was now out of the question, so Heisenberg concentrated on his other wartime research program, the study of cosmic radiation.[31]

The city of Göttingen was relatively intact at the end of the war, and Heisenberg was given several large rooms located in buildings formerly used for aeronautical research. However, precisely because Göttingen was better off than most German cities, too many people wanted to live there. The many refugees from the east had raised the population of the city to more than double the prewar level. It was almost impossible to find an appartment, or even to receive permission from the city for another scientist to move to Göttingen. Thus Heisenberg was in the position of needing more collaborators for his institute, but having to turn down friends and colleagues who wanted to join him and who had no other position. There was no room. Although as a scientist supported by the British authorities, Heisenberg and his family were certainly better off than most other Germans, he nevertheless found it difficult to provide for his children. As with many Germans, Heisenberg's family was the grateful recipient of aid from abroad, including CARE packages from America. Shoes and food for the children were among the most welcome gifts.[32]

Although Heisenberg wanted very much to return to Munich and finally to become Sommerfeld's successor, he found it difficult to leave the British zone. In February of 1947 he told his aging teacher that he could not come to Munich. Reason told Heisenberg that he should remain in Göttingen for the time being, until the "nonsense" was over. But his heart said something completely different, and conjured up before Heisenberg's eyes the small heavens of the Bavarian foothills, memories of his student days with Sommerfeld and the former brilliance of Munich. But then reason returned, and reminded Heisenberg of all the ruins in Munich, of the fact that his house there had been confiscated and that he lived very well in Göttingen. However, Heisenberg's heart would not give up, and reminded him of sailing on the Starnberger Sea, the powder snow at the Unterberger ski lodge, and the air in the spring when the Föhn wind blows from the mountains. What could one do, he asked Sommerfeld?[33]

By early 1947 Heisenberg had become optimistic about the next generation of German scientists and cautiously thought that the German economy would be in better shape in five to ten years. Heisenberg also made a comment which showed how much the experiences of the war and National Socialism had changed him for, from the historian's perspective, this statement would have been unthinkable before 1945. Heisenberg did not believe that Germany would become an independent state again, and doubted that it would be a good thing if it did. Heisenberg now considered it much better if a large part of Europe could be reorganized into one individual state without customs borders and immigration restrictions.[34]

Given the great animosity towards Germany and Germans after the fall of National Socialism and the great suffering that the German state had caused in Europe during the years of National Socialist rule, it is amazing how easily German scientists were reintegrated into the international community of science. There were three very different reasons why German scientists were reaccepted by foreign colleagues more quickly after the fall of the Third Reich than following the defeat of the Kaiser's armies in 1919: one political, one of conscience, and one very personal. As the postwar tensions between east and west grew and the Cold War turned harsh, the Americans and their allies looked more and more to the Germans in the three western zones for assistance in their political struggle against Soviet Russia. Previous collaboration with National Socialism was now forgiven and sometimes forgotten in exchange for opposition to Communism. However, for many others in the west, the lessons of history motivated their good will towards Germany. It was difficult to overlook the connection between the post-World War I ostracism of Germany and German science on one hand, and some of the support that was given by Germans to the National Socialist movement during the Weimar Republic on the other. Cooperation and forgiveness, not ostracism, appeared to be the answer. Finally, the personal reason arose from an individual's need to either apologize for, or to exorcise, the horrors of the National Socialist period, to put this evil behind him (or her), and to move on.[35]

One example of a scientist who wished to exorcise the National Socialist devil was Max Born. He had been planning to write to Heisenberg for quite some time, but events in October of 1946 provided a special opportunity for Born to set pen to paper. On the same day as the judgment of the

Nuremberg Trials of the Major War Criminals was announced, Born was asked by the British military government in Germany if he wanted to return to Göttingen. The university there offered him the professorship that had been taken away in 1933. Not only a great injustice, but also a small injustice, had been atoned for. But Born did not belong to those who are pleased by victories. He bemoaned the injury and injustice that had occurred, and did his best to ensure that there finally would be an end to revenge and violence. Born asked Heisenberg to inform the university that he would not come – though Born did return in the end and was one of the few to do so – for many reasons, one of which, he hardly wanted to mention lest wounds be reopened: the loss of so many relatives and friends, the annihilation of the tribe from which Born came. Although he did not wish to return at this time, Born did want to reestablish old bonds of friendship and went out of his way to contact Max von Laue, Max Planck, Robert Pohl, and Sommerfeld as well as Heisenberg.[36]

As a gesture of reconciliation, Heisenberg was invited to England for a six week lecture series in early 1948. However, not everyone was pleased about this symbolic gesture. Rudolf Peierls, a former student of Heisenberg, a Jewish refugee from Germany, and an important participant in the Manhattan District nuclear weapons project, thought that Heisenberg was the wrong choice. The first official invitation should have been extended to someone like Laue, whose conduct during the Third Reich was, in Peierls' opinion, more clear-cut and laudable. Peierls sent Heisenberg a draft article entitled "Our relations with German Scientists," which sharply criticized the behavior of the majority of senior German academics. According to Peierls, in contrast to junior German scientists, these senior scholars easily could have left their posts in protest when the National Socialists purged the universities. Moreover, this act of defiance might have had some effect, but instead the established scientists acquiesced and continued to serve under the new system. Although Peierls admitted that he did not know how he himself would have acted in a similar situation, he stressed that it was precisely this general inertia among the senior people that set the pattern for the younger scholars.[37]

In the eyes of many foreign colleagues, it was this question, why did Heisenberg and others like him stay in Germany, that cast a long shadow over Heisenberg throughout the postwar era, indeed beyond his death. As will be examined below, Heisenberg saw his responsibility differently. Heisenberg nevertheless thought that the trip to England was a success. The time he spent there had been pleasing in every way. Born had been as "friendly and nice" as in the old days. Simon and Peierls had also been very hospitable, but Heisenberg believed that they found it difficult to free themselves from the injustice they had suffered.[38]

Nazification and denazification

One of the few things that the four occupying powers could agree on was that Germany and the German people should be purged of National Socialism. The Potsdam Conference of July 1945 confirmed the policies of "demilitarization" and "denazification," but since there was no clear definition of who was or was not a "nazi," this effort perhaps was doomed to failure. National Socialism was not superimposed on top of Germany and Germans. Eventually the theory and practice of this ideology pervaded every aspect of life in Germany and affected every German to some degree. National Socialism succeeded because it was able to subsume and exploit existing ideologies and traditions, including anti-Semitism, trust in the German state, fear of socialism and communism, militarism, nationalism, and many more. Although the particular historical phenomenon of German National Socialism was dead after World War II, the social, economic, and ideological forces that had helped unleash it persisted.

Denazification in Germany was often haphazard and arbitrary. What was perhaps most unfair, was that after punishing the "little Hitlers" – for example local Party leaders – the entire denazification process was abandoned by the occupation authorities in the three western zones, thereby excluding the greater portion of the traditional German bureaucratic, business, industrial, and military elites. As of 1950, over 6 million denazification cases had been tried, of which two out of three received summary amnesty, more than 1 million were exonerated, 1 million were judged fellow travelers (*Mitläufer*), 150,000 as lesser offenders, 23,000 as offenders, and less than 2,000 as major offenders. In fact, of the Germans who returned the questionnaires in the American zone, three out of four could not even be charged under the criteria of denazification, but it is difficult to imagine the events of the Third Reich in a setting where more than three out of four Germans took no part in, and bore no responsibility for, the planning, adaptation, and implementation of National Socialist policy.[39]

What effect did denazification have on the German physics community and, in particular, on the German nuclear power project? Or to put it another way, how far did the "nazification" of the nuclear power project during the Third Reich go, and how was this "nazification" dealt with after the war? The term "nazi," a derogatory synonym for National Socialist, took on a special meaning in the postwar era. A "nazi" came to denote someone who – directly or indirectly – was personally responsible for some of the inhuman excesses committed by Germany and Germans during the years 1933 to 1945 and especially for the systematic extermination of millions of people during the last few years of the war. This admittedly vague definition was subjective. The same individual might be considered a "nazi" in some circles and a "victim of the nazis" in another. Rather than trying to decide whether a particular scientist or administrator was a "nazi" or not, let us search for other means of gauging the influence that National Socialism had on the German nuclear power project.

Taking seventy-one members of the extended nuclear power project – practically everyone directly or indirectly involved with research or administration – let us examine those who joined the National Socialist German Workers Party or relevant ancillary organizations (for although there was often great pressure to join, membership was not an official prerequisite for acquiring or staying at an academic or scientific post), discover when they did so, and try to analyze why. The first point to make is that rather than asking who was a "party comrade" (*Parteigenosse*), the reader might as well ask who was not. More than half of these men, 56 percent, were members of the National Socialist German Workers Party.[40]

Since most of these scientists and administrators were academics or wanted to be, membership in the National Socialist Teachers League (*Nationalsozialistischer Lehrerbund*) is also relevant. Of these researchers, 72 percent were either party comrades or members of the Teachers League (if one was already a Party member, he may well not have felt the need to join the Teachers League as well). If all the ancillary organizations are taken into account – and it is often difficult to judge the differences in degree of commitment to National Socialism between membership in different organizations – four out of five of these scientists and administrators were card-carrying, dues-paying participants in organized National Socialism. Indeed these figures represent minimum values. There is evidence that the records used to produce these statistics are incomplete.[41]

When did these scientists join the Party or the Teachers League? The remarkable answer sheds light on some of the motivations for membership. Of the thirty-two physicists and chemists who joined the Teachers League, twenty-six joined during the first three years of the Third Reich. Five of the six remaining signed up shortly after they had received their doctoral degrees and thereby had qualified for a university teaching position. The figures for Party membership are similar. Eight percent were "old fighters" and had joined before the National Socialist German Workers Party gained control of the government, 68 percent joined during the years 1933–38, 15 percent during the war, and for 9 percent the date of entry is unknown.[42]

The Party membership figures are even more striking when one takes into account that enrollment was frozen for the general population in 1934. In 1937 membership was reopened for certain favored groups, including academics and scientists, and of the forty total Party members, eighteen joined at that time, almost 50 percent. Thus two general trends are clear from the data. First of all, those scientists who joined the Teachers League did so immediately after the start of the National Socialist government or as soon thereafter as possible, which suggests opportunism. Secondly, the majority of the scientists who joined the Party did so just before the end of the period in which National Socialism had shown its best face to the world.[43]

For example, think of the spectacle of the 1936 Olympics, Adolf Hitler's repeated bloodless foreign policy coups, the celebrated return of universal military service, and the renunciation of the resented Treaty of Versailles. At this time, another world war was the last thing on the mind of the German public or these scientists. This flood of scientists into the National Socialist German Workers Party in the years just before the war cannot be explained merely by opportunism or by fear of political retribution alone. Many of these physicists and chemists sincerely wanted to take part in what contemporaries called the "National Socialist Revolution," a return to traditional German values after the brief aberrant Weimer Republic.[44]

On the other hand, with respect to Party membership, the German nuclear power project as a whole exhibited every extreme. For example, one physicist joined in 1929 at the age of twenty-three, while another joined in 1941 at the age of forty-six, and yet another was still waiting at the end of the war to hear whether his application had been approved. Several Austrian scientists joined the Austrian National Socialist German Workers Party at a time when this party was illegal in Austria and it was not at all clear that National Socialism would one day spread beyond Germany. Finally, one scientist was thrown out of the Party two years after he joined in 1940 because of his personal relations with his sister's former boyfriend, a Jew. This scientist was lucky. Since his relationship with the Jew had occurred before he entered the Party, he was merely expelled. If he had been a party comrade at the time, then his punishment would have been severe.[45]

Moving from the general to the specific, let us now examine the Institute for Physical Chemistry at the University of Hamburg. This institute has been chosen for study because of the richness of the available historical material. Of the six Hamburg scientists in the nuclear power project, all were members of the Teachers League or the Party, and five of the six were party comrades. When the dates of membership are examined – for one scientist such information is unavailable – those who joined the Teachers League did so either at the start of the Third Reich, or as soon as possible thereafter. Those who joined the Party did so in 1937 or 1938.[46]

Although in many respects statistical analysis is preferable to individual case studies, particular examples of scientists under National Socialism must be examined as well. In order to protect living scientists, their names will not be used. One of the most important steps in a German academic career was the *Habilitation*, in a sense a second doctoral degree which bestowed upon the bearer the right to teach at a particular university. In practice, this degree was a prerequisite for a call to a professorship. During the Third Reich the *Habilitation* process became politicized. The Reich University Teachers League (*Reichsdozentenbund*) – the political arm of National Socialism in the university faculties – held veto power over any *Habilitation*. During the course of the Third Reich, three of Paul Harteck's most valuable colleagues took this important professional step. As far as surviving documentation allows, these *Habilitation* processes will be examined as examples of the political pressure exerted on young, ambitious, and often patriotic and nationalistic scientists by National Socialism.[47]

One scientist, henceforth referred to as the "part-Aryan," applied for a job at Harteck's institute in 1937. According to his own account, the part-Aryan had joined a branch of the Party outside of Germany in 1934. He subsequently became a member of the German Party in 1938, yet the problem with his job application was not his Party membership, but rather his race. There was some doubt as to whether his four grandparents were of sufficiently Aryan origin. Since one of his grandfathers had been born in a now hostile country, in the end, his racial background remained questionable.[48]

When the part-Aryan applied for his *Habilitation* a few years later, the racial question surfaced again. The Dean of the Natural Sciences-Mathematical Faculty finally passed the problem on to higher authorities. The faculty had no objection to bestowing the right to teach when it came to the professional performance and personality of the scientist. However, the Dean recommended that, along with the Leader of the Hamburg University Teachers League, the University President carefully examine the question of "Aryan origin." Given the information available, the part-Aryan just fulfilled the requirements of the Nuremberg Laws, and received the *Habilitation*.[49]

Johannes Jensen, the theoretical physicist who collaborated with Harteck on isotope separation, presented a different case. When he received his *Habilitation* in 1936 he had been a member of the Teachers League for three years and was a candidate for membership in the Party, which came through the next year. In 1938 the Hamburg University Teachers League approved a stipend for Jensen, noting that the scientific report on Jensen was very positive. There was nothing negative known about his personality. Politically, Jensen had been in several organizations for a long time, and in the Party since 1937. The leader of the Hamburg University Teachers League made it clear that "active participation" was expected from Jensen, to which the scientist agreed. Moreover, Jensen had volunteered for military service, but had not been able to take part because of a sport accident. In June of 1941 Jensen was appointed extraordinary professor of theoretical physics at the Hanover Technical University.[50]

In 1947 Jensen was facing denazification proceedings. Werner Heisenberg wrote a "whitewash certificate" (*Persilschein*) for him, noting that he had met Jensen often during the war. In the many conversations that he had had with Jensen on the "political situation," Heisenberg noted that there had never been any doubt that Jensen had "inwardly" and completely rejected National Socialism. Whenever it was possible to protect any person, for example non-Aryan colleagues, from persecution by the National Socialist authorities, Heisenberg wrote that Jensen had always been ready to help with "all his might." According to Heisenberg, Jensen undoubtedly had joined the Party only in order to avoid unnecessary difficulties as a teacher. Jensen eventually became a professor in Heidelberg and subsequently won the Nobel Prize.[51]

Just as Jensen was under political pressure to participate actively in National Socialism, Wilhelm Groth also experienced difficulties with his *Habilitation*. When in 1937 Harteck requested an extension of Groth's assistant position in the institute, the leader of the Hamburg University Teachers League answered that he had no basic objections. However, this Party official added that it would be "desirable" if Groth began to demonstrate his readiness to serve "today's state" and gave up the political neutrality that he carried around "for show." However, by the end of the year the calls for Groth to change his ways had become more explicit. The Party representative in the university remained unconvinced that Groth had been penetrated by National Socialist "thought and will" and doubted that Groth was suited to educate students in the "National Socialist" sense. But as long as Groth was judged favorably by the University Teachers Academy, this Party official was willing to set aside his political objections.[52]

In 1938, Groth was recommended by the Mathematical–Natural Sciences Faculty for the *Habilitation*. His knowledge of physical chemistry was judged excellent. Shortly before Christmas of the same year, Groth received official notification of his enhanced academic status. Groth's reputation grew as the war dragged on, and in 1943 Abraham Esau recommended that the Reich Minister of Education give Groth a professorship. But Groth did not receive this honor until the postwar period, when with the blessing of the British military government he was appointed extraordinary professor of physical chemistry at Hamburg. In 1950 he accepted a call to a full professorship at the University of Bonn.[53]

Although every German university had been politicized, not every one was as strict as Hamburg. To put it another way, there was no general rule for the political conduct of academics or scientists throughout the Third

Reich. For example, when Karl Wirtz, a member of the Teachers League but not of the Party, applied for the *Habilitation* at the University of Berlin in 1940, the local head of the University Teachers League gave his approval. This political leader had some objections to Wirtz's candidacy, but in view of the shortage of theoretical physicists, set them aside.[54]

Although Wolfgang Gentner was only a member of the National Socialist Pilot Corps, and though his political behavior was described by the SS as "correct" towards the National Socialist State, but lacking "activity" and "readiness to serve," the Dean of the University of Frankfurt still approved his *Habilitation*. As with Wirtz's case, because of the shortage of young academics, especially in the physical and chemical subjects, it appeared necessary to give capable scientists, whose suitability of character was recognized and whose political conduct was irreproachable, the opportunity to become university instructors.[55]

Resistance or even political opposition to the regime was risky (and for this reason rare), but in some cases political neutrality and support of the state – apparent or otherwise – sufficed to allow scientists to pursue their academic careers. As Harteck emerged in the postwar period he found himself in a good position. Because of his relatively clean slate, the British military authorities – possibly with Goudsmit's backing – quickly placed him in powerful positions, both at the University of Hamburg and in the university denazification commission, responsibilities that Harteck accepted with mixed feelings.[56]

As the German physics community passed through the process of denazification, certain scientists acquired powerful positions as the authors of whitewash certificates. Werner Heisenberg, who had never belonged to the Party or any of its ancillary organizations, who had clashed publicly with the Party and the SS in 1936 and 1937, and who had been given a university chair and physics institute by the British occupation authorities, exerted great influence as a symbol of resistance against National Socialism. Thus many members of the nuclear power project, who now had a potentially compromising political past, turned to Heisenberg for help.

Because of lack of space, only two examples will be compared and contrasted here: Gottfried von Droste and a scientist henceforth referred to as "the fellow traveler." Both men joined the paramilitary National Socialist Storm Troopers (*Sturmabteilung*) in 1933 and the Party shortly after membership was reopened in 1937. Both asked Heisenberg for a whitewash certificate, though in different ways. Droste felt little need to apologize. He admitted that he had joined the Storm Troopers, but went on to imply that he had been taken into the Party against his will in 1938. Since Heisenberg knew Droste's attitude towards the "political events of the time," Droste felt able to ask him for a far-reaching "exoneration certificate" with a clear conscience. However, in fact no one joined the Party without personally applying and signing the application. Similarly no one remained a member without paying his dues.[57]

The second scientist put it to Heisenberg in a more thoughtful, but not completely apologetic way. He made no secret of the fact that he joined the Storm Troopers voluntarily for idealistic reasons, not without reservations or uncritically, but because of his belief that it was the duty of all decent people to take part in the apparently so constructive plan of national renewal. Later, during the war, the fellow traveler's sense of duty hindered disloyalty, and only after the war did he recognize where the higher duty lay. The fellow traveler admitted his political mistake, but since he had had only good intentions, he found it difficult to feel any personal guilt. He accepted denazification, since he appreciated that Hitler's "former followers" were more obliged to make reparations than other Germans. Unfortunately, the important things could not be made good anyway. Short and sweet, he wanted to be judged a "fellow traveler," which indeed he had been.

Heisenberg's whitewash certificates for his two colleagues shared a common theme. For Droste, Heisenberg wrote that between 1939 and 1943 he had often discussed "political questions" with Droste and had always found that Droste criticized the "crimes and errors" of National Socialism just as Heisenberg himself did. The Göttingen physicist had never had the impression that Droste had participated in the "bad side" of National Socialism. The whitewash certificate for the fellow traveler was a bit more sympathetic. Heisenberg had never noticed any sort of political activity by the fellow traveler in the "National Socialist sense," had discussed political questions openly with him during the war years, and found him always understanding of Heisenberg's criticism of the "politics of the times." The fellow traveler had always thought "professionally and impartially," Heisenberg recalled, political fanaticism was completely foreign to him. Heisenberg's compassion and readiness to help acquaintances, colleagues, and friends is laudable – he almost never turned down a request to write a whitewash certificate – but it would have been dangerous indeed if Heisenberg actually had discussed political questions openly and critically during the Third Reich with as many people as he subsequently claimed.[58]

Heisenberg had debts to pay at the end of the Third Reich. Several individuals in the Party, the SS, and the National Socialist government had helped Heisenberg's side in the *deutsche Physik* controversy, and now – when they faced denazification – these men turned to Heisenberg for help. Limiting himself to events he could remember, Heisenberg provided his former SS and Party allies with whitewash certificates that lauded their respective parts in the struggle against *deutsche Physik*. In the case of Johannes Juilfs, Heisenberg went far beyond his duty. Because of his SS record, this person had been incriminated by a denazification court and could not return to the university as teacher or researcher. In the summer of 1948 Heisenberg contacted a colleague at a research institute in the Rhineland – technically not part of the four zones of occupation – and asked whether they might have a place for Juilfs, since this physicist had intervened so energetically for the "reasonable side" during the struggle against *deutsche Physik*. Unfortunately, the Rhineland institute did not even have enough funding for the scientific workers they already employed.[59]

After the founding of the Federal German Republic, the fortunes of Johannes Juilfs improved dramatically. In 1950 he found a job as an industrial physicist. No less a personage than the Minister of Culture of the German state of Lower Saxony now intervened on his behalf, first to arrange a grant, then a temporary teaching position at a university. By the end of the decade, Johannes Juilfs was a full professor in physics at one of the West German institutions of higher learning. Although he was more incriminated than most other German scientists, his story is in many respects typical. At the beginning of the postwar period many scientists and other scholars lost their positions as part of the ongoing denazification process, but by the start of the new Federal German Republic, most of them were back in place.

Philipp Lenard was a very old man at the end of the war, so it was Johannes Stark – politically by far the more active of the two – who had to represent *deutsche Physik* in denazification court. In his denazification questionnaire, Stark noted that he should be cleared of all charges. Instead, the denazification court of Traunstein convicted and sentenced him as a major offender to four years of forced labor. Stark, seventy-three-years old and with failing health, appealed.[60]

The Munich court of appeal reversed the Traunstein judgment. The charge against Stark could be broken down into three groups: (1) conflicts with people in the region of Traunstein; (2) support of Hitler and National Socialism before 1933; and (3) activity as President of the German Research Community (*Deutsche Forschungsgemeinschaft*) from 1934 to 1936 and the Imperial Physical-Technical Institute from 1933 to 1939. The first charge was disposed of quickly, since Stark's accusers were less credible than the accused. While the second charge was undeniable, in the view of the Munich court, support of Hitler before the National Socialists gained power was not necessarily support of the subsequent National Socialist dictatorship, indeed Stark had withdrawn from the Party in 1943. The third charge was complicated by apparently false testimony given in Traunstein that Stark had employed only party comrades as scientists at the Imperial Physical–Technical Institute. The Munich court heard abundant evidence that – at least according to certain individuals – Stark had run this institute in a professionally correct manner.[61]

But the third charge also included Stark's attacks on the supporters of "Jewish science," so the Munich court solicited statements on this issue from Einstein, Heisenberg, and others on Stark's anti-Semitism and opposition to the theory of relativity. Since he was the sole member of the nuclear power project involved, Heisenberg's response will be examined here. The court asked him for his opinion on two basic questions: (1) was the difference between "dogmatic" (Heisenberg's side) and "pragmatic" physics (Stark's side) grounded in anti-Semitism, or in professionally justifiable research methods; and (2) did Stark play a role in the rejection and prohibition of the theory of relativity during the Third Reich?[62]

Heisenberg replied that he believed that the attack by Stark on him as a "white Jew" was not due to personal antagonism, instead Stark had wanted to block the former's call to the professorship at Munich. Agreeing with Einstein's statement to the court, Heisenberg doubted that anti-Semitism was at the roots of Stark's actions. Heisenberg believed that it was bitterness at not having been appreciated by his colleagues – at least in Stark's mind – that had led to his "preposterous" behavior. However, Heisenberg did make it clear who was responsible for *deutsche Physik*. The campaign against the theory of relativity, led by a small clique of National Socialists, was due almost exclusively to the activity of two people; Lenard and Stark, Heisenberg added, had successfully enticed "weak young" Party members into attacks against "senile and Jewishified" physics. The Munich court of appeals considered the *deutsche Physik* controversy to have been a scientific debate, which the court could not judge, and accordingly placed Stark in the group of lesser offenders and fined him 1,000 German Marks.[63]

Heisenberg's compassion towards Johannes Juilfs, an SS physicist who had held a high position on Himmler's staff and who had backed Heisenberg's side in the *deutsche Physik* debate, contrasts with his correct, yet cold, if not bitter, attitude towards Johannes Stark, the relatively harmless advocate of *deutsche Physik*. Although there were personal grounds for this difference – Heisenberg had lost the Munich professorship because of Stark, while his acquaintance had helped him to try to regain it – the contrast is also typical of one aspect of the postwar apologia disseminated by the German physics community. The *deutsche Physik* movement was retrospectively portrayed as having been the full extent of National Socialist influence in German physics, while Lenard, Stark, and their few followers were retrospectively described as having represented the full extent of the participation of German physicists in National Socialism. According to the post-1945 "party line," the "nazis" among the German physicists were Lenard, Stark, and their followers. A scientist who had backed Heisenberg's side in the *deutsche Physik* controversy – almost no matter what else he may have done during the Third Reich –

was no "nazi." By redefining retrospectively the interaction of National Socialism and the German physics community in this narrow way, German physicists were able to argue that they had "resisted" National Socialism by pointing to the victorious struggle with *deutsche Physik*.

Although during the Third Reich most Germans were unaware of the extent and magnitude of the crimes committed by their government and Armed Forces, the postwar Nuremberg Trials of the Major War Criminals by the four occupation powers publicized atrocities almost beyond belief that had been carried out at German concentration camps and elsewhere. Whatever a given German might or might not have known at the time of the atrocities, the legacy of National Socialism was now all too clear. As with many other political developments during and after the war, the nuclear power project was involved indirectly in the Nuremberg Trials. Along with other former members of the German Foreign Office, Ernst von Weizsäcker, former State Secretary and the father of the physicist Carl-Friedrich, was charged in 1947 with "crimes against humanity." The newspaper accounts of Weizsäcker's trial disturbed Heisenberg, a close friend of the Weizsäcker family, and for this reason in November 1947 Heisenberg set down his thoughts in a memo entitled "The Active and Passive Opposition in the Third Reich." This essay – apparently never published or circulated – will be examined in detail, since it offers a unique opportunity to get inside Heisenberg's mind.[64]

If the vast majority of Germans had turned away from and refused any collaboration with National Socialism in 1933, Heisenberg noted, then a great deal of misfortune would have been avoided. But this reaction did not occur. Rather, the National Socialist system had understood how to win the support of the uncritical masses. Once the National Socialists had gained control of the government, the relatively thin layer of people whose "certain instinct" told them that the new system was bad from the ground up, now only had the opportunity of "passive" or "active" opposition.[65]

Heisenberg noted that, on one hand, these people could have said that the "Hitler-System" was basically bad and would lead to a catastrophe for Germany and Europe, but there was nothing that could be done. Therefore, an individual could emigrate, or in any case deny any responsibility and wait until the system was overcome from the outside, despite the sacrifice in goods and blood connected with the war. Heisenberg designated this behavior as "passive" opposition. Another group, Heisenberg went on, judged the situation as follows: a war, even if it serves to overthrow National Socialism, is such a horrible catastrophe, and would cost so many millions of people their lives, that everything must be done to hinder this catastrophe, or, if it has started, to reduce and cut it short in order to help those who were suffering. Many people who thought so, but did not comprehend the stability of a modern dictatorship, tried the path of open, immediate resistance during the first years and ended up in a concentration camp.[66]

For others, Heisenberg argued, individuals who recognized the hopelessness of a direct attack on the dictatorship, the only path remaining was the acquisition or preservation of a certain amount of influence, conduct which Heisenberg recognized must have appeared to be collaboration. Heisenberg now claimed that such conduct had been the only way to bring about change and described this behavior, which alone offered the chance of replacing National Socialism with something better without "great sacrifice," as "active" opposition. Viewed from the outside, Heisenberg noted, this stance was much more difficult than the former, because a member of the "active" opposition repeatedly had to make concessions at "unimportant places" in order to be able to influence important matters.[67]

For Heisenberg, Ernst von Weizsäcker was one of those Germans who had chosen "active" opposition and attempted – and failed – to influence National Socialist foreign policy and to avoid war. In order to make the difficulty inherent in "active" opposition appear topical, Heisenberg made an analogy in the spirit of the times by hypothesizing that there might be an "active" opposition in Russia composed of people who officially acted as Communists and who made concessions to the party line, but who Heisenberg believed had the ethical standards of the Christian world in their hearts and secretly made every effort to prevent armed conflict with the West and to facilitate a change in Soviet policies. Should these men also one day be prosecuted as war criminals, Heisenberg asked?[68]

Heisenberg set down these reflections because he believed that the war crimes trials had been diverted from the "moral to the political" plane and this troubled him. Weizsäcker was found guilty of complicity in the deportation of Jews to extermination camps and, as Weizsäcker had been aware, to almost certain death. Weizsäcker's defense, that he stayed in office in order to aid the underground German resistance to Hitler and to be in a position to help negotiate peace, did not convince his judges. They rejected the argument that it was acceptable for someone to consent to, or implement, the commission of murder because by doing so he hopes some day to rid society of the chief murderer. The first was a crime of "imminent actuality" while the second was but a future hope.[69]

Heisenberg's memo is truly a "period piece," a classic example of postwar German apologia, which at the same time convinces the reader that the author was sincere, that Heisenberg had believed what he set down. Two of the points that Heisenberg brought up were exemplary of the apologetic Cold War age: (1) passive collaboration during the Third Reich retrospectively was reinterpreted as "active" opposition, and (2) the Cold War threat of European domination by Soviet Russia was set equal to the threat of National Socialism as perceived retrospectively after the end of the war.

It is all too easy from the perspective of the historian to criticize the actions of Heisenberg and his colleagues during the Third Reich, but in recognition of the often inhuman pressure exerted on Germans during these years, this historian will make no attempt to prescribe what Heisenberg or his colleagues should or should not have done. Nevertheless, Heisenberg's 1947 protrayal is very difficult to reconcile with his actions during the Third Reich. This memo tells us a great deal about how Heisenberg saw things in 1947, in the light of Hiroshima and the Nuremberg Trials, but it is difficult to believe that it tells us much about his thoughts between 1933 and 1945.

In particular, Heisenberg's tacit claim, that he recognized the basically and thoroughly evil character of the National Socialist system from the very beginning and set out to overthrow it or to change it into something better by working from within, is implausible. Indeed the National Socialist system did not exist in its final evil form in 1933 or 1934, but rather itself developed gradually over time in a not entirely planned or foreseen manner. Like most of his contemporaries, Heisenberg was disturbed by some aspects of National Socialism, but others fascinated and heartened him, at least temporarily, while still others were only revealed to him after the utter defeat of his fatherland. This seduction of Heisenberg and many other German scientists is a central aspect of the interaction of science and National Socialism, and must be recognized as such. Heisenberg's definition of "active" opposition describes what usually is called "inner exile". Such a psychological retreat certainly happened during the Third Reich, but itself developed and changed over time. For the German nuclear project, inner exile was very real, but it began in 1942 or 1943, not 1941, and certainly not 1933.

It is important to remember that the face that National Socialism showed to the world, and especially to most Germans, itself changed over time, and was very different from the one both revealed at the end of the war and now remembered. At the start of the Third Reich, the new National Socialist government appealed to many Germans in many different ways, an appeal which often overshadowed the dark side of National Socialism. Here is the problem behind Heisenberg's postwar claim that from the very beginning he had set out to oppose National Socialism. For a danger has to be recognized to be opposed or resisted. The Third Reich can be thought of as a slowly but steadily accelerating train. It is easy to get on or off at the beginning, as the train slowly picks up speed, but, just as one begins to be concerned about the speed or direction, trying to leave the train or to alter its course no longer seems such a good idea. Once the train has reached a certain speed, the danger is clear to all, but any attempt to get off now appears suicidal. All one can do is to hang on and wait for the end. "The Active and Passive Opposition in the Third Reich" should be read as a retrospective autobiographical defense of Heisenberg's harrowing ride through the Third Reich.

The Goudsmit/Heisenberg controversy

In many respects, by the time Samuel Goudsmit had received his discharge from the army, he was an embittered man. The loss of his parents and the horrific legacy of National Socialist Germany were blows that he would feel keenly the rest of his life. Understandably, Goudsmit no longer was objective when it came to Germany, German science, or German scientists. Immediately after the end of the war, he advocated a sink or swim policy for German science. The universities and research institutes should be reopened when the Germans could do so without outside help. Let them publish their research again if they can find the paper and presses themselves, he argued. Goudsmit believed that the common American worship of German science, even after its rapid decline, was detrimental to the progress and development of American research. But Goudsmit eventually came to soften and qualify his stance towards German science as a result of an emotional public and private debate with his colleague and former friend Werner Heisenberg.[70]

During the course of 1946, Goudsmit published three popular articles on physics under National Socialism. These essays had both a pedagogical function and a political aim. The folly of National Socialist science policy was illustrated vividly by the example of the German nuclear power project and used to argue against secrecy in science. Although Goudsmit presented his account as authoritative, he grossly misrepresented the German scientific achievement. His arguments were an often indiscriminate jumble of relevant information, irrelevant material, and unverifiable anecdotes. He showed that he had not yet read carefully through all the captured German reports concerned with nuclear power. Among other erroneous statements, Goudsmit claimed that the Germans conceived of an atomic bomb as a uranium machine gone out of control, and that the Germans did not seriously consider using plutonium for atomic bombs. Moreover, he implied incorrectly that the Germans had not recognized that uranium machines and nuclear explosives were linked inextricably.[71]

Perhaps Goudsmit's most misleading claim was his stress on Heisenberg. The latter was portrayed incorrectly as having dominated and controlled the entire German nuclear power project. Furthermore, according to Goudsmit, Heisenberg and the supposedly docile scientists around him had lacked vision, for none of Heisenberg's associates understood that the realization of nuclear power required more than academic laboratory efforts and entailed involved industrial capacities. But Goudsmit did go out of his way to soften the blow for one of the Germans. He felt certain that Heisenberg would have been one of the leading figures in the Manhattan Project, if he had been working on the Allied side.[72]

Heisenberg and Weizsäcker had tried to publish an account of the German nuclear power research project as soon as the Farm Hall scientists had been returned to Germany, but they were stopped by the British occupation officials. First of all, any such publication had to pass through the hands of censors in London and Washington. Secondly, the British officials thought that any public discussion of the German physicists and the atomic bomb would cause political difficulties in America as well as in Germany. After the publication of Goudsmit's articles, Weizsäcker was convinced that eventually some sort of statement had to be made and that the Germans needed the freedom to say what they wanted.[73]

Heisenberg did not have long to wait. By the end of November 1946, the British authorities had given him permission to publish an article on the German nuclear power project in the journal *Die Naturwissenschaften*. Heisenberg composed a preliminary draft – which fortunately has survived – and sent copies to Walther Bothe, Klaus Clusius, Siegfried Flügge, Walther Gerlach, and Paul Harteck for approval and criticism. Since Otto Hahn and Weizsäcker were in Göttingen, it is safe to assume that they saw this draft as well. Significantly Kurt Diebner, Esau, and Shumann were not consulted by Heisenberg.[74]

Heisenberg's article followed the pattern of the Farm Hall memorandum, but with one important difference. By this time Heisenberg had seen a copy of the Smyth Report and thus knew a considerable amount about the successful American nuclear weapons project. Before the published and draft versions of this article are discussed – the latter is written in a much less guarded form than the former, and consequently is more revealing – the importance of rhetoric must be stressed. This article is full of implications, statements that the author stops short of making explicit, but that he apparently wants his audience to infer. In order to get at the mentality lying behind the words, the form of presentation must be analyzed.[75]

When Heisenberg's article is compared to the history of the German nuclear power project as set out above, several important discrepancies emerge. First of all, the scientists connected to the Army Ordnance and those who held other high positions in the National Socialist science policy bureaucracy – particularly Diebner, Esau, and Schumann – were slighted by Heisenberg. For example, Heisenberg gave Walther Gerlach credit for several of Esau's innovations and accomplishments. With respect to the cube-lattice uranium machine design, clearly still a sensitive matter for

Heisenberg, even Bothe thought that Heisenberg's draft formulation was not entirely fair to Diebner's group. Bothe suggested some changes in the text to rectify this injustice, a suggestion which Heisenberg both accepted and implemented. This unfair treatment of Esau and the leading Army Ordinance scientists foreshadowed their progressive ostracism by large segments of the German physics community and certainly by the circle around Heisenberg. Although personal animosities played a role here, the roots of this "banishment" ran deeper and illustrate an important aspect of the postwar scientific apologia.[76]

These ostracized scientists were in many respects an embarassment to the rest of their colleagues in postwar Germany, for they had held highly visible positions in National Socialist Germany and, in the cases of Esau and Schumann were likely to be labeled "nazis" in the context of denazification. Even after the end of the war and the revelations with respect to the German atrocities, often these physicists admitted their wartime support of National Socialist Germany unrepentantly. In other words, they represented exactly what Heisenberg and others were trying to distance themselves from. Diebner and the rest now were unfairly labeled "incompetent scientists" (*Nichtkönner*), men who had received their positions only through political influence. In fact, Esau had become a full professor during the Weimar Republic, Schumann had managed a *Habilitation* (in acoustics) before the National Socialists gained power, and Diebner was a skilled administrator and a respectable, if not world-class, physicist. Since these scientists were unrepentantly supportive of at least some of the previously held goals of National Socialism, they were now attacked as having been "political" as well. Thus the conventions of the German physics community with respect to acceptable conduct were altered dramatically by the fall of the Third Reich. Support of National Socialism, an action that had been apolitical during the years 1933 to 1945, now was redefined as having been political.[77]

According to the postwar apolitical ideology of the German physics community, the competent apolitical scientists, who were said to have been aloof from, or to have resisted, National Socialism, were representative of German physics. The incompetent political scientists – if they even deserved the latter title – were classified as aberrations. The final step of this apologia should be clear. Competence was tied exclusively to apolitical behavior, and *vice versa*. Thus the physics community no longer had to explain why German physicists had supported National Socialism. All those perceived as having given such support were dismissed retroactively as incompetents. The affected physicists certainly felt mishandled, if not betrayed. Schumann wrote a book on the nuclear power project in response to Heisenberg's claims, but publication was blocked by the British occupation authorities. "Their" side only came out with the publication of a book by Diebner in 1957.[78]

The second discrepancy that stands out in the draft article, and one that no doubt surprised Bothe, was Heisenberg's assertion that Bothe's 1941 measurement of the diffusion length of neutrons in carbon had been a mistake that had hindered the further progress of the entire nuclear power project. Bothe protested, and Heisenberg again accepted the former's rewording. However, this theme, "if only we had tried graphite..." continued to circulate among Heisenberg's circle and beyond. Eventually Bothe became a scapegoat, the scientist who had made "the mistake" that had kept the Germans from achieving a chain reaction.[79]

As shown above, this insinuation was false. The reasonable and justifiable decision for heavy water and against carbon as a moderator was made on economic grounds by those responsible, the Army Ordnance, in full knowledge of the potential of carbon as a moderator. Why did Heisenberg now make this claim, in particular when carbon had not been mentioned in any way in the Farm Hall memorandum? By this time he had studied the Smyth Report and had noted that, in contrast to the Germans, the Americans had used graphite for the nuclear piles. As another part of the postwar apologia, the facts that the Americans had used graphite and succeeded, whereas the Germans had not and did not, were used to reach the dubious conclusion that the Germans would have succeeded, or certainly would have gone much farther, if only Bothe had not made his "error" and they had chosen graphite as their moderator. Heisenberg was not alone in making this judgment. Harteck also blamed Bothe's error for holding back the research.[80]

The third discrepancy concerned Weizsäcker's theoretical discovery of the explosive properties of plutonium, and here the form of Heisenberg's presentation is important. Taking the draft article first, Heisenberg mentions Weizsäcker's discovery that an operating uranium machine produces uranium 239, whose transuranic daughter products will have the same properties as uranium 235. Heisenberg thus wrote in the draft that an energy-producing uranium burner could be used to produce nuclear explosives. Heisenberg finished the paragraph by noting that the Americans had applied this process on a large scale in order to produce plutonium for atomic bombs. Apparently one of Heisenberg's colleagues thought that this passage was too explicit, for the published version was much more circumspect. Instead of stating flatly that nuclear explosives can be produced by an operating uranium machine, the sentence now allowed that Weizsäcker's work made it more probable that an energy-producing uranium machine could manufacture nuclear explosives, but immediately added that the "practical execution" of this process had not been discussed at that time. The form of the final version could imply that this lack of discussion was intentional.[81]

Almost halfway through the article, Heisenberg brought up the fourth important discrepancy: his description of the German decision that nuclear weapons could not influence the further course of the war. Here Heisenberg misrepresented grossly one important aspect of this question by attributing falsely the decision – not to shift the nuclear power research up to the industrial level of production – to the meeting of a small group of Kaiser Wilhelm Society scientists with Minister of Armaments Albert Speer in June of 1942. The role of Army Ordnance in this decision was slighted. Heisenberg's account laconically mentioned that, before the meeting with Speer, the project had been transferred from Army Ordnance to the Reich Research Council.[82]

This decision was made by Army Ordnance alone, more than half a year before the meeting with Speer, but that may explain Heisenberg's stress on the meeting with the Minister of Armaments. Yet another aspect of the postwar German nuclear power apologia was the "control" of research, in particular, the claim that the academic scientists – especially the circle around Heisenberg – exercised considerable if not complete control over the course of the nuclear power project. Given this argument, it is understandable that Heisenberg should have attributed the decision to the meeting with Speer, at which Heisenberg personally played a considerable role, and not to the Army Ordnance, whose scientists and science policy makers were discredited in the postwar era. In fact, the nuclear power research program was controlled by Army Ordnance and the Reich Research Council, for although Speer provided important support to this research project, he was not in control. It was Kurt Diebner, Abraham Esau, Walther Gerlach, and Erich Schumann who exercised the greatest influence. For example, throughout the war Diebner had far more control over nuclear fission research than did Bothe, Clusius, Hahn, Harteck, or Heisenberg.

To be fair to Heisenberg, most of his article presented an accurate account of nuclear power research under National Socialism. In the second-to-last paragraph of the published version, he presented an excellent summary of why the Germans had not attempted the production of nuclear weapons on an industrial scale, for it appeared that the project could not have succeeded before the war was over. After 1942, the steadily deteriorating state of the war hampered any further progress. Even as late as 1942, Heisenberg noted, the German leadership still anticipated an early end to the war and was uninterested in weapons which could not be used in the immediate future. As with a similar passage in the Farm Hall memorandum, this summary would have provided an accurate account of the German nuclear power project if Heisenberg had ended there. Once again, he did not.[83]

Both versions ended by implying that the German scientists – especially the circle around Heisenberg – had held themselves back from producing nuclear weapons for the National Socialist German state because of moral scruples. Indeed this passive resistance was supposed to have stopped the German production of such weapons. In the published article, Heisenberg wrote that the German physicists had striven from the very beginning to keep control of the project in their hands, and they used the influence which they had as experts to steer the research away from the manufacture of nuclear weapons. "External circumstances," and here he probably was referring to the course of the war, took the difficult decision, whether the German scientists should manufacture nuclear weapons, out of their hands. The preliminary draft included a much more explicit passage. Here Heisenberg wrote that for the researchers involved with nuclear power, the decision not to attempt the industrial production of nuclear weapons also had another, "human side." According to Heisenberg, these physicists had been aware of the great responsibility carried by a person who could release such natural forces, and from the very beginning they had "knowingly," and with "great effort," striven to keep control of the project in their own hands. From the beginning, they had had to consider whether the cause for which these great natural forces should be wielded was just.[84]

Of course it is possible that no single one of the German scientists who worked on nuclear power, including Heisenberg, either intended, or desired, that German nuclear weapons be created and used. In fact, the members and administrators of the German nuclear power project did not attempt to implement the industrial scale production of nuclear weapons during World War II, but according to the historical evidence, their motivations were economic, scientific, and technical, not moral. Heisenberg's claim, that these German scientists willfully hindered the creation of nuclear weapons for Hitler's government, is implausible. Why should they have feared what they knew could not be done before the end of the war?

Heisenberg's article should be taken for what it was, an honest, sincere account of his retrospective misgivings that he felt after the war, after the attack on Hiroshima, and after the revelations of the Nuremberg Trials about having worked on applied nuclear fission under the National Socialist German government. However, this article presented an inaccurate account of the actions of these German scientists during the war and represented another stage in the Myth of the German Atomic Bomb. In order to reconcile their wartime research with the realities of postwar Germany and the legacy of the National Socialist revolution, five historically false arguments were proposed and propagated by some or all members of the German physics community:

1 Bothe's "error" held back the nuclear power project.

2 The "peaceful" uranium machine was and is separable from the nuclear explosives it produces, and after 1942 the German scientists worked only on the "peaceful" uranium machine.

3 During the Third Reich all "good" "competent" scientists were "apolitical," while conversely all "political" scientists were neither good nor competent.

4 The influence of National Socialism in the German physics community and *vice versa* was equivalent to the *deutsche Physik* movement.

5 A group of academic scientists, especially the small circle around Heisenberg, controlled nuclear power research and steered the project away from nuclear weapons production because of their moral scruples when faced with the prospect of providing such weapons to the "nazis."[85]

Although he was not the only member of the German nuclear power project who could have taken his case to the public, Heisenberg was the only one to do so. Thus our historical perspective is biased. Did his colleagues agree with his retrospective postwar apologia? Fortunately the *FIAT Review of German Science* makes such a comparison possible. This series of volumes was sponsored by the American, British, and French occupation authorities in order to present a "complete and concise account" of the research carried out by German scientists during the war and included 2 volumes and over 400 pages on "Nuclear Physics and Cosmic Rays." Whereas Heisenberg had taken his case to the public and had written for a general audience, the FIAT volumes were written by scientists for scientists. With the significant exception of the members of the Gottow research group, almost every scientist involved with nuclear power research contributed to a FIAT volume.[86]

What about the two "Nuclear Physics and Cosmic Rays" volumes? Do they present a more accurate picture of the German nuclear power project than Heisenberg's article? The answer is no, and here what was important was not what was written, but rather what was left out. As Paul Harteck claimed, for example, in his section on the separation of isotopes, the goal of the German scientists was to set in motion a "so-called uranium machine" for the production of energy. According to Harteck, the task was either to create a sufficient amount of heavy water, or to enrich uranium 235 far enough so that natural water or graphite could be used as moderator, so that a chain reaction could be ignited in a uranium machine. Again, there was something missing here, the potential production of nuclear explosives, either by means of isotope separation – pure uranium 235 – or of the transuranics that are created in a uranium machine. Between Wilhelm Walcher and Harteck, all the isotope separation methods which had been investigated in Germany were discussed in the FIAT volumes, but each method was presented as either being concerned with isotope separation in general, or, if uranium isotope separation was mentioned, the sole goal of this process was portrayed as building a "peaceful" machine out of enriched uranium and ordinary water. There was no mention of the very military applications that Harteck and Groth had brought to the attention of the army authorities in the spring of 1939 and that had instigated the research into the separation of uranium isotopes.[87]

Any mention of the military applications of transuranic elements, which had been reported to the Army Ordnance in 1940, was avoided. Kurt Starke mentioned that he had enriched uranium 239 and subsequently discovered neptunium, but did not discuss the applications or explosive properties of this new element. Flügge wrote on the spontaneous fission of transuranics and with Kurt Sauerwein on resonance absorption in general, but the military consequences of these processes were not discussed. Fritz Houtermans surveyed experimental methods for measuring neutrons, and Weizsäcker did not even contribute to this volume, writing on astrophysics instead. Heisenberg and Wirtz confined themselves to a survey of the German uranium machine experiments. In the end, no one made any mention of the nuclear explosives which isotope separation or operating uranium machines produce.[88]

The FIAT "Nuclear Physics and Cosmic Rays" volumes were apolitical apologia written for scientists by scientists. Although they indicated rightly how much quality basic physics research was carried out during the war, they presented a false picture of German nuclear power. The German nuclear power project was applied science, was a goal-oriented research program, was sponsored by military as well as civilian authorities, and was directed at the military and economic applications of nuclear fission. But the FIAT authors and editors abstracted this research program away from the historical context, away from the military origins and goals of the research, and portrayed it as academic basic research. There are certainly good reasons for this misrepresentation. It hardly would have helped their already miserable living and working conditions after the war if these German scientists had bragged about their work on nuclear explosives under National Socialism. Nevertheless, neither the *Die Naturwissenschaften* article nor the FIAT reports accurately described the German nuclear power project. Heisenberg was one apologist among many.

Samuel Goudsmit was angered after reading a translation of Heisenberg's article in the British journal *Nature* and reviewed it in the *Bulletin of the Atomic Scientists*. According to Goudsmit, Heisenberg's account had all the earmarks of being meant for consumption and appeasement in Germany. In Goudsmit's opinon, Heisenberg had not owned up to the failures of the German nuclear power project, indeed the latter had told a "tale of success." The fact that Heisenberg had refrained from criticising National Socialism explicitly in his article also disturbed Goudsmit. But what really enraged Goudsmit was Heisenberg's apologia, for the latter's statements might make the casual reader believe that the German scientists had made a "deliberate decision" to refrain from making nuclear weapons, whereas Goudsmit argued that the Germans themselves had thought that they were progressing satisfactorily in that direction. Although not mentioned in his review, Goudsmit had a similar opinion of the FIAT reports, commenting that they had been edited so as to show only the "most favorable" aspects of the scientific research.[89]

Heisenberg's article was probably one reason why Goudsmit decided to take his case to a broader audience and wrote the popular book *Alsos* in 1947. In order that *Alsos* not go unnoticed, it was previewed in *Life* magazine on 20 October 1947. *Alsos* posed and answered a question of keen interest to Goudsmit. Why did German science fail where the Americans and British succeeded? His answer was that science under fascism was not, and probably could never be, the equal of science in a democracy. In Goudsmit's opinion, the "totalitarian climate" of National Socialist Germany led to complacency, politics in science, and hero worship, all of which adversely affected the German nuclear power project.[90]

Goudsmit's account of the Alsos Mission and the German nuclear power research program was basically the same as that set out in his earlier articles. Heisenberg was portrayed as a tragic figure, an extreme nationalist led astray by the nazis and made to appear foolish by the revelations of Hiroshima. But Goudsmit was concerned with issues larger than the German nuclear power project. All of science was to be covered by his argument that governmental control ruins research, as chapter 11, "The misorganization of German science," showed.[91]

Using Gestapo records which he himself considered suspect, Goudsmit dismissed Schumann, Mentzel, and other National Socialist science policy administrators unfairly as incompetent nazis and drew an arbitrary line of demarcation between the "good" – in the professional and moral senses – and the "nazi" scientists. Thus Goudsmit did exactly what Heisenberg had done, although for completely different reasons. In fact, without the skill, influence, and backing of these scientists the German nuclear power project could not have gone as far as it did. Almost all of the project scientists and administrators had connections to the National Socialist movement and there certainly was no inverse relation between the strength of an individual's commitment to National Socialism and his scientific abilities or performance.[92]

Science policy under National Socialism certainly had irrational aspects, and totalitarianism or fascism is not to be advocated as a congenial environment for science and technology, but the fact remains that at times National Socialist science policy worked very well. In particular, and in contradiction to Goudsmit's claims, the science policy makers, administrators, sponsors, and researchers connected with the German nuclear power project acted in a careful, justifiable, and reasonable manner. National Socialist science policy was able to work because the majority of German engineers and scientists willingly or unwillingly rallied to, or passively supported, the National Socialist revolution and later the war.[93]

But Goudsmit was more concerned with postwar American science than reliving the war and National Socialism. His concluding chapter, entitled "It can't happen here," sharply criticised what he saw as American complacency and attacked those who wanted to continue wartime restrictions on science. Goudsmit then went on to use the example of Heisenberg to make – as far as Goudsmit was concerned – his most important point, in all probability the main reason for the publication of *Alsos* and his previous articles. Isolation, secrecy, and governmental control ruin science. In other words, science should be apolitical.[94]

Cooperation is necessary for progress, Goudsmit argued. Whereas a small isolated group would probably be dominated by one man – and Heisenberg was his model – if the group was larger, then it would enjoy increased creativity and effectiveness. Goudsmit's conclusion clearly was meant to play a role in the postwar debate on the future of American nuclear power, and, in particular, whether there should be civilian or military control. Wartime restrictions on the exchange of scientific information should not be continued in peacetime. Goudsmit closed with a call for international scientific cooperation and reiterated his slogan. "Too much secrecy stifles the progress of science."[95]

Alsos touched off an emotional debate in the 1947 *Bulletin of the Atomic Scientists*. The wounds caused by National Socialism and the war were still open. Philip Morrison, a scientist who had also been involved with scientific intelligence, reviewed Goudsmit's book and attacked Heisenberg's suggestion that the Germans had not wanted to create nuclear weapons. No different from their counterparts in America and Britain, Morrison stated, the German scientists had worked for the military as best their circumstances allowed. But the difference, which Morrison found unforgivable, was that they worked for the "cause of Himmler and Auschwitz," for the burners of books and the takers of hostages. Morrison's review illustrates one reason for the strong anti-German sentiment that was found in the American scientific community after the war: the guilt associated with Hiroshima and the unleashing of nuclear fear that many American, British, and *émigré* scientists felt keenly. With justification, Morrison and others in America believed that the Germans were implying that they had been morally superior. Heisenberg and others in Germany emphasized ritually in the press and elsewhere that the Allies had built and used nuclear weapons while the Germans had not, hinting moreover that their lack of greater progress was the result of moral scruples, that they had "dragged their feet."[96]

Morrison's attack provoked a response from Laue, perhaps the only

German physicist who still could have commanded respect in America. Goudsmit had gone out of his way to paint Laue as one of the few who had remained untainted by National Socialism, and although this claim is debatable – Heisenberg and Weizsäcker arguably were no more tainted than their Berlin colleague – Laue nevertheless was perceived by American scientists as being one of the few Germans whose voice deserved to be heard. Laue's reply was published in German for home consumption as well as appearing in the April 1948 *Bulletin*. A German reader would have seen only Laue's forceful reply. Except for what Laue quoted in his article, neither Goudsmit's nor Morrison's criticism was translated.[97]

Laue's reply is disturbing when seen in its historical context, for his article both evokes sympathy by bringing up valid points about the difficult nature of science, or indeed life, under National Socialism, and provokes criticism by its apologia and – conscious or unconscious – distortion of key information. Noting that he had not read *Alsos*, Laue attacked Morrison for the "monstrous suggestion" that German scientists as a body had worked for Himmler and Auschwitz. Laue recognized that Goudsmit had lost many of his closest relatives in Auschwitz and other concentration camps and what unutterable pain the mere word Auschwitz must evoke in the Jewish physicist. But Laue then went on to draw the conclusion that therefore neither Goudsmit, nor his reviewer Morrison, was capable of an unbiased judgment.[98]

According to Laue, even since civilized states had relapsed into barbaric "total war," it had been difficult for an isolated citizen to withdraw himself from war service. In fact it was "relatively unimportant" whether a citizen put his heart into such service or not, or even whether he wanted to depose the government. Just because a few German scientists had managed to avoid being drawn into the maelstrom, Laue argued, did not mean that all could have. Laue claimed that whereas open refusal would have led to catastrophic consequences, often a fictitious compliance allowed German physicists to shield younger researchers from the war. Sometimes, Laue continued, "political suspects" were protected from concentration camps by assigning them work labeled "of military importance." Laue then ironically asked whether these scientists should be labeled "armorers of Himmler and Auschwitz?" He also pointed to the FIAT reports for the true story of what German scientists had done during the war. Finally Laue stated that articles such as Morrison's review kept "alive hate."[99]

Regretting that he had to take issue with Laue's "moving statement," Morrison pointed out correctly that Laue had distorted his book review. The American had written that German scientists had worked, not for Himmler, but for Himmler's cause, the victory of National Socialist Germany. This objection illustrates one of the many instances in the postwar period where the two sides talked past each other, unable or unwilling to agree on terms. For Morrison, Goudsmit, and many people who had been in, or had fled from countries dominated by or opposed to National Socialist Germany, working for a German victory in World War II was equivalent to working for the cause of Himmler and Auschwitz, especially in light of the revelations of the Nuremburg Trials. On the German side, during the Third Reich few Germans distinguished clearly between the known goals of the National Socialist government and those of Germany or the German people. But once the legacy of National Socialism was revealed and undeniable, many Germans – such as Laue and Heisenberg – advanced a retrospective argument that implied that efforts toward a German victory and for the good of the German people had been completely separable from allegiance towards or service rendered for National Socialism. This apologia is understandable, but historically inaccurate.[100]

In the same issue as the Morrison–Laue debate, Goudsmit contributed an essay which showed that he had changed his mind. Entitled "Our task in Germany," Goudsmit's article once again called for international scientific cooperation, but this time he re-extended his hand to Germans as well. Goudsmit believed that American scientists must morally support those German colleagues who were worthy of confidence, and added that there were many of them. Americans did not have to agree with all of their opinions but should make allowances for the disturbing circumstances under which these Germans have lived and are still living. Americans had to communicate with them as they had in the days before Hitler. It was as if Goudsmit had been converted by the disturbing forces that he had helped to unleash. However, the book *Alsos* reinforced germanophobia among American scientists and concentrated this prejudice towards those Germans whom Goudsmit had singled out as scapegoats, including Heisenberg and Weizsäcker.[101]

The publication of *Alsos* touched off a fascinating correspondence between Goudsmit and Heisenberg. This exchange brought out two important aspects of the postwar psychology: exorcizing or burying the past in order to be able to move on. Without having read *Alsos*, indeed there is no record that he *ever* did, Heisenberg wrote Goudsmit in the fall of 1947 and enclosed a copy of his article in *Die Naturwissenschaften*. Using polite language, Heisenberg remarked that he had seen several of Goudsmit's articles and had got the impression that Goudsmit was unaware both of the details of the German nuclear power research effort and the psychological situation in Germany during the war.[102]

Subtly reminding Goudsmit that at the end of the war he had told Heisenberg that the Americans had not worked on nuclear weapons, Heisenberg went on to describe the wartime situation in Germany in a manner difficult to reconcile with his conduct as a member of the nuclear power project and ambassador for German science during the war. On one hand, he wrote, it was clear to them what "heinous consequences" a victory of National Socialism in Europe would have, but on the other hand, in view of the hate with which National Socialism had saturated Europe, they could hardly look forward to the utter defeat of Germany. Such a situation, Heisenberg argued, led to a more "passive and humble" manner.[103]

Goudsmit finally replied to Heisenberg on 1 December 1947 by criticizing Heisenberg's justification of a more passive and humble manner. The American had been deeply disappointed to learn of Heisenberg's attempts at a compromise with the National Socialists. What surprised him most was that Heisenberg did not see that such a compromise was impossible. The attempts to convince the National Socialists of the soundness of relativity and quantum theory seemed so out of place. How, Goudsmit asked, could he have hoped to be successful, or thought that these were important issues? In Goudsmit's opinion, not under Hitler, but in the present was the right time for the "more humble manner" mentioned in Heisenberg's letter. Finally, Goudsmit sent his regards to those colleagues whom he last met under such "unusually dramatic" circumstances.[104]

Heisenberg replied in early 1948, and this time his tone was colder and less polite. First of all, he made it clear that he now considered the question, whether the Germans had known how an atomic bomb would have operated, to be most important. Heisenberg then went on correctly to refute Goudsmit's claims on this score by showing that the Germans had understood both fast-neutron chain reactions and the potential of plutonium. Letting a little sarcasm leak into his tone, Heisenberg remarked that obviously Goudsmit had accidently overlooked the reports which would give the correct picture. Only after they had agreed on the "facts" of the German scientific achievement would Heisenberg be willing to discuss the political motives behind the work.[105]

However, Heisenberg nevertheless wanted to comment on a few points raised by Goudsmit's letters. First of all, he pointed out that he had always believed that German science had suffered under National Socialism, especially because of the expulsion of many capable scholars from Germany and nonsensical theories such as *deutsche Physik*. Moreover, Heisenberg had made such comments public at a time when such action had been dangerous. Also, it never would have occurred to Heisenberg to think that the German physicists were any different from their Allied counterparts. But how could Goudsmit continue to overlook the fact that the German physicists also found themselves in a different psychological situation than did their colleagues in England and America?[106]

Heisenberg also commented on what Goudsmit had described as compromise with National Socialism by denying that he had been so naive as to believe that there was much chance of winning over Himmler, and bluntly stated that he would have "criminally" neglected his duty if he had not at least in his small circle tried to shatter the "delusion" of the dictatorship. In particular, Heisenberg had never had the slightest sympathy for the people who withdrew from all responsibility – by his standards, neither "passive," nor "active" opposition – but then in a safe dinner conversation would tell someone that Germany and Europe would be ruined, just wait and see.[107]

At the end of his letter, Heisenberg turned to the present situation in Germany and his views on dealing with the past. It was difficult to win the hearts and minds of people through the force of arms, especially because of the "indescribable misery" in Germany. What Germans needed was no hateful settling of accounts with the past, but instead a quiet reconstruction of a life worthy of a human being. In any case, Heisenberg assured Goudsmit that he could be certain that the German physicists would gladly participate in any effort that would contribute to a "better world understanding."[108]

At this point the Dutch mathematician Bartel L. van der Waerden, a friend and former colleague of Heisenberg, former countryman of Goudsmit, and a very perceptive observer, briefly entered the debate. Van der Waerden had spent the war at the University of Leipzig and came to the United States in 1947 to take a visiting position at The Johns Hopkins University. In March of 1948, van der Waerden got his hands on *Alsos*, read it with great interest, and subsequently wrote to both Goudsmit and Heisenberg. As van der Waerden told Goudsmit, there was one point in *Alsos* which he did not understand. Did he mean, van der Waerden asked, that these people, knowing who Hitler was, had planned "the horrible crime" of putting an atomic bomb into his hands? Goudsmit replied that such an act would not have been a crime, rather it was something that could not be stopped.[109]

According to Goudsmit, the Germans thought that making an atomic bomb was much more difficult than it actually was, and thus the question of conscience was not so urgent for them. This argument pervaded all of Goudsmit's publications on the German nuclear power project and was an attempt to reconcile the evidence that he had gathered with his profoundly ahistorical and non-contextual preconceptions of how science and technology work. In his view, since the Americans had succeeded in building an atomic bomb, the Germans should somehow have known that it was feasible. Since the German scientists and authorities had decided that this task was not feasible, Goudsmit concluded that this decision must have been a mistake, and searched until he "found" the German error: the concept of a nuclear pile as a bomb. Goudsmit was right to believe that the question of conscience had not been important for the Germans – certainly not as urgent as they claimed after Hiroshima – but he embraced a false cause. For the rest of his life, Goudsmit was unwilling to accept the claim that conscience had played a role in the German "non-development" of nuclear weapons. Thus he also refused to abandon his cause – that the Germans had made a gross scientific or technological mistake – no matter what evidence was presented to refute this claim.[110]

Van der Waerden wrote to Heisenberg immediately after his conversation with Goudsmit, who, unlike some scientists in the United States, did not hold Heisenberg and his colleagues responsible as acessories to the "heinous events" of the National Socialist period. Goudsmit impressed van der Waerden most as being concerned about the future and the reestablishment of international scientific ties. Van der Waerden noted that documents in Goudsmit's office verified Heisenberg's claims about what the Germans had known about plutonium and nuclear weapons, but added that in his opinion, questions such as the "complacency" of the German physicists or what Heisenberg and other scientists had understood or overlooked were insignificant. The two Dutch-born scientists had also discussed the "question of guilt." In the end they still disagreed over the psychological question, what Heisenberg's group would have done if they had made greater progress, but agreed that someone should not be condemned for what he might have done if the situation had been different. Goudsmit had thought this matter over and had had to admit that van der Waerden was right.[111]

Although van der Waerden was defending Heisenberg, he was also critical of his friend and former colleague. In a second letter, sent the very next day, van der Waerden asked Heisenberg for more information. Had Heisenberg considered the question of responsibility when he informed the higher authorities about the potential of nuclear explosives? Had that all been mere deception in order to get money for physics? As Heisenberg's "lawyer," he had enough evidence to defend him, but as Heisenberg's friend he also wanted so badly to believe that under any circumstances Heisenberg's decency would have been stronger than the combination of his nationalism and ambition. In the eyes of Heisenberg's foreign colleagues, one of the most damning accusations in *Alsos* was a remark that Heisenberg reportedly made during a 1944 lecture in Switzerland. According to Goudsmit, near the end of the war Heisenberg visited Switzerland and expressed regret that Germany would not win the war. Heisenberg now disputed this statement, although it would fit into the context of his other lecture tours during the war. Goudsmit was convinced that Heisenberg probably had made the statement, but perhaps had not given it the same meaning at that time as it now had in the postwar world.[112]

Van der Waerden made one last attempt to reconcile the two before he returned to Holland. Naturally Heisenberg was right, van der Waerden agreed, that the former's efforts in the *deutsche Physik* controversy represented a significant success. But on the other hand, van der Waerden could understand the negative reaction of Goudsmit and others towards those same efforts. This negative reaction was admittedly illogical. However, emotionally it was also comprehensible. Did Heisenberg remember what van der Waerden had said after seeing the 1937 article in *Das Schwarze Korps*? He had told Heisenberg that he could be proud of the title "white Jew," but instead, Heisenberg was annoyed. Heisenberg's lawyer agreed that it had been in the best interests of German physics that his client had handled matters as he did. But on the other hand, van der Waerden asked, could Heisenberg associate with such people, and exert influence over them, without compromising himself? Van der Waerden believed that he could, but could also understand if others did not.[113]

Only one of Heisenberg's replies to van der Waerden is available. In a letter written on 28 April 1948, Heisenberg again addressed the moral question. When he knew near the end of 1941 that the uranium machine would go and that nuclear weapons probably could be built, Heisenberg explained, he had been "shocked" by the thought of such weapons in the hands of some ruler, and not only Hitler. In any case, Heisenberg flatly stated that he would have considered it a crime to make atomic bombs for Hitler. But he also considered it unfortunate that these weapons were given to other rulers and were used by them. During the past few years, Heisenberg had learned something which his friends in the West did not want to understand: during such times, hardly anyone can avoid committing crimes or supporting them by doing nothing. Heisenberg, in an attempt to avoid any misunderstanding, hastened to assure van der Waerden that he did not mean that he had been prepared to commit any sort of crime "for Hitler." Van der Waerden's peace mission failed to reconcile the two sides.[114]

Beginning no later than the news of Hiroshima, Heisenberg's way of dealing with the past entailed a gradual retrospective reinterpretation of the German work on the uranium problem in the postwar light of the National Socialist legacy. Moreover, this apologia changed and adapted itself over time to the social, scientific, and political currents of the post World War II period. This retrospection reached a point with Heisenberg's letter to van der Waerden such that it cannot be reconciled with the historical evidence. Heisenberg's postwar claim, that early on he was shocked by the prospect of helping to produce nuclear weapons for the German war effort – in his words, making atomic bombs for Hitler – is difficult to believe. There is every reason to assume that his statement to van der Waerden was sincere, that by 1948 he had convinced himself that he had felt such emotions and that he had reacted in such a way, but the historical evidence of what he did during the Third Reich and especially during the war – his 1942 lecture before the Reich Research Council, his foreign lecture tours in 1943 and 1944, and so on – belie Heisenberg's claim. He was not that great a hypocrite.

Goudsmit wrote to Heisenberg in late September of 1948 and admitted that he had been wrong about certain details, but now grasped mistakenly at another perceived German deficiency by claiming that the Germans had not understood that the atomic bomb used a fast-neutron chain reaction. However, Goudsmit's main aim in this letter was again to stress how science had suffered under National Socialism and how political interference ruins science. As Goudsmit himself realized, the contents of this letter differed little from the previous one he had sent to Heisenberg.[115]

After spending several letters discussing the moral aspect of the German nuclear power project, only to have Goudsmit stubbornly continue to make false statements about the German scientific achievement, Heisenberg now dealt almost exclusively with the question of scientific competence. The German physicist noted Goudsmit's grudging partial admission of error with pleasure. Now that Goudsmit had agreed that the Germans had known about plutonium, Heisenberg wanted him to make this admission public, indeed in the *Bulletin of the Atomic Scientists*. But Heisenberg did more than gloat over Goudsmit's discomfiture. Naturally he agreed that a totalitarian system greatly damages science, but in *Alsos* this conclusion was based on false arguments, which Heisenberg found very unfortunate. Goudsmit found Heisenberg's answer "impertinent" in turn and could not understand why the recognition of the value of Heisenberg's scientific work meant so much to his German colleague. Heisenberg may well have been asking himself why Goudsmit could not recognize the admittedly modest German achievement.[116]

Before Goudsmit could write to his German colleague or publish anything in the *Bulletin*, Heisenberg took his case directly to the American people by means of an interview published in the *New York Times*. Heisenberg devoted most of this article to refuting Goudsmit's claims about the German scientific achievement, but he also addressed the moral question carefully: because of their sense of decency, most of the leading German scientists disliked the totalitarian system. Yet as patriots who loved their country, when called upon to work for the government, they could not refuse. Goudsmit responded in print by admitting that his portrayal in *Alsos* was an oversimplification, but insisted stubbornly that the Germans had had only a very vague notion of how an atomic bomb worked. Just as Heisenberg's interview had done, in general Goudsmit rehashed the same arguments that he had put forward throughout the debate. Heisenberg replied in turn by stressing that Goudsmit had now withdrawn some of the statements he had made in *Alsos*.[117]

On 11 February 1949 Goudsmit wrote to Heisenberg again, advanced the same arguments, and in an exasperated tone asked whether any further correspondence made any sense. Heisenberg responded with his most curt letter yet, stating bluntly that he would have preferred no public discussion of the German nuclear power research, that through his articles and book Goudsmit repeatedly had spread false information about the German work, that it was time that a correct description of the German research was presented in the newspapers for a change, and that he was disappointed that Goudsmit did not recognize Heisenberg's right to take his case to the public as Goudsmit had done so often. It is clear that in the end Goudsmit's unfair criticism of Heisenberg's scientific abilities and achievement exasperated and embittered the German physicist. The damage done to his reputation as a physicist may have come to bother him more than the criticism he received for serving the National Socialists. Heisenberg's reaction to Goudsmit's attacks on his scientific name is reminiscent of the former's embitterment over the attacks on his honor by Johannes Stark during the Third Reich.[118]

Both men had come very close to losing their tempers and realized that it was pointless to continue. Goudsmit wrote one last letter, repeated his litany of arguments, told Heisenberg that he would not bring up the matter again, and expressed the hope that they could continue to correspond about physics. Heisenberg replied immediately, and thanked him for his letter, which this time Heisenberg had been very happy to receive. Goudsmit could be certain, Heisenberg promised, that he would not stir up the controversies of the past few years again, and especially not in public. Exactly like Goudsmit, Heisenberg believed that it was more interesting to discuss physics than the unpleasant past. Both men worked very hard the rest of their lives to restore international cooperation in science. Despite the loss of his parents, Goudsmit went out of his way to assist German scientists. In 1950 Heisenberg visited Goudsmit at Brookhaven Laboratory in Long Island, New York, but they only discussed physics.[119]

7 ✧ The myth of the German atomic bomb

myth ... a story that is usually of unknown origin and at least partially traditional, that ostensibly relates historical events usually of such character as to serve to explain some practice, belief, institution, or natural phenomenon ... a story invented as a veiled explanation of a truth ... a person or thing existing only in imagination or whose actuality is not verifiable ... a belief given uncritical acceptance by the members of a group especially in support of existing or traditional practices and institutions ... a belief or concept that embodies a visionary ideal ...

"Myth," from *Webster's Third New International Dictionary*[1]

The "Myth of the German Atomic Bomb" means different things to different people. A German version of this fable emphasizes that (1) the scientists involved with nuclear power in Germany did not make atomic bombs during World War II, affirms that (2) these scientists had not wanted to create nuclear weapons, asserts that (3) they were good enough to have done the job, but their efforts were hindered by forces beyond their control, and finally avows that (4) even if they had been able to create nuclear explosives and had tried to produce such weapons, they would have denied atomic bombs to the Nazis. A second version, favored outside Germany, recognizes that (1) the Germans did not create nuclear weapons, but affirms that (2) these German scientists had wanted to unleash and wield nuclear power, asserts that (3) the German scientists must have been incompetent, for if they could have made atomic bombs, then they would have, and avows that (4) if such weapons had been created, then atomic bombs would have been placed at the disposal of the National Socialist government in order that Germany win the war. Thus the Myth of the German Atomic Bomb can be summed up in a single question: would German scientists have made atomic bombs for Adolf Hitler?[2]

But such "what if" questions have no definite answer, and perhaps exactly for this reason extraordinary and implausible significance has been attributed to a single symbol of the Myth of the German Atomic Bomb: Werner Heisenberg's mythical conversation with his Danish colleague, friend, and mentor Niels Bohr in occupied Copenhagen during the fall of

222

1941. After the war, Heisenberg lent his considerable authority to the journalist Robert Jungk's thesis that while in Copenhagen the German physicist had tried to enlist Bohr in a plan to forestall the creation of all nuclear weapons. But this same meeting was interpreted after the war by some members of the circle around Bohr in quite a different way: Heisenberg had been a spy for the National Socialist government.[3]

Neither alternative is credible. When the historical evidence that predates the end of the war is taken into account, it is clear that Heisenberg neither spied for the National Socialist government of Germany, nor attempted to slow down the research, nor advocated the hindrance or the manufacture of German nuclear weapons. Such historically inaccurate descriptions of Heisenberg's visit with Bohr are significant, both because they touch upon the important topics of political awareness and responsibility among scientists and their sponsors, and because they shed light upon the postwar apologia. Let us take a closer look at Heisenberg's mythical trip to Copenhagen, but with the eyes of a historian, not of an apologist or antagonist.

Heisenberg's 1941 trip to Denmark must be seen in three different contexts: the German nuclear power project, the war, and German cultural imperialism. Heisenberg and Weizsäcker actually did not go to Copenhagen exclusively to see Bohr, although that was certainly a bonus. They wanted to attend an astrophysics conference held at the German Cultural Institute in Copenhagen, perhaps in part as a contribution to the ongoing struggle against *deutsche Physik*. This meeting was being planned as early as April of 1941, before the German invasion of Russia and at a time when it appeared to most Germans that the war would soon be over, with Germany in a position to impose its terms upon most of Europe. The conference was held during the following September, after the surprise attack on the Soviet Union, as German armies were advancing quickly and deeply into European Russia. Once again, there was widespread hope in Germany that Russia would be forced to surrender soon and give in to the inevitable German victory. In short, both when this scientific meeting was being planned and when it was held, a German had every reason to believe that the war would soon be over, leaving Germany in command of Europe.[4]

As far as nuclear fission research was concerned, during this same period uranium isotope separation appeared to be a failure, the first small model uranium machine experiments had achieved modest results, and the supplies of uranium and moderator were quite limited. At this time, there was no reason for the Germans to believe that nuclear power was impossible, but it hardly seemed within easy reach. It was clear that the problem would not be solved in the near future. Therefore, if during September 1941 Heisenberg based his conclusions on the information that was available to him, he would have seen no connection between the imminent German victory and the realization of nuclear power sometime in the future, unless the conditions anticipated to follow such a victory would facilitate the further exploitation of nuclear fission.[5]

As already mentioned, the astrophysics conference was held at the Copenhagen German Cultural Institute. But why was a German scientific meeting held in Denmark? The answer to this question is bound up with the activities of the Weizsäcker family during the Third Reich, in particular, their participation in the German policy of cultural imperialism. The German Cultural Institutes were under the jurisdiction of the German Foreign Office, which was officially responsible for all German propaganda outside the Reich. Ernst von Weizsäcker, State Secretary in the Foreign Office, worked closely with the German occupation authorities in Denmark. Thus it is easy to understand why Carl-Friedrich von Weizsäcker, Ernst's son, was involved in the planning of an astrophysics conference at the Copenhagen German Cultural Institute. The younger Weizsäcker also wrote to Bohr, informed him that he and Heisenberg were going to speak at the astrophysics conference, and invited all of the Danish scientists to attend.[6]

This meeting represented an attempt to lure, or to coerce, Bohr and the rest of the Danish physicists at his institute into cultural collaboration with Germany and German policies. In other words, these Danes were pressed to justify and support the German occupation of their country and the reordering of Europe under German control. As Stefan Rozental, a physicist at Bohr's institute, recalled long after the war, when the Danes boycotted the astrophysics conference Heisenberg and Weizsäcker expressed regret at the unwillingness of their colleagues to hear their talks. In recompense, Bohr then invited Weizsäcker to speak at his institute. Weizsäcker then abused Bohr's hospitality by taking advantage of this opportunity to force Bohr into a meeting with the director of the German Cultural Institute, a confrontation that Bohr had avoided up until that time, with the result that Bohr was both alienated and compromised still further. Clearly Weizsäcker was involved in German attempts to encourage or force the Danes into cultural collaboration with the National Socialist government of Germany and thereby with National Socialist policies. Weizsäcker may have seen his role as part of the fight against *deutsche Physik*, but his Danish colleagues considered him a most unwelcome interloper. Therefore it was no surprise that, after the war, the Danes were reluctant to reaccept Weizsäcker into their circle. For his part, while in town for the astrophysics conference, Heisenberg had lunch several times at Bohr's institute and callously offended the Danes by remarking that war was a "biological necessity" and by expressing pleasure at the successful German campaign in the East.[7]

On one occasion during his visit to Copenhagen, Heisenberg had an important private conversation with Bohr. All accounts agree that the two scientists discussed two difficult yet important questions. Should physicists contribute to the war effort in their respective countries? Should the great potential of nuclear power be used as a weapon? Again, by all accounts, the conversation was broken off, leaving both men disturbed and damaging their friendship severely. After the war, after the attack on Hiroshima, and after the public revelations of the atrocities carried out by the German state during the Third Reich, Bohr and Heisenberg gave irreconcilable descriptions of the discussion that they had held during the fall of 1941. Both of these accounts must be seen in the context of the postwar apologia and germanophobia.

The earliest, and arguably most accurate account of Bohr's impressions of Heisenberg's visit, is given in a 23 October 1946 letter from the American physicist Rudolf Ladenburg to Samuel Goudsmit. Niels Bohr told Ladenburg that when Heisenberg and Weizsäcker had visited him in 1941, they had expressed their "hope and belief" that if the war lasted long enough, then nuclear weapons would win the war for Germany. The earliest, and arguably most accurate account of Heisenberg's impressions of his conversation with Bohr, is given in his 28 April 1948 letter to Bartel van der Waerden, also cited above. According to this account, when Heisenberg spoke with Niels Bohr, he broached the following question: did a physicist have the "moral right" to work on problems in atomic physics during, and relevant to, the war? Bohr asked a question in turn: did his younger colleague believe that a warlike application of nuclear power was possible? Heisenberg answered yes, and repeated his question. Heisenberg recalled that then, to his amazement, Bohr replied that on both sides the mobilization of physicists for the war effort was unavoidable, and therefore justified. Obviously, Heisenberg told van der Waerden, Bohr had considered implausible Heisenberg's tacit proposal, that physicists in all countries should "band together" in opposition to their governments.[8]

Although it was not mentioned in Ladenburg's letter to Goudsmit, eventually a story emerged among Bohr's friends and acquaintances to the effect that Heisenberg had wanted to extract information concerning the Allied nuclear weapons project from Bohr. The idea of Heisenberg as an intelligence agent is implausible, as demonstrated above. Heisenberg's relationship with National Socialism is open to criticism, but not in such a grotesque fashion. On the other hand, when the great pressure that Bohr and the other scientists at his institute were under is taken into account, for Bohr was in constant danger of betrayal, then it is understandable that Heisenberg's Danish mentor might have overreacted and misinterpreted Heisenberg's intentions.[9]

Heisenberg's retrospective claim, that by proposing an international "strike" among the physicists of the world, he tried to forestall the creation of nuclear weapons in Germany as well as in America, is exactly as implausible as the thought of him as a nazi agent. When Heisenberg traveled to Copenhagen in 1941, it appeared to most Germans, and very probably to him as well, that the war would soon end with a German victory in Europe. Heisenberg would not have seen nuclear weapons as a way to end, or to decide, the outcome of the war then raging in Europe. His fatherland was winning the war with conventional weapons. Nuclear weapons appeared feasible, but far off, and furthermore the Germans believed that they were ahead of the Allies with respect to nuclear power.[10]

Furthermore, why would Heisenberg have a dangerous confidential meeting with Bohr in the fall of 1941, only to describe vividly the destructive potential of nuclear fission in a lecture before representatives of the German Armed Forces and the Reich Research Council in February of 1942? He was not forced to make so striking a speech, for in the spring of 1943, when the need for wonder weapons was more pressing than in 1942, he delivered a lecture that implied that nuclear weapons were impossible within the constraints of the war economy.[11]

It is easy to understand the causes of Heisenberg's historically inaccurate account of his visit with Bohr. This story is an important part of his postwar apologia, as described above. There is no reason to question Heisenberg's sincerity when he told van der Waerden that he had wanted to work with Bohr to forestall the creation of nuclear weapons. By 1947 Heisenberg obviously had convinced himself that he had had such feelings and intentions, but this retrospective account is nevertheless an inaccurate description of his actions and intentions during 1941, or for that matter throughout the war. The story of Heisenberg's 1941 trip to Copenhagen formed the last piece of the Myth of the German Atomic Bomb: the tacit claim that one of the reasons, if not the main reason, why the Germans did not create nuclear weapons during the Third Reich was the recognition by the members of the nuclear power project of the evil consequences of a National Socialist victory in World War II and the subsequent un-willingness on the part of these same scientists to put so powerful a weapon into the hands of Adolf Hitler and his followers. As Heisenberg himself told the writer Robert Jungk in 1957, he and his colleagues had instinctively felt that a "a decent man" could not make nuclear weapons. There is no reason to doubt that, after the war, the scientists who had been involved with nuclear fission believed that it would have been a crime to contribute to a National Socialist victory in this way, but such an attitude is very, very difficult to reconcile with their actions during the Third Reich.[12]

Since neither Bohr's nor Heisenberg's retrospective account of their conversation is likely to be accurate, let us try to reconstruct the historical context of Heisenberg's visit. This German physicist did not come to Denmark just to see Bohr. He also wanted to speak at the German Cultural Institute in Copenhagen, an act that alienated Bohr and the other Danish scientists. As we have seen from Heisenberg's other lecture tours inside Greater Germany, although he never spread explicit National Socialist propaganda, Heisenberg both approved of, and enthusiastically supported, the German policy of cultural imperialism. There is no reason to assume that Heisenberg acted any differently in Denmark during 1941 than he did in Holland two years later, or in Hungary, in the Slovakian Protectorate, or in the General Government. There is no reason to assume that Heisenberg's attitude towards the German Cultural Institutes was any different in 1941 than the enthusiastic support that he gave this institution in 1943 and 1944. But in a manuscript that Heisenberg composed sometime after the war, he presented a retrospective, apologetic, and implausible justification for his 1941 lecture at the German Cultural Institute. A few years after Heisenberg and Weizsäcker had spoken at the astrophysics conference in Copenhagen, but before the war was over, the physicist Johannes Jensen visited Bohr. Upon his return, Jensen informed Heisenberg that Bohr had disapproved of Heisenberg's 1941 lecture at the German Cultural Institute. Apparently Jensen's message was news to Heisenberg. After the war, Heisenberg wrote that this participation surely had been the "smallest price" to pay for successful intercession on Bohr's behalf with the German ambassador to Denmark.[13]

By this time Heisenberg had inverted the cause and effect of his 1941 visit to Copenhagen. In 1944 he did travel north in order to help the scientists at Bohr's institute. But in 1941 he went to Denmark to speak at the German Cultural Institute because he wanted to and because he supported the aims of this institution. Heisenberg then took advantage of this opportunity to visit Bohr. In the eyes of the Danes, in 1941 Heisenberg appeared as a German nationalist and apologist. Thus it should be no surprise that when Heisenberg discussed the military applications of nuclear power with Bohr, the Danish physicist interpreted the remark as a desire to use German nuclear weapons in order to attain a German victory in arms. Similarly, it is no surprise that Heisenberg reacted as he did. Throughout the war and the immediate postwar period, he remained apparently unable, or unwilling, to understand why his foreign colleagues disapproved of his intimate association with German aggression and imperialism. It is understandable that he sought to excuse his own actions during the Third Reich and brought himself to believe in a story that made his actions seem morally justifiable, that made it appear that he had been firmly in control of his research, and that generally put him in the best possible light. But when the conversation between Bohr and Heisenberg is placed into the context of the German nuclear power project, it demonstrates the opposite of Heisenberg's postwar assertions. The German scientists were not in control of their research, they apparently did not contemplate the consequences of a German military victory during World War II, other than to desire this end, and as "apolitical men" they apparently did not understand the political responsibility of all citizens, including scientists. They were troubled – hence the conversation with Bohr in the first place – but they did not understand.[14]

A distinction must be made between criticism of actions taken and decisions made during the Third Reich – which although warranted, is very hard, given the inhuman pressures on these scientists – and an exposé of the much more difficult to justify postwar apologia. The Myth of the German Atomic Bomb has left behind a dangerous legacy, both in Germany and elsewhere. This fable should be exposed, not because someone lied, although that sometimes was the case, and not because some scientists reconstructed their memory in order to believe retrospectively in a historically inaccurate story, which definitely happened, but rather because this myth reinforces and perpetuates a very dangerous aspect of the apolitical ideology of science: the belief that respectable, moral, and apolitical scientists, or their science, cannot go astray. In essence, Heisenberg and many other German scientists claimed after the war that as decent, humane men, they had not wanted to, and therefore did not, build weapons of destruction. As decent, humane men, they had opposed National Socialism because they had recognized its evil character. As decent, humane men, they had understood the social and political significance of nuclear power. And as decent, humane, and responsible men, they had not created nuclear weapons for Adolf Hitler.

The scientists who worked in the German nuclear power project were indeed decent, moral, and humane men, but unfortunately these attributes alone were not enough. They refused to recognize the "political" nature of science and therefore could not comprehend the political responsibilities that their profession entailed. Many were seduced by the National Socialists' vision of a return to German power and only recognized the true nature of the Third Reich as Germany lay in ruins. They clung to their apolitical ideology and limited themselves to asking whether, and how quickly, nuclear weapons could be produced. All other decisions were left up to their leaders. Throughout the war, the most important question that faced these scientists remained unasked. If nuclear power can be used to kill, should it? The Myth of the German Atomic Bomb was both an obviation of, and a retrospective answer to, this question.[15]

Conclusion

Therefore a repressed idea or thought can penetrate into the consciousness, under the condition that it can be denied. The denial is a way to take notice of the repressed thought, even a termination of the repression, but certainly no admission of the repressed thought.

Sigmund Freud, "The Denial" (1925)[1]

What historical lesson, if any, does the German quest for nuclear power teach us? This book has used the German efforts to harness nuclear fission as a vehicle for investigating how science, technology, and society can interact, and has emphasized four topics towards this end: ideology, "resistance," apologia, and science policy. A brief summary of these points, as well as how they interact, forms the conclusion of this history.

The relationship between the German physics community and the National Socialist German state was one of collaboration and compromise, in simpler terms, of give and take. The ideological, political, and economic policies of the state forced scientists to embrace applied science, especially the inherent industrial and military utility of scientific research. The scientists, with the powerful backing of industrialists and military leaders, in turn forced the state to make significant ideological concessions, including a rehabilitation of modern physics, in order to enlist the wholehearted support of physicists for the war effort and to ensure the availability of the general scientific training of engineers, scientists, and technicians for the armaments industry.[2]

But what effect did ideology have on science? The interaction of ideology and physics during the Weimar Republic contrasts with the relationship between physics and National Socialism, mainly because paradoxically many German physicists perceived the Third Reich as a less hostile environment, at least at first. Because of the traditional German trust in the strong authoritarian state, the physics community was divided and conquered almost effortlessly by the National Socialists. This assimilation of science by National Socialism often produced divided loyalties among scientists, and the attitude of German scientists towards the purge of the universities and towards cultural and scientific imperialism within Greater Germany was inconsistent. Remorse was felt and expressed for the plight of individual friends and colleagues, but the same sympathetic German scientists generally either supported, or acquiesced in, the National Socialist policies that had brought about their colleague's misfortune. The conventions of the German apolitical ideology did not change very much from the height of the German Empire to the heart of the Third Reich, but the political and cultural environment that this ideology had to work within became progressively more extreme during the course of the National Socialist period. The apolitical ideology predisposed these scientists to be susceptible towards exploitation by any authoritarian ideology. It was in fact the National Socialist movement that became powerful in Germany and seduced them, but they might well have been swayed by a different appeal for a rebirth of German power.[3]

A point which has been repeated over and over during this book, but which also deserves such emphasis, is that black-and-white characterizations of scientists under Hitler are invalid. This study has dealt with neither nazis nor anti-nazis, but rather with people who stood somewhere in between, as most Germans did during the Third Reich. Resistance, opposition, and non-conformity towards National Socialism necessarily were constrained by the degree to which scientists recognized the dangers inherent in this political movement. In sharp contradiction to many postwar claims, few scientists realized the danger until it was too late, and even then the most common response was an understandable concern with self-preservation. Moreover, the changing historical context must be taken into account when judging their behavior. Werner Heisenberg's tactics in his struggle against *deutsche Physik*, for example, appeared acceptable during the first few years of the Third Reich, but after the war, these same actions no longer seemed justifiable to many of his peers. This change was a result of the unforeseen evolution of the Third Reich and the resulting alteration in the context of Heisenberg's actions.[4]

But no matter how sympathetic a historian may be, to characterize the behavior of honorable men such as Otto Hahn, Werner Heisenberg, Max von Laue, Max Planck, and others as "resistance" is to debase the term. They opposed limited and isolated aspects of National Socialism, supported others, and acquiesced in, or were unaware of, a great many more. Let us take the example of Otto Hahn, the discoverer of nuclear fission. Hahn devoted most of his personal research effort during the war to the study of fission fragments, which at the time were not perceived as having military significance. However, he was also director of the Kaiser Wilhelm Institute for Chemistry during this period, where experimental and theoretical work of direct relevance to the military applications of nuclear fission took place. Hahn certainly was aware of the potential of this research. In his regular progress reports to the army, this chemist went out of his way to stress the possible future military significance of the work being carried out at his institute. Obviously Hahn was under pressure to justify military support, and in any case would have asserted that the research carried out at his institute was important. But Hahn's motivations are not the point. Rather it is *what* he did, bringing the warlike potential of nuclear fission to the attention of the army, and what *effects* his actions had, heightening interest among military officials and providing them with accurate information with respect to nuclear weapons, that are significant.[5]

Hahn and his partner Fritz Strassmann also were involved with the research on nuclear power. No one tried harder than Otto Hahn, or wanted more, to produce small samples of plutonium and analyze them chemically, and it was exactly this crucial first step, taken successfully by Philip Abelson, Edwin McMillan, Glen Seaborg and others in a joint effort at the University of California, that allowed the United States government to commit itself early on to large-scale plutonium production. At the end of the war – but significantly before the announcement of the attack on Hiroshima – Hahn was asked by American officials about the military significance of his research. He responded that yes, he knew that the transuranic elements that he had been studying might be used as a nuclear explosive, but dismissed the matter by adding that he expected this application to be realized only in the distant future. After the news of Hiroshima, Hahn expressed misgivings about his research, and – again significantly – his subsequent public response was to create the deliberately misleading impression that he and his institute had only engaged in "pure research" – both in the scientific and moral senses – during the Third Reich. Hahn neither wanted, nor consciously attempted, to create nuclear weapons for the National Socialists, but his research nevertheless was heading towards that goal.[6]

The Myth of the German Atomic Bomb was only one small part, although a highly visible one, of the postwar apologia. In general, after the war Germans hastened to portray the Third Reich as a historical accident, whereby a small group of nazis somehow had taken control of the country, but fortunately were all gone or already had been punished. For the German physics community, the equivalent argument equated the total influence of National Socialism in their profession with the *deutsche Physik* group. This claim, along with the postwar ostracism of Kurt Diebner, Abraham Esau, Erich Schumann, and others, was an important part of the apologia. The German physics community thereby denied its past, and purged itself of those elements that hindered its acceptance back into the international scientific community and that belied, or at the very least might expose, the change in apolitical conventions that this community undertook consciously after the fall of Hitler.[7]

The role of Heisenberg as spokesman for the German nuclear power project was important for the apologia as well, for his erroneous claim, that he had been in control of nuclear power research, was accepted uncritically by friends and critics alike. In part, this acceptance is to be attributed to the perception of science by scientists and laymen as reducible to the work of a few "great" scientists. Control is the key aspect of the apologia, for only if Heisenberg and his colleagues had been in command of their research, could their claim, that they had steered it deliberately away from nuclear weapons and towards "peaceful nuclear energy," appear believable.[8]

The Heisenberg/Goudsmit controversy illustrated what was important to Heisenberg and Samuel Goudsmit, as well as showing how scientists and the general public can react to such a controversy. For Goudsmit and Heisenberg, the main concerns were their professional scientific reputations and the preservation of the apolitical nature of their science, although they did not fail to wrestle with difficult moral issues as well. With respect to the public and private reactions to this controversy, it is striking how almost everyone assumed that *either* Heisenberg *or* Goudsmit was right and that one side or the other should be, and usually was, accepted at face value. In fact, neither physicist was unbiased nor was unwilling to take considerable liberties with information and presentation when it came to making his case.[9]

What does this story, including the brief comparison with the Manhattan Project, tell us about how science, politics, and society interact? The obvious question is one that Goudsmit raised in his book *Alsos*. How does science under totalitarianism – or if you like, under fascism – compare with science in a democracy? Of course there was a great difference, but this disparity was not so great as to allow only democracies to harness science and technology for peace and war. Perhaps the German science policy makers and structures of science administration were not quite as good as their counterparts in America, but they were good enough to deliver the goods, as the German rocket project demonstrated, although often at an inhuman cost, as illustrated by the widespread German use of slave labor in the war economy. Goudsmit's claim that because of scientists' need for professional intellectual freedom, science can flourish only in a democracy, was naive and dangerously presumptuous. Scientists, science administrators, and scientific communities showed themselves quite willing to work under National Socialism, even at an often humiliating cost.[10]

A study by Charles C. Gillispie of science and politics in late eighteenth-century France has argued, in so many words, that scientists will serve any master. My history of nuclear power under Hitler hardly conflicts with this claim, but I want to emphasize as well that this readiness to serve does not mean that scientists are necessarily indifferent to, or uninfluenced by, the sort of master they have, or the type of society in which they live. Scientists, scientific communities, and sciences can be bent to an amazing degree and in astonishing directions by forces in their cultural, ideological, and political environments. A historian can follow a slightly extended generation of German physicists from the German empire to the postwar division of Germany and see that when scientists are put under ideological or political pressure, they are ready and able to adapt to the changing cultural currents, are opportunistic, and are willing to make considerable sacrifices in order to retain some degree of professional autonomy and self-respect, whether real or imagined. But what is perhaps most striking is the ability, and perhaps need, of scientists and scientific communities retrospectively to convince themselves and subsequent generations of science students that they had acted in a professionally acceptable manner, even if they have to revise their own memories to do it.[11]

Finally, I have tried to demonstrate the importance of historical perspective and context. By dividing the scope of this history up into distinct time periods, and limiting myself within each section as much as possible to historical evidence from that interval, I meant to illustrate how retrospective evidence can obscure important aspects of a story – for example cultural and scientific imperialism during the Third Reich – by focusing on matters that are more the concerns of present day readers than of the actors in a historical drama. Perhaps the crudest example is the argument that, since the American nuclear power project resulted in useful nuclear weapons and the German effort did not, where did the Germans fail? As I have shown, there was no German failure. The German nuclear power project took the course it did because of the cultural, economic, ideological, political, and scientific environment in which it took place, a very different one from that found in America. Anyone who wants to understand why nuclear weapons were an American, and not a German invention, should ponder the subtleties of politics, ideology, economics, and culture as well as science and technology.

Notes

1 Robert Merton, "Science in the social order," *Philosophy of Science*, 5 (1938), reprinted in *The Sociology of Science: Theoretical and Empirical Investigations*, pp. 254–66, 257.

2 See Spencer Weart, *Scientists in Power*, although I use "power" in a different sense.

3 Michael Eckert and Helmut Schubert, *Kristalle, Elektronen, Transistoren*, pp. 25–48; John Beer, *The Emergence of the German Dye Industry*; Paul Forman, John L. Heilbron, and Spencer Weart, "Physics circa 1900: personnel, funding, and productivity of the academic establishments," *HSPS*, 5 (1975), 1–185.

4 Eckert and Schubert, pp. 49–53; Lothar Burchardt, *Wissenschaftspolitik im Wilhelminischen Deutschland*; Günter Wendel, *Die Kaiser Wilhelm Gesellschaft 1911–1914*; *Dokumente zur Gründung der Kaiser-Wilhelm-Gesellschaft und der Max-Planck-Gesellschaft zur Förderung der Wissenschaften*, p. 47.

5 Georg Friedrich Nicolai, *The Biology of War*, pp. xi–xiv.

6 John L. Heilbron, *The Dilemmas of an Upright Man: Max Planck as Spokesman for German Science*, pp. 69–79; Michael Eckert, Willibald Pricha, Helmut Schubert, and Gisela Torkar, *Geheimrat Sommerfeld – Theoretischer Physiker: Eine Dokumentation aus seinem Nachlass*, p. 129.

7 Lewis Pyenson, *Cultural Imperialism and Exact Sciences. German Expansion Overseas 1900–1930*; Lewis Pyenson, "The limits of scientific condominium: geophysics in Western Samoa," in N. Reingold and M. Rothberg (eds.), *Scientific Colonization: A Cross-Cultural Comparison*, pp. 251–95; Eckert, Pricha, Schubert, Torkar, 130.

8 Arnold Sommerfeld, *Süddeutsche Monatshefte* (15 May 1918).

9 Gerald Feldman, *Army, Industry, and Labor in Germany, 1914–1918*, pp. 45–6; Ludwig Haber, *The Poisonous Cloud: Chemical Warfare in the First World War*, pp. 24, 27, 30, 34, 39; Wendel, 210–15.

10 Eckert, Pricha, Schubert, Torkar, 132; Fritz Ringer, *The Decline of the German Mandarins: The German Academic Community, 1890–1933*; Paul Forman, "The environment and practice of atomic physics in Weimar Germany: a study in the history of science," 1967; Paul Forman, "Weimar culture, causality, and quantum theory, 1918–1927: adaptation by German

physicists and mathematicians to a hostile environment," *HSPS*, 3 (1971),
1–115; Paul Forman, "Scientific internationalism and the Weimar physicists: the ideology and its manipulation in Germany after World War I,"
Isis, 64 (1973), 151–80; Paul Forman, "The financial support and political
alignment of physicists in Weimar Germany," *Minerva*, 12 (1974), 39–66;
Paul Forman, "*Kausalität, Anschaulichkeit*, and *Individualität*, or how cultural
values prescribed the character and lessons ascribed to quantum mechanics,"
in Nico Stehr and Volker Meja (eds.), *Society and Knowledge: Contemporary
Perspectives in the Sociology of Knowledge*, pp. 333–47.

11 Also see Forman, *Isis*, 64 (1973), 170; Clifford Geertz, *The Interpretation of
Cultures*, pp. 193–233; Daniel Greenberg, *The Politics of Pure Science*, pp.
3–48 and 68–96; Joseph Haberer, *Politics and the Community of Science*, pp.
1–13, 103–84, and 299–332; Ringer; and Fritz Stern, *The Failure of
Illiberalism: Essays on the Political Culture of Modern Germany*, pp. 3–25.

12 For only one example of scientists susceptible to the political currents of their
social and economic environment, see Forman, *HSPS*, 3 (1971), 1–115, and
Forman, "*Kausalität*,"

13 Ringer; Brigitte Schröder-Gudehus, "Challenge to transnational loyalties:
international scientific organizations after the First World War," *SCIS*, 3
(1973), 93–118; Daniel Kevles, "'Into hostile camps': the reorganization of
international science in World War I," *Isis*, 62 (1970), 47–60; Daniel Kevles,
The Physicists: The History of a Scientific Community in Modern America, pp.
139–54.

14 Schröder-Gudehus, *SCIS*, 3 (1973), 93–118; Forman, *Isis*, 64 (1973), 156,
163; Eckert, Pricha, Schubert, Torkar: 117–27; Michael Eckert, "Propaganda in science: Sommerfeld and the spread of the electron theory of
metals," *HSPS*, 17 (1987), 191–233.

15 Schröder-Gudehus, *SCIS*, 3 (1973), 93–118; Forman, *Isis*, 64 (1973), 156,
163; Eckert, Pricha, Schubert, Torkar: 117–27; Eckert, *HSPS*, 17 (1987)
191–233.

16 Forman, *Minerva*, 12 (1974), 39–66; Brigitte Schröder-Gudehus, "The
argument for the self-government and public support of science in Weimar
Germany," *Minerva*, 10 (1972), 537–70.

17 Martin Broszat, *The Hitler State*, pp. 1–95.

18 Gerda Friese, "Autonomie und Anpassung – Das Selbstverständnis von
Naturwissenschaftlern im Nationalsozialismus," in Rainer Brämer (ed.),
Naturwissenschaft im NS-Staat, pp. 31–58, 39.

19 Broszat, *State*, pp. 198, 245; Gordon Craig, *Germany, 1866–1945*, p. 579;
Alan Beyerchen, *Scientists under Hitler: Politics and the Physics Community in
the Third Reich*, pp. 12–14; Hans Mommsen, *Beamtentum im Dritten Reich:
Mit ausgewählten Quellen zur nationalsozialistischen Beamtenpolitik*, pp. 39–61.

20 Beyerchen, pp. 12–14, 40, 47–50; Edward Hartshorne, *The German
Universities and National Socialism*; Benno Müller-Hill, *Murderous Science:
Elimination by Scientific Selection of Jews, Gypsies and Others, Germany,
1933–1945*, pp. 9, 24–5.

21 Friese, "Anpassung," p. 37; Heisenberg to Born (2 June 1933), reprinted in

Karl von Meyenn, Armin Hermann, and Viktor Weisskopf (eds.), *Wolfgang Pauli: Wissenschaftliches Briefwechsel mit Bohr, Einstein, Heisenberg*, u.a. Band II: *1930–1939*, p. 186.

22 Kristie Macrakis, "Wissenschaftsförderung durch die Rockefeller-Stiftung im 'Dritten Reich': Die Entscheidung, das Kaiser-Wilhelm-Institut für Physik finanziell zu unterstützen, 1934–39," *GG 12* (1986), 348–79; Heilbron, pp. 177–9; Müller-Hill, pp. 9, 24–25.

23 Heisenberg to Born (2 June 1933), reprinted in von Meyenn, Hermann, and Weisskopf, p. 186.

24 Harold James, *The German Slump: Politics and Economics 1924–1936*, chapter 10; Dieter Petzina, *Autarkiepolitik im Dritten Reich: Der nationalsozialistische Vierjahresplan*; Michael Geyer, "The dynamics of military revisionism in the interwar years. Military politics between rearmament and diplomacy," in Wilhelm Deist (ed.), *The German Military in the Age of Total War*, pp. 100–51; Wolfram Wette, "From Kellogg to Hitler (1928–1933), German public opinion concerning the rejection or glorification of war," in Wilhelm Deist (ed.), *The German Military in the Age of Total War*, pp. 71–99; Schumann to Harteck (17 July 1937) EBK; Harteck to Oberkommando des Heeres (26 Aug. 1937) EBK; Planck to employees of the Kaiser Wilhelm Society (11 Nov. 1935) MPSB.

25 Ian Kershaw, *The "Hitler Myth": Image and Reality in the Third Reich*, pp. 121–32; *The Olympic Year in Germany*; Born to Rutherford (10 Oct. 1936), reprinted in *Der Luxus des Gewissens: Max Born James Franck Physiker in ihrer Zeit*, p. 127.

26 Ian Kershaw, "The Führer image and political integration: the popular conception of Hitler in Bavaria during the Third Reich," in Gerhard Hirschfeld and Lothar Kettenacker (eds.), *Der "Führerstaat": Mythos und Realität*, pp. 133–63, 133–4; also see Detlev J. K. Peukert, *Inside Nazi Germany: Conformity, Opposition, and Racism in Everyday Life*, and Martin Broszat and Elke Fröhlich, *Alltag und Widerstand – Bayern im National-sozialismus*.

1 Lightning war

1 Boberach, Heinz (ed.), *Meldungen aus dem Reich: Die geheimen Lageberichte des Sicherheitsdienstes der SS 1938–1945*, vol. 8, p. 2787.

2 For the "Crystal Night" see Ian Kershaw, *Popular Opinion and Political Dissent in the Third Reich: Bavaria 1933–1945*, pp. 257–74.

3 Otto Hahn to Lise Meitner (19 Dec. 1938) 29-023 IMC; Lise Meitner to Otto Hahn (21 Dec. 1938) 29-026 IMC; for the work of Hahn, Meitner, and Strassmann, see Spencer Weart, "The discovery of fission and a nuclear physics paradigm," in William Shea (ed.), *Otto Hahn and the Rise of Nuclear Physics*, pp. 91–133.

4 Hahn's diary (22 Dec. 1938) 29-021 IMC; Otto Hahn and Fritz Strassmann, "Nachweis der Entstehung aktiver Bariumisotope aus Uran und Thorium durch Neutronenbestrahlung: Nachweis weiterer aktiver Bruchstücke bei

der Uranspaltung," *NW*, 27 (1939), 11–15, reprinted in Horst Wohlfarth (ed.), *40 Jahre Kernspaltung*, pp. 65–76; Weart, "Discovery."

5 Lise Meitner and Otto Frisch, "Disintegration of uranium by neutrons: a new type of nuclear reaction," *Nature*, 143 (1939), 239–40, in Wohlfarth, pp. 97–100.

6 Meitner and Frisch, *Nature*, 143 (1939), 239–40; for the French work, see Weart, *Power*, chapters 4–10; Siegfried Flügge and Gottfried von Droste, "Energetische Betrachtungen zu der Entstehung von Barium bei der Neutronenbestrahlung von Uran," *ZPCB*, 42 (1939), 274–80; several researchers came independently to this conclusion, see Louis Turner, "Nuclear fission," *RMP*, 12 (1940), 1–29, 8; for a list of the papers see Turner, *RMP*, 12 (1940), 7–10; Bohr's announcement is mentioned in R. Roberts, R. Meyer, and L. Hafstad, "Droplet fission of uranium and thorium nuclei," *PR*, 55 (1939), 416–17.

7 Otto Hahn and Fritz Strassmann, "Zur Folge nach der Entstehung des 2,3 Tage-Isotopes des Elements 93 aus Uran," *NW*, 27 (1939), 89–95, in Wohlfarth, 78–96, here 93; also see Turner, *RMP*, 12 (1940), 11–13; Hans von Halban, Frédéric Joliot, and Lew Kowarski, "Liberation of neutrons in the nuclear explosion of uranium," *Nature*, 143 (1939), 470–1, in Wohlfarth, pp. 111–14.

8 von Halban, Joliot, Kowarski, "Liberation," *Nature*, 143 (1939), 470–1; Hans von Halban, Frédéric Joliot, and Lew Kowarski, "Number of neutrons liberated in the nuclear fission of uranium," *Nature*, 143 (1939), 470–1, 680; Herbert Anderson, Enrico Fermi, and H. B. Hanstein, "Production of neutrons in uranium bombarded by neutrons," *PR*, 55 (1939), 797–8; Gottfried von Droste and H. Reddemann, "Über die beim Zerspalten des Urankerns auftretenden Neutronen," *NW*, 27 (1939), 371–2; Turner, *RMP*, 12 (1940), 7–13, 20–1; for the French work, also see Weart, *Power*, chapters 4–10.

9 Lise Meitner, Otto Hahn, and Fritz Strassmann, "Über die Umwandlungsreihen des Urans die durch Neutronenbestrahlung erzeugt werden," *ZP*, 106 (1937), 249–70; several researchers independently noticed this contradiction, see Turner, *RMP*, 12 (1940), 17–20.

10 Niels Bohr, "Resonance in uranium and thorium disintegrations and the phenomena of nuclear fission," *PR*, 55 (1939), 418–19; Herbert Anderson, E. Booth, J. Dunning, Enrico Fermi, G. Glasoe, and F. Slack, "The fission of uranium," *PR*, 55 (1939), 511–12; A. Grosse, E. Booth, and J. Dunning, "The fission of protactinium," *PR*, 56 (1939), 382; Niels Bohr and John Wheeler, "The mechanism of nuclear fission," *PR*, 56 (1939), 426–50, in Wohlfarth, 142–90.

11 Siegfried Flügge, "Kann der Energieinhalt der Atomkerne technisch nutzbar gemacht werden?" *NW*, 27 (1939), 402–10, in Wohlfarth, 119–40; Siegfried Flügge, "Die Ausnutzungen der Atomenergie," *DAZ* (15 Aug. 1939).

12 Turner, *RMP*, 12 (1940), 7–21.

13 Wilhelm Deist, Manfred Messerschmidt, Hans-Erich Volkmann, and Wolfram

Wette, "Causes and preconditions of German aggression," in Wilhelm Deist (ed.), *The German Military in the Age of Total War*, pp. 336–53; Geyer, "Dynamics," pp. 100–51.

14 Esau to Bothe (24 Apr. 1939) MPSB; Esau to General? (13 Nov. 1939) 29-098 IMC; interview with Nikolaus Riehl; Riehl was an expert in luminescence, see Nikolaus Riehl, *Physik und technische Anwendungen der Lumineszenz.*

15 Schumann to Harteck (17 July 1937) EBK; Harteck to Army Ordnance (26 Aug. 1937) EBK; Harteck and Groth to Army Ordnance (24 Apr. 1939), translated in Goudsmit to Furman (25 May 1945) 29-058 IMC; interview with Wilhelm Hanle; interview with Nikolaus Riehl; interview with Paul Harteck.

16 Basche to Harteck (22 Aug. 1939) EBK; Esau reported his conversation with Mentzel in the letter Esau to General? (13 Nov. 1939) 29-098 IMC; interview with Wilhelm Hanle; interview with Carl-Friedrich von Weizsäcker.

17 For only one example of partial integration, see Peter Hayes, *Industry and Ideology: IG Farben in the Nazi Era.*

18 Erich Bagge, Kurt Diebner, and Kenneth Jay, *Von der Uranspaltung bis Calder Hall*, pp. 20–4; interview with Georg Hartwig; for an example of Diebner's work see Kurt Diebner and E. Grassmann, *Künstiche Radioaktivität: Experimentale Ergebnisse*; "Notiz für Professor Schnadel, Betreff Dr. K. Diebner," (?) 29-1195 IMC.

19 Interview with Erich Bagge; Bagge's diary (11, 13, 14, 17, 25, and 26 Sept. 1939) EBK, also 29-106 IMC; Bagge, Diebner, Jay, pp. 20–4.

20 Debye to Tisdale (7 Oct. 1939) MPSB; Telschow, memo (17 Oct. 1939) MPSB; Debye to Sommerfeld (31 Sept. 1939) 1977–?? (A, 61, 18) GMM; Debye to Hochheim (8 Jan. 1940) MPSB; memo (22 Jan. 1940) MPSB; Schumann to Kaiser Wilhelm Society (25 Jan. 1940) MPSB; memo (1 Mar. 1940) MPSB; "Niederschrift über die Sitzung des Senates der KWG" (31 July 1941) R26 III 701 FGAK.

21 For the role of I. G. Farben in the rearmament see Hayes; for Vögler's relations to the National Socialist German Workers Party see Karl-Heinz Ludwig, *Technik und Ingenieure im Dritten Reich*, p. 122; for Göring and Rust's support of Vögler see memo (31 July 1941) MPSB; personal communication from Kristie Macrakis.

22 Harteck to Army Ordnance (18 Sept. 1939) EBK; Basche to Harteck (19 Oct. 1939) EBK; Harteck to Army Ordnance (23 Nov. 1939) EBK; Schumann to Harteck (15 Dec. 1939) EBK.

23 The "G-reports" are listed by number only in the footnotes, for complete information, see the bibliography; *G-39*; *G-40*; Turner, *RMP*, 12 (1940), 28–9; Harteck to Army Ordnance (15 Jan. 1940) EBK; Harteck to Heisenberg (15 Jan. 1940) EBK; Harteck to Bonhoeffer (4 Feb. 1940) B1 F6 RPI.

24 Alfred Nier, E. Booth, J. Dunning, and A. Grosse, "Nuclear fission of separated uranium isotopes," *PR*, 57 (1940), 546; Alfred Nier, E. Booth, J. Dunning, and A. Grosse, "Further experiments on fission of separated uranium isotopes," *PR*, 57 (1940), 748; E. Booth, J. Dunning, A. Grosse, and Alfred

Nier, "Neutron capture by uranium (238)," *PR*, 58 (1940), 475–6; Willibald Jentschke, F. Prankl, and F. Hernegger, "Die Spaltung des Ioniums unter Neutronenbestrahlung," *NW*, 28 (1940), 315–16.

25 Enrico Fermi, "Possible production of elements of atomic number higher than 92," *Nature*, 133 (1934), 898–9; Meitner, Hahn, Strassmann, *ZP*, 106 (1937), 249–70.

26 Edwin McMillan and Philip Abelson, "Radioactive element 93," *PR*, 57 (1940), 1185–6.

27 *G-113*; This was subsequently published in Kurt Starke, "Anreicherung des künstlich radioaktiven Uran-Isotops U^{239} und seines Folgeproduktes 93^{239} (Element 93)," *NW*, 30 (1942), 577–82; *G-151*; this was subsequently published in Otto Hahn and Fritz Strassmann, "Zur Folge nach der Entstehung des 2,3 Tage-Isotopes des Elements 93 aus Uran," *NW*, 30 (1942), 256–60.

28 McMillan and Abelson, *PR*, 57 (1940), 1185–6; *G-55*; *G-112*; *G-111*; interview with Kurt Starke.

29 *G-59*; *G-94*; *G-190*; interview with Kurt Sauerwein; Turner, *PR*, 57 (1940), 157.

30 *G-59*.

31 *Energiegewinnung aus Uran*, 9 EBK.

32 Fermi, *Nature*, 133 (1934), 898–9; Halban, Joliot, Kowarski, "Liberation," *Nature*, 143 (1939), 470–1; Anderson, Fermi, Hanstein, *PR*, 55 (1939), 797–8; Leo Szilard and Walter Zinn, "Instantaneous emission of fast neutrons in the interaction of slow neutrons with uranium," *PR*, 55 (1939), 799–800, This is also discussed by Flügge, *NW*, 27 (1939), 402–10; *G-39*; *G-40* 1a.

33 Harteck to Army Ordnance (8 Feb. 1940) EBK; Harteck to Army Ordnance (12 Apr. 1940) EBK; Herold to Harteck (15 Apr. 1940) EBK; Harteck to Army Ordnance (19 Apr. 1940) EBK.

34 Army Ordnance to Harteck (25 Apr. 1940) EBK; Heisenberg to Harteck (29 Apr. 1940) EBK.

35 Harteck to Heisenberg (30 Apr. 1940) EBK; Harteck to Diebner (9 May 1940) EBK; Pose to Harteck (22 May 1940) EBK; Army Ordnance to Harteck (27 May 1940) EBK; Harteck to Army Ordnance (3 June 1940) EBK; *G-36*; *Energiegewinnung*, 94 EBK.

36 *G-12*; *G-71*.

37 *G-46*; *G-85*; *G-71*; interview with Wilhelm Hanle.

38 *Energiegewinnung*, 87–8 EBK; *G-39* 24; *G-40* 1a.

39 *Energiegewinnung*, 121 EBK; interview with Karl Wirtz; Harteck to Army Ordnance (24 June 1940) EBK; Army Ordnance to Harteck (1 Feb. 1940) EBK; interview with Paul Harteck.

40 Harteck to Heisenberg (15 Jan. 1940) EBK; Heisenberg to Harteck (18 Jan. 1940) EBK; *G-21*; *G-61*; Harteck to Army Ordnance (24 Jan. 1940) EBK; Army Ordnance to Harteck (1 Feb. 1940) EBK; Harteck to Army Ordnance (8 Feb. 1940) EBK; Harteck to Bonhoeffer (9 Feb. 1940) EBK; Bonhoeffer to Harteck (28 Feb. 1940) EBK; *G-23*.

41 *Energiegewinnung*, 15, 127 EBK; Army Ordnance to Harteck (18 June 1941)

EBK; *G-86*, 1–2; *G-341 v.3* (1 Oct. 1941, 4 Oct. 1941, 8 Oct. 1941, 20 Oct. 1941); Paul Harteck, "Bericht über den Stand der SH 200 Gewinnung" (15 Apr. 1944) 29-762 IMC.

42 *G-86*.

43 *G-86*; *Energiegewinnung*, 15 EBK; *G-341 v.3* (20 Oct. 1941); *G-341 v.3* (around 8 Oct. 1941).

44 *G-39*; *G-50*; *G-49*; Klaus Clusius and Gerhard Dickel, "Neues Verfahren zur Gasentmischung und Isotopentrennung," *NW*, 26 (1938), 546.

45 Clusius and Dickel, *NW*, 26 (1938), 546; the figure is taken from Klaus Clusius and Gerhard Dickel, "Das Trennrohr," *ZPCB*, 44 (1939), 459.

46 Horst Korsching and Karl Wirtz, "Zur Trennung von Flüssigkeitsgemischen im Clusiusschen Trennrohr (Trennung der Zinkisotope)," *NW*, 27 (1939), 367–8, here 368; Horst Korsching and Karl Wirtz, "Trennung von Flüssigkeitsgemischen mittels kombinierter Thermo-Diffusion und Thermo-siphonwirkung," *NW*, 27 (1939), 110; Klaus Clusius and Gerhard Dickel, "Das Trennrohrverfahren bei Flüssigkeiten," *NW*, 27 (1939), 148–9; Klaus Clusius and Gerhard Dickel, "Zur Trennung der Chlorisotope," *NW*, 27 (1939), 148; Klaus Clusius and Gerhard Dickel, *NW*, 27 (1939), 487.

47 Gustav Hertz, "Ein Verfahren zur Trennung von gasförmigen Isotopen-gemischen und seine Anwendung auf die Isotope des Neons," *ZP*, 79 (1932), 108–21; Gustav Hertz, "Ein Verfahren zur Trennung von Isotopengemischen durch Diffusion in strömendem Quecksilberdampf," *ZP*, 91 (1934), 810–15; Wilhelm Groth, "Versuche zur Anreicherung der Xenonisotope und deren Nachweis," *NW*, 27 (1939), 260–1; Clusius and Dickel, *ZPCB*, 44 (1939), 447; Wilhelm Groth and Paul Harteck, "Anreicherung der Quecksilberisotope nach einem Trennrohrverfahren," *NW*, 27 (1939), 584.

48 Alfred Nier, "The isotopic constitution of uranium and the half-lives of the uranium isotopes," *PR*, 55 (1939), 150.

49 Harteck to Ruff (25 Sept. 1939) EBK; Harteck to Diebner (9 Oct. 1939) EBK; Harteck to Army Ordnance (23 Nov. 1939) EBK; Harteck to Army Ordnance (4 Dec. 1939) EBK; Harteck to Diebner (9 Oct. 1939) EBK; Harteck to Army Ordnance (4 Dec. 1939) EBK; Schumann to Harteck (15 Dec. 1939) EBK; Basche to Harteck (5 Jan. 1940) EBK; Harteck to Army Ordnance (8 Jan. 1940) EBK; Harteck to Army Ordnance (18 Jan. 1940) EBK; *G-32*; Harteck to Diebner (9 Oct. 1939) EBK; Harteck to Army Ordnance (4 Dec. 1939) EBK; Schumann to Harteck (15 Dec. 1939) EBK; Basche to Harteck (5 Jan. 1940) EBK; Harteck to Army Ordnance (8 Jan. 1940) EBK; Harteck to Army Ordnance (18 Jan. 1940) EBK; Harteck to Army Ordnance (26 June 1940) EBK.

50 *G-33*; *G-89*, 1; Harteck to Army Ordnance (17 Apr. 1941) EBK.

51 *G-83*.

52 Wilhelm Walcher, "Isotopentrennung," *EEN*, 18 (1939), 155–228; Wilhelm Walcher, "Über einen Massenspektrographen hoher Intensität und die Trennung der Rubidiumisotope," *ZP*, 108 (1938), 376–90; interview with Wilhelm Walcher; *G-18*; *G-27*; Clusius to Army Ordnance (18 July 1940) EBK; *G-19*; *G-20*; *G-73*; *G-172*; *G-102*; Erich Bagge, "Rasch

arbeitendes Verfahren zur Entmischung von Isotopen (Isotopenschleuse)"
(24 Nov. 1940) EBK, also 29-304 IMC; Bagge's diary (2, 20 Aug.; 5–7,
11 Sept.; 22 Nov. 1941) EBK, also 29-106 IMC; *G-88.*

53 Martin to Allied High Command (16 May 1945) SGNY; *G-95*; Groth's diary
(5, 11 Aug.; 11 Oct. 1941) SGNY; Harteck to Army Ordnance (23 Sept.
1941) EBK; Harteck to Army Ordnance (1 Nov. 1941) EBK; for example
Jesse Beams and C. Skarstrom, "The concentration of isotopes by the
evaporative centrifuge method," *PR*, 56 (1939), 266–72; *G-82*, 2–4.

54 *G-82*; *G-83.*

55 *G-88*; *Energiegewinnung*, 103–4 EBK; interview with Paul Harteck.

56 *Energiegewinnung*, 12 EBK.

57 *G-39*; *G-40*; Halban, Joliot, Kowarski, "Liberating," *Nature*, 143 (1939),
470–1; Herbert Anderson, Enrico Fermi, and Leo Szilard, "Neutron
production and absorption in uranium," *PR*, 56 (1939), 284–6.

58 Harteck's suggestion is mentioned in Hahn's diary (26 Sept. 1939) 29-021
IMC; *G-39*, 18; *G-40*, 8.

59 *G-39*; *G-93*, 3.

60 Interview with Carl-Friedrich von Weizsäcker; interview with Karl-Heinz
Höcker.

61 *G-60*; *G-42*; *G-51*; *G-53*; *G-43*; *G-41*; *G-52*; *G-122*; *G-13*; *G-14*; *G-128*;
G-92.

62 *Energiegewinnung*, 71 EBK; *G-17*; *G-25*; *G-26*; *G-67*; *G-68*; *G-66*; *G-72*;
G-74; *G-70*; *G-98*; *G-81*; *G-38*; *G-56*; *G-37*; *G-116*; *G-117*; *G-118*; *G-91*;
G-22; *G-24*; *G-48*; *G-77*; *G-78*; *G-110*; *G-79*; *G-44*; *G-99*; for the work in
Geiger's institute also see David Cassidy, "Gustav Hertz, Hans Geiger und das
Physikalische Institut der Technischen Hochschule Berlin in den Jahren
1933 bis 1945," in R. Rürup (ed.) *Wissenschaft und Gesellschaft: Beiträge zur
Geschichte der Technischen Universität Berlin, 1879–1979*, pp. 373–87.

63 *Energiegewinnung*, 13 EBK.

64 Basche to Harteck (6 Jan. 1940) EBK; Heisenberg to Harteck (29 Apr. 1940)
EBK; Esau to General? (13 Nov. 1939) SGNY; *G-41*; interview with Nikolaus
Riehl.

65 *G-93*; 22 GR; *Energiegewinnung*, 97 EBK; the figure is taken from Walther
Bothe and Siegfried Flügge (eds.), *Kernphysik und kosmische Strahlen*, vol. 14,
part II, p. 152.

66 *G-74*; *G-75*; *Energiegewinnung*, 99 EBK; the figure is taken from Bothe and
Flügge, part II, p. 150.

67 *Energiegewinnung*, 15 EBK.

68 Lothar Burchardt, "The impact of the war economy on the civilian
population of Germany during the First and Second World Wars," in
Wilhelm Deist (ed.), *The German Military in the Age of Total War*, pp. 40–70;
Bernard Kroener, "Squaring the circle. Blitzkrieg strategy and manpower
shortage, 1939–1949," in Wilhelm Deist (ed.), *The German Military in the Age
of Total War*, pp. 282–303; for Wirtz's reaction see the interrogation of Paul
Rosebaud (5 Aug. 1945) 29-1174 IMC.

69 Basche to Harteck (1 Feb. 1940) EBK; interview with Paul Harteck; Harteck
to Army Ordnance (10 Oct. 1940) EBK; Hahn's ties to industry are discussed

in Weart, "Discovery," 126; interview with Heinz Ewald; interview with Carl-Friedrich von Weizsäcker; interview with Karl-Heinz Höcker.

70 Interviews with Gerhard Borrmann, Werner Czulius, Werner Maurer, Kurt Starke, and Carl-Friedrich von Weizsäcker.

71 Interview with Karl-Heinz Höcker.

72 Werner Heisenberg (ed.), *Kosmische Strahlung*; interview with Gerhard Borrmann; Harteck to Army Ordnance (26 June 1940) EBK; Schumann to Harteck (15 Dec. 1939) EBK; Harteck to Army Ordnance (24 Jan. 1940) EBK; Harteck to Army Ordnance (10 Oct. 1940) EBK; Telschow to Bothe (21 Feb. 1938) MPSB; Bothe to Debye (18 Mar. 1938) MPSB; Bothe to Helmholtz Society (13 May 1938) MPSP; Pohl to Vögler (16 May 1938) MPSB; Bothe to Hoffmann (19 May 1938) MPSB; Hoffmann to Bothe (20 May 1938) MPSB; Bothe to Hoffmann (20 May 1938) MPSB; Bothe to Helmholtz Society (24 May 1938) MPSB; Bothe to Lawrence (3 June 1938) MPSB; Peterson to Bothe (5 Oct. 1938) MPSB; Bothe to Debye (19 Dec. 1938) MPSB; Bothe to Mentzel (17 Mar. 1939) MPSB; Telschow to Bothe (30 Mar. 1939) MPSB; Mentzel to Kaiser Wilhelm Society (11 Apr. 1939) MPSB; Telschow to Bothe (17 Oct. 1939) MPSB; Bothe to Telschow (23 Oct. 1939) MPSB; Bothe to Schmidt-Ott (29 July 1940) MPSB; Bothe to Laue (17 Aug. 1940) MPSB; Schmidt-Ott to Bothe (1 Nov. 1940) MPSB; Bothe to Stifterverband (7 Nov. 1940) MPSB; Bothe to Schmidt-Ott (16 June 1941) MPSB; Schmidt-Ott to Bothe (24 June 1941) MPSB.

73 *G-34*; *G-84*.

2 The war slows down

1 Boberach, *Meldungen*, vol. 9, p. 3124.

2 For the course of the war see Craig, *Germany* pp. 714–64, 730–2; also see Christian Streit, *Keine Kameraden: Die Wehrmacht und die sowjetischen Kriegsgefangenen 1941–1945*; for a discussion of the radicalization, see Kershaw, *Myth*, and *Popular*.

3 See Kershaw, *Myth*, pp. 149–89, and *Popular*, part II for the changing aspects of popular opinion and repression during the war.

4 Bonhoeffer to Harteck (9 Jan. 1942) B1 F7 RPI; Bonhoeffer to Harteck (24 Jan. 1942) B1 F7 RPI.

5 For the upheaval felt in German military and armaments circles during the last stages of the lightning war, see Ludwig, *Technik*, pp. 370–403; for popular impressions of the war fortune, see Kershaw, *Myth*, pp. 149–89; also see Boberach, *Meldungen*, vols. 1–8; for the plunder of Europe see Craig, *Germany* pp. 744–6, Burchardt, "Impact," pp. 40–70, and Kroener, "Blitzkrieg," pp. 282–303; interview with Georg Hartwig.

6 Schumann to Harteck (5 Dec. 1941) EBK; *Energiegewinnung*, 133–4 EBK, the surviving copy of this report, titled "Energiegewinnung aus Uran," was unsigned, but the joint authors probably included F. Berkei, Werner Czulius, Kurt Diebner, Georg Hartwig, and W. Herrmann.

7 *Energiegewinnung*, 8, 12–13, 134 EBK.

8 Ibid., 13–16, 133 EBK.

9 Ibid., 134 EBK.
10 Vögler to Leeb (27 Feb. 1942) MPSB; Mentzel to Görnert (8 Dec. 1942) 29-1046 IMC.
11 Schumann to Harteck (24 Jan. 1942) EBK; Harteck to Schumann (31 Jan. 1942) EBK; Army Ordnance to Harteck (16 Feb. 1942) EBK; program of conference (26–28 Feb. 1942) 29-998 IMC; Schumann to Harteck (4 Feb. 1942) EBK; President of the Reich Research Council to Harteck (21 Feb. 1942) EBK; Heisenberg to Rust (20 Feb. 1942) WHM; Rust to Lorenz (12 Feb. 1942) 29-993 IMC.
12 These estimates have been taken from an examination of all nuclear power scientific reports written during the war; interview with Otto Haxel.
13 Boberach, *Meldungen*, vol. 4, pp. 1049–51.
14 Program of conference (26–28 Feb. 1942) 29-998 IMC; *G-147*; Erich Bagge's diary (5–23 Jan. 13, 17–9 Feb. 1942) EBK, also 29-106 IMC; *G-124*; *G-174*; *G-133*; *G-132*; *G-196*.
15 *G-159*; *G-194*; *G-134*; *G-198*.
16 *G-197*; *G-127*; *G-373*; *G-140*; *G-185*; *G-151*; *G-186*; the figure is taken from Bothe and Flügge, part II, p. 154.
17 Schumann to Harteck (4 Feb. 1942) EBK; President of the Reich Research Council to Harteck (21 Feb. 1942) EBK; Heisenberg to Rust (20 Feb. 1942) WHM; Rust to Lorenz (12 Feb. 1942) 29-993 IMC.
18 Samuel Goudsmit, *Alsos*, pp. 168–71.
19 *G-150*; *G-154*.
20 The figure is taken from a subsequent talk, *G-217*; Werner Heisenberg, "Die theoretischen Grundlagen für die Energiegewinnung aus der Uranspaltung" (26 Feb. 1942), 2–3 SGNY, 29-1005 IMC, and reprinted in Werner Heisenberg, *Gesammelte Werke/Collected Works*, vol. A II (forthcoming)
21 Heisenberg to Goudsmit (5 Jan. 1948) SGNY; Heisenberg, "Theoretischen," 3 SGNY.
22 Heisenberg, "Theoretischen," 4–5 29-1005 IMC.
23 Heisenberg, "Theoretischen," 5–9 29-1005 IMC.
24 Hahn's diary (26 Feb. 1942) 29-021 IMC; newspaper clipping (paper unknown) (27 Feb. 1942) "Physik und Landesverteidigung," MPSB; Finkelnburg to Heisenberg (6 May 1942) WHM.
25 Joseph Goebbels, *The Goebbels Diaries 1942–1943*, p. 140.
26 Vögler to Leeb (27 Feb. 1942) MPSB; Telschow to Vögler (24 July 1942) MPSB.
27 Telschow memo (22, 26 Jan. 1942) MPSB.
28 Telschow memo (22, 26 Jan. 1942) MPSB; Maria Osietzki, "Kern-physikalische Grossgeräte zwischen naturwissenschaftlicher Forschung und ökonomischer Praxis: Zur Entwicklung der ersten deutschen Teilchen-beschleuniger bei Siemens 1935–43" (manuscript).
29 Leeb to Vögler (4 Mar. 1942) MPSB; Vögler to Leeb (6 Mar. 1942) MPSB.
30 David Joravsky, *The Lysenko Affair*. For a history of the *deutsche Physik* movement, see Beyerchen, as well as Andreas Kleinert, "Von der science allemande zur deutschen Physik," *Francia*, 6 (1978), 509–25, as well as "Nationalistische und antisemitische Ressentiments von Wissenschaftlern

gegen Einstein," *Lecture Notes in Physics*, 100 (1979), 501–16, and Steffen Richter, "Die 'Deutsche Physik,'" in Herbert Mehrtens and Steffen Richter (eds.), *Naturwissenschaft, Technik und Ideologie: Beiträge zur Wissenschafts-geschichte des Dritten Reiches*, pp. 116–41. Beyerchen's path-breaking history is concerned with much more than *deutsche Physik*, and provides a broad, general account of the ideological, professional, and political aspects of German physics during the Weimar Republic and Nationalist Socialist period. For information on the *deutsche Mathematik* movement, an interesting complement to *deutsche Physik*, as well as the history of mathematics under Hitler, see the writings of Herbert Mehrtens: "Naturwissenschaft und Nationalsozialismus," in Steffen Harbordt (ed.), *Wissenschaft und National-sozialismus*, pp. 101–14; "'Die Gleichschaltung' der mathematischen Gesellschaften im nationalsozialistischen Deutschland," *JM* (1985), 83–103; "Angewandte Mathematik und Anwendungen der Mathematik im national-sozialistischen Deutschland," *GG*, 12 (1986), 317–47; "The social system of mathematics and National Socialism: a survey," *Sociological Inquiry*, 57 (1987), 159–82 "Ludwig Bieberbach and 'Deutsche Mathematik,'" in E. Phillips (ed.), *Studies in the History of Mathematics*, pp. 195–241.

31 Beyerchen, pp. 141–67.

32 Ibid., pp. 79–167.

33 Ibid.

34 *VB* (29 Jan. 1936), p. 5; *VB* (28 Feb. 1936), p. 6; Heisenberg to Sommerfeld (14 Feb. 1936) 1977-28/A, 136/13 GMM; Beyerchen, pp. 142–3; *SK* (15 July 1937), p. 6; Bayerisches Staatsministerium für Unterricht und Kultur an den Reichs- und Preussischen Minister für Wissenschaft, Erziehung und Volksbildung (9 Mar. 1937) Heisenberg BDC.

35 Beyerchen, pp. 159; Heisenberg to Sommerfeld (12 Feb. 1938) 1977-28/A, 136/16 GMM.

36 Heisenberg to Sommerfeld (23 Feb. 1938) 1977-28/A, 136/18 GMM; (14 Apr. 1938) 1977-28/A, 136/18 GMM.

37 Prandtl to Himmler (12 July 1938) LPG.

38 Ibid.

39 Himmler to Prandtl (21 July 1938) Heisenberg BDC; Himmler to Heisenberg (21 July 1938) SGNY, reprinted in Goudsmit, *Alsos*, p. 116; Himmler to Heydrich (21 July 1938) SGNY; Heisenberg to Sommerfeld (23 July 1938) 1977-28/A, 136/21 GMM.

40 Heisenberg to Himmler (23 July 1938) SGNY; Heisenberg to Sommerfeld (23 July 1938) 1977-28/A, 136/21 GMM; (24 Nov. 1938) 1977-28/A, 136/?? GMM; Prandtl to Heckmann (29 Nov. 1938) Heckmann BDC.

41 Heisenberg to Sommerfeld (30 Jan. 1939) 1977-28/A, 136/25 GMM; (15 Feb. 1939) 1977-28/A, 136/26 GMM; (3 Mar. 1939) 1977-28/A, 136/28 GMM; (13 May 1939) 1977-28/A, 136/30 GMM; Himmler to Heisenberg (7 June 1939) SGNY; Heisenberg to Himmler (14 June 1939) SGNY; Heisenberg to Voigt (11 Feb. 1950) WHM.

42 Heisenberg to Sommerfeld (13 May 1939) 1977-28/A, 136/30 GMM; for the rivalry between Party and state see Broszat, *State*; Himmler to Heisenberg

(7 June 1939) SGNY; Heisenberg to Himmler (4 Feb. 1943) WHM; Heisenberg to Sommerfeld (8 June 1939) 1977-28/A, 136/31 GMM.

43 Heisenberg to Sommerfeld (13 May 1939) 1977-28/A, 136/30 GMM; Ludwig Prandtl, "Über die theoretische Physik" (20 Apr. 1941) LPG; Heisenberg to Sommerfeld (17 Dec. 1939) 1977-28/A, 136/33 GMM; Beyerchen, pp. 166.

44 Heisenberg to the Ministry of Education (11 Dec. 1942) WHM; the Ministry of Education to the Kaiser Wilhelm Society (22 July 1942) MPSB; the Ministry of Education to Johannes Jensen (22 Apr. 1941) Nat. – Math. 76 HSA; Beyerchen, pp. 169–74; Hartshorne; Bechtold to Härtle (18 Nov. 1941) MA 116/17 HA Wissenschaft Weizsäcker ICHM; Reichsforschungsrat to Hirt (4 Oct. 1943) R26 III/29 FGAK; Himmler to Sievers (July 1942) R26 III 729 FGAK; Goudsmit, *Alsos*, pp. 73–5.

45 Goudsmit, *Alsos*, pp. 66–73; Beyerchen, pp. 176–86; Finkelnburg to Heisenberg (6 May 1942) WHM.

46 Bechtold to Härtle (18 Nov. 1941) ICHM.

47 Bechtold to Härtle (18 Nov. 1941) M116/17 HA Wissenschaft Weizsäcker ICHM; Borger to Party Chancellery (17 Nov. 1941) HA Wissenschaft Weizsäcker ICHM.

48 Borger to Party Chancellery (17 Nov. 1941) M116/17 HA Wissenschaft Weizsäcker ICHM; Erxleben to Bechtold (28 Nov. 1941) M116/17 HA Wissenschaft Weizsäcker ICHM.

49 Dean of Math. – Scientific Faculty, University of Berlin to Heisenberg (23 July 1942) WHM; Heisenberg to the Dean (31 July 1942) WHM; Weizsäcker to Sommerfeld (4 July 1942) GMM; Borger to Party Chancellery (2 Oct. 1942) MA 612 59821-4 ICHM.

50 Heisenberg to Sommerfeld (17 Feb. 1941) GMM; Ramsauer to Rust (20 Jan. 1942) LPG; Wolfgang Finkelnburg, "Der Kampf gegen die Partei-Physik" (post 1945), 9 WHM; Beyerchen, pp. 176–9.

51 Ramsauer to Rust (20 Jan. 1942) LPG; Finkelnburg, "Kampf," 9 WHM; Beyerchen, pp. 176–9, 192; Heisenberg to Sommerfeld (4 Dec. 1941) LPG; invitation to the physics retreat (7 Oct. 1942) WHM; Heisenberg to University Teachers League (14 Oct. 1942) WHM; Heisenberg to Sauter (24 June 1950) WHM; Goudsmit, *Alsos*, pp. 153.

52 Ramsauer to Rust (20 Jan. 1942) LPG; Finkelnburg, "Kampf," 9 WHM; Beyerchen, pp. 176–9, 192; Heisenberg to Sommerfeld (4 Dec. 1941) LPG; invitation to the physics retreat (7 Oct. 1942) WHM; Heisenberg to Reich University Teachers League (14 Oct. 1942) WHM; Heisenberg to Sauter (24 June 1950) WHM; Goudsmit, *Alsos*, pp. 153.

53 Heisenberg to Sommerfeld (8 Oct. 1942) WHM.

54 Sommerfeld to Becker (15 Oct. 1942) WHM; Sommerfeld to Heisenberg (19 Oct. 1942) WHM; the third volume of Sommerfeld's lectures on theoretical physics, including his treatment of the theory of relativity, was not published until 1948 and contains many references to Einstein and his work.

55 Prandtl to Himmler (12 July 1938) LPG; Himmler to Prandtl (21 July 1938) Heisenberg BDC; Himmler to Heydrich (21 July 1938) SGNY; Vahlen to

Heisenberg (8 Sept. 1942) WHM; Heisenberg to Vahlen (10 Sept. 1942) WHM; Heisenberg to Bosech (26 June 1942) WHM; Thürring to Heisenberg (14 Oct. 1942) WHM; Heisenberg to Bosech (10 Dec. 1942) WHM; Heisenberg to Himmler (4 Feb. 1943) WHM; Bosech to Heisenberg (15 Feb. 1943) WHM; Werner Heisenberg, "Die Bewertung der 'modernen theoretischen Physik,'" *ZGN*, 9 (1943), 201–12.

56 Heisenberg, *ZGN*, 9 (1943), 201–2.

57 Ibid., 209–10.

58 Ibid., 204–5.

59 Clusius to Heisenberg (18 Jan. 1944) WHM.

60 Mentzel to Laue (22 May 1943) WHM; Laue to Weizsäcker (26 May 1943) 29-1065 IMC; Weizsäcker to Laue (2 June 1943) 29-1065 IMC; Laue to Weizsäcker (4 June 1943) 29-1065 IMC.

61 Interrogation of Paul Rosbaud (5 Aug. 1945) 29-1174 IMC.

62 Heisenberg to Sommerfeld (4 Sept. 1939) 1977-28/A, 136/32 GMM; Heisenberg to Himmler (4 Feb. 1943) WHM.

63 Goudsmit, *Alsos*, p. 6, the Reich Ministry of Education to the President of the University of Leipzig (22 Sept. 1942) WHM; Rust to Heisenberg (26 Feb. 1943) WHM; "Niederschrift über die Sitzung des Senates der Kaiser-Wilhelm-Gesellschaft zur Förderung der Wissenschaften" (24 Apr. 1942) R26 III 701 FGAK.

64 Prandtl to Göring (28 Apr. 1941) LPG; Ludwig Prandtl, "Über die theoretische Physik" (28 Apr. 1941) LPG.

65 The second State Secretary for the plenipotentiary of the Four Year Plan to Prandtl (19 May 1941) LPG; Prandtl to Milch (13 Nov. 1941) LPG; Prandtl to the second State Secretary for the plenipotentiary of the Four Year Plan (27 May 1941) LPG; Prandtl to Ramsauer (8 June 1941) LPG.

66 Prandtl to Joos (29 May 1941) LPG; Ramsauer to Prandtl (9 June 1941) LPG; Joos to Prandtl (6 June 1941) LPG.

67 Ramsauer to Prandtl (31 Oct. 1941) LPG; Prandtl to Milch (13 Nov. 1941) LPG; Lucht to Prandtl (3 Dec. 1941) LPG.

68 Joos to Prandtl (6 June 1941) LPG; Finkelnburg to Heisenberg (6 May 1942) WHM; Ramsauer to Rust (20 Jan. 1942) LPG.

69 Ramsauer to Rust (20 Jan. 1942) LPG.

70 Ibid.

71 Ibid.

72 Finkelnburg to Heisenberg (6 May 1942) WHM; Heisenberg to Finkelnburg (22 May 1942) WHM; Prandtl to Ramsauer (28 Jan. 1942) LPG; Heisenberg to Jordan (31 July 1942) WHM; Sommerfeld to Heisenberg (19 Oct. 1942) WHM.

73 Albert Speer, *Inside the Third Reich*, pp. 225–6; also see a review of Speer's memoirs, Karl-Heinz Ludwig, "Die wohlreflektierten 'Erinnerungen' des Albert Speer. Einige kritische Bemerkungen zur Funktion des Architekten, des Ingenieurs und der Technik im Dritten Reich," *GWU*, 21 (1970), 695–708; for a discussion of Speer's debt to Todt, see chapters 9 and 10 in Ludwig, *Technik*.

74 Speer, pp. 225–6; for a discussion of the transfer of the Reich Research Council, see chapter 6 in Ludwig, *Technik*.

75 Speer, pp. 225–6; Heisenberg, "theoretischen" SGNY; Craig, pp. 751–3.

76 Forstmann to Heisenberg (13 Oct. 1942) WHM; Heisenberg to Telschow (11 Jan. 1943) WHM; Heisenberg to Müller (11 Jan. 1943) WHM; Vögler to Heisenberg (31 Oct. 1944) MPSB.

77 Vögler to Leeb (11 May 1942) MPSB; Leeb to Vögler (16 May 1942) Vögler to Leeb (27 May 1942) MPSB; Laue, memo (24 June 1942) MPSB.

78 Party Chancellery to Härtle (8 July 1942) MA 116/5 HA Wissenschaft Heisenberg ICHM; Erxleben to Party Chancellery (9 Sept. 1942) MA 116/5 HA Wissenschaft Heisenberg ICHM.

79 Erxleben to Borger (10 July 1942) MA 116/5 HA Wissenschaft Heisenberg ICHM; Borger to Party Chancellery (9 Sept. 1942) ICHM.

80 Norwegian Hydro to Harteck and Wirtz (9 Feb. 1942) *G-341 v.3* GR; Harteck to Army Ordnance (23 Mar. 1942) EBK; Norwegian Hydro to W Stab N (21 Apr. 1942) 1977-28/A, 136/*G-341 v.3* GR; Norwegian Hydro to W Stab N (23 Apr. 1942) *G-341 v.3* GR; "Niederschrift über die Besprechung bei Norsk Hydro am 25.9.1942 in W Stab N," *G-341 v.3* GR; Karl Wirtz, "Bericht über den Besuch in Rjukan vom 13. bis 15.11.42" (17 Nov. 1942) SGNY.

81 Minutes of a meeting on heavy water production (16 July 1942) EBK; Harteck to Army Ordnance (1 Dec. 1942) EBK; *G-189*.

82 Bütefisch to Harteck (23 Mar. 1942) EBK; Bütefisch to Harteck (20 Apr. 1942) EBK; Hayes, pp. 163–317.

83 Harteck to Diebner (26 June 1942) EBK; Harteck to Army Ordnance (26 June 1942) EBK.

84 Groth's diary (15 Apr., 10 May 1942) 29-814 IMC; Groth to Army Ordnance (27 June 1942) EBK; *G-146*; Groth's diary (7 Aug. 1942) 29-814 IMC; *G-149*; Groth to Army Ordnance (12 Dec. 1942) 29-751 IMC.

85 *G-139*, 1–2, 15; the figure is taken from Bothe and Flügge, part II, p. 99; Von Ardenne's research was hampered, and finally ended by the war, see Manfred von Ardenne, *Mein Leben für Forschung und Fortschritt*.

86 *G-162*; Auler to Heisenberg (20 May 1942) WHM.

87 *G-136*, 9, 12.

88 *G-135*.

89 *G-161*; Harteck to Army Ordnance (12 Oct. 1942) EBK; *G-161*; Zimmer to Heisenberg (19 Aug. 1942) WHM; Bothe to Heisenberg (1 Sept. 1942) WHM; Bothe to Heisenberg (14 Sept. 1942) WHM; Heisenberg to Bothe (23 Oct. 1942) WHM; the figure is taken from Bothe and Flügge, part II, p. 156.

90 Ludwig, *Technik*, pp. 234–7 for the Reich Research Council; Decree by Hitler (9 June 1942) SGNY; Wirtz to Heisenberg (20 Aug. 1942) WHM; Vögler to Göring (29 Aug. 1942) SGNY; Harteck to Martin (16 May 1942) EBK; contract between Army Ordnance and Kaiser Wilhelm Society (24 June 1942) MPSB; Telschow to Heisenberg (6 July 1942) WHM; Telschow to Diebner (19 Oct. 1942) MPSB; Telschow memo (3 Aug. 1942) MPSB.

91 Telschow to Vögler (24 July 1942) MPSB.

92 Goerens to Heisenberg (12 May 1942) WHM.

93 Heisenberg to Goerens (15 May 1942) WHM.
94 Telschow to Vögler (24 July 1942) MPSB; Wirtz to Telschow (28 Aug. 1942) WHM; Esau to Mentzel (24 Nov. 1942) SGNY; Osietzki.
95 Esau to Mentzel (26 Nov. 1942) SGNY; Bagge's diary (4 Dec. 1942) EBK, also 29-106 IMC.

3 The war comes home

1 Boberach, *Meldungen*, vol. 14, p. 5620.
2 Göring to Esau (8 Dec. 1942) 29-1044 IMC; Mentzel to Görnnert (8 Dec. 1942) 29-1046 IMC.
3 Mentzel to Görnnert (8 Dec. 1942) 29-1046 IMC; Schumann to Harteck (8 Mar. 1943) *G-341 v.4*; Esau to Harteck (19 Mar. 1943) *G-341 v.4*.
4 Telschow to Heisenberg (8 Feb. 1943) WHM; Telschow to Mentzel (1 Mar. 1943) 29-1049 IMC; Mentzel to Telschow (4 Mar. 1943) MPSB; Vögler to Mentzel (4 Mar. 1943) MPSB; Mentzel to Vögler (9 Mar. 1943) MPSB; Schumann to Mentzel (31 Mar. 1943) 29-1057 IMC; Mentzel to Esau (31 Mar. 1943) 29-1057 IMC.
5 Craig, pp. 753–4; Kershaw, *Myth*, pp. 189–99; Willi Boelcke (ed.), *"Wollt Ihr den totalen Krieg?": Die geheimen Goebbels-Konferenzen 1939–1943*.
6 Ludwig, *Technik*, pp. 436–44.
7 Boberach, *Meldungen*, pp. 5413–5416.
8 Mentzel to Heisenberg (7 Sept. 1942) WHM; Heisenberg to Mentzel (10 Sept. 1942) WHM; for example, the binders in the Heisenberg Papers holding correspondence and papers from inventors dwarf Heisenberg's general correspondence for certain years; Fischer to Heisenberg (9 June 1943) WHM; Heisenberg to Fischer (15 June 1943) WHM.
9 Reich Minister for Armaments and Munitions to Heisenberg (13 July 1943) WHM; Heisenberg to Reich Minister for Armaments and Munitions (15 July 1943) WHM; Reich Minister for Armaments and War Production to Heisenberg (8 Oct. 1943) WHM.
10 Heisenberg to Reich Minister for Armaments and War Production (11 Oct. 1943) WHM; unfortunately Günther's reply to Heisenberg has apparently not survived; Bahr to Heisenberg (11 Jan. 1944) WHM; Heisenberg to Bahr (21 Jan. 1944) WHM; Bahr to Heisenberg (13 Mar. 1944) WHM; Bahr to Günther (13 Mar. 1944) WHM.
11 Ludwig, *Technik*, pp. 436–44; Esau to Mentzel (26 Nov. 1942) 29-1035 IMC; Mentzel to Görnnert (8 Dec. 1942) 29-1044 IMC.
12 Mentzel to Görnnert (8 July 1943) 29-1068 IMC; for example, the possibility of nuclear explosives is mentioned in Werner Osenberg, memo (8 May 1943) 29-1065 IMC.
13 Heisenberg to Army Ordnance (13 Jan. 1943) WHM; Schumann to Heisenberg (18 Jan. 1943) WHM; Heisenberg to Hahn (22 Jan. 1943) WHM; Ramsauer to Prandtl (12 May 1942) LPG; *G-241*.
14 Bothe to Heisenberg (10 Feb. 1943) WHM; Heisenberg to Bothe (12 Feb. 1943) WHM; *G-214*; *G-213*; *G-216*; *G-207*; *G-205*.
15 *G-217*; too much should not be made of this linguistic change. The term

"burner" was only used by Heisenberg's immediate circle, and only from July, 1942 to the beginning of 1944, when they returned to use of the term "machine."

16 *G-217.*

17 Telschow to Diebner (2 June 1942) MPSB; Heisenberg to Weizsäcker (16 Dec. 1942) WHM.

18 Interviews with Gerhard Borrmann, Werner Czulius, and Georg Hartwig.

19 *G-125,* from which the figure is taken; interview with Georg Hartwig.

20 *G-125,* also for the figure; interview with Georg Hartwig; interview with Werner Czulius.

21 *G-221; G-164; G-218; G-222;* interview with Karl-Heinz Höcker.

22 *G-218; G-222.*

23 *G-218; G-222; G-125.*

24 Heisenberg to Telschow (25 Mar. 1943) WHM.

25 *G-211; G-212,* from which the figure is taken; Georg Hartwig recalls that Czulius, Herrmann, Pose, and himself developed the cube idea together.

26 Heisenberg to Telschow (25 Mar. 1943) WHM; (7 May 1943) *G-341 v.4;* interview with George Hartwig; Höcker to Heisenberg (20 Apr. 1943) WHM; Heisenberg to Höcker (30 Apr. 1943) WHM.

27 (7 May 1943) *G-341 v.4;* Esau to Harteck (29 May 1943) *G-341 v.4;* interview with Karl Zimmer.

28 Bothe to Heisenberg (14 Sept. 1942) WHM; Bothe to Heisenberg (30 July 1943) WHM; *G-206.*

29 Riehl and Zimmer to Heisenberg (15 July 1943) WHM; Riehl and Zimmer to Heisenberg (19 Aug. 1943) WHM; Heisenberg to Vögler (25 Aug. 1943) WHM; Fischer to Heisenberg (9 Sept. 1943) WHM; Heisenberg to Bothe (13 Dec. 1943) WHM.

30 Abraham Esau (21 Aug. 1944) 29-1101 IMC; *G-240.*

31 *G-210;* Abraham Esau (21 Aug. 1944) 29-1101 IMC; the figure is taken from Bothe and Flügge, part II, p. 159.

32 Höcker to Heisenberg (30 July 1943) WHM; Wirtz to Heisenberg (23 Nov. 1943) WHM; *G-223.*

33 Werner Heisenberg, "Auswertung des Gottower Versuches G III," WHM.

34 Heisenberg to Ministry of Education, (9 Apr. 1943) WHM; Gerlach to Stückelberg (29 Dec. 1943) WGM; Mentzel to Laue (22 May 1943) WHM; Rektor of Hamburg University to Harteck (12 May 1938) HSW D- & PA IV 367 HSA; Goudsmit and Wardenburg to ? (8 Dec. 1944) SGNY; two visits, to Switzerland in 1944 and to Denmark in 1941, will not be discussed until chapter 6 and 7, respectively, because only postwar sources are available for these two events; Also see Dieter Hoffmann, "Zur Teilnahme deutscher Physiker an den Kopenhagener Physikerkonferenzen nach 1933 sowie am 2. Kongress Für Einheit der Wissenschaft, Kopenhagen 1936," *NTM. Schriftenreihe für Geschichte der Naturwissenschaften, Technik, und Medizin,* 25 (1988), 49–55.

35 Memo (1 June 1942) WHM; memo (1 Mar. 1943) WHM.

36 Memo (1 June 1942) WHM; memo (1 Mar. 1943) WHM.

37 The institutes in Portugal and Spain were named "*Deutsches Kulturinstitut*";

Ministry of Education to Heisenberg (21 Oct. 1942) WHM; Memo (1 June 1942) WHM; Memo (1 Mar. 1943) WHM.

38 Scherrer to Heisenberg (26 May 1942) WHM; Heisenberg to Scherrer (10 June 1942) WHM; Heisenberg to Dean of Leipzig University philosophical faculty (10 June 1942) WHM; Stueckelberg to Heisenberg (20 Aug. 1942) WHM; student organization of the University of Bern to Heisenberg (7 Sept. 1942) WHM; Fischer to Heisenberg (23 Oct. 1942) WHM; student organization of the University of Basle to Heisenberg (2 Nov. 1942) WHM; Ministry of Education to Heisenberg (21 Oct. 1942) WHM; National Socialist German Workers Party to Heisenberg (28 Oct. 1942) WHM.

39 Elisabeth Heisenberg, *Inner Exile: Recollections of a Life with Werner Heisenberg*; Werner Heisenberg, *Physics and Beyond: Encounters and Conversations.*

40 Heisenberg to Ministry of Education (trip to Switzerland) (11 Dec. 1942) WHM.

41 Heisenberg to German Congress Center (17 Nov. 1942) WHM; Heisenberg to Ministry of Education (trip to Hungary) (11 Dec. 1942), WHM; for more information on Planck's lectures in Greater Germany, see Heilbron, pp. 183–91.

42 Ministry of Education to Heisenberg (24 Feb. 1943) WHM; Heisenberg to Ministry of Education (9 Apr. 1943), WHM; Heisenberg to German Academic Exchange Service (9 Mar. 1943) WHM.

43 Heisenberg to Coster (16 Feb. 1943) WHM.

44 Ibid., Coster to Laue (7 June 1943) SGNY.

45 Boettcher to Heisenberg (21 Apr. 1943) WHM.

46 Ibid.; Heisenberg to Boettcher (30 Apr. 1943) WHM.

47 Ministry of Education to Heisenberg (15 June 1943) WHM; (31 July 1943) WHM; Heisenberg to Ministry of Education (11 Aug. 1943) WHM.

48 Kramers to Heisenberg (29 July 1943) WHM.

49 Ibid. (5 July 1944) WHM.

50 Heisenberg to Ministry of Education (20 Aug. 1943) WHM; Heisenberg to Kramers (20 Aug. 1943) WHM; Kramers to Heisenberg (1 Sept. 1943) WHM; Ministry of Education to Heisenberg (6 Sept. 1943) WHM; Reich Commissioner for the occupied Dutch territories to Heisenberg (15 Sept. 1943) WHM.

51 Heisenberg to Ministry of Education (10 Nov. 1943), WHM.

52 Ibid.

53 Kuiper to Fischer (30 June 1945) GKT; I have not visited the archives of the University of Arizona in person, but I would like to thank Ron Doel, who has researched in Tucson and allowed me to view this document; Hendrik Casimir, *Haphazard Reality*, pp. 191–210, and "Heisenberg im Urteil seiner Schüler," *BW* (1985), 142, 144–45.

54 Heisenberg to Hiby (1 Nov. 1943) WHM.

55 Rosenfeld to Heisenberg (10 Dec. 1943) WHM, (14 Apr. 1944) WHM; Kramers to Heisenberg (5 July 1944) WHM; interview with Stefan Rosental.

56 Heisenberg to Schwarz (14 Feb. 1944) WHM.

57 Coblitz to Dennhardt (8 Dec. 1943) R 52 IV/152 FGAK; Christoph Klessmann, "Osteuropaforschung und Lebensraumpolitik im Dritten Reich,"

in Peter Lundgreen (ed.), *Wissenschaft im Dritten Reich*, pp. 350–83, especially 364–6; Martin Broszat, *Nationalsozialistische Polenpolitik: 1939–1945*, especially pp. 68–84, 177–92; Mehrtens, *GG*, 12 (1986), 317–47; Max Weinreich, *Hitler's Professors: The Part of Scholarship in Germany's Crimes against the Jewish People*, pp. 95–7.

58 Coblitz to Heisenberg (20 May 1941) WHM; Coblitz to Dennhardt (8 Dec. 1943) R52IV/152 FGAK; Coblitz to Heisenberg (20 May 1941) WHM; Heisenberg to Coblitz (6 June 1941) WHM; Ministry of Education to Heisenberg (13 May 1943) WHM; Coblitz to Heisenberg (25 May 1943) WHM; Heisenberg to Coblitz (26 May 1943) WHM; Heisenberg to Coblitz (3 June 1943) WHM.

59 Borger to Heisenberg (7 June 1943) WHM; Heisenberg to Borger (11 June 1943) WHM.

60 Coblitz to Heisenberg (15 July 1943) WHM; Coblitz to Heisenberg (29 Sept. 1943) WHM; Heisenberg to Coblitz (11 Oct. 1943) WHM; Heisenberg to Coblitz (29 Oct. 1943) WHM; Heisenberg to German Congress Center (29 Oct. 1943) WHM; Coblitz to Heisenberg (18 Nov. 1943) WHM; Coblitz to Dennhardt (8 Dec. 1943) R 52 IV/152 FGAK.

61 "Rapport over Begivenhederne under Besættelsen af Universitetets Institut for teoretisk Fysik fra d.6.December 1943 til d.3.Februar 1944" (1944 or 1945) BGC; I want to thank Finn Aaserud and Gro Naes for translating this document for me.

62 "Rapport" BGC.

63 Ibid.; Euler to Heisenberg (8 Jan. 1944) WHM; Weizsäcker to Heisenberg (translation) (16 Jan. 1944) NAARS; Heisenberg to Euler (1 Feb. 1944) WHM; J. G. Crowther, *Science in Liberated Europe*, pp. 106–8; Heisenberg to Johannes Jensen (1 Feb. 1944) WHM.

64 Ministry of Education to Heisenberg (1 Mar. 1944) WHM; German Research Community to Heisenberg (28 Mar. 1944) WHM; Heisenberg to Höfler (27 Apr. 1944) WHM.

65 Klinger to Heisenberg (28 June 1949) WHM; Heisenberg to Klinger (4 July 1949) WHM; Heisenberg to Höfler (27 Apr. 1944) WHM; Höfler to Heisenberg (12 Jan. 1947) WHM.

66 Heisenberg to Klinger (4 July 1944) WHM; interview with Stefan Rosental.

67 Interview with Stefan Rosental; Kuiper to Fischer (30 June 1945) GKT.

68 Burchardt, "Impact," pp. 40–70.

69 Paul Harteck and Karl Wirtz (20 Oct. 1941) *G-341 v.3.*

70 (11 Jan. 1943) *G-341 v.3*; Harteck to Army Ordnance (20 Jan. 1943) *G-341 v.3*; for more information on the espionage efforts directed at the Norwegian Hydro, see David Irving, *The German Atomic Bomb: The History of Nuclear Research in Nazi Germany*, pp. 132–45, 155–70, 192–6, 200–11.

71 W Stab N to Army Ordnance (2 Mar. 1943) *G-341 v.3.*

72 (13 Mar. 43) *G-341 v.3.*

73 Harteck to Diebner (14 Apr. 1943) *G-341 v.4*; (7 May 1943) *G-341 v.4.*

74 Paul Harteck, (27 May 1943) *G-341 v.4*; Heisenberg to Esau (21 May 1943) WHM.

75 G-341 v.3; (11 Dec. 1943) *G-341 v.3*; Paul Harteck (2 Oct. 1943) *G-341 v.4.*

76 Paul Harteck (2 Oct. 1943) *G-341 v.4*; Bütefisch to Esau (8 Dec. 1943) 29-759 IMC.

77 *G-158*; the diagram is taken from Konrad Beyerle, Wilhelm Groth, Paul Harteck, and Johannes Jensen, *Über Gaszentrifugen: Anreicherung der Xenon-, Krypton- und der Selen-Isotope nach dem Zentrifugenverfahren*, p. 9; Harteck to Diebner (14 Apr. 1943) *G-341 v.4*; Groth's diary (1, 2 July; 5, 6 Nov. 1943) 29-814 IMC.

78 Esau to Harteck (15 July 1943) *G-341 v.4*; Harteck to Esau (21 July 1943) *G-341 v.4*.

79 Beuthe to Harteck (3 Aug. 1943) *G-341 v.4*; Beuthe to Harteck (11 Sept. 1943) *G-341 v.4*; Harteck to Diebner (16 Sept. 1943) *G-341 v.4*.

80 Harteck to Oberleutnant Gieser (15 Dec. 1943) *G-341 v.4*; Harteck to Esau (15 Dec. 1943) *G-341 v.4*.

81 Heisenberg to Kaiser Wilhelm Gesellschaft (1 Apr. 1943) WHM; C. H. F. Müller Aktiengesellschaft to Heisenberg (14 Dec. 1943) WHM; Forstmann to Heisenberg (13 Apr. 1943) WHM; circular from the Reich Minister for Armaments and Munitions (15 Apr. 1943) WHM.

82 Ludwig, *Technik*, p. 252; Ramsauer to Rust (20 Jan. 1942) LPG; *G-241*; Telschow to Heisenberg (10 Mar. 1943) WHM; Wirtz to Kaiser Wilhelm Gesellschaft (19 Apr. 1943) WHM; interview with Heinz Maier-Leibnitz; interview with Julius Hiby; interview with Willibald Jentschke.

83 Laue to Heisenberg (20 Aug. 1943) WHM; Harteck to Diebner (16 Sept. 1943) *G-341 v.4*; Harteck to Heisenberg (24 Nov. 1943) WHM; Rosenfeld to Heisenberg (10 Dec. 1943) WHM; Döpel to Reichsforschungsrat (10 Dec. 1943) WHM; Döpel to Heisenberg (12 Dec. 1943) WHM; Bonhoeffer to Harteck (27 Dec. 1943) B1 F7 RPI; Bonhoeffer to Harteck (?1943) B1 F7 RPI.

84 Hahn to Heisenberg (5 Aug. 1943) WHM; Bothe to Helmholtz Gesellschaft (16 Mar. 1943) Bothe G1 MPSB; Bothe to Esau (1 June 43) ? IMC; Osietzki.

85 Program of "Kernphysikalische Tagung 1943" 29-1078 IMC.

86 "Tagung" 29-1078 IMC; *G-206*; *G-240*; *G-249*; *G-144*; *G-202*.

87 "Tagung" 29-1078 IMC; *G-204*; *G-280*; *G-297*; Karl G. Zimmer, "Bericht über Dosimetrie schneller Neutronen," 30-643 IMC.

88 Interview with Kurt Starke.

89 Grobbrügge to Harteck (25 June 1948) HSWD- & PA I 206 B.1 HSA; Harteck to Grobbrügge (29 July 1948) HSWD- & PA I 206 B.1 HSA.

90 "Auszug aus dem Protokoll des Universitätssenats" (26 June 1945) Universität I- D.10.10 Bd. I HSA; Koch's betrayal of Harteck was common knowledge after the war, for example, see Robert Jungk, *Brighter than a Thousand Suns*, p. 96; for the academic politics within the Hamburg physics community see Monika Renneberg, "Die Physik und die physikalischen Institute an der Universität Hamburg im Dritten Reich," two different manuscripts (1 Apr. 1985 and 15 Apr. 1986); for Harteck's personal interest in calling a nuclear physicist see Harteck to Jensen (15 Aug. 1944) *G-341 v.6*.

91 Interview with Paul Harteck; also see Peukert, *Nazi Germany*.

4 The war is lost

1 Boberach, *Meldungen*, vol. 16, p. 6215.

2 Burchardt, "Impact," pp. 40–70; Esau to Mentzel (28 Oct. 1943) 29-1082 IMC; Mentzel to Görnnert (6 Nov. 1943) 29-1082 IMC; Mentzel to Goerner (6 Nov. 1943) 29-1082 IMC; Mentzel to Görnnert (12 Nov. 1943) 29-1082 IMC; Kershaw, *Myth*, pp. 200–4.

3 Mentzel to Görnnert (12 Nov. 1943) 29-1082 IMC; Mentzel to Görnnert (3 Dec. 1943) 29-1082 IMC; Göring to Plendl (2 Dec. 1943) 29-1082 IMC; Mentzel to Görnnert (8 Dec. 1943) 29-1082 IMC; Ludwig, *Technik*, p. 457; interrogation of Gerlach (13 May 1945) 29-1253 IMC.

4 Heisenberg to Harteck (8 Dec. 1943) WHM; Harteck to Esau (4 Oct. 1944) *G-341 v.6*; Clusius to Heisenberg (18 Jan. 1944) WHM; interview with Georg Hartwig; interview with Kurt Starke.

5 Gerlach to Mentzel (26 May 1944) 29-1110 IMC; Abraham Esau, "Bericht über den Stand der Arbeiten auf dem Gebiete der Kernphysik am 31.12.43." 29-1101 IMC.

6 Göring to Gerlach (2 Dec. 1943) 29-1082 IMC; Gerlach to Bingel (9 Dec. 1943) WGM; Mentzel to Gerlach (5 Jan. 1944) 29-1082 IMC; Gerlach to Harteck (24 Jan. 1944) *G-341 v.2*; Gerlach, "Arbeitsbescheinigung" (25 Apr. 1945) 29-1158 IMC; interrogation of Gerlach (13 May 1945) 29-1253 IMC; Gerlach to Heisenberg (28 June 1946) WHM.

7 Harteck to Gerlach (5 Feb. 1944) *G-341 v.2*.

8 Mentzel to Gerlach (16 Mar. 1944) 29-1101 IMC; Diebner to Mentzel (18 Apr. 1944) 29-1110 IMC; Gerlach to Mentzel (26 May 1944) 29-1110 IMC; Mentzel to Gerlach (26 May 1944) 29-1110 IMC.

9 Heisenberg to Stetter (2 July 1943) WHM; Heisenberg to Hornung (20 Aug. 1943) WHM; Heisenberg to the Dean of Math–Science Faculty of University of Berlin (2 Oct. 1943) WHM; "Niederschrift über die Direktorenbesprechung am 9.11.1943 im Harnack-Haus," R21/592 FGAK; Osenberg to Harteck (28 Mar. 1944) *G-341 v.2*; Berkei to Harteck (26 Apr. 1944) *G-341 v.2*; Clusius to Walcher (17 Dec. 1943) WPB; Gerlach, "Declaration" (2 Mar. 1945) 29-1158 IMC; Bagge's diary (Aug.–Sept. 1943) EBK, also 29-106 IMC; Laue to Heisenberg (18 Apr. 1944) WHM.

10 Hiby to Heisenberg and Wirtz (20 Jan. 1944) WHM; "Niederschrift über die Direktorenbesprechung am 9.11.1943 im Harnack Haus," R21/592 FGAK; Bagge's diary (13 Apr. 1944) EBK, also 29-106 IMC; "Affidavit of SS Captain Karl Sommer" (4 Oct. 1946) Document NI-1065 from Staatsarchiv Nürnberg, is reprinted in Benjamin Ferencz, *Lohn des Grauens*, p. 270.

11 Benjamin Ferencz, *Less than Slaves*; Hayes, pp. 325–83; Ulrich Herbert, *Fremdarbeiter: Politik und Praxis des "Ausländer-Einsatzes" in der Kriegswirtschaft des Dritten Reiches*; Streit; Jürgen Förster, "The Wehrmacht and the war of 'Weltanschauungen' 1941," in Wilhelm Deist (ed.), *The German Military in the Age of Total War*, pp. 304–22; "Affidavit by Rudolf Höss" (12 Mar. 1947), reprinted in Ferencz, *Slaves*, p. 203.

12 Interview with Kurt Starke; interview with Kurt Sauerwein; Heisenberg to Kopfermann (18 Jan. 1944) WPB.

13 Bagge's diary (5 Aug., Aug–Sept. 1943, 20 Feb., 13 Apr., 2 May – 19 Aug. 1944) EBK, also 29-106 IMC; Diebner to Harteck (11 July 1944) *G-341 v.2*; Diebner to Harteck (4 Aug. 1944) *G-341 v.2*; Bagge's diary (10–17 Aug. 1944) EBK, also 29-106 IMC; Wirtz to Hiby (23 Feb. 1944) WHM; Horst Korsching, *NW*, 32 (1944), 220 (31 May 1944).

14 Bothe to Helmholtz Society (10 Jan. 1944) Bothe G1 MPSB; Telschow to Bothe (17 Sept. 1944) Bothe G2 MPSB; Bothe to Telschow (15 July 1944) Bothe G2 MPSB; interview with Kurt Starke; Riezler to Bothe (10 Oct. 1944) Bothe 11 MPSB; Mentzel to Vögler (27 Oct. 1944) 29-1143 IMC; Osietzki.

15 Döpel to Heisenberg (12 Dec. 1943) WHM; Döpel to Reich Research Council (10 Dec. 1943) WHM; Heisenberg to Döpel (18 Dec. 1943) WHM; Hund to Heisenberg (3 Jan. 1944) WHM; Catel to Heisenberg (21 Apr. 1944) WHM; Döpel to Heisenberg (10 Apr. 1944) WHM; Heisenberg to Catel (24 Apr. 1944) WHM; Heisenberg to Sommerfeld (8 Aug. 1944) 1977-28/A, 132/42 GMM.

16 Laue to Heisenberg (23 Nov. 1943) WHM; Heisenberg to Kramers (10 Jan. 1944) WHM; Hahn to Heisenberg and Laue (25 Feb. 1944) WHM; Thiessen to Heisenberg (5 Apr. 1944) WHM; Heisenberg to Döpel (26 Apr. 1944) WHM; Hacmann to Heisenberg (19 Mar. 1944) WHM; Heisenberg to Hacmann (31 Mar. 1944) WHM.

17 Harteck to Clusius (18 Jan. 1944) *G-341 v.6*; Harteck to Bonhoeffer (9 May 1944) *G-341 v.6*; Harteck to Hauptwirtschaftsamt (14 Nov. 1944) *G-341 v.6*.

18 Craig: 671; Ralf Dahrendorf, *Society and Democracy*, pp. 392–3; Kershaw, *Myth*, pp. 215–20; Heisenberg, *Beyond*, chapter 15.

19 Harteck to Osenberg (19 July 1944) *G-341 v.6*; Gerlach to Harteck (22 July 1944) *G-341 v.2*; telegram Kwasnik to Groth *G-341 v.5*; telegram Harteck to Kwasnik (1 Sept. 1944) *G-341 v.5*; Kwasnik to Groth (14 Sept. 1944) *G-341 v.5*; Gerlach, memo, *G-341 v.2*; Groth to Kwasnik (28 Sept. 1944) *G-341 v.5*.

20 Mentzel to Gerlach (2 Sept. 1944) R26 III 515 FGAK; Gerlach to Reich Research Council (26 Feb. 1945) 29-1158 IMC; Speer to Gerlach (19 Dec. 1944) A3/1579 FGAK.

21 Clusius to Gerlach (9 Sept. 1944) R26 III 446a FGAK; Martin Bormann, "Rundschreiben" (3 Sept. 1944) 31-1062 IMC; Klopfer to Osenberg (12 Aug. 1944) 31-1062 IMC; Gerlach to Bormann (16 Dec. 1944) 29-1156 IMC; Bagge's diary (early 1945) EBK, also 29-106 IMC.

22 Abraham Esau, "Bericht über den Stand der Arbeiten auf dem Gebiete der Kernphysik am 31.12.43." (21 Aug. 1944) 29-1101 IMC; Vögler to Heisenberg (27 Jan. 1944) WHM; Harteck to Gerlach (5 Feb. 1944) *G-341 v.2*; Diebner to Harteck (8 Jan. 1944) *G-341 v.2*.

23 Harteck to Diebner (16 Feb. 1944) *G-341 v.5*.

24 Ibid.

25 Schoepke to Harteck (2 Mar. 1944) *G-341 v.3*; Harteck to Herold (10 Mar. 1944) *G-341 v.5*; Harteck to Herold (10 Mar. 1944) *G-341 v.5*; Walther Gerlach, "Bericht über die Arbeiten auf kernphysikalischem Gebiet vom 1. Feb. bis 31 März 1944" (30 May 1944) 29-1118 IMC.

26 Harteck to Herold (10 Mar. 1944) *G-341 v.5*; Walther Gerlach, "Bericht

über die Arbeiten auf kernphysikalischem Gebiet vom 1. Feb. bis 31 März 1944" (30 May 1944) 29-1118 IMC; *G-303*; Kurt Diebner, "Fusionsprozesse mit Hilfe konvergenter Stosswellen – einige ältere und neuere Versuche und Überlegungen," *Kerntechnik*, 4 (1962), 89–93.

27 Paul Harteck, "Bericht über den Stand der SH 200-Gewinnung" (15 Apr. 1944) 29-762 IMC.

28 Paul Harteck (9 Jan. 1945) *G-341 v.3*.

29 Ibid. Harteck to von der Bey (12 Feb. 1945) *G-341 v.6*.

30 Rosbaud to Harteck (14 Jan. 1944) *G-341 v.6*; Harteck to Rosbaud (17 Jan. 1944) *G-341 v.6*; Harteck to Rosbaud (4 Feb. 1944) *G-341 v.6*.

31 Harteck to Rosbaud (4 Feb. 1944) *G-341 v.6*; Rosbaud to Harteck (8 Feb. 1944) *G-341 v.6*.

32 Harteck to Bonhoeffer (5 Oct. 1944) *G-341 v.6*; Harteck to SS-Führungshauptamt SS-Sanitätsamt (11 Mar. 1944) *G-341 v.6*; Ludwig, *Technik*, pp. 473–514.

33 Abraham Esau, "Bericht über den Stand der Arbeiten auf dem Gebiete der Kernphysik am 31.12.43" (21 Aug. 1944) 29-1101 IMC; (11 Jan. 1944) *G-341 v.5*; Harteck to Heisenberg (13 Mar. 1944) *G-341 v.6*; Hans Suess (26 Jan. 1944) *G-341 v.5*; Hans Suess, *G-341 v.5*; Hoyer to Harteck (4 Feb. 1944) *G-341 v.6*; Harteck to Diebner (16 Feb. 1944) *G-341 v.5*.

34 Harteck to Herold (10 Mar. 1944) *G-341 v.5*; Harteck to Herold (4 Apr. 1944) *G-341 v.5*; IG Farben to Gerlach (1 Apr. 1944) *G-341 v.5*.

35 IG Farben to Harteck (1 June 1944) *G-341 v.2*; Suess to Gerlach (29 June 1944) *G-341 v.5*; Harteck to Army Ordnance (18 July 1944) *G-341 v.2*; Harteck to Army Ordnance (20 July 1944) *G-341 v.2*; Hans Suess (21 July 1944) *G-341 v.2*.

36 Harteck to Clusius (29 June 1944) *G-341 v.6*; Paul Harteck, "Bericht über den Stand der SH 200-Gewinnung" (15 Apr. 1944) 29-762 IMC.

37 Walther Gerlach, "Bericht über die Arbeiten auf kernphysikalischem Gebiet von 1. Feb. bis 31 März 1944" (30 May 1944) 29-1118 IMC; *G-296*; Gerlach to Harteck (18 Apr. 1944) *G-341*; Wirtz to Gerlach (20 Sept. 1944) *G-341 v.6*; Harteck to Gerlach (10 Nov. 1944) *G-341 v.6*; Clusius to Harteck (18 Apr. 1944) *G-341 v.6*; Harteck (2? May 1944) *G-341 v.2*; Heisenberg to Harteck (22 May 1944) *G-341 v.6*; Harteck to Bonhoeffer (31 May 1944) *G-341 v.6*; Bonhoeffer to Harteck (7 June 1944) *G-341 v.6*; Bonhoeffer to Diebner (12 June 1944) *G-341 v.6*; Wirtz to Harteck (27 June 1944) *G-341 v.6*; Silica Gel Gesellschaft to Reichsforschungsrat (27 Aug. 1944) *G-341*.

38 Paul Harteck (9 May 1944) *G-341 v.2*.

39 Ibid.; Harteck (2? May 1944) *G-341 v.2*; Harteck to Clusius (31 July 1944) *G-341 v.6*; Harteck to Clusius (15 Aug. 1944) *G-341 v.6*.

40 Herold to Harteck (26 May 1944) *G-341 v.5*; Gerlach to Herold (28 July 1944) *G-341 v.2*; Herold to Gerlach (23 Aug. 1944) *G-341 v.5*; Gerlach to Herold (14 Sept. 1944) *G-341 v.4*; Gerlach to Röcke (14 Sept. 1944) *G-341 v.1*.

41 Paul Harteck (20 Nov. 1944) *G-341*; Paul Harteck, "Termine" (2? May 1944) *G-341 v.2*; Paul Harteck (2, 15 Nov. 1944) *G-341 v.5*; Diebner to Harteck (3 Mar. 1945) *G-341 v.2*; Harteck to Gerlach (7 Feb. 1945) *G-341*.

42 Harteck to Diebner (28 Sept. 1944) *G-341 v.2*; Walther Gerlach (2 May

1945) 29-1158 IMC; IG Farben to Harteck (6 Jan. 1945) *G-341 v.5*; Harteck to Herold (9 Mar. 1945) *G-341 v.5.*

43 Harteck to Noack (10 Mar. 1944) *G-341 v.5*; Noack to Harteck (9 May 1944) *G-341 v.5*; Harteck to Noack (20 May 1944) *G-341 v.5*; Noack to Harteck (11 July 1944) *G-341 v.5*; Harteck to Noack (17 Aug. 1944) *G-341 v.5*; Harteck to Riehl (15 Mar. 1944) *G-341 v.6*; (24 Mar. 1944) *G-341 v.2*; *G-391.*

44 (24 Mar. 1944) *G-341 v.2*; Höcker to Harteck (19 May 1944) *G-341 v.6*; Harteck to Gerlach (7 Feb. 1945) *G-341*; Paul Harteck, *G-391* (?1944).

45 Harteck to Oberleutnant Gieser (15 Dec. 1943) *G-341 v.4*; Harteck to Esau (15 Dec. 1943) *G-341 v.4*; Diebner to Harteck (8 Jan. 1944) *G-341 v.2*; Abraham Esau, "Bericht über den Stand der Arbeiten auf dem Gebiete der Kernphysik am 31.12.43" (21 Aug. 1944) 29-1101 IMC; *G-330*; Gerlach to Osenberg (18 Aug. 1944) *G-341 v.2*; Harteck to Diebner (16 Feb. 1944) *G-341 v.5*; Walther Gerlach, "Bericht über die Arbeiten auf kernphysikalischem Gebiet vom 1 Feb. bis 31 März 44" (30 May 1944) 29-1118 IMC.

46 Harteck to Diebner (25 Mar. 1944) *G-341 v.2.*

47 Ibid.; Paul Harteck (2? May 1944) *G-341 v.2.*

48 Harteck to Diebner (28 July 1944) *G-341 v.2*; Konrad Beyerle, "Niederschrift über meine Reise nach Freiburg und Kandern in der Zeit vom 2.8 bis 13.8.44," 29-775 IMC; Beyerle to Harteck (17 Aug. 1944) 29-775 IMC; Konrad Beyerle, "Niederschrift über den Besuch von Herrn Professor Harteck bei Anschütz u. Co. am 16.8.44" (17 Aug. 1944) 29-775 IMC; "Niederschrift von einer Besprechung bei Anschütz" (8 Sept. 1944) 29-775 IMC; Beyerle to Harteck (8 Sept. 1944) 29-775 IMC; "Niederschrift von einer Besprechung zwischen Harteck und Beyerle über die Ultrazentrifuge" (9 Sept. 1944) 29-775 IMC; *G-245.*

49 Harteck to Gerlach (15 Aug. 1944) *G-341 v.5*; Gerlach to Harteck (28 Aug. 1944) *G-341 v.2.*

50 Harteck to Gerlach (29 Sept. 1944) *G-341 v.2*; Paul Harteck, "Aktennotiz" (18 Oct. 1944) *G-341 v.2.*

51 Goudsmit to Bush (15 Aug. 1945) SGNY; see Introduction, above.

52 Harteck to Diebner (9 Jan. 1945) *G-341 v.2*; Harteck to Gerlach (7 Feb. 1945) *G-341*; Manhattan District History Volume 14: Intelligence and Security, 4.34 NAARS.

53 Harteck to Gerlach (6 Feb. 1944) *G-341 v.2*; *G-161*; Bothe to Heisenberg (14 Sept. 1942) WHM; Bothe to Heisenberg (30 July 1943) WHM; Fischer to Bothe (26 Aug. 1943) WHM; Fünfer to Bopp (25 Oct. 1943) WHM; Heisenberg to Fünfer (25 Oct. 1943) WHM; Bothe to Heisenberg (7 Dec. 1943) WHM; Heisenberg to Bothe (13 Dec. 1943) WHM; Heisenberg to Döpel (18 Dec. 1943) WHM; Abraham Esau, "Bericht über den Stand der Arbeiten auf dem Gebiete der Kernphysik am 31.12.43" (21 Aug. 1944) 29-1101 IMC; Vögler to Heisenberg (18 Jan. 1944) WHM.

54 Heisenberg to Bothe (13 Dec. 1943) WHM; Bothe and Flügge, part II, p. 157.

55 Bothe to Heisenberg (14 Sept. 1942) WHM; Bothe to Heisenberg (30 July 1943) WHM; *G-249*; Wirtz to Heisenberg (15 Mar. 1944) WHM; Wirtz to Heisenberg (16 Mar. 1944) WHM; Walther Gerlach, "Bericht über die Arbeiten auf kernphysikalischem Gebiet von 1 Feb. bis 31 März 44" (30 May

1944) 29-1118 IMC; Heisenberg to Bothe (29 Apr. 1944) WHM; *G-300*;
Bothe and Flügge, part II, pp. 153–7.

56 Wirtz to Heisenberg (23 Nov. 1943) WHM.
57 Report from Samuel Goudsmit (2 May 1945) SGNY; (24 Mar. 1944) *G-341 v.2*; Vögler to Heisenberg (31 Oct. 1944) MPSB.
58 BIOS Final Report No. 675. Item No. 21 (?1945) 31-929 IMC; (24 Mar. 1944) *G-341 v.2*; Walther Gerlach, "Bericht über die Arbeiten auf kernphysikalischem Gebiet von 1 Feb. bis 31 März 44" (30 May 1944) 29-1118 IMC; *G-391*; Manhattan, 4.29 NAARS.
59 Bothe and Flügge, part II, pp. 158–62, the figure is on p. 159.
60 Manhattan, 4.29 NAARS; Bothe and Flügge, part II, pp. 158–62.

5 The German achievement in the American shadow

1 Fernand Braudel, *On History*, p. 174.
2 See below; Assistant Army Chief of Staff to Chief of Staff (25 Sept. 1943) NAARS; Assistant Army Chief of Staff to Chief of Staff (1 Apr. 1944) NAARS; Assistant Army Chief of Staff to Chief of Staff (11 May 1944) NAARS; Goudsmit, *Alsos*, p. 15.
3 Pash to Chief of Military Intelligence Service (24 July 1944) NAARS; Pash to Chief of Military Intelligence Service (1 Sept. 1944) NAARS; Pash to Chief of Military Intelligence Service (7 Sept. 1944) NAARS; Samuel Goudsmit, Interview with "F.J.," Paris, Tuesday, 28 August 1944 (31 Aug. 1944) M1108 File 26 NAARS; interview with Professor F. Joliot, London, September 5th and 7th 1944, M1108 File 26 NAARS; Manhattan, 4.3-.7, 4.9 NAARS; Goudsmit, *Alsos*, p. 34; Joliot did eventually gain this information, see Weart, *Power*, p. 205.
4 Goudsmit, *Alsos*, pp. 46–9.
5 Manhattan, 4.12 NAARS; Goudsmit, *Alsos*, p. 67.
6 Goudsmit and Wardenburg, Report, (16 Dec. 1944) NAARS; see above, chapter 1.
7 Goudsmit to Major Frank Smith (29 Jan. 1945) NAARS.
8 *G-343*.
9 Report presumably written by Fleischmann, *G-343*, the description of a uranium machine as a bomb is unclear, and only Goudsmit's rough translation is available.
10 Goudsmit, *Alsos*, p. 75; memorandum to General Groves (6 Mar. 1945) M1109 File 7C NAARS; Groves to Marshall (7 Mar. 1945) M1109 File 7C NAARS; Spaatz to Marshall (19 Mar. 1945) M1109 File 7C NAARS; Leslie Groves, *Now It Can Be Told*, pp. 222, 224–30, 234; large portions of Groves' memoirs are virtually identical to the declassified Manhattan NAARS, written by an unnamed historian; Nikolaus Riehl, *Zehn Jahre im goldenen Käfig*; John Gimbel, "U.S. Policy and German Scientists: The Early Cold War," *PSQ*, 101 (1986), 433–51.
11 Walther Bothe, "Bericht über die Arbeit des Instituts während des Krieges" (11 July 1945) SGNY; Manhattan, 4.14–18 NAARS; Goudsmit, *Alsos*, pp. 78–80.
12 Walther Bothe, "Bericht über die Arbeit des Instituts während des Krieges"

(11 July 1945) SGNY; Manhattan, 4.14–18 NAARS; Goudsmit, *Alsos*, pp. 78–80.

13 Manhattan, 4.25 NAARS; Goudsmit, *Alsos*, pp. 88–90, 179–81; Gerlach to Mentzel (18 Nov. 1944) in Goudsmit, *Alsos*, p. 180.

14 Manhattan, 4.36 NAARS; Groves to Marshall (23 Apr. 1945) M1109 File 7E NAARS, also reprinted in Groves, pp. 238–9; John Lansdale, Capture of Material (10 July 1946) M1109 File 7E NAARS; Groves, pp. 222, 224–9, 234, 242; Gimbel, *PSQ*, 101 (1986), 433–51.

15 Goudsmit, *Alsos*, p. 97; Manhattan 4.30 NAARS; Bopp to Kaiser Wilhelm Society (3 June 1945) 29-1172 IMC; Heisenberg to Sethe (30 July 1946) WHM.

16 Eugene Hamion, Special "T" Forces, Wurtemberg Area, Southwestern Germany (29 Apr. 1945) RG165 Box 140 NAARS; Manhattan, 4.30 NAARS; Bopp to Kaiser Wilhelm Society (3 June 1945) 29-1172 IMC; Lansdale to Groves (5 May 1945) M1109 File 7B NAARS; John Lansdale, Operation Harborage (10 July 1946) M1109 File 7B NAARS; Goudsmit, *Alsos*, p. 108.

17 Manhattan, 4.30 NAARS; Goudsmit, *Alsos*, pp. 100–5; Bopp to Kaiser Wilhelm Society (3 June 1945) 29-1172 IMC; John Lansdale, Operation Harborage (10 July 1946) M1109 File 7B NAARS.

18 George Eckmann, Alsos Special Operation, Southwest Germany, 21 April to 29 April 1945 (14 May 1945) RG160 Box 93 F334 NAARS; Manhattan, 4.40, 4.41 NAARS; Goudsmit, *Alsos*, p. 101.

19 Boris Pash, Alpine Operation (10 May 1945) RG160 Box 93 F334 NAARS; R. C. Hahn, Munich Operation (12 May 1945) RG160 Box 93 F334 NAARS; Manhattan, 4.43–5 NAARS; Goudsmit, *Alsos*, pp. 122–3.

20 Manhattan, 4.46 NAARS; Alsos Report (3 Sept. 1945) SGNY; Goudsmit, *Alsos*, pp. 128–32; Henry Smyth, *Atomic Energy for Military Purposes*.

21 Samuel Goudsmit, Report Alsos Mission, (7 Dec. 1945) SGNY; Goudsmit to Bush (15 Aug. 1945) SGNY.

22 R. V. Jones, "Introduction," in Goudsmit, *Alsos*, p. xiv; Max von Laue to Theodore von Laue (7 Aug. 1945) SGNY.

23 Max von Laue to Theodore von Laue (7 Aug. 1945) SGNY.

24 Transcript of 9.00 p.m. BBC news broadcast (6 Aug. 1945) 31-1310 IMC.

25 Max von Laue to Theodore von Laue (7 Aug. 1945) SGNY; Gerlach's diary (7 Aug. 1945) 29-1339 IMC.

26 Bagge's diary (7 Aug. 1945) EBK, also 29-145 IMC; Max von Laue to Theodore von Laue (7 Aug. 1945) SGNY.

27 BBC News Report, 6.00 p.m. (6 Aug. 1945) 31-1310 IMC; Max von Laue to Theodore von Laue (7 Aug. 1945) SGNY.

28 Manuscript (7 Aug. 1945) WHM; a partial English version of this document was reprinted in Groves, pp. 336–7, although it is not clear that the British authorities actually allowed the release of this memo.

29 Manuscript (7 Aug. 1945) WHM.

30 Ibid.

31 Ibid.

32 Ibid.; *G-34*; *G-84*.

33 Manuscript (7 Aug. 1945) WHM.

34 Ibid.

35 See above, especially chapters 1 and 2.

36 Manuscript (7 Aug. 1945) WHM.

37 Ibid.

38 Smyth, *Atomic*; Werner Heisenberg, "Über die Arbeiten zur technischen Ausnutzung der Atomkernenergie in Deutschland," *NW*, 33 (1946), 325–9; Henry Smyth, *Atomenergie und ihre Verwertung im Kriege*; The immense yet unsatisfying literature on the Manhattan Project cannot be cited here in full; along with the Smyth Report, the interested reader is directed to Weart, *Power*, and Richard Rhodes, *The Making of the Atomic Bomb*.

39 Smyth, *Atomic*, pp. 27–9; see above, chapter 1.

40 Smyth, *Atomic*, pp. 34–6; see above, chapter 1.

41 Smyth, *Atomic*, pp. 34, 36, 38; see above, chapters 1 and 3.

42 Smyth, *Atomic*, pp. 37, 63, 101.

43 See above, chapters 1, 2 and 4; Crowther, *Science*, p. 57; Osietzki.

44 Smyth, *Atomic*, pp. 40–1.

45 See above, chapter 1.

46 Smyth, *Atomic*, p. 42; see above, chapter 1.

47 Smyth, *Atomic*, pp. 56, 58–9; see above chapters 1 and 3; personal communication from Spencer Weart.

48 Smyth, *Atomic*, pp. 64–5; see above, chapters 1 and 3.

49 Smyth, *Atomic*, pp. 52, 66, 187, 189; see above, chapters 1 and 3; see "The Frisch-Peierls Memorandum" and "The Maud Reports" (30 June 1941), reprinted in Margaret Gowing, *Britain and Atomic Energy 1939–1945*, pp. 389–436; Osietzki.

50 Smyth, *Atomic*, p. 67; see above.

51 Smyth, *Atomic*, pp. 69–70; see above, chapters 1 and 2.

52 Smyth, *Atomic*, pp. 70–71.

53 Ibid., 73; see above, chapter 1.

54 Smyth, *Atomic*, pp. 71–72; Gowing, *Britain*, pp. 389–436.

55 Smyth, *Atomic*, pp. 71–74.

56 See above, especially chapter 2; Peierls to the author (26 Jan. 1988).

57 See above, chapters 1 and 2.

58 Bothe to Debye (19 Dec. 1938) Bothe 64 MPSB; Monika Renneberg, "Die Physik und die physikalischen Institute an der Universität Hamburg im Dritten Reich," two manuscripts (1 Apr. 1985, 15 Apr. 1986); Osietzki.

59 Smyth, *Atomic*, pp. 75, 82; see above, chapter 2.

60 Smyth, *Atomic*, pp. 79, 82–3.

61 Ibid., pp. 92–3.

62 Ibid., pp. 96, 98, 239; the Smyth report gives merely the amount of metal uranium in the nuclear pile, 12,400 pounds; the number of scientists taking part in the experiment and the amounts of materials used are taken from Enrico Fermi, "Experimental production of a divergent chain reaction." *AJP*, 26 (1952), 536–58, reprinted in Wohlfarth, *40 Jahre*, pp. 322–70, here 323, 334, 351–4; see above, chapters 2 and 3.

63 Smyth, *Atomic*, pp. 168, 148–9.

64 Ibid., pp. 223–4.
65 Goudsmit to Hemke (16 Jan. 1950) SGNY; Harteck to Goudsmit (2 Nov. 1950) SGNY; Goudsmith to Hemke (18 Jan. 1951) SGNY; Hemke to Goudsmit (22 Jan. 1951) SGNY; Harteck to Goudsmit (27 Nov. 1951) SGNY.
66 *G–344.*
67 *G–371.*
68 *G–371;* this point has been made in Spencer Weart, "Secrecy, simultaneous discovery, and the theory of nuclear reactors," *AJP,* 45 (1977), 1049–60 here 1059, footnote 40.
69 *G–371.*
70 *G–371.*

6 The legacy of German National Socialism

1 Philip Morrison, "Alsos: the story of German science," *BAS,* 3 (1947), 365.
2 Volker Berghahn, *Modern Germany: Society, Economy and Politics in the Twentieth Century,* pp. 177–96.
3 Gimbel, *PSQ,* 101 (1986), 433–51; Clarence Lasby, *Project Paperclip;* Eckert to Heisenberg (20 Mar. 1946) WHM; Heisenberg to Eckert (26 Mar. 1946) WHM.
4 Jentschke to Bothe (25 Jan. 1946) Bothe 46 MPSB; Ramm to Heisenberg (28 Sept. 1947) WHM; Heisenberg to Ramm (6 Oct. 1947) WHM.
5 Volz to Heisenberg (28 Nov. 1946) WHM; Heisenberg to Volz (4 Dec. 1946) WHM; Heisenberg to Sommerfeld (7 Feb. 1947) GMM; Volz to Heisenberg (17 Jan. 1947) WHM; Gimbel, *PSQ,* 101 (1986), 433–51; Lasby, *Paperclip;* Heisenberg to Die Welt (9 Nov. 1948) WHM; Harteck to Schulverwaltung, Hochschulabteilung (23 Sept. 1950) HSA HSW D- & PA N367 HSA.
6 Bothe to Pohl (7 Nov. 1945) Bothe 11 MPSB; Samuel Goudsmit, Interview with F. J., Paris, Tuesday, 28 August 1944 (31 Aug. 1944) M1108 File 26 NAARS; interview with Professor F. Joliot, London, September 5th and 7th 1944, M1108 File 26 NAARS.
7 Bothe to Hahn (22 Mar. 1946) Bothe 11 MPSB; Bothe to Regener (10 Aug. 1946) Bothe 53 MPSB; Bothe to Mattauch (5 Mar. 1947) Bothe 11 MPSB; Bothe to Dänzer (18 Oct. 1947) Bothe 12 MPSB; interview with Heinz Maier-Leibnitz; interview with Kurt Starke.
8 Bothe to Oldenburg (10 Aug. 1946) Bothe 11 MPSB; Bothe to Schwug (23 July 1947) Bothe 12 MPSB; Wirtschaftsministerium to Bothe (13 May 1947) Bothe 45 MPSB; Bothe to Oldenburg (19 May 1948) Bothe 13 MPSB; Bothe to Dänzer (16 Feb. 1946) Bothe 14 MPSB; eventually Willibald Jentschke and Kurt Starke returned to the Federal Republic of Germany; Osietzki.
9 Samuel Goudsmit, "German scientists in army employment: I – the case analyzed," *BAS,* 3 (1947), 64, 67; Hans Bethe and H. S. Slack, "German scientists in army employment: II – a protest," *BAS,* 3 1947, 65, 67.
10 Bethe and Slack, "German scientists," *BAS,* 3 1947, 65, 67.
11 Otto Hahn and Friedrich Rein, "Gelehrtenexport nach Amerika," *GUZ* (21 Feb. 1947), reprinted in *PB,* 3 (1947), 33–5.

12 Hahn and Rein, *PB*, 3 (1947), 34.
13 Army Service Forces, Office of the Chief Signal Officer (10 Oct. 1945) RG160 Box 93 NAARS; Alsos Report (3 Sept. 1945) 31-1085 IMC; interview with Werner Czulius; interview with Nikolaus Riehl; interview with Karl Zimmer.
14 Samuel Goudsmit, 'Report on Interrogation of Kallmann' (14 Aug. 1945) 31-1085 IMC; Döpel to Heisenberg (30 Apr. 1947) WHM; Pose to Heisenberg (18 June 1946) WHM; Heinz and Elsi Barwich, *Das Rote Atom*; Nikolaus Riehl, *Zehn Jahre im goldenen Käfig. Erlebnisse beim Aufbau der sowjetischen Uran-Industrie*; interview with Werner Czulius; interview with Nikolaus Riehl; interview with Karl Zimmer.
15 Riehl; Barwich, *Atom*.
16 Gimbel, *PSQ*, 101 (1986), 433–51; Lasby, *Paperclip*; Gerlach to Heisenberg (28 June 1946) WHM.
17 Pose to Heisenberg (18 July 1946) WHM.
18 Heisenberg to Pose (29 July 1946) WHM.
19 Seelinger to Heisenberg (14 Feb. 1947) WHM; Heisenberg to Seelinger (7 Mar. 1947) WHM; Heisenberg to Vietinghoff-Scheel (15 Apr. 1947) WHM; Heisenberg to Kravre (2 July 1947) WHM; Gimbel, *PSQ*, 101 (1986), 433–51.
20 Bonhoeffer to Heisenberg (7 Mar. 1946) WHM; Bonhoeffer to Heisenberg (1 Apr. 1947) WHM; Hund to Heisenberg (1 Mar. 1946) WHM; Gimbel, *PSQ*, 101 (1986), 433–51.
21 Bonhoeffer to Heisenberg (7 Mar. 1946) WHM; Gimbel, *PSQ*, 101 (1986), 433–51; Hund to Heisenberg (1 Mar. 1946) WHM; Bonhoeffer to Heisenberg (1 Apr. 1947) WHM.
22 Bopp to Kaiser Wilhelm Gesellschaft (3 June 1945) 29-1172 IMC; Bopp to Heisenberg (5 Feb. 1946) WHM.
23 Bopp to Heisenberg (5 Feb. 1946) WHM; Bopp to Rochard (19 Aug. 1945) WHM.
24 Bopp to Heisenberg (5 Feb. 1946) WHM; Schüler to Heisenberg 19 Jan. 1946) WHM; Gentner to Hahn (5 May 1947) WHM.
25 Heisenberg to Joerges (6 May 1946) WHM; Heisenberg to Gerlach (7 May 1946) WHM; Butenandt to Heisenberg (15 Nov. 1946) WHM; Schüler to Hahn and Heisenberg (18 Nov. 1946) WHM.
26 Hahn to Heisenberg (25 Nov. 1949) Grü 23 MPSB; Protokoll der Kommissionssitzung über die Zukunft des Hechinger Physikinstituts am 17.11.1949 (17 Nov. 1949) WHM; Hiby to Heisenberg (7 Jan. 1950) WHM.
27 Heisenberg to Blackett (5 Oct. 1945) WHM; Heisenberg to Sommerfeld (5 Feb. 1946) 1977-28/A, 136/43 GMM; Jürgen Brautmeier, *Forschungspolitik in Nordrhein-Westfalen: 1945–1961*, pp. 12–21.
28 Fraser to Heisenberg (Jan./Feb. 1947) WHM; Ernst Telschow, "Antwort auf die Fragen" (18 May 1947) Grü 12 MPSB.
29 Müller-Hill; see above.
30 Telschow to Heisenberg (9 Apr. 1948) WHM.
31 Heisenberg to Sommerfeld (5 Feb. 1946) 1977-28/A, 136/43 GMM.
32 Heisenberg to Scherzer (11 June 1946) WHM; Heisenberg to Ramin (7 Oct.

1946) WHM; Calver to Heisenberg (10 Feb. 1946) WHM; Heisenberg to Calvert (30 Dec. 1946) WHM; van der Waerden to Heisenberg (22 Dec. 1947) WHM; Heisenberg to Schmitt (17 July 1946) WHM.

33 Heisenberg to Harteck (9 Dec. 1947) WHM; Heisenberg to Sommerfeld (7 Feb. 1947) 1977-28/A, 136/47 GMM.

34 Heisenberg to Hund (21 Feb. 1947) WHM; Heisenberg to Bank (3 Mar. 1947) WHM.

35 See Introduction.

36 Born to Heisenberg (2 Oct. 1946) WHM.

37 Heisenberg to Regener (13 Dec. 1947) WHM; interview with Rudolf Peierls; Peierls to Heisenberg (11 Feb. 1948) WHM; Rudolf Peierls, "Our Relations with German Scientists" (manuscript) WHM; Heisenberg to Sommerfeld (31 Mar. 1948) WHM.

38 Heisenberg to Regener (13 Dec. 1947) WHM; interview with Rudolf Peierls; Peierls to Heisenberg (11 Feb. 1948) WHM; Peierls, 'Relations' WHM; Heisenberg to Sommerfeld (31 Mar. 1948) WHM.

39 Berghahn, pp. 186–7.

40 The full list of seventy-one scientists – both Party members and scientists not in the Party – includes: Erich Bagge, Karl-Friedrich Bonhoeffer, Fritz Bopp, Gerhard Borrmann, Walther Bothe, Klaus Clusius, Werner Czulius, Gerhard Dickel, Kurt Diebner, G. Robert Döpel, Gottfried von Droste, Abraham Esau, Heinz Ewald, Wolfgang Finkelnburg, Erich Fischer, Arnold Flammersfeld, Rudolf Fleischmann, Siegfried Flügge, Erwin Fünfer, Ewald Fünfer, Hans Geiger, Wolfgang Gentner, Walther Gerlach, Wilhelm Groth, Otto Hahn, Wilhelm Hanle, Paul Harteck, Georg Hartwig, Otto Haxel, Otto Heckmann, Werner Heisenberg, Julius Hiby, Karl-Heinz Höcker, Johannes Jensen, Peter Jensen, Willibald Jentschke, Georg Joos, Johannes Juilifs, Alfred Klemm, Friedrich Knauer, Peter Koch, Hans Kopfermann, Horst Korsching, Karl Lintner, Heinz Maier-Leibnitz, Hans Martin, Josef Mattauch, Werner Maurer, Rudolf Mentzel, Wolfgang Paul, Hans Pose, Carl Ramsauer, Nikolaus Riehl, Wolfgang Riezler, Kurt Sauerwein, Fritz Sauter, Erich Schumann, W. Seelmann-Eggebert, Kurt Starke, Fritz Strassmann, Georg Stetter, Hans Suess, K. Albert Suhr, Ernest Telschow, Albert Vögler, Helmut Volz, Wilhelm Walcher, Ludwig Waldmann, Carl-Friedrich von Weizsäcker, Karl Wirtz, and Karl Zimmer. The statistical information comes from research in BDC.

41 The statistical information comes from research in BDC.

42 Ibid.

43 Ibid.; Michael Kater, *The Nazi Party: A Social Profile of Members and Leaders, 1919–1945.*

44 The statistical information comes from research in BDC.

45 Ibid.; Arbeiterpartei Gaugericht München/Obb. (8 June 1942) Waldmann BDC.

46 These scientists are included in the above list; the statistical information comes from research in BDC.

47 The information comes from research in BDC.

48 NSDAP Dozentenbund to Hamburg Rektor (14 June 1937) HSW D-PA IV

917 HSA; Dekan to Rektor of Hamburg University. (19 Nov. 1940) Nat. – Math. 131 HSA.

49 NSDAP Dozentenbund to Hamburg Rektor (14 June 1937) HSW D-PA IV 917 HSA; Dekan to Rektor of Hamburg University (19 Nov. 1940) Nat. – Math. 131 HSA.

50 The information comes from research in BDC; Dozentenbundführer der Universität Hamburg to Reichsamtsleitung des NSD-Dozentenbundes (10 May 1938), Johannes Jensen BDC.

51 Heisenberg to Jensen (14 July 1942) WHM.

52 Rektor to Erziehungsministerium (15 Mar. 1937) HSW D- & PA IV 330 HSA; Gaudozentenführer to Bothe, Syndicus der Hanseschen Universität (30 Dec. 1937) HSW D- & PA IV 330 HSA.

53 Dekan Math–NW Fakultät to Staatsverwaltung der Hansestadt Hamburg Hochschulwesen (28 Nov. 1938) HSW D- & PA I 194 HSA; Dekan to Groth (19 Dec. 1938) HSW D- & PA I 194 HSA; Esau to Reichsminister für Wissenschaft (25 Feb. 1943) BDC; Dekan to Bürgermeister von Hamburg (20 Oct. 1945) HSW D- & PA I 194 HSA; Groth to Harteck (6 Aug. 1946) HSW D- & PA IV 330 HSA; Groth to Rektor University Hamburg (31 Oct. 1950) HSW D- & PA I 194 HSA.

54 Dozentenführer der Universität Berlin to Rektor Universität Berlin (20 Dec. 1940) Wirtz BDC.

55 NSDAP to Reichsstatthalter in Sachsen (14 Aug. 1937) Gentner BDC; SD to Sächs. Min. für Volksbildung (20 Nov. 1937) Gentner BDC; Rektor, Universität Frankfurt to ? (10 Sept. 1937) Gentner BDC.

56 See Introduction for the discussion of "resistance," "opposition," and "nonconformity"; British Military Government to whom it may concern (10 Sept. 1946) HSW D- & PA II 367 HSA; interview with Paul Harteck.

57 Droste to Heisenberg (22 Dec. 1946) WHM.

58 Heisenberg to Droste (8 Jan. 1947) WHM.

59 See above, chapter 2; Erler to Heisenberg (13 Apr. 1947) WHM; Heisenberg to Erler (25 Apr. 1947) WHM; Heisenberg to Borger (6 June 1947) WHM.

60 Andreas Kleinert, "Das Spruchkammerverfahren gegen Johannes Stark," *SUAR*, 67 (1983), 13–24, here 14.

61 Ibid., 16–18.

62 Ibid., 22, Kleinert does not mention Heisenberg's personal involvement with Stark's second trial; Berufungskammer München to Heisenberg (18 May 1949) WHM.

63 Heisenberg to Berufungskammer München (24 May 1949) WHM; Kleinert, SUAR, 67 (1983), 22.

64 *Trials of War Criminals Before the Nüremberg Military Tribunals*, vols. 12–14; Werner Heisenberg, "Die aktive und passive Opposition im Dritten Reich" (12 Nov. 1947) WHM.

65 Heisenberg, "Opposition" WHM.

66 Ibid.

67 Ibid.

68 Ibid.

69 Ibid. *Trials*, vol. 14, pp. 497–8.
70 Heisenberg to Escales (9 Dec. 1947) WHM; Goudsmit to Ladenburg (14 Oct. 1946) SGNY; Goudsmit to Bush (23 Aug. 1945) SGNY.
71 Samuel Goudsmit, "War physics in Germany," *RSI*, 17 (Jan. 1946), 49–52; Samuel Goudsmit, "How Germany lost the race," *BAS*, 1 (1946), 4–5; Samuel Goudsmit, "Secrecy or science?" *SI*, 1 (1946), 97–9.
72 Goudsmit, *RSI*, 17 (Jan, 1946), 49–52; Goudsmit, *BAS*, 1 (1946), 4–5; Goudsmit, *SI*, 1 (1946), 97–9.
73 Brücke to Weizsäcker (20 Aug. 1946) WHM; Weizsäcker to Brücke (27 Aug. 1946) WHM; Die Neue Zeitung to Heisenberg (25 June 1946) WHM; Heisenberg to Krugmann (16 July 1946) WHM; Weizsäcker to Heisenberg (27 Aug. 1946) WHM.
74 Werner Heisenberg (manuscript), "Über die Arbeiten zur technischen Ausnutzung der Atomkernenergie in Deutschland," Bothe MPSB; Heisenberg to Bothe, Clusius, Flügge, Gerlach, and Harteck (29 Nov. 1946) WHM.
75 Heisenberg, "Ausnutzung" Bothe MPSB; Heisenberg to Bothe, Clusius, Flügge, Gerlach, and Harteck (29 Nov. 1946) WHM; Heisenberg, *NW*, 33 (1946), 325–9.
76 Heisenberg, "Ausnutzung" Bothe MPSB; Bothe to Heisenberg (7 Dec. 1946) Bothe MPSB.
77 See the introduction; Schumann to Dekan der Philosophischen Fakultät, Universität Berlin (22 May 1941) BDC; "Notiz für Professor Schnadel, Betreff Dr. K. Diebner," 29-1195 IMC; personal communication from Kristie Macrakis.
78 Gerlach to Winkhaus (29 Jan. 1949) WGM; Bagge, Diebner, and Jay.
79 Heisenberg, "Ausnutzung" Bothe MPSB; Bothe to Heisenberg (7 Dec. 1946) Bothe MPSB.
80 Harteck to Heisenberg (15 Jan. 1947) Harteck B1 F12 RPI.
81 Heisenberg, "Ausnutzung" Bothe MPSB.
82 Heisenberg, *NW*, 33 (1946), 327.
83 Ibid., 329.
84 Ibid., Heisenberg, "Ausnutzung" Bothe MPSB.
85 Heisenberg's retrospective and historically inaccurate portrayal of events and intentions has been accepted uncritically by most subsequent writers in full or part, for example see Jungk, pp. 87–104, 164–71, 214–20; Heisenberg, *Beyond*, chapters 14–16; Armin Hermann, *Die Jahrhundertswissenschaft*, pp. 148–70, Jost Herbig, *Kettenreaktion*; Heisenberg, *Exile*, chapters 4–6; for a recent reaffirmation of the Myth of the German Atomic Bomb, see Armin Hermann, "Die fünf historischen Epochen in der Geschichte der Atomenergie," in Armin Hermann and Rolf Schumacher eds., *Das Ende des Atomzeitalters? Eine sachlich-kritische Dokumentation*, pp. 11–22 and Armin Hermann, "Heisenberg und das deutsche Atomprojekt," *Bild der Wissenschaft*, 10(1988), 140–45; David Irving's book is an exception in that this author did considerable research into primary documents, conducted interviews, and was critical of the leading figures in the German nuclear power project. For example, Irving did not accept the thesis that the Germans deliberately held themselves back from making bombs for Hitler because of

moral scruples. Irving nevertheless wrote his book under considerable influence from Heisenberg. For only one example of an argument adopted from Heisenberg's apologia, see Irving's uncritical repetition of the thesis that Bothe's "mistake" derailed the German nuclear power project. Irving also places an implausible amount of significance on the Allied sabotage of heavy water production in Norway. For a critique of Irving's use of historical evidence and preconceptions – criticism of a different book by Irving, but instructive in this case as well – see Martin Broszat, "Hitler and the genesis of the 'Final Solution': an assessment of David Irving's theses," in H. W. Hoch (ed.), *Aspects of the Third Reich*, pp. 390–429.

86 Bothe and Flügge, *Kernphysik*, vols. 1 and 2.
87 Ibid., vol. 2, pp. 94–107, 181–93.
88 Ibid., vol. 1, 208–20, vol. 2, 13–24, 127–24, 143–65.
89 Samuel Goudsmit, "Heisenberg on the German nuclear power project," *BAS*, 3 (1947), 64, 67; Goudsmit to Kaempffert (8 Apr. 1949) SGNY.
90 Goudsmit, *Alsos*, pp. xxvii–xxix; Samuel Goudsmit, "Nazis' atomic secrets," *Life*, 23 (20 Oct. 1947), 123–34.
91 Goudsmit to Bohr (2 Dec. 1947) spool 28, 46–62 BSC; Goudsmit, *Alsos*, pp. 114, 128–39, 140–59.
92 Goudsmit, *Alsos*, pp. 140–59, 177, and 243.
93 Goudsmit, *RSI*, 17 (Jan. 1946), 49–52; Goudsmit, *BAS*, 1 (1946), 4–5; Goudsmit, *SI*, 1 (1946), 97–9; Goudsmit, *Alsos*, pp. 114, 128–39, 140–59; 177, and 243.
94 Goudsmit, *Alsos*, pp. 234–5, 245–6.
95 Ibid.
96 Morrison, *BAS*, 3 (1947), 354–5; see Spencer Weart, *Nuclear Fear*.
97 Finkelnburg to Heisenberg (6 Feb. 1948) WHM; Max von Laue, "Die Kriegstätigkeit der deutschen Physiker," *PB*, 4 (1947), 425–5; Max von Laue, "The wartime activities of German scientists," *BAS*, 4 (1948), 103.
98 Laue, *BAS*, 4 (1948), 103.
99 Ibid.
100 Philip Morrison, "A reply to Dr. von Laue," *BAS*, 4 (1948), 104.
101 Samuel Goudsmit, "Our task in Germany," *BAS*, 4 (1948), 106; Finkelnburg to Heisenberg (6 Feb. 1948) WHM.
102 Heisenberg to Goudsmit (23 Sept. 1947) SGNY.
103 Ibid.
104 Goudsmit to Heisenberg (1 Dec. 1947) SGNY.
105 Heisenberg to Goudsmit (5 Jan. 1948) 29-1185 IMC.
106 Ibid.
107 Ibid.
108 Ibid.
109 I want to thank Bartel L. van der Waerden for generously translating the letters written in Dutch for me; van der Waerden to Goudsmit (17 Mar. 1948) SGNY; van der Waerden to Heisenberg (18 Mar. 1948) WHM; Goudsmit to van der Waerden (Mar. 1948) SGNY.
110 Goudsmit to van der Waerden (Mar. 1948) SGNY.
111 van der Waerden to Heisenberg (19 Apr. 1948) WHM.

112 Ibid.; Goudsmit, *Alsos*, p. 114; van der Waerden to Heisenberg (28 Apr. 1948) WHM; Goudsmit to van der Waerden (26 Apr. 1948) SGNY.

113 van der Waerden to Heisenberg (28 Apr. 1948) WHM.

114 Heisenberg to van der Waerden (28 Apr. 1948) SGNY.

115 Goudsmit to Heisenberg (20 Sept. 1948) SGNY.

116 Heisenberg to Goudsmit (3 Oct. 1948) 29-1185 IMC; Goudsmit to Weisskopf (7 Dec. 1948) SGNY.

117 Waldemar Kaempffert, "Nazis spurned idea of an atomic bomb," *NYT* (28 Dec. 1948); Samuel Goudsmit, "German war research," *NYT* (9 Jan. 1949); Werner Heisenberg, "German atom research," *NYT* (30 Jan. 1949).

118 Goudsmit to Heisenberg (11 Feb. 1949) SGNY; Heisenberg to Goudsmit (20 Apr. 1949) SGNY.

119 Goudsmit to Heisenberg (3 June 1949) SGNY; Heisenberg to Goudsmit (22 June 1949) SGNY; Harteck to Goudsmit (2 Nov. 1950) SGNY; Goudsmit to Hemke (18 Jan. 1951) SGNY; Harteck to Goudsmit (27 Nov. 1951) SGNY; Report of Alien Visitor to Brookhaven National Laboratory (4 Oct. 1950) SGNY.

7 The myth of the German atomic bomb

1 *Webster's Third New International Dictionary*, p. 1497.

2 The classic account of the German version is Jungk, pp. 91–104, 164–66, 214–20; as discussed above, the classic account of the version favored outside of Germany is Goudsmit, *Alsos*.

3 Jungk, pp. 100–4; the most recent claim that Heisenberg spied for the nazis is found in Arnold Kramish, *The Griffin: Paul Rosbaud and the Nazi Atomic Bomb that Never Was*; both claims are discussed below.

4 Weizsäcker to Deutscher Akademischer Austauschdienst (22 July 1941) *G-343*; Weizsäcker to Bohr (15 Aug. 1941) Bohr Scientific Correspondence BSNY; see above, chapter 1.

5 See above, chapter 1.

6 Weizsäcker to Deutscher Akademischer Austauschdienst (22 July 1941) *G-343*; Heisenberg to Ernst von Weizsäcker (25 July 1947) WHM; Weizsäcker to Bohr (15 Aug. 1941), Bohr Scientific Correspondence BSNY; Ernst von Weizsäcker left the Foreign Office before the end of the war; see above, chapter 6.

7 Crowther, pp. 106–8; Aage Bohr, "The war years and the prospects raised by the atomic weapons," in Stefan Rozental (ed.), *Niels Bohr*, p. 193; Stefan Rozental, *NB. Erindringer om Niels Bohr*, pp. 44–5; interview with Stefan Rozental; I want to thank Per Als for his translation of the passages in Danish.

8 Ladenburg to Goudsmit (23 Oct. 1946) SGNY; Heisenberg to van der Waerden (28 Apr. 1947) 29-1185 IMC; Stanley Goldberg has brought an earlier letter from Ladenburg to my attention, from which it is clear that one German scientist had believed that Heisenberg was trying to delay the nuclear power project. This claim should be disregarded. See Mark Walker, "Uranium machines, nuclear explosives, and National Socialism: The

German quest for nuclear power, 1939–1949," 382–3, as well as Stanley Goldberg, "Before the Manhattan Project: The decision to build the bomb" (manuscript).

9 For the most recent account of Heisenberg as an agent of the nazis, see Kramish, *Griffin,*

10 See above, especially chapter 1.

11 See above, chapters 2 and 3.

12 See above, especially chapter 6; Heisenberg to Jungk (18 Jan. 1957) WHM.

13 See above, chapter 3; Werner Heisenberg, manuscript (1946?) WHM.

14 See above, chapters 3, 5 and 6.

15 See above, especially chapter 6.

Conclusion

1 Sigmund Freud, "Die Verneinung," *Gesammelte Werke,* vol. 14, p. 12.

2 See above, chapter 2.

3 See above, Introduction and chapters 2 and 3, and 4.

4 See above, especially Introduction and chapters 2 and 6.

5 See above, Introduction and chapter 1.

6 See above, chapters 1, 2 and 5.

7 Introduction and chapters 2, 5 and 6. Herbert Mehrtens has discerned analogous tactics in the German mathematics community in the case of Ludwig Bieberbach, see Mehrtens, *Sociological Inquiry,* 57 (1987), 159–82.

8 See above, chapters 2, 3, 5, and 6.

9 See above, chapter 6.

10 See above, Introduction and chapters 4, 5, and 6; Herbert; Ferencz; Streit.

11 Charles C. Gillispie, *Science and Polity in France at the End of the Old Regime,* pp. 549–52; see above, Introduction and chapters 2, 3, 4, and 6.

Bibliography

German reports cited

Copies of the "German reports" are available at the Karlsruhe Nuclear Research Center in the Federal Republic of Germany, and at the Niels Bohr Library of the American Institute of Physics in New York City.

G-12 (7 June 1940) Walther Bothe, "Die Diffusionslänge für thermische Neutronen in Kohle."

G-13 (28 June 1940) Walther Bothe, "Die Abmessungen endlicher Uranmaschinen."

G-14 (17 July 1941) Walther Bothe, "Die Abmessungen von Maschinen mit rückstreuendem Mantel."

G-17 (9 May 1940) Walther Bothe and Wolfgang Gentner, "Die Energie der Spaltungsneutronen aus Uran."

G-18 (1 June 1940) Klaus Clusius, "I. Bericht über Trennversuche von Metallionen mit Hilfe des Nernstschen Verteilungssatzes," also 31-068 IMC.

G-19 (28 July 1940) Klaus Clusius and M. Maierhauser, "II. Bericht," also 31-068 IMC.

G-20 (13 Jan. 1941) Klaus Clusius, Gerhard Dickel, and M. Maierhauser, "III. Bericht," also 31-091 IMC.

G-21 (24 June 1940) Erika Cremer and Karl Wirtz, "Untersuchungen des Schwerwassergehaltes einiger technischer Elektrolyseure in Deutschland."

G-22 (5 Dec. 1940) Robert Döpel, K. Döpel, and Werner Heisenberg, "Bestimmung der Diffusionslänge thermischer Neutronen in Präparat 38."

G-23 (7 Aug. 1940) Robert Döpel, K. Döpel, and Werner Heisenberg, "Bestimmung der Diffusionslänge thermischer Neutronen in schwerem Wasser."

G-24 (24 Sept. 1940) Gottfried von Droste, "Bericht über einen Versuch mit 2t Natriumuranat."

G-25 (21 May 1940) Arnold Flammersfeld, Peter Jensen, and Wolfgang Gentner, "Die Energietönung der Uranspaltung."

G-26 (24 Sept. 1940) Arnold Flammersfeld, Peter Jensen, and Wolfgang Gentner, "Die Aufteilungsverhältnisse und Energietönung bei der Uranspaltung."

G-27 (3 July 1940) Rudolf Fleischmann, "Ein mögliches Verfahren zur Isotopentrennung von Uran," also 31-112 IMC.

G-32 (5 Dec. 1940) "Korrosionsversuche an zwei angesändten Metallegierungen (Stahllegierung und Leichtmetallegierung) mit Uranhexafluorid."

G-33 (5 June 1940) Wilhelm Groth, "Stand der Arbeiten zur Trennung der Isotope 235U und 238U."

G-34 (10 Dec. 1940) Otto Hahn, "Bericht über die Arbeiten des Kaiser Wilhelm-Instituts für Chemie über 'Präparat 38'."

G-36 (19 Aug. 1940) Paul Harteck, Johannes Jensen, Friedrich Knauer, and Hans Suess, "Über die Bremsung, die Diffusion und den Einfang von Neutronen in fester Kohlensäure und über ihren Einfang in Uran."

G-37 (17 Dec. 1940) Otto Haxel and Helmut Volz, "Über die Absorption von Neutronen in wässerigen Lösungen."

G-38 (11 June 1940) Otto Haxel and Helmut Volz, "Bestimmung von Absorptionsquerschnitten für langsame Neutronen. Methode I. Konzentrationsabhängigkeit."

G-39 (6 Dec. 1939) Werner Heisenberg, "Die Möglichkeit der technischen Energiegewinnung aus der Uranspaltung," also 29-374 IMC.

G-40 (29 Feb. 1940) Werner Heisenberg, "Bericht über die Möglichkeit technischer Energiegewinnung aus der Uranspaltung (II)," also 29-398 IMC.

G-41 (6 June 1940) Karl-Heinz Höcker, "Die Abhängigkeit des Energiegewinnes in der Uranmaschine von der Dichte des Urans und der Dichte der Bremssubstanz," also 29-451 IMC.

G-42 (20 Apr. 1940) Karl-Heinz Höcker, "Berechnung der Energieerzeugung in der Uranmaschine. II Kohle als Bremssubstanz," also 29-427 IMC.

G-43 (3 June 1940) Karl-Heinz Höcker, "Berechnung der Energiegewinnung in der Uranmaschine. IV Wasser."

G-44 (Aug. 1940) Willibald Jentschke and F. Prankl, "Energien und Massen der Urankernbruchstücke."

G-46 (29 Mar. 1940) Georg Joos to Army Ordinance, also 31-110 IMC.

G-48 (20 Dec. 1940) Josef Mattauch, "Über die Anzahl der bei der Spaltung von 235 U und 238 U gebildeten Neutronen," also 29-465 IMC.

G-49 (1941) Paul Müller, "Die Energiegewinnung aus dem Uranspaltungsprozess durch schnelle Neutronen."

G-50 (May 1940) Paul Müller, "Eine Bedingung für die Verwendbarkeit von Uran als Sprengstoff," also 29-437 IMC.

G-51 (25 Apr. 1940) Paul Müller, "Die Neutronenabsorption in Kugelschalen aus Uran."

G-52 (30 Sept. 1940) Paul Müller, "Über die Temperaturabhängigkeit der Uranmaschine," also 29-456 IMC.

G-53 (29 Apr. 1940) Paul Müller, "Berechnung der Energieerzeugung in der Uranmaschine. III Schweres Wasser." 29-434 IMC.

G-55 (10 Dec. 1940) Josef Schintlmeister and F. Hernegger, "Über ein bisher unbekanntes, alpha-strahlendes chemisches Element," also 31-001 IMC.

G-56 (11 June 1940) Ernst Stuhlinger, "Bestimmung von Absorptionsquerschnitten für langsame Neutronen."

G-59 (17 July 1940) Carl-Friedrich von Weizsäcker, "Eine Möglichkeit der Energiegewinnung aus U 238," also 29-451 IMC.

G-60 (26 Feb. 1940) Carl-Friedrich von Weizsäcker, Paul Müller, and Karl-Heinz Höcker, "Berechnung der Energieerzeugung in der Uranmaschine."

G-61 (19 Jan. 1940) Karl Wirtz, "Bericht II. Eine 10-stufige Elektrolyseuranlage zur Gewinnung von schwerem Wasser."

G-66 (28 Mar. 1941) Walther Bothe, "Einige Eigenschaften des U und der Bremsstoffe. Zusammenfassender Bericht über die Arbeiten," also 31-117 IMC.

G-67 (20 Jan. 1941) Walther Bothe and Arnold Flammersfeld, "Die Wirkungsquerschnitte von 38 für thermische Neutronen aus Diffusionsmessungen."

G-68 (8 Mar. 1940) Walther Bothe and Arnold Flammersfeld, "Resonanzeinfang an einer Uranoberfläche."

G-69 (26 May 1941) Walther Bothe and Arnold Flammersfeld, "Messungen an einem Gemisch von 38-Oxyd und -Wasser; der Vermehrungsfaktor K und der Resonanzeinfang w," also 31-140, IMC.

G-70 (11 July 1941) Walther Bothe and Arnold Flammersfeld, "Die Neutronenvermehrung bei schnellen und langsamen Neutronen in 38 und die Diffusionslänge in 38 Metall und Wasser."

G-71 (20 Jan. 1941) Walther Bothe and Peter Jensen, "Die Absorption thermischer Neutronen in Elektrographit."

G-72 (12 May 1941) Walther Bothe and Peter Jensen, "Resonanzeinfang an einer Uranoberfläche."

G-73 (1941) Klaus Clusius, M. Maierhauser, and Gerhard Dickel, "Bericht über die im Jahre 1940/41 ausgeführten Versuche zur Entwicklung eines Auswaschverfahrens zur Isotopentrennung," also 31-128 IMC.

G-74 (28 Apr. 1941) Walther Bothe and Arnold Flammersfeld, "Versuche mit einer Schichtenanordnung von Wasser und Präp. 38," also 29-548 IMC.

G-75 (28 Oct. 1941) Robert Döpel, K. Döpel, and Werner Heisenberg, "Versuche mit Schichtenanordnungen von D_2O und 38."

G-77 (24 July 1941) Gottfried von Droste, "Über die Vermehrung der Neutronen im Präparat 38."

G-78 (1941) Gottfried von Droste, "Über den Spaltprozess bei Präparat 38."

G-79 (26 June 1941) Erich Fischer, "Bestimmung des Absorptionsquerschnittes von Uran für langsame Neutronen."

G-81 (10 Oct. 1941) Erwin Fünfer and Walther Bothe, "Absorption thermischer Neutronen und die Vermehrung schneller Neutronen in Beryllium," also 30-098 IMC.

G-82 (14 Dec. 1941) Wilhelm Groth, "Stand der Arbeiten zur Herstellung einer Ultrazentrifuge," also 29-857 IMC.

G-83 (Dec. 1941) Wilhelm Groth, "Stand der Arbeiten zur Trennung der Isotope des Präparats 38."

G-84 Otto Hahn, "Zur Arbeitstagung vom 13. bis 14. März 1941 im Kaiser-Wilhelm-Institut für Physik."

G-85 (18 Apr. 1941) Wilhelm Hanle, "Über den Nachweis von Bor und Cadmium in Kohle."

G-86 (Dec. 1941) Paul Harteck, "Die Produktion von schwerem Wasser," also 29-670 IMC.

G-88 (Dec. 1941) Paul Harteck, "Die Trennung der Uranisotope," also 29-678 IMC.

G-89 (18 Feb. 1941) Paul Harteck and Johannes Jensen, "Der Thermo-diffusionseffekt im Zusammenspiel mit der Konvektion durch mechanisch bewegte Wände und Vergleich mit der Thermosiphonwirkung," also 30-004 IMC.

G-91 (4 Aug. 1941) Otto Haxel, Ernst Stuhlinger, and Helmut Volz, "Über die Absorption und Verlangsamung von Neutronen in Berylliumoxyd."

G-92 (1941) Werner Heisenberg, "Über die Möglichkeit der Energieerzeugung mit Hilfe des Isotops 238."

G-93 (May 1941) Werner Heisenberg, "Bericht über Versuche mit Schichten-anordnungen von Präparat 38 und Paraffin am Kaiser Wilhelm Institut für Physik in Berlin-Dahlem," also 29-471 IMC.

G-94 (Aug. 1941) Fritz Houtermans, "Zur Frage der Auslösung von Kern-Kettenreaktionen," also 30-794, 30-545 IMC.

G-95 (Dec. 1941) Johannes Jensen, "Über die Ultrazentrifugenmethode zur Trennung der Uranisotope," also 80-080 IMC.

G-98 (28 July 1941) Peter Jensen, "Eine weitere Bestimmung des Absorption-squerschnittes von 38 für thermische Neutronen."

G-99 (16 Sept. 1941) Willibald Jentschke, "Energien und Massen der Urankern-brüchstücke bei Bestrahlung mit schnellen (Rn + Be)-Neutronen."

G-102 (5 Sept. 1941) Horst Korsching, "Trennung von schwerem und leichtem Benzol durch Thermo-Diffusion in flüssiger Phase."

G-110 (Nov. 1941) Kurt Sauerwein, "Untersuchungen über den Resonanzeinfang von Neutronen bei Uran."

G-111 (23 May 1941) Josef Schintlmeister, "Die Stellung des Elementes mit Alphastrahlen von 1,8 cm Reichweite im periodischen System, III Bericht," also 31-031 IMC.

G-112 (May 1941) Josef Schintlmeister and F. Hernegger, "Weitere chemische Untersuchungen an dem Element mit Alphastrahlen von 1,8 cm Reichweite. II Bericht," also 31-018 IMC.

G-113 (20 May 1941) Kurt Starke, "Anreicherung des künstlich radioaktiven Uran-Isotops U^{239} und seines Folgeproduktes 93^{239} (Element 93)," also 29-513 IMC.

G-116 (1941) Helmut Volz, "Über die Absorption des Urans im Resonanzgebiet," also 30-116 IMC.

G-117 (1941) Helmut Volz, "Über die Geschwindigkeitsverteilung der Neutronen in einem Gemisch von schwerem Wasser und Uran," also 30-066 IMC.

G-118 (1 Feb. 1941) Helmut Volz and Otto Haxel, "Über die Absorption von Neutronen im Uran."

G-122 (2 Aug. 1941) Carl-Friedrich von Weizsäcker, "Bemerkungen zur Berechnung von Schichtenanordnungen."

G-124 (16 Mar. 1942) Erich Bagge, "Über die Möglichkeit einer Anreicherung der leichten Uranisotope mit der Isotopenschleuse," also 29-316, 30-214 IMC.

G-125 (before 26 Nov. 1942) F. Berkei, Werner Czulius, Kurt Diebner, Georg Hartwig, W. Herrmann, Gerhard Borrmann, Karl-Heinz Höcker, Heinz Pose, and Ernst Rexer, "Bericht über einen Würfelversuch mit Uranoxyd und Paraffin," also 30-322 IMC.

G-127 (Mar. 1942) Fritz Bopp, Erich Fischer, Werner Heisenberg, Carl-Friedrich von Weizsäcker, and Karl Wirtz, "Untersuchungen mit neuen Schichten-anordnungen aus U-Metall und Paraffin," also 30-122 IMC.

G-128 (7 Dec. 1941) Walther Bothe, "Maschinen mit Ausnutzung der Spaltung durch schnelle Neutronen," also 30-025 IMC.

G-132 (20 Feb. 1942) Klaus Clusius, Gerhard Dickel, and Ludwig Waldmann, "Über die Beeinflussung des Wirkungsgrades von Draht-Trennrohren durch Zentrierung und Einbau von Scheiben," also 30-193 IMC.

G-133 (Mar. 1942) Klaus Clusius and M. Maierhauser, "Über die Weiterentwicklung des Verfahrens zur Isotopentrennung mittels des Nernst'schen Verteilungssatzes," also 30-186 IMC.

G-134 (24 Feb. 1942) Klaus Clusius and Kurt Starke, "Zur Gewinnung von schwerem Wasser," also 30-179 IMC.

G-135 (9 July 1942) Robert Döpel, "Bericht über zwei Unfälle beim Umgang mit Uranmetall," also 29-539, 30-298 IMC.

G-136 (July 1942) Robert Döpel, K. Döpel, and Werner Heisenberg, "Der experimentelle Nachweis der effektiven Neutronenvermehrung in einem Kugel-Schichten-System aus D_2O und Uran-Metall," also 29-527 IMC.

G-139 (3 May 1942) Heinz Ewald, "Eine neue Methode zur magnetischen Isotopentrennung," also 30-289 IMC.

G-140 (27 Jan. 1942) Siegfried Flügge, "Zur spontanen Spaltung von Uran und seinen Nachbarelementen," also 30-057 IMC.

G-144 (19 Nov. 1942) Walter Fritz and Eduard Justi, "Bericht über die Leistung der Uranmaschine," also 30-415 IMC.

G-146 (27 June 1942) Wilhelm Groth, "Trennung der Uranisotope nach dem Ultrazentrifugenverfahren. I. Anreicherung der Xenonisotope in einer einstufigen Ultrazentrifuge," also 30-251 IMC.

G-147 (23 Mar. 1942) Wilhelm Groth, "Die Trennung der Uranisotope nach dem Trennrohr- und dem Ultrazentrifugenverfahren," also 29-887, 30-211 IMC.

G-149 (17 Aug. 1942) Wilhelm Groth and Albert Suhr, "Trennung der Uranisotope nach dem Ultrazentrifugenverfahren," also 30-258 IMC.

G-150 (26 Feb. 1942) Otto Hahn, "Die Spaltung des Urankerns."

G-151 (27 Feb. 1942) Otto Hahn and Fritz Strassmann, "Zur Folge nach der Entstehung des 2,3 Tage-Isotops des Elements 93 aus Uran," also 30-158 IMC.

G-154 (26 Feb. 1942) Paul Harteck, "Die Gewinnung von schwerem Wasser."

G-158 (Feb. 1943) Paul Harteck and Johannes Jensen, "Berechnung des Trenneffektes und der Ausbeute verschiedener Zentrifugenanordnungen zur Erhöhung des Wirkungsgrades einer einzelnen Zentrifuge," also 30-388 IMC.

G-159 (?) Paul Harteck, Johannes Jensen, and Albert Suhr, "Über den Zusammenhang zwischen Ausbeute und Trennschärfe bei der Niederdruckkolonne," also 30-199 IMC.

G-161 (31 July 1942) Werner Heisenberg, "Bemerkungen zu dem geplanten halbtechnischen Versuch mit 1,5 to D_2O und 3 to 38-Metall," also 30-228 IMC.

G-162 (30 Oct. 1942) Werner Heisenberg, Fritz Bopp, Erich Fischer, Carl-Friedrich von Weizsäcker, and Karl Wirtz, "Messungen an Schichtenanordnungen aus 38-Metall und Paraffin," also 30-342 IMC.

G-164 (26 Nov. 1942) Karl-Heinz Höcker, "Auswertung des Würfelversuchs mit Uranoxyd und Paraffin in der Versuchsstelle Gottow des Heereswaffenamts."

G-172 (1942) Alfred Klemm, "Anreicherung des leichten Kupferisotops," also 30-115 IMC.

G-174 (25 Feb. 1942) Horst Korsching, "Zur Frage des Isotopeneffekts bei Thermodiffusion in flüssiger Phase," also 30-210 IMC.

G-185 (28 Jan. 1942) Kurt Sauerwein and Siegfried Flügge, "Untersuchungen I und II über den Resonanzeinfang von Neutronen beim Uran," also 30-035 IMC.

G-186 (26 Feb. 1942) Josef Schintlmeister, "Die Aussichten für eine Energieerzeugung durch Kernspaltung des 1,8 cm Alphastrahlers," also 30-168 IMC.

G-189 (29 June 1942) Klaus Clusius und Kurt Starke, "Zur Theorie der fraktionierten Destillation von H_2-HD-D_2 Gemischen," also 30-309 IMC.

G-194 (23 Mar. 1942) Hans Suess, "Die Gewinnung von Deuterium durch Austausch bei zwei verschiedenen Temperaturen," also 30-205 IMC.

G-196 (Mar. 1942) Wilhelm Walcher, "Bericht über den Stand der in Kiel durchgeführten massenspektroskopischen Arbeiten," also 30-217 IMC.

G-197 (Mar. 1942) Carl-Friedrich von Weizsäcker, "Verbesserte Theorie der Resonanzabsorption in der Maschine," also 30-165 IMC.

G-198 (26–28 Feb. 1942) Karl Wirtz, "Die elektrolytische Schwerwassergewinnung in Norwegen," also 30-175 IMC.

G-202 (29 May 1943) Erich Bagge, "Die Anreicherung des leichten Silberisotops mit der Isotopenschleuse," also 30-514 IMC.

G-204 (29 June 1943) Walther Bothe, "Über Strahlenschutzwände," also 30-489 IMC.

G-205 (5 May 1943) Walther Bothe, "Die Forschungsmittel der Kernphysik," also 31-173 IMC.

G-206 (6 Dec. 1943) Walther Bothe and Erwin Fünfer, "Schichtenversuche mit Variation der U- und D_2O-Dicken," also 30-437 IMC.

G-207 (5 May 1943) Klaus Clusius, "Isotopentrennung," also 31-173 IMC.

G-210 Kurt Diebner, Werner Czulius, W. Herrmann, Georg Hartwig, F. Berkei, and E. Kamin, "Über die Neutronenvermehrung einer Anordnung aus Uranwürfeln und schwerem Wasser (G III)," also 31-247 IMC.

G-211 (Apr. 1943) Kurt Diebner, Georg Hartwig, W. Herrmann, H. Westmeyer, Werner Czulius, F. Berkei, and Karl-Heinz Höcker, "Vorläufige Mitteilung über einen Versuch mit Uranwürfeln und schwerem Eis als Bremssubstanz."

G-212 (Jul. 1943) Kurt Diebner, Georg Hartwig, W. Herrmann, H. Westmeyer, Werner Czulius, F. Berkei, and Karl-Heinz Höcker, "Bericht über einen Versuch mit Würfeln aus Uran-Metall und schwerem Eis."

G-213 (5 May 1943) Abraham Esau, "Herstellung von Leuchtfarben ohne Anwendung von Radium," also 31-173 IMC.

G-214 (5 May 1943) Abraham Esau, "Einleitung," also 31-173 IMC.

G-216 (5 May 1943) Otto Hahn, "Künstliche Atomumwandlung und Atomkernspaltung," also 31-173 IMC.

G-217 (6 May 1943) Werner Heisenberg, "Die Energiegewinnung aus der Atomkernspaltung," also 31-173 IMC.

G-218 (25 Jan. 1943) Karl-Heinz Höcker, "Über die Anordnung von Uran und Streusubstanz in der U-Maschine."

G-221 Karl-Heinz Höcker, "Zur Auswertung der Grossversuche," also 30-357 IMC.

G-222 (23 June 1943) Karl-Heinz Höcker, "Über die Abmessungen von Uran und schwerem Wasser in einer Kugelstrukturmaschine," also 30-414 IMC.

G-223 (Nov. 1943) Karl-Heinz Höcker, "Vergleich der bei L-VI bestimmten Neutronendichte mit der Theorie."

G-240 (12 Oct. 1943) Heinz Pose and Ernst Rexer, "Versuche mit verschiedenen geometrischen Anordnungen von Uranoxyd und Paraffin," also 30-453 IMC.

G-241 (2 Apr. 1943) Carl Ramsauer, "Über Leistung und Organisation der angelsächsischen Physik: Mit Ausblicken für die deutsche Physik," also 31-154 IMC.

G-248 (12 Dec. 1944) Konrad Beyerle, "Die Gaszentrifugenanlage für den Reichsforschungsrat."

G-249 Fritz Bopp and Erich Fischer, "Einfluss des Rückstreumantels auf die Neutronenausbeute des U-Brenners," also 30-418 IMC.

G-280 R. Rajewsky, "I. Zur Frage des Strahlenschutzes," also 30-496 IMC.

G-296 (8 Aug. 1944) Karl Wirtz, "Einrichtung der Elektrolyse zur Aufbearbeitung von schwerem Wasser."

G-297 Karl G. Zimmer, "Bericht über die Untersuchungen der relativen Wirksamkeit von Röntgenstrahlen und schnellen Neutronen bezügl. der Erzeugung von Chromosomenmutationen," also 30-641 IMC.

G-300 (3 Jan. 1945) Fritz Bopp, Walther Bothe, Erich Fischer, Erwin Fünfer, Werner Heisenberg, O. Ritter, and Karl Wirtz, "Bericht über einen Versuch mit 1,5 to D_2O und U und 40 cm Kohlerückstreumantel. (B7)," also 29-656 IMC.

G-303 (1944) W. Herrmann, Georg Hartwig, H. Rockwitz, W. Trinks, and H. Schaub, "Versuche über die Einleitung von Kernreaktionen durch die Wirkung explodierender Stoffe," also 31-688 IMC.

G-330 correspondence and reports concerning centrifuge research, selected items also in IMC.

G-341, volumes 1–6, Paul Harteck's institute papers.

G-343 excerpts from documents found in Strassburg by the Alsos Mission.

G-344 (9 Apr. 1946) Jesse W. Beams, "Report on the use of the centrifuge method for the concentration of U235 by the Germans," also 29-791 IMC.

G-371 (6 Nov. 1945) Weinberg and Nordheim to Compton, also 31-1182 IMC.

G-373 (Mar. 1942) Robert Döpel, K. Döpel, and Werner Heisenberg, "Die Neutronenvermehrung in einem D_2O-38-Metallschichtensystem," also 30-120 IMC.

G-391 (? 1944) Paul Harteck, untitled.

Publications cited (before 1950)

Anderson, Herbert, Booth, E., Dunning, J., Fermi, Enrico, Glasoe, G., and Slack, F., "The fission of uranium," *Physical Review*, 55 (1939), 511–12.

Anderson, Herbert, Fermi, Enrico, and Hanstein, H. B., "Production of neutrons in uranium bombarded by neutrons," *Physical Review*, 55 (1939), 797–8.

Anderson, Herbert, Fermi, Enrico, and Szilard, Leo, "Neutron production and absorption in uranium," *Physical Review*, 56 (1939), 284–6.

Beams, Jesse W., and Skarstrom, C., "The concentration of isotopes by the evaporative centrifuge method," *Physical Review*, 56 (1939), 266–72.

Bethe, Hans and Slack, H. S., "German scientists in army employment: II-a protest," *Bulletin of the Atomic Scientists*, 3 (1947), 65, 67.

Bohr, Niels, "Resonance in uranium and thorium disintegrations and the phenomena of nuclear fission," *Physical Review*, 55 (1939), 418–19.

Bohr, Niels, and Wheeler, John, "The mechanism of nuclear fission," *Physical Review*, 56 (1939), 426–50.

Booth, E., Dunning, J., Grosse, A., and Nier, Alfred, "Neutron capture by uranium (238)," *Physical Review*, 58 (1940), 475–6.

Bothe, Walther and Flügge, Siegfried (eds.), *Kernphysik und kosmische Strahlen, Naturforschung und Medizin in Deutschland 1939–1946*, vol. 14 (Weinheim, Chemie, 1948).

Clusius, Klaus, and Dickel, Gerhard, "Neues Verfahren zur Gasentmischung und Isotopentrennung," *Die Naturwissenschaften*, 26 (1938), 546.

"Zur Trennung der Chlorisotope," *Die Naturwissenschaften*, 27 (1939), 148.

"Das Trennrohrverfahren bei Flüssigkeiten," *Die Naturwissenschaften*, 27 (1939), 148–9.

"Isolierung des leichten Chlorisotopes mit dem Atomgewicht 34,979 im Trennrohr," *Die Naturwissenschaften*, 27 (1939), 487.

"Das Trennrohr," *Zeitschrift für physikalische Chemie*, B 44 (1939), 397–473.

Crowther, J. G., *Science in Liberated Europe* (London, Pilot, 1949).

Diebner, Kurt and Grassmann, E., *Künstliche Radioaktivität. Experimentale Ergebnisse* (Leipzig, Hirzel, 1939).

von Droste, Gottfried and Reddemann, H., "Über die beim Zerspalten des Urankerns auftretenden Neutronen," *Die Naturwissenschaften*, 27 (1939), 371–2.

Fermi, Enrico, "Possible production of elements of atomic number higher than 92," *Nature*, 133 (1934), 898–9.

Flügge, Siegfried, "Die Ausnutzung der Atomenergie," *Deutsche Allgemeine Zeitung* (15 Aug. 1939).

"Kann der Energieinhalt der Atomkerne technisch nutzbar gemacht werden?" *Die Naturwissenschaften*, 27 (1939), 402–10.

Flügge, Siegfried and von Droste, Gottfried, "Energetische Betrachtungen zu der Entstehung von Barium bei der Neutronenbestrahlung von Uran," *Zeitschrift für physikalische Chemie*, B 42 (1939), 274–80.

Freud, Sigmund, "Die Verneinung" (1925), *Gesammelte Werke* (Frankfurt am Main, Fischer, 1948), vol. 14, p. 12.

Goebbels, Joseph, *The Goebbels Diaries 1942–1943* (New York, Doubleday, 1948).

Goudsmit, Samuel, *Alsos*, 2nd edn (Los Angeles, Tomash, 1983).

"German scientists in army employment: I – the case analyzed," *Bulletin of the Atomic Scientists*, 3 (1947), 343.

"German war research," *New York Times* (9 Jan. 1949).

"Heisenberg on the German nuclear power project," *Bulletin of the Atomic Scientists*, 3 (1947), 64, 67.

"How Germany lost the race," *Bulletin of the Atomic Scientists*, 1 (1946), 4–5.

"Nazis' atomic secrets," *Life*, 23 (20 Oct. 1947), 123–34.

"Our task in Germany," *Bulletin of the Atomic Scientists*, 4 (1948), 106.

"Secrecy or science?" *Science Illustrated*, 1 (1946), 97–9.

"War physics in Germany," *The Review of Scientific Instruments*, 17 (Jan. 1946), 49–52.

Grosse, A., Booth, E., and Dunning, J., "The fission of protactinium," *Physical Review*, 56 (1939), 382.

Groth, Wilhelm, "Versuche zur Anreicherung der Xenonisotope und deren Nachweis," *Die Naturwissenschaften*, 27 (1939), 260–1.

Groth, Wilhelm and Harteck, Paul, "Anreicherung der Quecksilberisotope nach einem Trennrohrverfahren," *Die Naturwissenschaften*, 27 (1939), 584.

Hahn, Otto and Rein, Friedrich, "Gelehrtenexport nach Amerika," *Göttinger Universitäts-Zeitung* (21 Feb. 1947), reprinted in *Physikalische Blätter*, 3 (1947), 33–5.

Hahn, Otto and Strassmann, Fritz, "Über den Nachweis und das Verhalten der bei der Bestrahlung des Urans mittels Neutronen entstehenden Erdalkalimetalle," *Die Naturwissenschaften*, 27 (1939), 11–5.

"Nachweis der Entstehung aktiver Bariumisotope aus Uran und Thorium durch Neutronenbestrahlung: Nachweis weiterer aktiver Bruchstücke bei der Uranspaltung," *Die Naturwissenschaften*, 27 (1939), 89–95.

"Zur Folge nach der Entstehung des 2,3 Tage-Isotopes des Elements 93 aus Uran," *Die Naturwissenschaften*, 30 (1942), 256–60.

von Halban, Hans, Joliot, Frédéric, and Kowarski, Lew, "Liberation of neutrons in the nuclear explosion of uranium," *Nature*, 143 (1939), 470–1.

"Number of neutrons liberated in the nuclear fission of uranium," *Nature*, 143 (1939), 680.

Hartshorne, Edward, *The German Universities and National Socialism* (London, Allen & Unwin, 1937).

Heisenberg, Werner, "Die Bewertung der 'modernen theoretischen Physik,'" *Zeitschrift für die gesamte Naturwissenschaft*, 9 (1943), 201–12.

"German atom research," *New York Times* (30 Jan. 1949).

Heisenberg, Werner (ed.), *Kosmische Strahlung* (Berlin, Springer, 1943).

Heisenberg, Werner, "Die theoretischen Grundlagen für die Energiegewinnung aus der Uranspaltung," in *Gesammelte Werke/Collected Works*, Volume A II (Heidelberg, Springer, 1988 – forthcoming).

"Über die Arbeiten zur technischen Ausnutzung der Atomkernenergie in Deutschland," *Die Naturwissenschaften*, 33 (1946), 325–9.

Hertz, Gustav, "Ein Verfahren zur Trennung von gasförmigen Isotopengemischen und seine Anwendung auf die Isotope des Neons," *Zeitschrift für Physik*, 79 (1932), 108–21.

"Ein Verfahren zur Trennung von Isotopengemischen durch Diffusion in strömendem Quecksilberdampf," *Zeitschrift für Physick*, 91 (1934), 810–15.

Jentschke, Willibald, Prankl, F., and Hernegger, F., "Die Spaltung des Ioniums unter Neutronenbestrahlung," *Die Naturwissenschaften*, 28 (1940), 315–16.

Joliot, Frédéric, *Comptes Rendus*, 208 (1939), 313–14.

Kaempffert, Waldemar, "Nazis spurned idea of an atomic bomb," *New York Times* (28 Dec. 1948).

Korsching, Horst, "Ein abgeändertes Verfahren bei der Trennung von Lösungsbestandteilen durch Thermodiffusion in der Flüssigkeit," *Die Naturwissenschaften*, 32 (1944), 220.

Korsching, Horst, and Wirtz, Karl, "Trennung von Flüssigkeitsgemischen mittels kombinierter Thermo-Diffusion und Thermosiphonwirkung," *Die Naturwissenschaften*, 27 (1939), 110.

"Zur Trennung von Flüssigkeitsgemischen in Clusiusschen Trennrohr (Trennung der Zinkisotope)," *Die Naturwissenschaften*, 27 (1939), 367–8.

von Laue, Max, "The wartime activities of German scientists," *Bulletin of the Atomic Scientists*, 4 (1948), 103.

"Die Kriegstätigkeit der deutschen Physiker," *Physikalische Blätter*, 4 (1948), 424–5.

McMillan, Edwin, and Abelson, Philip, "Radioactive element 93," *Physical Review*, 57 (1940), 1185–6.

Meitner, Lise, and Frisch, Otto, "Disintegration of uranium by neutrons: a new type of nuclear reaction," *Nature*, 143 (1939), 239–40.

Meitner, Lise, Hahn, Otto, and Strassmann, Fritz, "Über die Umwandlungsreihen des Urans die durch Neutronenbestrahlung erzeugt werden," *Zeitschrift für Physik*, 106 (1937), 249–70.

Merton, Robert, "Science in the social order," *Philosophy of Science*, 5 (1938), reprinted in *The Sociology of Science: Theoretical and Empirical Investigations* (Chicago, University of Chicago, 1973), pp. 254–66.

Morrison, Philip, "Alsos: the story of German science," *Bulletin of the Atomic Scientists*, 3 (1947), 354, 365.

"A reply to Dr. von Laue," *Bulletin of the Atomic Scientists*, 4 (1948), 104.

Nicolai, Georg Friedrich, *The Biology of War* (New York, Century, 1918).

Nier, Alfred, "The isotopic constitution of uranium and the half-lives of the uranium isotopes," *Physical Review*, 55 (1939), 150.

Nier, Alfred, Booth, E., Dunning, J., and Grosse, A., "Nuclear fission of separated uranium isotopes," *Physical Review*, 57 (1940), 546.

"Further experiments on fission of separated uranium isotopes," *Physical Review*, 57 (1940), 748.

The Olympic Year in Germany (Berlin, Volk und Reich, 1936).

Riehl, Nikolaus, *Physik und technische Anwendungen der Lumineszenz* (Berlin, Springer, 1941).

Roberts, R., Meyer, R., and Hafstad, L., "Droplet fission of uranium and thorium nuclei," *Physical Review*, 55 (1939), 416–7.

Das Schwarze Korps (15 July 1937), p. 6.

Smyth, Henry, *Atomic Energy for Military Purposes* (Princeton, Princeton University, 1945).

Atomenergie und ihre Verwertung im Kriege (Basel, Reinhardt, 1947).

Sommerfeld, Arnold, *Süddeutsche Monatshefte* (15 May 1918).

Starke, Kurt, "Anreicherung des künstlich radioaktiven Uran-Isotops U^{239} und seines Folgeproduktes 93^{239} (Element 93)," *Die Naturwissenschaften*, 30 (1942), 577–82.

Szilard, Leo, and Zinn, Walter, "Instantaneous emission of fast neutrons in the interaction of slow neutrons with uranium," *Physical Review*, 55 (1939), 799–800.

Trials of War Criminals Before the Nüremberg Military Tribunals (Washington, US Government, 1949), vols. 12–14.

Turner, Louis, "The nonexistence of transuranic elements," *Physical Review*, 57 (1940), 157.

"Nuclear fission," *Reviews of Modern Physics*, 12 (1940), 1–29.

Völkischer Beobachter (29 Jan. 1936), p. 5; (28 Feb. 1936), p. 6.

Walcher, Wilhelm, "Isotopentrennung," *Ergebnisse der exakten Naturwissenschaften*, 18 (1939), 155–228.

Walcher, Wilhelm, "Über einen Massenspektrographen hoher Intensität und die Trennung der Rubidiumisotope," *Zeitschrift für Physik*, 108 (1938), 376–90.

Weinreich, Max, *Hitler's Professors: The Part of Scholarship in Germany's Crimes against the Jewish People* (New York, YIVO, 1946).

Publications cited (after 1949)

von Ardenne, Manfred, *Mein Leben für Forschung und Fortschritt* (Munich, Nymphenburger, 1984).

Bagge, Erich, Diebner, Kurt, and Jay, Kenneth, *Von der Uranspaltung bis Calder Hall* (Hamburg, Rowohlt, 1957).

Barwich, Heinz and Elsi, *Das Rote Atom* (Munich, Scherz, 1967).

Beer, John, *The Emergence of the German Dye Industry*, 2nd edn (New York, Arno, 1981).

Berghahn, Volker, *Modern Germany: Society, Economy and Politics in the Twentieth Century* (Cambridge, Cambridge University Press, 1982).

Beyerchen, Alan, *Scientists under Hitler: Politics and the Physics Community in the Third Reich* (New Haven, Yale University Press, 1977).

Beyerle, Konrad, Groth, Wilhelm, Harteck, Paul, and Jensen, Johannes, *Über Gaszentrifugen: Anreicherung der Xenon-, Krypton- und der Selen-Isotope nach dem Zentrifugenverfahren* (Weinheim, Chemie, 1950).

Boberach, Heinz (ed.), *Meldungen aus dem Reich: Die geheimen Lageberichte des Sicherheitsdienstes der SS 1938–1945* (Herrsching, Pawlak, 1984).

Boelcke, Willi (ed.), *"Wollt Ihr den totalen Krieg?": Die geheimen Goebbels-Konferenzen 1939–1943* (Stuttgart, DVA, 1967).

Bohr, Aage, "The war years and the prospects raised by the atomic weapons," in Stefan Rozental (ed.), *Niels Bohr* (Amsterdam, North-Holland, 1967), p. 193.

Braudel, Fernand, *On History* (Chicago, University of Chicago Press, 1980).

Brautmeier, Jürgen, *Forschungspolitik in Nordrhein-Westfalen: 1945–1961* (Düsseldorf, Schwann, 1983).

Broszat, Martin, *Nationalsozialistische Polenpolitik: 1939–1945* (Stuttgart, DVA, 1961).

The Hitler State (New York, Longman, 1981).

"Hitler and the genesis of the 'Final Solution': an assessment of David Irving's theses," in H. W. Hoch (ed.), *Aspects of the Third Reich* (New York, St. Martin's, 1985), pp. 390–429.

Broszat, Martin and Elke Fröhlich, *Alltag und Widerstand-Bayern im Nationalsozialismus* (Munich, Piper, 1987).

Burchardt, Lothar, *Wissenschaftspolitik im Wilhelminischen Deutschland* (Göttingen, Vandenhoeck & Ruprecht, 1975).

"The impact of the war economy on the civilian population of Germany during the First and Second World Wars," in Wilhelm Deist (ed.), *The German Military in the Age of Total War* (Dover, Berg, 1985), pp. 40–70.

Casimir, Hendrik, *Haphazard Reality* (New York, Harper & Row, 1983).

"Heisenberg im Urteil seiner Schüler," *Bild der Wissenschaft* (1985), 142, 144–5.

Cassidy, David, "Gustav Hertz, Hans Geiger und das Physikalische Institut der Technischen Hochschule Berlin in den Jahren 1933 bis 1945," in R. Rürup (ed.) *Wissenschaft und Gesellschaft: Beiträge zur Geschichte der Technischen Universität Berlin, 1879–1979* (Heidelberg, Springer, 1979). pp. 373–87.

Craig, Gordon, *Germany, 1866–1945* (Oxford, Oxford University Press 1978).

Dahrendorf, Ralf, *Society and Democracy* (New York, Norton, 1979).

Deist, Wilhelm, Messerschmidt, Manfred, Volkmann, Hans-Erich, and Wette, Wolfram, "Causes and Preconditions of German Aggression," in Wilhelm Deist (ed.), *The German Military in the Age of Total War* (Dover, Berg, 1985), pp. 336–53.

Diebner, Kurt, "Fusionsprozesse mit Hilfe konvergenter Stosswellen – einige ältere und neuere Versuche und Überlegungen," *Kerntechnik*, 4 (1962), 89–93.

Dokumente zur Gründung der Kaiser-Wilhelm-Gesellschaft und der Max-Planck-Gesellschaft zur Förderung der Wissenschaften (Munich, MPG, 1981).

Eckert, Michael, "Propaganda in science: Sommerfeld and the spread of the electron theory of metals," *Historical Studies in the Physical and Biological Sciences*, 17 (1987), 191–233.

Eckert, Michael, Pricha, Willibald, Schubert, Helmut, and Torkar, Gisela, *Geheimrat Sommerfeld – Theoretischer Physiker: Eine Dokumentation aus seinem Nachlass* (Munich, Deutsches Museum, 1984).

Eckert, Michael, and Schubert, Helmut, *Kristalle, Elektronen, Transistoren* (Reinbek, Rowohlt, 1986).

Feldman, Gerald, *Army, Industry, and Labor in Germany. 1914–1918* (Princeton, Princeton University Press, 1966).

Ferencz, Benjamin, *Less than Slaves* (Cambridge, Harvard University Press, 1979). *Lohn des Grauens*, 2nd edn (Frankfurt am Main, Campus, 1986).

Fermi, Enrico, "Experimental production of a divergent chain reaction," *American Journal of Physics*, 26 (1952), 536–58.

Forman, Paul, "The environment and practice of atomic physics in Weimar Germany: a study in the history of science" (Berkeley, University of California Ph.D., 1967).

"Weimar culture, causality, and quantum theory, 1918–1927: adaptation by German physicists and mathematicians to a hostile environment," *Historical Studies in the Physical Sciences*, 3 (1971), 1–115.

"Scientific internationalism and the Weimar physicists: the ideology and its manipulation in Germany after World War I," *Isis*, 64 (1973), 151–80.

"The financial support and political alignment of physicists in Weimar Germany," *Minerva*, 12 (1974), 39–66.

"*Kausalität, Anschaulichkeit,* and *Individualität,* or how cultural values prescribed the character and lessons ascribed to quantum mechanics," in Nico Stehr and

Volker Meja (eds.), *Society and Knowledge: Contemporary Perspectives in the Sociology of Knowledge* (New Brunswick, Transaction Books, 1984), pp. 333–47.

Forman, Paul, Heilbron, John L., and Weart, Spencer, "Physics circa 1900: personnel, funding, and productivity of the academic establishments," *Historical Studies in the Physical Sciences*, 5 (1975), 1–185.

Friese, Gerda, "Autonomie und Anpassung – Das Selbstverständnis von Naturwissenschaftlern im Nationalsozialismus," in Rainer Brämer (ed.), *Naturwissenschaft im NS-Staat* (Marburg, Soznat, 1983), pp. 31–58.

Geertz, Clifford, "Ideology as a cultural system," in *The Interpretation of Cultures* (New York, Basic Books, 1973), 193–233.

Geyer, Michael, "The dynamics of military revisionism in the interwar years. Military politics between rearmament and diplomacy," in Wilhelm Deist (ed.), *The German Military in the Age of Total War* (Dover, Berg, 1985), pp. 100–51.

Gillispie, Charles Coulston, *Science and Polity in France at the End of the Old Regime* (Princeton, Princeton University Press, 1980).

Gimbel, John, "U.S. policy and German scientists: the early Cold War." *Political Science Quarterly*, 101 (1986), 433–51.

Gowing, Margaret, *Britain and Atomic Energy 1939–1945* (London, St. Martin's, 1964).

Greenberg, Daniel, *The Politics of Pure Science* (New York, New American Library, 1967).

Groves, Leslie, *Now It Can Be Told*, 2nd edn (New York, Da Capo, 1983).

Haber, Ludwig, *The Poisonous Cloud: Chemical Warfare in the First World War* (Oxford, Clarendon, 1986).

Haberer, Joseph, *Politics and the Community of Science* (New York, Van Nostrand, 1969).

Hayes, Peter, *Industry and Ideology: IG Farben in the Nazi Era* (Cambridge, Cambridge University Press, 1987).

Heilbron, John L., *The Dilemmas of an Upright Man: Max Planck as Spokesman for German Science* (Berkeley, University of California, 1986).

Heisenberg, Elisabeth, *Inner Exile: Recollections of a Life with Werner Heisenberg* (Boston, Birkhäuser, 1984).

Heisenberg, Werner, *Physics and Beyond: Encounters and Conversations* (New York, Harper & Row, 1971).

Herbert, Ulrich, *Fremdarbeiter: Politik und Praxis des "Ausländer-Einsatzes" in der Kriegswirtschaft des Dritten Reiches* (Berlin, Dietz, 1985).

Herbig, Jost, *Kettenreaktion* (Munich, DTV, 1979).

Hermann, Armin, *Die Jahrhundertwissenschaft* (Stuttgart, DVA, 1977).

"Heisenberg und das deutsche Atomprojekt," *Bild der Wissenschaft*, 10 (1988), 140–45.

"Die fünf historischen Epochen in der Geschichte der Atomenergie," in Armin Hermann and Rolf Schumacher (eds.), *Das Ende des Atomzeitalters? Eine sachlich-kritische Dokumentation* (Gräfelfing, Moss & Partner, 1986), pp. 11–22.

Hoffmann, Dieter, "Zur Teilnahme deutscher Physiker an den Kopenhagener Physikerkonferenzen nach 1933 sowie am 2. Kongress für Einheit der

Wissenschaft, Kopenhagen 1936", *NTM. Schriftenreihe für Geschichte der Naturwissenschaften, Technik, und Medizin*, 25 (1988), 49–55.

Irving, David, *The German Atomic Bomb: The History of Nuclear Research in Nazi Germany*, 2nd edn (New York, Da Capo, 1983).

James, Harold, *The German Slump: Politics and Economics 1924–1936* (Oxford, Clarendon, 1986).

Joravsky, David, *The Lysenko Affair* (Cambridge, Harvard University Press, 1970).

Jungk, Robert, *Brighter than a Thousand Suns* (New York, Harcourt, 1958).

Kater, Michael, *The Nazi Party: A Social Profile of Members and Leaders, 1919–1945* (Cambridge, Harvard University Press, 1983).

Kershaw, Ian, *The "Hitler Myth": Image and Reality in the Third Reich* (Oxford, Clarendon, 1987).

"The Führer image and political integration: the popular conception of Hitler in Bavaria during the Third Reich," in Gerhard Hirschfeld and Lothar Kettenacker (eds.), *Der "Führerstaat": Mythos und Realität* (Stuttgart, Klett, 1981), pp. 133–63.

Popular Opinion and Political Dissent in the Third Reich: Bavaria 1933–1945 (Oxford, Clarendon, 1983).

Kevles, Daniel, *The Physicists: The History of a Scientific Community in Modern America* (New York, Vintage, 1979).

"'Into hostile camps': the reorganization of international science in World War I," *Isis*, 62 (1970), 47–60.

Kleinert, Andreas, "Von der science allemande zur deutschen Physik: Nationalismus und moderne Naturwissenschaft in Frankreich und Deutschland zwischen 1914 und 1940," *Francia: Forschungen zur westeuropäischen Geschichte*, 6 (1978), 509–25.

"Nationalistische und antisemitische Ressentiments von Wissenschaftlern gegen Einstein," *Lecture Notes in Physics*, 100 (1979), 501–16.

"Das Spruchkammerverfahren gegen Johannes Stark," *Sudhoffs Archiv*, 67 (1983), 13–24.

Klessmann, Christoph, "Osteuropaforschung und Lebensraumpolitik im Dritten Reich," in Peter Lundgreen (ed.), *Wissenschaft im Dritten Reich* (Frankfurt am Main, Suhrkamp, 1985), pp. 350–83.

Kramish, Arnold, *The Griffin: Paul Rosebaud and the Nazi Atomic Bomb that Never Was* (Boston, Houghton Mifflin, 1986).

Kroener, Bernard, "Squaring the circle. Blitzkrieg strategy and manpower shortage, 1939–1949," in Wilhelm Deist (ed.), *The German Military in the Age of Total War* (Dover, Berg, 1985), pp. 282–303.

Lasby, Clarence, *Project Paperclip* (New York, Atheneum, 1971).

Ludwig, Karl-Heinz, *Technik und Ingenieure im Dritten Reich*, 2nd edn (Düsseldorf, Droste, 1979).

"Die wohlreflektierten 'Erinnerungen' des Albert Speer. Einige kritische Bemerkungen zur Funktion des Architekten, des Ingenieurs und der Technik im Dritten Reich," *Geschichte in Wissenschaft und Unterricht*, 21 (1970), 695–708.

Der Luxus des Gewissens: Max Born James Franck Physiker in ihrer Zeit (Berlin, Staatsbibliothek Preussischer Kulturbesitz Berlin, 1982).

Macrakis, Kristie, "Wissenschaftsförderung durch die Rockefeller-Stiftung im 'Dritten Reich': Die Entscheidung, das Kaiser-Wilhelm-Institut für Physik finanziell zu unterstützen, 1934–39," *Geschichte und Gesellschaft*, 12 (1986), 348–79.

Mehrtens, Herbert, "'Die Gleichschaltung' der mathematischen Gesellschaften im nationalsozialistischen Deutschland," *Jahrbuch Überblicke Mathematik* (1985), 83–103.

"Angewandte Mathematik und Anwendungen der Mathematik im national-sozialistischen Deutschland," *Geschichte und Gesellschaft*, 12 (1986), 317–47.

"The social system of mathematics and National Socialism: a survey," *Sociological Inquiry*, 57 (1987), 159–82.

"Das 'Dritte Reich' in der Naturwissenschaftsgeschichte: Literaturbericht und Problemskizze," in Herbert Mehrtens and Steffen Richter (eds.), *Naturwissenschaft, Technik und Ideologie: Beiträge zur Wissenschaftsgeschichte des Dritten Reiches* (Frankfurt am Main, Suhrkamp, 1980), pp. 15–87.

"Naturwissenschaft und Nationalsozialismus," in Steffen Harbordt (ed.), *Wissenschaft und Nationalsozialismus* (Berlin, TU Berlin, 1983), pp. 101–14.

"Ludwig Bieberbach and 'Deutsche Mathematik'," in E. Phillips (ed.), *Studies in the History of Mathematics* (Mathematical Association of America, 1987), pp. 195–241.

von Meyenn, Karl, Hermann, Armin, and Weisskopf, Viktor (eds.) *Wolfgang Pauli: Wissenschaftlicher Briefwechsel mit Bohr, Einstein, Heisenberg, u.a. Band II: 1930–1939* (Berlin, Springer, 1985).

Mommsen, Hans, *Beamtentum im Dritten Reich: Mit ausgewählten Quellen zur nationalsozialistischen Beamtenpolitik* (Stuttgart, DVA, 1966).

Müller-Hill, Benno, *Murderous Science: Elimination by Scientific Selection of Jews, Gypsies, and Others, Germany, 1933–1945* (Oxford, Oxford University Press, 1988).

Petzina, Dieter, *Autarkiepolitik im Dritten Reich: Der nationalsozialistische Vier-jahresplan* (Stuttgart, DVA, 1968).

Peukert, Detlev J. K., *Inside Nazi Germany: Conformity, Opposition, and Racism in Everyday Life* (New Haven, Yale University, 1987).

Pyenson, Lewis, *Cultural Imperialism and Exact Sciences. German Expansion Overseas 1900–1930* (New York, Peter Lang, 1985).

"The limits of scientific condominium: geophysics in Western Samoa," in N. Reingold and M. Rothberg (eds.), *Scientific Colonization: A Cross-Cultural Comparison* (Washington, Smithsonian Institution, 1987), pp. 251–95.

Rhodes, Richard, *The Making of the Atomic Bomb* (New York, Simon & Schuster, 1986).

Richter, Steffen, "Die 'Deutsche Physik'," in Herbert Mehrtens and Steffen Richter (eds.), *Naturwissenschaft, Technik und Ideologie: Beiträge zur Wissenschafts-geschichte des Dritten Reiches* (Frankfurt am Main, Suhrkamp, 1980), pp. 116–41.

Riehl, Nikolaus, *Zehn Jahre, im goldenen Käfig. Erlebnisse beim Aufbau der sowjetischen Uran-Industrie* (Stuttgart, Riederer, 1988).

Ringer, Fritz, *The Decline of the German Mandarins: The German Academic Community, 1890–1933* (Cambridge, Harvard University Press, 1969).

Rozental, Stefan, *NB. Erindringer om Niels Bohr* (Copenhagen, Gylendal, 1985).

Schröder-Gudehus, Brigitte, "The argument for the self-government and public support of science in Weimar Germany," *Minerva*, 10 (1972), 537–70.

"Challenge to transnational loyalties: international scientific organizations after the First World War," *Science Studies*, 3 (1973), 93–118.

Speer, Albert, *Inside the Third Reich* (New York, Macmillan, 1970).

Stern, Fritz *The Failure of Illiberalism: Essays on the Political Culture of Modern Germany* (New York, Knopf, 1972).

Streit, Christian, *Keine Kameraden: Die Wehrmacht und die sowjetischen Kriegsgefangenen 1941–1945* (Stuttgart, DVA, 1978).

Walker, Mark, "Uranium machines, nuclear explosives, and National Socialism: The German quest for nuclear power, 1939–1949" (Princeton, Princeton University Ph.D., 1987).

Weart, Spencer, *Nuclear Fear* (Cambridge, Harvard University Press, 1988).

Scientists in Power (Cambridge, Harvard University Press, 1979).

"Secrecy, simultaneous discovery, and the theory of nuclear reactors," *American Journal of Physics*, 45 (1977), 1049–60.

"The discovery of fission and a nuclear physics paradigm," in William Shea (ed.), *Otto Hahn and the Rise of Nuclear Physics* (Dordrecht, Reidel, 1983), pp. 91–133.

Webster's Third New International Dictionary (Springfield, Merriam, 1976), 1497.

Wendel, Günter, *Die Kaiser Wilhelm Gesellschaft 1911–1914* (Berlin, Akademie Verlag, 1975).

Wette, Wolfram, "From Kellogg to Hitler (1928–1933), German public opinion concerning the rejection or glorification of war," in Wilhelm Deist (ed.), *The German Military in the Age of Total War* (Dover, Berg, 1985), pp. 71–99.

Wohlfarth, Horst (ed.), *40 Jahre Kernspaltung* (Darmstadt, Wissenschaftliche Buchgesellschaft, 1979).

Index